Readings In Contemporary Transportation

Donald F. Wood
San Francisco State University

James C. Johnson
St. Cloud State University

BOOKS

Petroleum Publishing Company
Tulsa, Oklahoma 74101

Manufactured in the United States of America

Library of Congress Catalog Card Number 79-90688

ISBN 0-87814126-X
1 2 3 4 83 82 81 80 79

Dedication

TO: Tammy
   Frank
   Rufus
   Amy
   Lori
   Sebby

Contents

Preface

Transportation — like the air we breathe — is such a pervasive force that it is often taken for granted. Nevertheless, in the United States, freight transportation accounts for approximately ten percent of the Gross National Product. Passenger transportation accounts for another ten percent of G.N.P.

This book is designed to dramatically illustrate that transportation, besides being a dominant aspect of the economy, is also an **outstanding career area**. The editors have selected seventy articles from twenty-three different professional publications that vividly indicate the challenge, excitement, and opportunities available under the broad umbrella of transportation.

The articles in **Readings In Contemporary Transportation** have been carefully selected with three basic criteria in mind. First, the article had to present an interesting and highly readable discussion of the topic. Second, it had to be a first-class article regarding its ability to succinctly discuss the major aspects of each topic. Finally, the articles had to live up to the title of the book — they had to be **contemporary**! Almost all the articles are from 1978 to 1979 sources.

A unique feature of this book is that the selections are printed in a fascimile format. This style was chosen because it helps the reader grasp the true flavor of the original article. It also permits excellent reproduction of graphs, charts, and pictures.

The editors believe that **Readings In Contemporary Transportation** can be utilized in several ways. Its primary purpose is to serve as an up-to-date supplement to an introductory transportation course. It can also be used as a primary source book in more advanced classes in transportation. Finally, these articles will act as an excellent refresher for the practicing transportation and distribution executive.

The editors wish to thank the authors and publishers for allowing their articles to be reprinted in this book. A special thank you is due to Mrs. Diane McClure for her efficient assistance in the manuscript preparation.

Donald F. Wood
San Francisco, California

James C. Johnson
St. Cloud, Minnesota

October, 1979

Overview of Readings In Contemporary Transportation

Readings in Contemporary Transportation is divided into ten chapters. The first chapter provides an introduction to transportation as a career. After presenting a sketch of both the freight and passenger sides of transportation, career patterns are examined.

The next four chapters examine the five basic modes of transportation. Chapter 2 looks at the problems and opportunities in the trucking industry. The following topics are illustrative of material covered in this chapter: (a) trucking service standards, (b) computer usage, (c) potential and actual fuel savings, (d) future truck designs, (e) truck leasing issues, (f) management of specialized trucking operations, and (g) highway research activities.

Railroads are the subject of Chapter 3. The chapter starts by examining the strengths and weaknesses of one of the best managed railroads in the United States — The Rio Grande. Additional topics discused in this chapter include: (a) proposed changes in the Interstate Commerce Act to help the railroad industry, (b) unit-trains, (c) rail transportation of coal, (d) intermodal (piggyback) transportation, (e) railroad mergers, (f) the advent of contract rates in the railroad industry, (g) deregulation of agricultural products for railroads, (h) railroad financial analysis, and (i) the future of Amtrak.

Chapter 4 deals with air carriers. Both passenger and air freight problems and opportunities are examined. Specific topics include: (a) fuel availability, (b) pricing issues in both passenger and freight markets, (c) aircraft of the 1980's, (d) inventory strategy using air freight, (e) deregulation of air freight, (f) scheduling of aircraft, and (g) accessibility of airports in the next decade.

Pipelines and domestic water carriers are the subject of Chapter 5. An overview of the pipeline industry is presented, along with an examination of the alternative pipelines proposed to transport Alaska crude oil from the West Coast to the central United States. Barge transportation is virtually unregulated, therefore, prices must be negotiated on a day-to-day basis, as examined in the article entitled, "Bid Competition on Barge Delivery." Other aspects of domestic water transportation which are discussed include: (a) a comparison chart showing the carrying capacity of barges versus rail cars and truck trailers, (b) a technical discussion, from two viewpoints, on why the Great Lakes freighter, **The Edmund Fitzgerald**, sank November 10, 1975, with all twenty-nine crew members aboard, and (c) a discussion of techniques which enable domestic water carriers to operate longer during the winter season.

Chapter 6 examines the complexities of international transportation. The initial articles note **why** international transportation is more complicated, especially in regard to the documentation required. Next, articles examine international air policy and the benefits of air freight when one ships internationally. The remaining selections examine the usage of ocean shipping. Topics discussed are: (a) cargo preference laws, (b) containerization, (c) the ocean shipping conference system, (d) port facilities, (e) current status of the shipbuilding industry, (f) the "cold war" in ocean shipping between the United States and Russia, and (g) changing patterns in the liner cargo business.

Chapter 7 takes a broader perspective than the previous six chapters. It examines physical distribution and logistics. In the first article, physical distribution and logistics consultant, E. Grosvenor Plowman, noted, "Physical distribution management provides the **right** material from the **right** location, via the **right** routing and in the **right** equipment, to the **right** destination in the **right** quantity for receiving at the **right** time and at the **right** total cost for all factors required." The articles in this chapter clearly indicate where transportation fits into a physical distribution and logistics system. They illustrate that transportation is one of the many important functional areas that combine to form a physical distribution and logistics department.

Traffic management is the topic of Chapter 8. It examines the transportation function from the shipper's viewpoint. The following topics are examined: (a) how traffic managers select carriers, (b) freight loss and damage matters, (c) advantages and disadvantages of a private truck fleet, and (d) whether the private truck fleet operator should apply to the ICC for common or contract carrier operating rights.

Chapter 9 examines another important aspect of transportation — mass transit. This involves the transportation of people in an urban environment. Mass transit systems are typically operated by public authorities because it is difficult to operate these systems at a profit. This chapter examines a number of problems, opportunities, and challenges in both bus and rail mass transit systems.

Undoubtedly the most controversial subject in transportation today is whether the railroad and trucking industries should be **deregulated**. This is the topic of Chapter 10. As a general statement, it appears the most fervent supporters of complete deregulation are federal government officials and academicians. Both shipper and carrier executives are much more reluctant to change a regulatory system that has produced an excellent transportation system in the United States. The articles in this Chapter **do not** represent a balanced discussion of the pros and cons of deregulation. Instead, they indicate the concern and trepidation that most carrier and shipper executives have regarding significant transportation deregulation.

Chapter 1
Introduction

Modal excellence key to transport policy

By **THE HONORABLE BROCK ADAMS**
Secretary of Transportation

☆ The Department of Transportation Act's declaration of purpose sets out in broad language the directions in which we must move in the effort to shape a safer, more efficient and economical transportation system. But, as thoughtful as that language may be, it reflects the vantagepoint of 1966. It does not, for instance, truly reflect today's concern for transportation's effect upon both the natural and social environments, nor does it fully address today's problem of transportation's voracious consumption of energy and the resulting drain on scarce resources with the consequences of imbalance of foreign trade and inflation.

With all due respect toward legislative language and its intent that some 12 years of service in Congress has engendered, I suggest that it is the success accorded the legislative proposals and the wisdom and integrity of his executive decisions that measure best a Secretary of Transportation's influence on molding policy.

My statement of national transportation policy, issued in February, is based for the most part on actions we have already taken, actions we are in the process of taking and those actions we contemplate taking in the future. In this article, I shall limit my comments to those areas of policy which can be expected to most directly affect the interests of domestic shippers.

Nothing has so impelled the need to rethink national transportation policy as the change in the world's energy economy. We have witnessed in just a few years a drastic shift from cheap to costly energy. As transportation adapts to this change, conservation of energy through efficient use of transportation resources becomes essential.

Economic growth with its resulting maximum demand on our transportation systems remains a primary national goal, but in meeting that demand we shall place top priority on achieving more efficient use of existing systems as opposed to investment in new systems. This is not to say we have shut the door on expansion of the transportation network, but expansion has a low priority except in cases of high payoff, such as increasing the ability to move coal.

As we move from the former emphasis on new transportation construction and investment we shall concentrate on the improvement and integration of our transportation services, on increasing operational efficiency and on eliminating wasteful redundancy. We must transcend the parochial interests of individual transportation modes and treat all in the best interests of a national system of transportation.

By applying these precepts to the elements of the interstate transportation network we have set these specific goals:

● Expediting the completion of the essential segments of the Interstate Highway System;

● Upgrading, rehabilitating and maintaining existing and needed railway, waterway, airway and highway systems;

● Encouraging decisions to eliminate redundant railway facilities and improve the quality of rail service;

● Improving integration of service within and between transportation modes, especially surface freight movements.

Also, to the maximum extent possible, we must eliminate direct and indirect subsidies to freight transportation. The public should not underwrite through taxation a major part of product shipping costs. Waterway user charges should be imposed to recover a substantial portion of federal waterway expenditures, and aviation and highway user charges should be periodically reexamined to insure that the transportation industries pay their fair share of the cost of constructing and maintaining airways and highways.

To the extent that space permits, I shall discuss the effect of new transportation policy on the major freight-hauling modes.

Highways. It is time to finish the job of completing the Interstate Highway System. We shall accelerate the completion of unfinished essential gaps in the system, then give priority on a continuing basis to the maintenance of this valuable network.

Railways. Federal financial assistance, possibly more than provided by existing legislation, is a necessary step in the restoration of the nation's rail system. Federal aid must be applied only to those facilities needed for the future movement of freight, and the most effective use of such aid will be in support of restructuring and rationalizing the system—a job the industry should do itself. Federal aid alone will not solve the rail industry's problems. We must look for solutions that do not lead to federal dependency.

Waterways. The federal policy toward inland and intercoastal waterways has been promotional and interrelated with regional economic development. For the most part, the principal opportunities for extension have been exploited. A funding system supporting the future operation, maintenance and rehabilitation of the inland waterway system involving substantial contribution from commercial users is needed, and the Administration strongly supports legislation to this end.

Airways. For the most part the major airport and airway facilities needed for the forseeable future are authorized or in place. We must now improve the use and management of these facilities, and continue to take advantage of new technologies that increase safety and productivity.

We shall place top priority on achieving more efficient use of existing systems.

Even a letter-perfect transportation policy devised by the federal executive branch will inevitably be frustrated unless implemented in a compatible economic regulatory environment.

The existing economic regulatory system treats each mode of transportation differently, often inhibits management initiative, and can encourage inefficiency by frustrating competition.

We shall strive for a system that treats all similar traffic moving between comparable origins and destinations the same, regardless of the mode of transportation. Meaningful reform will require statutory change and new legislative directions, as well as compatible actions by the independent regulatory agencies.

We shall encourage and attempt to foster marketplace decisions, integration of transportation services, incentives for energy conservation and competition where it can be efficiently supported. And at the same time, we shall not lose sight of the fact that a primary purpose of regulation is to provide the consumer with reliable non-monopolistic service. ★

Meeting the needs of commerce

By **WILLIAM T. COLEMAN, JR.**
SECRETARY OF TRANSPORTATION
1975 TO 1977

☆ Ever since Alexander Hamilton published his seminal essay in 1789 entitled "The State of Manufacturing in the United States," the sophisticated political leader has realized that the economic growth, vitality and welfare of the United States depend upon the construction and maintenance of a transportation system that meets efficiently the needs of commerce.

Because the Federal Government's transportation concerns were fragmented throughout many goverment departments and independent agencies, President Johnson exercised great wisdom and leadership in 1967 in creating the Department of Transportation which sought to place the principal transportation decision making responsibility and operational activities of the Federal executive branch in one department. Complete integration was prevented at that time by political choices and compromises—a wholesome attitude in any free, democratic society.

My predecessors in office, Secretaries Boyd, Volpe, and Brinegar made great strides in attempting to integrate the diverse transportation modes and elements, and many of the good policies and facilities now in place were the result of their effort and foresight.

One responsibility that Congress gave the Department of Transportation was to develop and aid in carrying out a national transportation policy. Obviously, since transportation services are provided for the most part by private concerns and state and local governments, and since different Federal agencies remain responsible for various transportation programs, the Department of Transportation is limited to providing guidance and coordination after it has articulated its concept of what the national transportation policy should be.

In the first official Statement of National Transportation Policy of September 17, 1975, and in "National Transportation: Trends and Choices" (to the year 2000) issued in early January 1977, I attempted to discharge my statutory responsibility. These documents did engender some public debate, and the Congress is now appropriately in the process of developing its ideas about what the national transportation policy should be.

It is my judgment that, as of now, emphasis and priority with respect to the transport of commercial and government freight should be on the following:

4

1. The Federal Government must use the tools now available under the Railroad Revitalization and Regulatory Reform Act signed by President Ford in 1976 to help create a modern efficient freight railroad system that will permit trains to operate in an integrated system coast to coast and north and south at average speeds of at least 80 miles per hour. Preferably, there should be two or three east and west continental freight railroad systems and at least two north and south systems. Ideally each major city and seaport should be served by at least two competing freight railroad systems. Each system should be supplemented by regional freight rail systems which serve the less concentrated manufacturing and farming activities of the country.

Such a modernized freight railroad system could be called upon to serve passenger needs if the country experienced a petroleum crisis which would make impossible the use of the private automobile, buses or airplanes.

2. The motor freight system is in good shape, but we must insist that our interstate highway system be completed in the next five to eight years and be kept modern. Greater federal involvement in financing the maintenance of this system is inevitable. Regulatory reform is urgently needed to promote greater efficiency and productivity, eliminate outmoded restrictions and conserve energy, but the financial investment of truckers in their operating certificates must be protected. Efficient intermodal transfers, including central distribution terminals, should be encouraged and supported by Federal funding. Prohibitions on the ownership of motor freight carriers by railroads should be eliminated. Serious consideration should be given to placing the highway gasoline tax on a percentage basis rather than on a fixed cent per gallon (now 4 cents) since revenues would increase as and if the cost of gasoline increased.

3. Air freight has tremendous potential, and innovation and competition in the air freight industry should be encouraged without economic regulation. The air system in this country must be kept modern, and we must make sure that we place airports where needed. We must have the political courage to locate new airports where they will meet the demands of the future. The aviation noise policy adopted in the Ford Administration must be completed and carried out, but we must make sure that unnecessary noise restrictions, such as curfews and antiquated regulatory policies, do not prevent the growth of the air freight system.

4. We must continue to improve on the delivery of transportation services. For the Department this means substantial reorganization to enable more effective, equitable, and balanced national, regional, and local decision making and financing. The present organization tends to emphasize decision making on the basis of the mode rather than the area to be serviced. The present financial assistance functions of FRA, UMTA, FHWA, and *perhaps part* of FAA, should be reorganized into an Interstate Surface Administration and an Urban and Rural Administration. Improved delivery also requires freeing up transportation carriers from the inequitable and unnecessary intrusion of government economic

---

Improved delivery requires freeing carriers from inequitable and unnecessary intrusion of government economic regulation

---

regulation. This means regulatory reform of the type suggested by President Ford and basically adopted by President Carter.

5. The construction and operation of transportation facilities are greatly affected by the public interest and thus require active public participation and public decision making. The decisions of the Federal Government must embrace policies that will assure that minorities actively participate and receive a significant share of contract and employment opportunities. Moreover, the government should work creatively in the construction and operation of facilities to reduce unemployment. Financing for needed transportation facilities should be viewed not only as transportation improvement but also as an activity which will reduce unemployment, improve the urban and rural environment, and aid in community and business development. ★

PASSENGER TRANSPORTATION:
People in Perpetual Motion

By John H. Jennrich

I F AMERICA could have only one symbol, it would be the wheel.

That would symbolize transportation, the lifeblood of a nation that moved its people from a toehold in Virginia to fill up a country that covers more than 3.5 million square miles.

Americans like to move. They move for business, for pleasure, and sometimes just because they're restless. The

play where it suits us. It promotes economic development and ties the nation together, both commercially and socially. On the other hand, it clogs courts and jams hospitals, pollutes air and water, disturbs tranquillity, razes neighborhoods, and has made us overly dependent on foreign oil.

But America wouldn't be America without mobility. Even with telephones,

of the National Transportation Policy Study Commission, says transportation's capital needs between now and 2000 will exceed $4 trillion, with $1 trillion to come from public funds.

Because passenger transportation is so big and so public, there is little about it that isn't funded and usually regulated by some government agency.

Mouths of rivers

Actually, government involvement wasn't always bad. The government took over the private postal service and moved it from horseback to stagecoach to railroad to airplanes.

In the earliest days, boats were vital. Cities developed first at the mouths of major rivers, then upriver. Fulton's steamboat in 1807 and canal barges in the mid-1820s extended waterborne traffic into the interior.

Roads followed—first corduroy, with logs across the road, then plank roads, only slightly better. Then came the English macadam method using crushed stone; the National Road from Cumberland, Md., to Wheeling, W. Va., was built this way in 1815-1818.

In the 1830s, the steam railroad, with all its infant problems of derailments and varying track gauges, created a mobility explosion. The first rail line of any appreciable distance was built in 1834 from Charleston, S. C., to the Savannah River 165 miles away. Soon, it carried 600 passengers a week on the same route previously served by only three stagecoaches a week.

Getting to the plane on time was never so easy. These monorail cars carry passengers from parking lots to the main terminal at Dallas-Fort Worth Airport.

average American today makes the equivalent of three transcontinental trips every year. Most of those trips are in motor vehicles, but America's wheel symbol shows signs of sprouting wings, too, as deregulated commercial aviation expands.

Passenger transportation, American-style, has been praised and damned. It allows us to live where we are comfortable, work where we are productive, and

computers, and other electronic communication, people still need to move from one place to another, whether across town or around the world.

Passenger transportation accounts for 12.5 percent of America's gross national product. One fifth of the labor force— more than 14 million workers—is involved in motor vehicle transportation alone.

Rep. Bud Shuster (R.-Pa.), chairman

Outer space

But the biggest boom of all came at the turn of the century with automobiles, quickly followed by buses. Between them, they increased domestic mobility at an unprecedented rate.

Commercial air travel came of age in the early 1930s, but it wasn't until the first scheduled commercial jet service in 1958 that aviation really began to move multitudes of people.

Next is outer space, with air shuttles and satellite communities. As an ordinary commercial venture, space travel won't occur until the 21st century—but that's only 21 years away. There are people alive today who remember the invention of the automobile, and they overlap the lives of people who witnessed the first steamboats, barges, and railroads. Someone born this month will no doubt travel in space some day with as much unconcern as we have in hopping on a local bus.

Projected growth

Despite the energy problems, most observers see Americans traveling more, not less. Fuel shortages won't reduce travel but will change the vehicle. There will be more fly-drive trips as people go long distance the quickest way, then move around locally in the vehicle that gives them the most freedom.

Air travel, the largest commercial passenger carrier, has the greatest projected growth.

The policy study commission will issue its report next month. Rep. Shuster's figures show that a moderate growth of air travel, including general aviation, between 1975 and 2000 will more than triple intercity passenger miles. Aviation's share of total intercity passenger miles—including air, rail, bus, and private auto—will rise from 11.2 percent to 20.2

percent. And that's without considering the effects of deregulation.

But growth won't come without problems. Dr. George W. James, senior vice president for economics and finance for the Air Transport Association of America, sees a need for airline capital investment of $60 billion during the 1980s alone, compared to $10 billion in the 1960s and $15 billion in the 1970s. The reason is the large number of jet aircraft delivered during the 1960s. By the 1980s, most of these will have to be replaced. The total fleet is now about 2,260 aircraft.

Dr. James says airlines are moving to larger planes with more efficient designs, including redesigned engines that will reduce fuel use. The Boeing 747 jumbo jets, which can now carry as many as 500 passengers, may be stretched to carry even more. One Boeing design calls for adding 25 feet to the fuselage, which would accommodate another 120 passengers.

Fuel economy is vital for the new generation of jets to offset rising prices. In 1973, jet fuel cost 12 cents a gallon and amounted to 12 percent of operating costs; by 1978, the cost had risen to 40 cents a gallon, accounting for 20 percent of operating costs. Each penny per gallon raises costs $100 million.

Labor also costs more. Average salaries are now up to $26,000, with top

pilots getting as much as $100,000 a year. The total labor force is slightly more than 308,000, a fairly constant figure in the past decade.

Labor and fuel equal two thirds of operating costs, says Dr. James, and with both rising at more than ten percent a year, "you have a devil of a time getting your costs down." While new aircraft designs will help, he says, increased productivity will have to come in other areas such as ticketing, computer systems, and maintenance.

Fuller loads

Airlines obviously have to increase their income but cannot count on raising fares to pay the bills because deregulation will increase the pressure to compete with low fares. Although fares will rise, the key is to increase the year-round load factor, which the airlines are already doing. In the early 1970s, planes averaged slightly more than 50 percent of capacity. By 1978, that figure had risen to 62 percent.

To the layman, says Dr. James, that seems like a lot of capacity to fill. But it's not. Many planes are flying full, especially during peak hours. On the other hand, quite a few planes must fly lightly loaded. Example: New York to Miami in winter is full; the return trip flies light. Another example: A plane flying several legs may not fill up until the final leg, but it has to fly light at first to reach the final, full-up leg.

One result of this airline strategy, says Dr. James, is that passengers must make reservations far in advance, especially if they want to fly a popular route or at peak time. Last-minute changes in flights won't be possible, he says, and there may be a penalty for canceling.

No-frills fares

Another possibility for increasing airline productivity is higher density seating configurations such as nine abreast in wide-bodied, three-engine jets and ten abreast in 747s. Airlines are also reducing service along with fares; the no-frills fares and other low-price tickets are inducing more people to fly.

The push toward greater productivity and mass transit is changing the way airlines operate. Dan A. Colussy, president and chief operating officer of Pan American World Airways, Inc., sees no breakthroughs in aircraft technology in the foreseeable future. New aircraft—such as the Boeing 757 and 767—will replace the old 707s designed for cheap fuel, "but they do not justify the replacement of more recent fleets." Supersonic planes or the use of hydrogen fuel "will

The "Americar" Way

A study by Congress's Office of Technology Assessment in Washington, D. C., finds that:

1. Americans have built a way of life based on mobility—provided mainly by private automobiles—and will give it up only as a last resort.

2. No other transportation is likely to satisfy this need to any significant extent over the foreseeable future.

3. The prospect of inadequate fuel supplies is the prime threat to the American way of life. All other problems are a distant second when compared to autos without gas.

4. Getting 27.5 miles per gallon may not reduce total fuel consumption because the number of miles will increase—more drivers, more automobiles, and more miles driven per car.

5. Even without man-made fuel crises, Mother Nature will cut production of oil, most likely in the 1990s.

6. Large increases in fuel prices

might reduce auto use. But in Western Europe and Japan, auto usage is still increasing, even at prices much higher than current U. S. prices.

7. Revolutionary changes in technology are long in coming. The steam engine, the diesel, and the jet engine required 20 to 50 years to progress from conception to commercial use.

OTA director Russell W. Peterson says: "The automobile industry has demonstrated that you do not need a 5,000-pound vehicle with a 300-horse-power engine and 40 gallons of gas to move a 200-pound person 400 miles.

"The industry has shown that the job can be done with a 2,000-pound vehicle, a 50-horsepower engine, and ten gallons of fuel. This is a phenomenal change.

"If everyone bought such a light vehicle, we could raise the fleet average to at least 40 mpg. The challenge is to get people out of heavy cars and into light ones."

Shipowners scramble to increase capacity while cruises boom as glamorous vacations. With new ships costing a fortune, one line cuts its ships in two and adds a middle section to accommodate more people. This Cunard liner is in St. Thomas.

By 2000, the airplane's share of intercity passenger miles will double, rising to one fifth of the total.

Amtrak's Broadway Ltd. rounds Horseshoe Curve in Pennsylvania. Despite promotion, trains are losing their share of traffic.

Intercity buses serve 15,000 towns in the U.S. Bus companies are struggling to upgrade image and cut government regulation.

Motor vehicles permeate passenger transportation, a fact of life that will continue well into the 21st century.

not have a major impact on commercial aviation until the 1990s,'' he says.

The big shift will be in airline management, no longer shackled by government regulation. The next decade, says Mr. Colussy, ''should bring to the fore professional business managers with training and experience in business administration, marketing, economics, and engineering.''

He suggests that the ''myth of the uniqueness of the airline business'' will disappear. Also, the impact on prices will be great: ''Fare structures will have all the simplicity and tranquillity of an oriental bazaar,'' he adds.

Trains are moving away

Back on the ground, one of America's oldest forms of transportation—the train—is moving away from the masses and, critics say, away from service, too.

Trains, according to Rep. Shuster, had a 0.41 percent share of intercity noncommuter traffic in 1975 with 5.4 billion passenger miles. By 2000, he says, rail travel will increase by only 14 percent—the smallest gain of all transport—to 6.2 billion passenger miles, a 0.26 percent share.

The overwhelming presence in the passenger train industry is Amtrak, more formally known as the National Railroad Passenger Corp. Amtrak trains cover nearly 100 percent of the noncommuter rail passenger miles in the United States.

Amtrak is marketing its services aggressively, but a recent report by the Interstate Commerce Commission shows that in fiscal 1978 Amtrak fell below 1977 performance—revenue was down 0.4 percent, number of passengers, down 1.5 percent, and passenger miles, down 6.9 percent.

''The slight downturn in Amtrak ridership,'' says the ICC, ''may be attributed in part to traveler uncertainty about schedules and services, since funding problems led to disruption of schedules and changes in route frequencies and service availability early in the year.''

Fiscal conservatism

To help cut costs, Transportation Secretary Brock Adams has proposed to cut Amtrak's rail system by 43 percent, trackage that Mr. Adams says carries only nine percent of Amtrak's riders.

''It pains me to say that I support Secretary Adams,'' says Rep. Shuster, who stands to lose a rail line through his district.

''I'd love to say that Amtrak is successful; I can't in good conscience say it's anything but a disaster.'' The line

through Altoona, Pa., in his district was found to carry only 28 riders a day. While those 28 riders are potential votes, Rep. Shuster's fiscal conservatism won out.

''If you want to get somewhere fast,'' he says, ''take the airplane.''

Amtrak, of course, doesn't agree. President Alan S. Boyd predicts improvements in 1979, including gains of 5.6 percent in ridership and 13.5 percent in revenues. While he does not anticipate that Amtrak will turn a profit anytime soon, he points out that Amtrak receives a relatively minor amount of federal money compared with highways, aviation, and urban mass transit.

Other entrepreneurs are trying to capitalize on the efficiency of rail travel and America's attachment to the family car. The Autotrain of the East runs from Virginia to Florida. In Texas, a new outfit called the American Intermodal Transportation Corp. proposes to start a short-haul autotrain service in the Dallas-Houston corridor.

A direct competitor to the train is the

intercity bus, which now serves about 15,000 communities. According to the American Bus Association, there are 46 Class I carriers, out of a total 1,050 carriers, that travel just under two thirds of the 25.7 billion bus passenger miles in 1977. The major carriers employ about 30,000 people.

Cheaper air fares affect the bus, too,

especially the Class I carriers that emphasize scheduled, rather than chartered, trips. An ABA spokesman says there were 15.95 billion Class I passenger miles in 1978, down from 16.4 billion in 1977.

Rep. Shuster's projection for intercity passenger miles by bus is a 23 percent increase from 25.4 billion in 1975 to 31.2 billion in 2000. That's a drop in the transportation share of passenger miles from 1.9 to 1.3 percent.

Leading the list

Buses are fuel efficient, both within and between cities. The Motor Vehicle Manufacturers Association compared auto, air, bus, and rail travel on the basis of energy consumed—measured in British Thermal Units—per intercity passenger mile.

The bus led the list with the lowest number of BTUs consumed, 1,070; followed by trains, 2,730; automobiles, 3,250; and airplanes, 9,300.

A major change in bus operations is

Rental cars will play an even greater role in passenger transportation by 2000. Fly-drive trips for business and pleasure will be popular.

likely if the federal government decides to deregulate the industry as it has airlines. Trailways, Inc., was the first bus company to call for such deregulation. J. Kevin Murphy, Trailways president, says deregulation would result in lower fares, better equipment, and more frequent service.

''If one bus company drops service,''

he says, "a competitor will jump right in. Maybe it will be a small firm. Maybe it will be us."

The greatest influence in transportation by far is the ubiquitous automobile. It accounts for 85 percent of intercity passenger miles. With projected growth of 63 percent between now and 2000, the auto's share of the market will drop to 78 percent, still four times larger than the next category, aviation.

Greatest by far

Autos rack up more than 90 percent of domestic passenger miles, or nearly 2.4 trillion miles out of a total of 2.6 trillion. By comparison, intercity and local transit buses have 2.7 percent; intercity and commuter rail have 0.4 percent; and commercial air carriers, 5.8 percent.

Autos alone—their purchase, maintenance, fees, use, and repairs—account for ten percent of America's gross national product. All other passenger transportation adds only two percentage points to the GNP.

Despite, or because of, its popularity, the automobile has come in for a great deal of criticism. It uses too much energy, pollutes the air, kills people, and clogs city and suburban streets.

The auto, which averaged 14 miles per gallon in 1974, is now required by law to average nearly twice that by 1985. And that may double by 2000.

Peter G. Koltnow, chairman of the executive committee of the Transportation Research Board, an arm of the National Academy of Science, and president of the Highway Users Federation, thinks the auto of 2000 will be like today's.

"It will be a box on four wheels with an internal combustion engine," he says.

Engineers at the American Automobile Association see the future car in finer detail. D. James McDowell and John Fobian predict an average 2,500-pound car, slightly lighter than the present Ford Fairmount, "that can hold four comfortably, five squashed."

Spare tires

They see more use of plastics and exotic materials such as graphite to reduce weight and more front-wheel drive. Spare tires and traditional tune-ups will be obsolete.

One thing is certain about the car of the future; the price is going up.

"Those people without two cars now will have a difficult time owning two of them in the future," says V. J. Adduci, president of the Motor Vehicle Manufacturers Association.

Rising costs will affect use as well as ownership, but Mr. Adduci isn't sure how much. "Will more expensive gas cause Americans to drive less or will they give up fancy food and drive just as much?"

The president of AAA, J. B. Creal, sees nothing in the next few decades to replace liquid fuels for cars.

Mr. Creal favors a more positive, supply-and-demand, nonregulated approach by the federal government. "The government should make it clear," he says, "that we don't intend to back out of the world as an industrial power or lower our high standard of living."

Fuel is the key element in passenger transportation for the next generation. Fuel's scarcity and cost will affect how every American travels. Costly fuel may put more commuters on buses and trains and more vacationers in planes and rental cars, but lack of fuel could stop America in its tracks.

Failure to solve fuel supply problems, concludes Secretary Adams, will result in transportation system breakdowns "overwhelming us by the mid-1980s." □

 To order reprints of this article, see page 12.

Airline ticket counters will get busier as America approaches the 21st century, and aviation doubles its share of intercity passenger miles in only 25 years.

On the Roads

America has 3.84 million miles of roads; 16.7 percent are urban, and 81 percent are surfaced.

The best-known highway is the interstate system; it includes one percent of America's roadways yet carries 20 percent of the traffic. The system is 91 percent complete. If finished, it will amount to 42,500 miles.

There are more than 563,000 bridges, 75 percent of which are more than 45 years old. More than 100,000 are structurally deficient or obsolete. According to Peter G. Koltnow, president of the Highway Users Federation, bridges fail on the average of one every other day.

A major source of funding for roads, at both federal and state levels, is the motor fuel tax. But as cars become more fuel efficient, less money goes into highway coffers.

About 3.5 percent of the federal budget is devoted to transportation, but the highway share of that has dropped from about two thirds to one half. Likewise, the highway portion of state and local budgets has dropped from 12 to six percent. The federal highway trust fund has a surplus of more than $10 billion, says Mr. Koltnow, who advocates spending that money soon.

"We need to improve our deteriorating roads or soon we'll be riding on another Penn Central Railroad."

DISTRIBUTION CAREER PATTERNS

Distribution executives are rising higher in their companies, earning more money, and spending less time on distribution matters, according to the authors' survey of the career patterns of distribution executives at U.S. companies.

The annual survey, now in its seventh year, was funded by the Logistics Research Fund of the Ohio State University.

The 1978 survey sought answers to a number of basic industry questions: How is distribution organized within companies? What are distribution managers' functions? How much are distribution executives compensated? Are there distinctive educational, occupational and age patterns for these executives? Do they see a need for specific education or background for their positions? What factors are shaping the distribution environment?

How much are executives
in distribution paid?
Where do they stand in
the corporate hierarchy?
In what areas do they
feel undereducated?
How do these executives
spend their time?
These are but a few
of the questions
asked in this survey
of career patterns
in distribution.

By DR. BERNARD J. LaLONDE,
Riley Professor of
Marketing and Logistics,
and **JEROME J. CRONIN,**
Research Associate,
Ohio State University

Data used in the study came from responses to a three-page questionnaire mailed to 368 members of the National Council of Physical Distribution Management during the summer of 1978.

The authors received 141 responses, a return of 38 percent. Of those, 119 responses were usable. The response rate, similar to rates in earlier years, was down from a 48 percent response to the 1977 survey. The response rate is still considered adequate in terms of level and representation, the authors note.

Finally, the authors warn readers to be wary of "generalizing year-to-year comparisons" with earlier surveys. Since the responses are made anonymously, they explain, there is no way to insure that the same respondents replied during both 1977 and 1978.

Continued

REPORTING RELATIONSHIPS OF DISTRIBUTION EXECUTIVES

Figures 1 and 2 show that the largest number of distribution executives still report to a functional vice president. However, on a percentage basis, those reporting in such a manner have dropped from 56 percent in the 1977 study to 40 percent this year.

The largest gain disclosed by this table can be found in the executive (group) vice president category. The number reporting in this category increased from 3 percent in 1977 to 16 percent in 1978.

This, combined with a corresponding drop (from 13 percent in 1977 to 2 percent in 1978) in the number of executives reporting to general managers, would seem to indicate that the P.D. function has continued to be upgraded from a sub-function of a department to a co-equal departmental status in a significant number of respondent companies.

Similarly, the number of distribution executives reporting directly to corporate presidents reversed its trend and increased during 1978. This seems to indicate a growth in the number of distribution vice presidents.

Conclusion: There has been a trend away from the distribution executive reporting to a functional vice president. This trend is at least partly due to organizational restructuring in many companies that has elevated the distribution function to the vice president level.

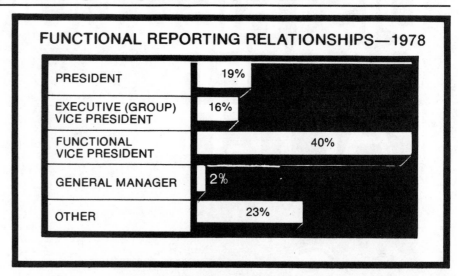

FUNCTIONAL REPORTING RELATIONSHIPS—1978

PRESIDENT	19%
EXECUTIVE (GROUP) VICE PRESIDENT	16%
FUNCTIONAL VICE PRESIDENT	40%
GENERAL MANAGER	2%
OTHER	23%

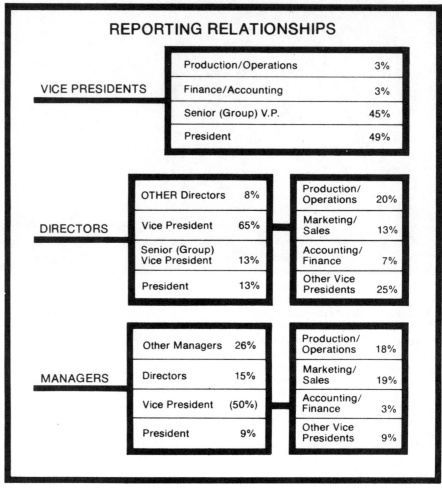

REPORTING RELATIONSHIPS

VICE PRESIDENTS

Production/Operations	3%
Finance/Accounting	3%
Senior (Group) V.P.	45%
President	49%

DIRECTORS

OTHER Directors	8%	Production/Operations	20%
Vice President	65%	Marketing/Sales	13%
Senior (Group) Vice President	13%	Accounting/Finance	7%
President	13%	Other Vice Presidents	25%

MANAGERS

Other Managers	26%	Production/Operations	18%
Directors	15%	Marketing/Sales	19%
Vice President	(50%)	Accounting/Finance	3%
President	9%	Other Vice Presidents	9%

HOW DISTRIBUTION EXECUTIVES SPEND THEIR WORK TIME

The table below shows that 23 percent of this year's sample of distribution executives have full international distribution responsibility for their companies. This represents a substantial increase over the past five years, indicating the growing importance of international markets to many firms.

Percent of Distribution Executives with Full International Distribution Responsibility

YEAR	PERCENT
1974	9.5%
1975	16.0%
1976	22.1%
1977	19.0%
1978	23.0%

The allocation of the distribution executive's time between distribution and non-distribution functions is illustrated in Figure 3.

The typical distribution executive now spends between 60 and 70 percent of work time on distribution-related tasks. This closely approximates the average range of the past several years' studies.

The pattern suggests that the higher the corporate positioning of the function, the more likely the executive is to spend time outside the traditional functional activities of distribution.

Of the non-distribution-related activities, general marketing functions require the most time while production-related activities follow as the second largest time user. Together, these two account for approximately 63 percent of the non-distribution-related time requirements of the typical P.D. executive.

A third and final observation which comes from this section is that the time requirement for finance-related interactions still falls far behind marketing and production requirements.

Conclusion: The distribution executive is spending less time in the purely distribution area and more time in general administration and interfacing with other major functional areas of the firm. This is particularly evident in the decline in the amount of time spent in the traffic and warehousing functions.

Continued

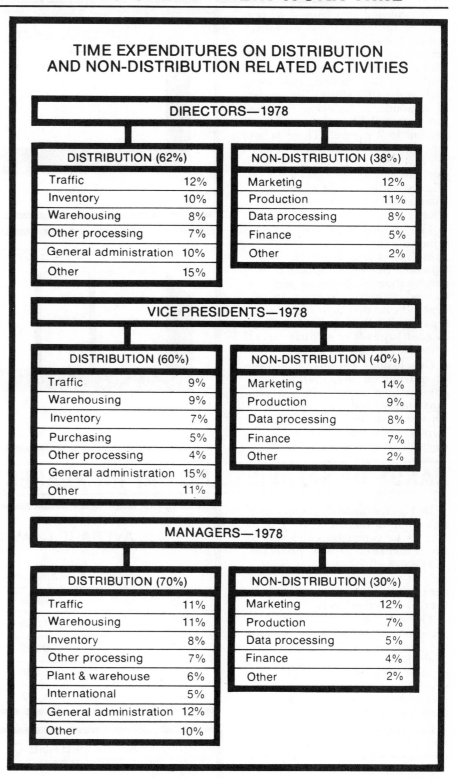

TIME EXPENDITURES ON DISTRIBUTION AND NON-DISTRIBUTION RELATED ACTIVITIES

DIRECTORS—1978

DISTRIBUTION (62%)		NON-DISTRIBUTION (38%)	
Traffic	12%	Marketing	12%
Inventory	10%	Production	11%
Warehousing	8%	Data processing	8%
Other processing	7%	Finance	5%
General administration	10%	Other	2%
Other	15%		

VICE PRESIDENTS—1978

DISTRIBUTION (60%)		NON-DISTRIBUTION (40%)	
Traffic	9%	Marketing	14%
Warehousing	9%	Production	9%
Inventory	7%	Data processing	8%
Purchasing	5%	Finance	7%
Other processing	4%	Other	2%
General administration	15%		
Other	11%		

MANAGERS—1978

DISTRIBUTION (70%)		NON-DISTRIBUTION (30%)	
Traffic	11%	Marketing	12%
Warehousing	11%	Production	7%
Inventory	8%	Data processing	5%
Other processing	7%	Finance	4%
Plant & warehouse	6%	Other	2%
International	5%		
General administration	12%		
Other	10%		

ORGANIZATION OF THE DISTRIBUTION FUNCTION

As indicated by Figure 4, 87 percent of the respondent executives possess both line and staff responsibilities within their organizations. This represents an increase of 8 percent over the number indicating such in the 1977 study. The number of respondents believing they had line responsibilities decreased by 4 percent to 9 percent. Those believing they had staff responsibilities fell to 4 percent. However, these reductions cannot be considered significant, as they could merely be attributed to year-to-year sample variation.

The findings presented in Figure 5 indicate that 40 percent of the responding firms have their distribution functions organized as a combination of divisional and centralized activities. Another 18 percent indicate that their firms have a separate distribution division. These percentages show only small changes from the 1977 study.

Conclusion: The dominant form of distribution organization which has emerged since 1970 is a combination line and staff organization. This has shifted away from the purely staff organization of the early 1970s.

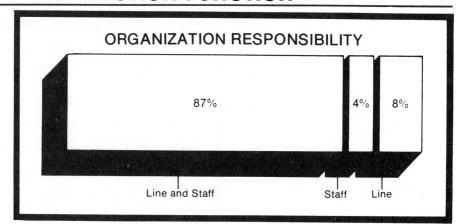

ORGANIZATION RESPONSIBILITY

87%   4%   8%

Line and Staff   Staff   Line

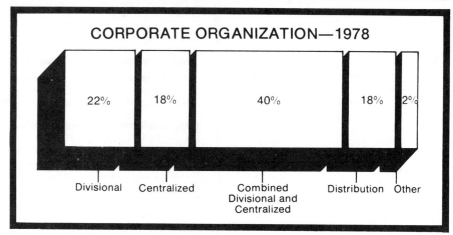

CORPORATE ORGANIZATION—1978

22%   18%   40%   18%   2%

Divisional   Centralized   Combined Divisional and Centralized   Distribution   Other

RANGE OF SALARIES AND PAY INCREASES

In Figures 6 and 7, average compensation levels of 1978 and increases in compensation levels for the period 1977-1978 are presented.

The overall salary levels, particularly at the director and vice president levels, have risen substantially over 1977 survey levels.

The only soft spot in the survey occurred in the higher ranges for the manager of distribution. This could be due to sampling variation or due to moves by many senior managers of distribution into the director or vice president levels in their organizations.

Conclusion: Compensation levels for distribution executives continue to outpace the rate of inflation. These increases undoubtedly also reflect the upward restructuring of the distribution function. The distribution director and vice president also tend to achieve their rank in the organization at a younger age (except for sales and marketing executives) than their functional counterparts in the firm.

AVERAGE COMPENSATION—1978

	Manager	Director	Vice President
Top quarter	$47,600	$58,900	$78,400
Second quarter	$34,000	$46,400	$57,000
Third quarter	$30,700	$39,900	$49,500
Lowest quarter	$25,200	$30,900	$38,100
Average	$34,375	$44,025	$55,750

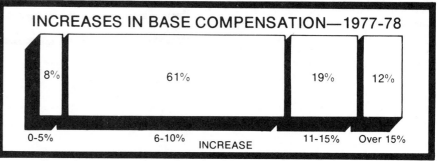

INCREASES IN BASE COMPENSATION—1977-78

8%   61%   19%   12%

0-5%   6-10%   INCREASE   11-15%   Over 15%

OCCUPATIONAL, EDUCATIONAL AND AGE BACKGROUNDS

As illustrated by Figure 8, the largest number of distribution executives still begin their careers in the production-manufacturing area.

However, while the number of managers indicating such a background remained fairly stable from 1977 to 1978, the three functional areas of traffic, distribution and marketing saw increases in the number of executives who began their careers within those areas.

Perhaps this is an indication that the distribution function is maturing and is seen as becoming more able to train its own executives, with some importation from other departments as needed.

The educational profile of the distribution executive, shown in Figures 9 and 10, saw only some random sample variations from the previous year. Emphasis is still on the college educated executive, as 95 percent of this year's respondents had at least some college and 89 percent had a college degree or more.

The percentage of P.D. executives with post-graduate work also increased during 1978 to a full 40 percent. Likewise, as indicated by Table 13, business administration and engineering and science backgrounds continued to dominate the undergraduate preparations of the executives in distribution capacities.

The age distribution of P.D. executives, as illustrated by Figure 11, remained similar to the patterns of recent years. The 40-49 age bracket continued to be the dominant age category of every job classification (manager, director, vice president).

Conclusion: There is a small but growing number of young, well-educated (usually with M.B.A. degree) distribution executives who have been formally educated in the distribution area and who are taking their places in the executive ranks of their firms. In the early 1970s it was unusual to find a distribution executive formally educated in the area who began his business career in the distribution area.

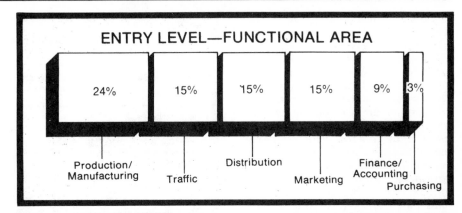

ENTRY LEVEL—FUNCTIONAL AREA

24% Production/Manufacturing — 15% Traffic — 15% Distribution — 15% Marketing — 9% Finance/Accounting — 3% Purchasing

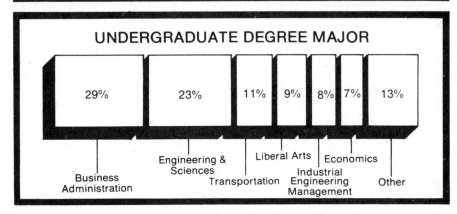

EDUCATIONAL BACKGROUND—1978

5% High school graduate — 6% College, non-degree — 49% College graduate — 9% Graduate school non-degree — 31% Master's degree

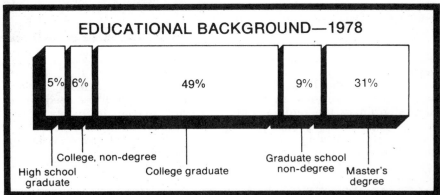

UNDERGRADUATE DEGREE MAJOR

29% Business Administration — 23% Engineering & Sciences — 11% Transportation — 9% Liberal Arts — 8% Industrial Engineering Management — 7% Economics — 13% Other

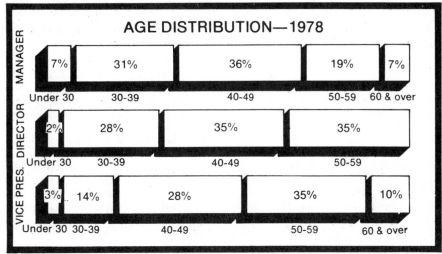

AGE DISTRIBUTION—1978

MANAGER: 7% Under 30 — 31% 30-39 — 36% 40-49 — 19% 50-59 — 7% 60 & over

DIRECTOR: 2% Under 30 — 28% 30-39 — 35% 40-49 — 35% 50-59

VICE PRES.: 3% Under 30 — 14% 30-39 — 28% 40-49 — 35% 50-59 — 10% 60 & over

PERCEIVED EDUCATIONAL NEEDS

Distribution executives again this year indicated by a wide margin that finance was the one academic area where they felt they could use additional educational foundation (Figure 12). Data processing, marketing and distribution planning were other areas of concern to the respondents. There was no significant change from the concerns noted in previous surveys.

The concern for more financial knowledge would appear to be unrelated to the time spent interacting and performing joint duties with the finance area within the firm, according to data gathered in this study.

Conclusion: There have been significant changes in the scope of responsibility of the distribution executive during the 1970s. The upward restructuring noted earlier has shifted primary job requirements away from the managing of activities (i.e., transportation and warehousing) to the management of a goal-directed organization. This, in turn, has prompted the need for a different set of managerial skills and knowledge. These needs are reflected in the desire of the distribution executive to learn more about the area of finance, data processing and planning skills.

EDUCATIONAL NEEDS—1978		
Area	First Choice	Second Choice
Finance	34%	12%
Data Processing	8%	10%
Distribution Planning	7%	9%
Marketing	4%	10%
Transportation	5%	3%
Organizational Behavior	4%	6%
Economics	4%	2%

THE FUTURE DISTRIBUTION ENVIRONMENT

The problem of distribution costs continued to be foremost on the minds of distribution executives. As illustrated by Figure 13, the two highest rated determining factors were distribution costs and "the economy." The inflationary pressures linking these two factors apparently caused such concern over cost factors that a better than three-fold increase was evidenced in their levels over 1977.

Customer service was also a frequently mentioned factor which would help determine the future P.D. environment. Again, this seems to be at least marginally related to the cost concerns as the service level connotes a cost-service trade-off. This concern also could be a carry-over of the weather-related difficulties encountered in many parts of the U.S. during the past two winters.

It also seemed significant that concern over energy dropped off of this year's list of factors. Evidently, the respondents felt that energy would be available and they may have lumped their concern over the cost and availability of fuels into the "economy" response category.

Conclusion: Along with the shift in responsibilities noted above has come a concern with a broader perspective of the management task. The distribution executive of today is concerned with both the external environment (energy, inflation, etc) and in integrating the important functional interfaces with the distribution function in a total corporate planning context. ■

FACTORS SHAPING THE FUTURE DISTRIBUTION ENVIRONMENT		
Factor	Most Important	2nd Most Important
Distribution Costs	40%	15%
Customer Service	6%	16%
Economy	8%	10%
Top Management's View of Physical Distribution	5%	6%
EDP—New Technology	7%	7%

Editorial

A Transportation Career — An Honorable Calling

Although we are mindful of the continuing and pervasive interest of American traffic and transportation professionals in the issues generated by the ongoing debate about relaxation or abolition of transportation regulation, we believe there's enough reading material about that debate on other pages of this issue to justify our giving attention on this page to another subject we deem no less important. It's the subject of striving for increased interest in, and betterment of the opportunities for, careers in the transportation field.

In our opinion, based on dozens of years of acquaintanceship with people employed in various levels of income-producing activities associated with transportation or physical distribution, the quality and trustworthiness and good citizenship of transportation careerists are unexcelled anywhere. The transportation management profession (which in our book includes management of physical distribution or business logistics functions) is truly an honorable and essential profession. Any participant in a transportation endeavor is a participant in a kind of service without which the commerce and industry of the United States could not exist.

To any young person who is intelligent, industrious, has a cooperative attitude and is about to start working for a typical transportation company or industrial or commercial traffic department we'd like to say: "You are beginning an employment experience in which your life will be enriched by friendships of business associates and acquaintances whom you will admire more and more as time goes on. I congratulate you on your choice of a career; it may not bring you great riches, but it *will* give you much happiness and, in the normal course of events, will enable you to live comfortably."

That young person might ask us, "What can I do, or what should I do, in addition to handling my work assignments diligently, to gain recognition and promotion as rapidly as possible?" We would include in our reply the advice that it would be helpful to the young worker to become a certificated member of the American Society of Traffic and Transportation, by preparing for, taking and passing the series of examinations that lead to acquisition of the "CM" (certified member) designation for successful examinees. It has been a special pleasure for us to see increases in the number of leaders in the managements of transportation companies and of physical distribution responsibilities who are in the "CM" category of AST & T membership.

For advice on what textbooks and other reading material you should study in preparing to take any or all of the AST & T examinations, you should address your inquiry to the AST & T headquarters, 543 West Jackson Boulevard, Chicago, Ill. 60606, where Carter M. Harrison, the executive director of the Society, and Mrs. Jo Ann Mangrum, its registrar, have their offices. Worthy of mention, we think, is the fact that all the national officers of the Society (except one, who is an educator member) are certified members.

The 1979 spring series of AST & T examinations will be held May 10 and 11 at centers as conveniently accessible as possible for the candidates for the examinations. We'll be delighted when and if we get a report that the candidate list for those examinations is the largest ever.

It seems appropriate to quote at this point parts of the speech made by Robert H. Curlette at the Society's 1978 annual meeting, last August 25, in Pittsburgh, after he had been elected as the Society's national president:

"Every class of members has responsibilities for helping the Society move toward its goals by encouraging women as well as men to enter the examination program, to assist those who falter to pick up and complete the examinations, including the research paper, and to urge certified members whose interest may have flagged to work with those at hand who are prospective candidates to pursue that professional aspiration within the Society's educational guidelines. . . . We owe a debt to our profession to help increase its value to ourselves by representing it, by supporting it, and by assisting the newcomers to come aboard. . . ."

Entitled to much commendation for the help it has given the AST & T and for the other contributions it has made to the cause of transportation education and the launching of professional careers in this field is the Delta Nu Alpha Transportation Fraternity, about which we'll have more to say at a later date. Valuable contributions to the encouragement and promotion of transportation education and of recruitment of talented young people for transportation jobs has been given also by the National Defense Transportation Association. It devoted an important part of its 1978 Transportation and Logistics Forum program, last October, in Washington, D.C., to discussion of "Careers and Educational Opportunities in Transportation." One of the speakers on that subject, Maj.-Gen. Rufus L. Billups, director of logistics plans and programs at the U.S. Air Force Headquarters, said that "our potential managers and corporate level executives should possess at least a master's degree in transportation and related fields." He added that "ideally, if they followed the course guide to certification in such professional societies as the American Society of Traffic and Transportation they would have met the course requirements of a qualified middle and upper level transportation executive." Another member of the NDTA transportation education panel, Dr. Charles A. Taff, professor of transportation and distribution at the University of Maryland, counseled that a combination of an undergraduate major in transportation or physical distribution or logistics with an MBA is "an extremely hard combination to beat as one moves up the managerial ladder." That's good advice and it has been used by many who have moved or are moving to top positions in the highly honorable calling of transportation management.

Chapter 2
Motor Carriers

ON-LINE, OVER THE ROAD

Sophisticated computers used by top motor carriers today provide shippers with more than just a better tracing capability. They give shippers better access to equipment, reduced OS&D and more reliable service

By THOMAS A. FOSTER, Editor

The Distribution Manager was really on the spot.

Unless he was absolutely certain two shipments of electrical components moving by motor carrier would arrive that afternoon, an entire 200-man production line would have to be closed down immediately.

The VP of production was on the phone, and he wanted an answer now. Would the shipments arrive in time?

Normally, it would take an expeditor hours to track down the vital shipments with absolute certainty, but the Distribution Manager had a new tool at his disposal.

He had an assistant punch a few numbers into a small computer terminal in the outer office, and within seconds the answer came back directly from the motor carrier handling the shipments. Fortunately, one trailer was just a few hours away and another one with the other components was even closer.

The Distribution Manager told the VP to keep the line open. The components would be on hand, even if it meant picking them up at the carrier's terminal.

Scenes like this one aren't exactly commonplace yet, but a few hundred shippers do have this type of direct electronic data interchange (EDI) with common carriers. And virtually any shipper dealing with one of the top motor carriers in the country can get tracing information within minutes by just using the phone.

"We have about 115 shippers of all types of commodities hooked into our computer, giving them direct tracing inquiry capability," says Gary Paler. He is vice-president of management systems for Spector Freight, which has one of the most advanced motor carrier computer systems.

"All a shipper needs is a teletype or equivalent equipment, and we are adding more shippers to the system almost every day," says Paler. "But it now seems many shippers find auto-reporting terminals linked to our computer more useful. The devices print out a daily computer log of shipments in our system headed for their location. In effect, they have a complete tracing report each morning. Such a report has the side benefit of allowing the consignee to monitor his suppliers.

"We also are working on an EDI program with shippers that will handle freight settlements directly between our computer and theirs," Paler continues. "This would be a giant step in eliminating much of the paperwork associated with motor carriage."

Motor carriers are now one of the most computer-oriented modes in the U.S. Applications of EDP and EDI are not limited to tracing and billing. Most of the top truck lines have on-line systems that monitor the flow of traffic as it moves.

The vastly improved control these systems give the motor carrier over the movement of freight benefits the shipper in quite a few ways he probably never knows about.

"Having an on-line system means we know what is happening to the freight right at that moment," says Charles Hardesty, senior vice-president of marketing for Mason & Dixon Lines in Kingsport, Tenn. "If problems occur, we can do something about it immediately. Without this on-line, real-time capability, we could only document foul-ups after they happen, and that wouldn't help us or the shipper."

The system developed by Mason & Dixon is fairly representative of the more advanced programs in use today. Called MADIX, the system eliminates much of the paperwork normally associated with motor carriage.

The customer bill of lading is turned over to a clerk at the truck terminal by the pickup driver. The information is keyed into a remote computer terminal by the clerk. No paper documents again come into play until the shipment arrives at the final terminal. At this time, another remote terminal prints out a completed freight bill for the consignee. All the information needed to move the shipment from origin to destination is held in the MADIX computer and can be accessed at anytime by any terminal.

On-line reports

The MADIX system also features centralized rating. No freight bills are rated at the individual terminals. A specialized crew of rate clerks at the headquarters in Kingsport access the basic freight bill information on CRTs and add the proper rates. According to Mason & Dixon, this system has cut the cost of rating in half and has reduced errors by at least 10%.

Not all motor carriers have chosen to include centralized rating, however, and one carrier in the West actually removed the central rating from its on-line system because of persistent technical problems.

Quite a few shippers, even large ones, are not entirely convinced all the "behind-the-scenes" reports generated by motor carrier computers benefit them.

"We know most of the larger carriers we use have recently developed sophisticated computer systems, but the actual service payoff to us, as a shipper, is difficult to measure," says Larry Foley, assistant traffic manager for Detroit Diesel Allison in Detroit.

"One thing that is immediately apparent is the benefit of the direct tracing link to the carrier computer which one trucker offers," says Foley. "This capability is especially useful to our distributors since they have to instantly know what parts are on their way. If this direct computer link could be expanded to provide forwarding information, freight charges and probable arrival *Continued*

INBOUND LOG

F/B	CONSIGNEE	S/N	SHIPPER	PCS	WT	REV	TRL
22050739	K MART 3383	103212	TAMPAX INC *	8	122	1780	07451P
22050746	*K MART 4016	103205	TAMPAX INC *	9	116	1840	07451P
09169816	KARTHRYN'S C	NS	FO MERZ & CO	3	85	1570	R5069C
38050779	KIMBERLY CLA		E L WIEGAND	1	3800	24928	09264C
27216887	LANDRUM MILL		YORK SAW & M	1	310	2396	YRK C
01371954	M&D	SUPPLIES	M&D	1	20	D/H	41350
02181423	MASTERCRAFT	0668640	ARTLEE FABRI*	4	350	RATE	09292
22050742	*MCKESSON & R	103202	TAMPAX INC *	6	129	1840	07451P
08083253	*MOFFATT BRG		NICE BALL BE	5	258	2504	LAN C
04105425	MOORES #92	20575	MOORES SUPER	2	70	1258	S6038C
09169830	MOORES SUPER	NS	AZ BOGERT CO	12	576	2742	07842P
24152795	MORGAN BROS	17537	BINNEY & SMI	31	161	1980	41225C
47083644	MORSE SHOE O	00869	MORSE SHOE I	16	400	5478	48323P
01371480	MRE PAT FORT		TRI-STATE RE	25	398	2300	ASH C
33021074	*MURPHEE-TAT	31134	MARTIN INDUS	20	2377	10505	41144C
32036766	RCA/DISTRIBU	05606	FORBES DIST	48	2547	16072	41224C
38050796	REVCO DRUG #		BRINN CHINA	11	365	2774	09264C
38050797	REVCO CHINA		BRINN CHINA	11	420	3192	09264P
11031504	*REVCO INC	BILL2	GENERAL ELEC	2	30	1766	41373P
47083627	*RICHWAY C/O	00887	MORSE SHOE I	24	600	6384	48323P
47083628	*RICHWAY C/O	00885	MORSE SHOE I	17	425	5320	48323P
47083634	*RICHWAY C/O	00886	MORSE SHOE I	17	425	5320	48323P
57024579	RONS WATCH R	982	GERMANOW SIM	3	195	2968	07686C
16179295	SA DEHART SO	436396	GEORGIA BOOT*	5	212	1688	41329C

Each terminal receives an outbound log every morning from the central computer. All shipments scheduled to leave that day are listed by the shippers' names, which are arranged alphabetically. The report is used by the terminal manager to load out his trailers. It also serves as an outbound tracing index. The freight bill number, which is needed to make an inquiry, is easily found if the name of the shipper is known.

OUTBOUND LOG

F/B	SHIPPER	S/N	CONSIGNEE	PCS	WGT	REV	TRL	DES
113697	ADA CO INC	08059	PHILADELPHIA	10	904	9570	ASH	BIN C
113589	AIR PREHEATIX	097282	GENERAL INTE	1	2750	RATE	09086MIL	
113684	AIR PREHEATAPX	57085	SUN O LIN CH	1	50	1600	09086WIL	C
113544	AMERICAN WOO	33402	OHIO VALLEY	8	104	RATE	41355MFS*	
113695	AMERICAN EN	T2422	SHIRLO KNITS	65	6572	23988	09086ATN	P
113694	*BARCLAY HOM	242577	SS KRESGE	337	5428	45649	08021MFS	C
113630	BEACON MFG 1104	1960	DAYS INN	63	693	11095	48333FTW*	C
113698	BLUE RIDGE	1825	SYRACUSE CON	3	213	1923	ASH	SYR C
113699	BLUE RIDGE	1818	GALLI READY	32	1410	7592	ASH	WPT C
113519	*CARO KNIT I	180943	CHEROKEE BOA	7	1526	5478	KNX	KNX C
113706	CAROLINA SH		DIXIE WESTER	4	110	1336	ASH	BHM C
113707	CAROLINA SH		NEW HOLLAND	68	2900	17777	ASH	YRK C
113743	CHAMPION PA		COPCO PAPERS	816	38641	47915	41151COL	P
113483	CTS	01807	BUNNELL PLAS	2	96	1634	09245BRL	C
109587A	DAVID MORGA	2733	CHAIR IMPORT	1	20	MEMO	SEC	SEC*C
113664	DAVID MORGA	1673	YOUNGSTOWN D	5	240	3110	09086BUF*	C
113665	DAVID MORGA	1674	KERSTEN BROT	8	547	13429	08021MFS*	C
113675	DAYCO CORP	07802	T B A SUP CO	29	485	3620	09086ATN	P
11376	DAYCO CORP	PB101310	INTERNATIONA	37	435	4040	08021FTW	P
113677	DAYCO CORP	07898	HERR & CO IN	4	136	1645	09086YRK	P
113585	DIAMOND BRA	06591	CHIMNEY MOUN	20	600	RATE	A0415SYR	
113701	DIAMOND BRA	06576	BOY SCOUTS O	28	510	4376	ASH	NBK C
113702	DIAMOND BRA	06568	CAMP YANKEE	4	156	1780	ASH	NHC*P
113680	E & W HOISE		SCHECTER & R	6	180	2396	09086SEC	C
113599	*E I DUPONT	242300	AIr8PC US AR	1	128	2157	09080SEC	C
113430	*ETHAN ALLEN	754343	GAMBLE BROS	2	2000	12100	LOU	LOU C

Each terminal also receives an inbound log every morning from the computer. All shipments loaded out that day for that terminal are listed on the log by the consignees' names, which are arranged alphabetically. The report helps the terminal manager plan for inbound freight handling, and it serves as an inbound tracing index. The freight bill number, which is needed to make an inquiry, is easily found if the name of the consignee is known.

MANIFEST

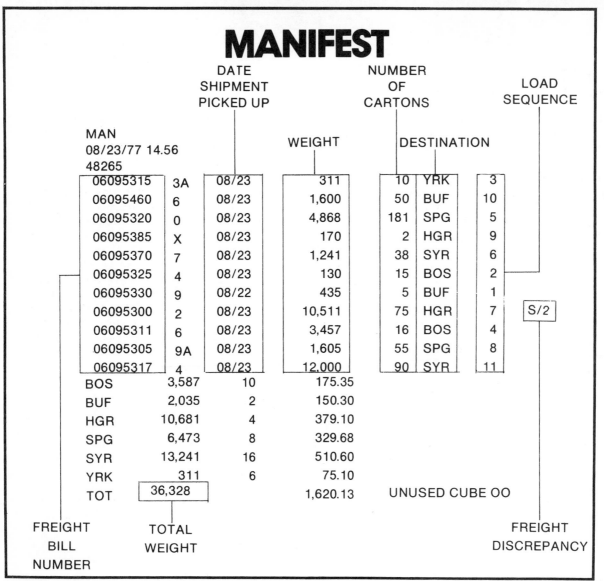

MAN
08/23/77 14.56
48265

FREIGHT BILL NUMBER		DATE SHIPMENT PICKED UP	WEIGHT	NUMBER OF CARTONS	DESTINATION	LOAD SEQUENCE
06095315	3A	08/23	311	10	YRK	3
06095460	6	08/23	1,600	50	BUF	10
06095320	0	08/23	4,868	181	SPG	5
06095385	X	08/23	170	2	HGR	9
06095370	7	08/23	1,241	38	SYR	6
06095325	4	08/23	130	15	BOS	2
06095330	9	08/23	435	5	BUF	1
06095300	2	08/23	10,511	75	HGR	7
06095311	6	08/23	3,457	16	BOS	4
06095305	9A	08/23	1,605	55	SPG	8
06095317	4	08/23	12,000	90	SYR	11

S/2 (FREIGHT DISCREPANCY)

	TOTAL WEIGHT		
BOS	3,587	10	175.35
BUF	2,035	2	150.30
HGR	10,681	4	379.10
SPG	6,473	8	329.68
SYR	13,241	16	510.60
YRK	311	6	75.10
TOT	36,328		1,620.13

UNUSED CUBE OO

As shipments are loaded on the trailer, the freight bill number is fed into the computer. When the trailer is loaded, the manifest is automatically produced. It includes the freight bill number (sometimes called the pro number) of each shipment, date when the shipment was picked up, weight and number of pieces in each shipment, destination of each shipment, load sequence, total weight of the freight, and any discrepancies such as overs or shorts.

TRACING INQUIRY BY TRAILER NUMBER

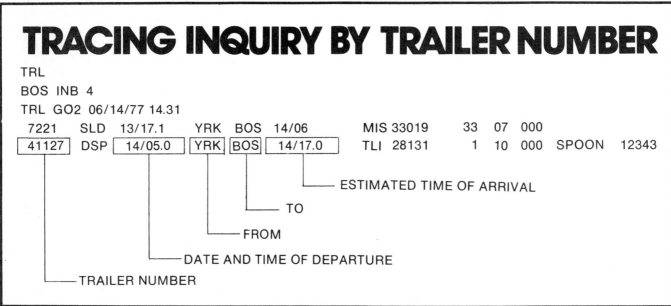

TRL
BOS INB 4
TRL GO2 06/14/77 14.31

7221	SLD	13/17.1	YRK	BOS	14/06	MIS 33019	33	07	000
41127	DSP	14/05.0	YRK	BOS	14/17.0	TLI 28131	1	10	000 SPOON 12343

- ESTIMATED TIME OF ARRIVAL
- TO
- FROM
- DATE AND TIME OF DEPARTURE
- TRAILER NUMBER

When a trailer departs this report is automatically sent to the destination terminal so the manager there can prepare for its arrival. He will request a manifest and freight bills for all shipments terminating in his area.

times, our distributors could greatly improve their inventory control systems."

Computerized tracing reports directly from the carrier are, of course, the most obvious benefit to the shipper from a carrier's EDP system. But before this capability is expanded to provide other data, there are probably going to be significant changes in existing programs.

"I think a few carriers went off half-cocked with their direct inquiry/response programs," says a shipper who is active on several joint carrier-shipper committees working on EDI projects. "While these existing systems certainly work and are extremely useful to the shipper, there is an obvious lack of standardization.

"As more carriers develop their own home-grown systems and put their remote terminals into shipper locations, the problem is going to get worse. Every carrier has developed his own format, codings and data elements, so no two direct response systems are exactly the same.

"Just in the last week or so, a joint shipper-carrier committee at the Transportation Data Coordinating Committee adopted data standards for truck status inquiry/response reports," the shipper explains.

Data standards

"Future EDI tracing systems linking carriers and shippers will probably use these standards. It just makes sense, so the carriers with existing systems will eventually have to conform to these standards," the shipper says.

Despite these minor differences in formats, most of the computer systems used by the top motor carriers today are fairly similar in design and capability.

The heart of practically all of these on-line systems is a data bank made up of two files: a freight bill file and a carrier equipment file. When the freight bill is keyed into the computer,

the data is captured and is married to the particular trailer carrying the shipment. Every time the shipment changes trailers the computer remarries the two data elements.

The key to the freight bill file is the freight bill number (sometimes called the pro number). The key to the equipment file is the trailer number. By inquiring about either number, the system can locate both.

"With up-to-the-minute data on just these two data elements, we can produce dozens of reports that help keep the freight moving," says A. Lowry Doggett, director of information systems for Mason & Dixon.

"We can get the outbound loading status of all trailers at any terminal right now, which tells us when a particular shipment left that terminal. If we see that a trailer has been sitting at the terminal for a few hours, we can find out why and make corrections. There is a similar report for inbound trailers.

"The MADIX system also allows us to get the equipment the shipper needs when he needs it," says Doggett. "Whether he needs an insulated trailer, an open-top or some other special piece of equipment, we can find the closest one in seconds just by asking the computer.

"Problems with overs and shorts are greatly reduced because every piece of freight we ever pick up is keyed into the computer," Doggett explains. "One person sitting in front of a CRT can match more overs and shorts than any army of freight hustlers rummaging through cartons on a loading dock.

"If an over or short shows up on a shipment at the loading dock, the terminal manager immediately enters that information into the computer," says Doggett. "All these overs and shorts then appear on a special OS&D report that is constantly updated.

"More often than not, this re-

port will place the overs and shorts right next to each other, even if in reality one carton is going to Cincinnati and the rest are headed for Jacksonville. With this information available so fast, we often can have shorts headed back in the right direction before the rest of the shipment is delivered."

Service reports

These on-line capabilities bring the most benefit to shipper. There are also a number of service reports produced by most carriers that may be on-line or batch processed. These would include reports of trailers or shipments that exceeded service standards for a particular route, and perhaps an analysis of how late the shipments actually were.

The carrier uses these to correct on-going problems at a particular terminal, but the shipper can also use the information.

"Our company has a customer service project that included monitoring transit times to our distributors," says a distribution manager for a Midwest chemical company. "We recently installed an automatic tracing terminal that allows a couple motor carriers to give us daily reports on inbound and outbound shipments. This data, when combined with service reports we get from all carriers, gives us a pretty good idea of the service we provide our customers and, at the same time, an idea of the service various carriers are giving us."

Right now, only about 50 motor carriers across the country have truely advanced computer systems with on-line processing that gives them—or will give them—the capability to tie in with shippers' data terminals or computers.

"A motor carrier has to have monthly revenues of $3 million to $5 million to make an on-line network worthwhile," says Jerry Yarborough, vice-president of Arkansas Best Corporation's Data-

CISS—An Idea Whose Time Has Come

Truckers call it "haulin' post holes," but by any name empty backhauls are a waste of time, money and gasoline. Needless to say, they also are an important cause of ever-increasing motor carrier rates.

Common carriers log 701 million empty backhaul miles each year, according to the American Trucking Association. An estimated 35 million gallons of diesel fuel are wasted on these trips.

ATA is trying to cut down on the waste with a trailer exchange program called Computerized Interchange Substituted Service (CISS). The stated goal of the program, which began in April, is to save 180 million backhaul miles and to conserve over 8 million gallons of diesel fuel.

The five-month-old CISS program is off to a slow start, according to ATA sources. Slowing its progress are carriers who are either not ready or not willing to get involved. For example, one major carrier's nationwide system couldn't use CISS because the carrier lacked a central computer.

When hooked into CISS, a carrier can post information on excess loads, available drivers and extra power units. A second carrier then can connect with the first to match his needs. The company getting help pays the accompanying carrier 70 cents per ton-mile, which is about 15 cents over normal operating costs for over-the-road carriage.

The carrier can easily recover CISS costs, according to ATA, because one match would more than cover one month's computer rental fee.

One carrier, for example, says his computer leases for slightly over $50 a month. One match with another carrier saved him $244, he says.

Most shippers interviewed by DW had not heard of CISS, but said they've been aware of manually operated equipment-interchange operations. Most were not convinced these manual operations improved service or reduced delays.

"Many times the carrier will hold onto our freight waiting to balance his loads in both directions, so he could make those runs more profitably," says the TM of a major New York drug house. "I'm in favor of a pooling of carrier resources, but only if it helps avoid delays and doesn't cause them. The CISS network might be the key to helping the carrier and the shipper."

Shippers who have heard of CISS seem to support it, but perhaps have a few reservations.

"The only concern my company would have with CISS is if an unreliable carrier were given my freight without our knowing it," says R. J. Gallagher, traffic manager for Honeywell.

"There are some carriers I just wouldn't use, and I would like to think I could reserve the right to restrict a carrier from getting our freight," Gallagher says.

"But other than the problem with unacceptable carriers, I don't care who hauls my freight," says Gallagher. "As long as I know what rates I'm getting and the approximate service I can expect, it doesn't matter."

And CISS seems to have given some distribution experts hope where there was once nothing but resignation.

In 1975, Dr. Nicholas Glaskowsky, of the University of Miami, and two of his colleagues conducted an independent evaluation of critical issues within the trucking industry.

"There have been many lurid claims made over the years about the amount of empty backhaul mileage in the trucking industry," the management and logistics experts wrote in the treatise that followed the 1975 study. "It is obvious that the backhaul problem is not a solvable problem, but is rather a fact of transport operations with which we live."

"CISS makes sense," Glaskowsky says today. "It's a scientific method of linking up trucks and shippers' goods and schedules that has to be an overall net gain. You're reducing empty ton-miles. The shipper automatically benefits."

Most shippers agree with Glaskowsky, particularly on the subject of keeping down costs.

"I'm for anything that holds down a carrier's expenses," comments Armour-Dial TM Frank Post. "Anything that saves somebody backhauls and reduces empty miles is an obvious benefit to the shipper."

Post does have one nudging, bothersome thought. "I have to wonder," he worries, "knowing all of the petty jealousies that go on in this industry, whether the program in fact has any chance at success."

CW Transports' Robert Shaw agrees there is a problem. "One of the things we have to eliminate is the carriers' reluctance to have somebody else haul their freight. I think every carrier has the same resistance. It's one of the first things that has to change if the program is to succeed." □

---

tronics division. "Right now, relatively few carriers fall into that category. Besides developing the computer system for ABF, our division is in the business of developing the EDP capabilities of smaller truck lines, so we are looking forward to the time when more carriers will be able to advance their systems. I don't think that day is too far off because,

overall, computer technology is actually becoming less expensive.

"When more trucking companies have advanced EDP or EDI systems, the smaller shipper will be the ultimate beneficiary," explains Yarborough. "The big shippers that have their own advanced computer systems and understand the value of on-line information are the ones who can

best take advantage of the EDP systems used by the top motor carriers today.

"As smaller shippers and motor carriers become more educated in the uses of computer technology, I think the overall quality of highway transportation will increase greatly," says Yarborough. "The technology already exists; it's just a matter of learning how to apply it." ∎

Highway transportation:

Technology fuels conservation

The gut reaction of many a trucker when the 55-mph speed limit went into force was defiance. The image of the angry trucker was glamorized by the popular press, and convoys of speeding truckers chattering in CB lingo quickly joined older American legends. In actuality, however, the self-proclaimed outlaws of the highway are a small minority whose actions are opposed by the regulated carriers. Enforcement will always be a problem, but at least the trucking associations are on record in support of the 55 mph limit. Meanwhile, efforts are well underway to maximize truck productivity at the 55 mph speed.

The Regular Common Carrier Conference of the American Trucking Associations, the Society of Automotive Engineers, and the U.S. Department of Transportation ran a National Truck Fuel Economy Test in St. Louis last year. It brought together 50 trucks from around the country to test various fuel-saving devices. Results:

- A tractor towing a 48-foot trailer can haul 10 percent more freight using virtually the same amount of fuel than one pulling a 45-footer.
- Air deflectors save 2.6 to 3.8 percent in fuel at highway speeds; 4.2 percent at 40 mph.
- Tractors pulling smooth-sided trailers consumed 2.1 percent less fuel than ones with exterior-post trailer.
- Tractors with synthetic lubricants in the engine, transmission, and rear axles burned 3.4 percent less fuel than ones with oil-base lubes.
- Engines with low-intake system restrictions got 1.2 percent better mileage, and radiator shutters increased efficiency by 1.8 percent.
- Radial tires improved mileage by 2.8 percent over bias-ply tires, and tires inflated to manufacturer's specifications got 9.7 percent better mileage than under-inflated tires.

Engineers with the Regular Common Carrier Conference estimate that the average over-the-road, for-hire tractor/trailer rig employing all these fuel-saving devices at one time could save up to 5,750 gallons of fuel over 130,000 miles.

Engines that power. Detroit Diesel Allison has developed an engine that should play a big role in "dieselizing" the trucking industry. The "Fuel Pincher" is a medium-duty model of the company's larger "Fuel Squeezer." The "Pincher" uses diesel fuel, which has a higher energy content than gasoline; it is meant to replace gas engines in lighter trucks.

The new diesel gives superior performance to gasoline engines because it uses a fuel injection system instead of a carburetor and has no spark plug or electrical ignition system. The engine comes with either 155 horsepower (certified for California) or 170 hp.

Cummins Engine, in order to maintain a constant 55-mph and improve fuel economy, has switched from the constant-horsepower-variable-speed engine to one that maintains constant speed with variable horsepower. A constant-speed engine enables a truck to maintain its speed against headwinds and up grades, with power in reserve that kicks in only when needed. These engines make for less shifting, less fatigue, faster trip time, and better fuel economy.

Strick Corporation's Cab-Under gives more payload, but must be proven safe and win driver approval.

Convert-a-body from Leaseway Transportation offers user choice of van, flatbed, tanker (not pictured), or stake body on one truck.

Improved turbochargers and combustion systems on the Formula 350 maintain good cruise fuel consumption, but increase the power in reserve from 80 to 135 hp. Increased power enables the Formula 350 to maintain 55 mph on 1.3-percent grades without a slowdown.

The NTC-400 engine is exactly like the Formula 350 except that the increased power in reserve goes from 135 to 170 hp. The NTC-400 can maintain a constant 55 on a grade of 1.5 percent.

Eaton Corporation has been experimenting with a fuel-saving valve-selector system that automatically kills cylinders when not needed. An eight-cylinder engine might at times run on only four cylinders.

So far, the valve-selector has been tested only in gasoline engines in cars and light trucks. Fuel savings average 15 percent. But the device would work on modified diesels. It probably would not be too effective on loaded tractor/trailer rigs, which need full power most of the way, but it would save fuel on trucks deadheading and during long periods of idling.

The trucks that pull. GMC Truck offers a medium truck with a nondriving tag axle used in combination with a driving axle. The advantages over tandem driving axles include improved fuel economy, operating economy, and weight reduction.

GMC's General model has a lightweight, welded, all-aluminum cab and aluminum battery box which reduce weight substantially. Most heavy-duty trucks can be equipped with other fuel savers such as dragfoilers, radial tires, and fan clutches.

Ford offers powertrain combinations that range from 270 through 600-hp diesels, with either Cummins, Detroit Diesel, or Caterpillar engines. The cabs are of aluminum alloy to increase payload and performance.

Operating economy and fuel efficiency are the bywords on Chevrolet's heavy-duty trucks. Models come with Detroit Diesel "Fuel Squeezer" and Cummins Formula 290 diesel engines and compatible six-, seven-, and nine-speed transmissions teamed with economical rear-axle ratios.

The new 142-inch wheelbase for the Titan DC290 diesel series fills the need for a "short" tractor to pull 45-foot trailers in 55-foot-length-limit states. The Titan has several aluminum options to increase fuel economy: battery box, clutch housing, front wheels, frame rails, and dual 50-, 75-, and 100-gallon fuel tanks.

The trailers. Truck fleet operators have turned to a variety of devices in their efforts to reduce aerodynamic drag on trailers. Nosecone bubbles, airfoils on tractor tops, air vanes on trailer faces, and more. Perhaps the most basic idea is to use smooth-sided rather than outside-post trailers, where operations permit.

GM Astro 95 highway tractor has luxury features inside (right) and stylish exterior (below) that appeal to owner-operators. Includes sports steering wheel and AM/FM radio with tape player and CB radio.

Ford's diesel CL-9000 has many engineering details which give drivers control and comfort.

Fruehauf had so many improvements that the company made them all standard equipment on Model F-Plus.

Trucking's future look? International Harvester illustrates its "Very Energy Efficient Vehicle."

Chevrolet's medium-duty truck lineup has a broad range of gasoline- and diesel-powered engines.

In a market dominated by aluminum for many years, the Budd Co. Trailer Division has begun to push steel trailers. Weight and rust have always been steel's drawbacks, but Budd believes it has solved the rust problem and that durability may outweigh the weight factor. The steel trailers are made of hot-dipped galvanized carbon steel covered on both sides with a coat of epoxy primer and sealed with an acrylic top coat. The combination is said to resist fading, chalking, blistering, cracking, and peeling.

United States Steel says that its Galvan siding is at least 31 percent more puncture resistant and 30 percent more resistant to buckling than aluminum. Although the steel trailers carry a premium price tag, it may not always be so if the price of aluminum continues to rise faster than steel.

Fruehauf has introduced its Model F-Plus trailer which boasts these improvements: zero torque, rear-door closing rods; two inches of added height; non-core all-metal doors; anti-snag roof bows; welded, high-strength steel subframe (to save up to 400 lbs.); and spring hangers for even distribution of braking and impact loads over the subframe.

A future for electrics. President Carter called the energy crisis "the moral equivalent of war." He urged a two-pronged attack in the battle—conserving our present resources and developing new ones. One imperative of the battle is to shift from our heavy use of scarce resources like petroleum and natural gas to more plentiful resources such as coal.

Trucks are not likely candidates for conversion to electric power. Secretary of Transportation Brock Adams has awarded three contracts worth over $500,000 to investigate ways to improve the fuel efficiency of heavy-duty trucks, but the quantum leap in reducing gas consumption will only come when electric passenger vehicles become a reality.

Public Law 94-413, passed in September 1976, over a presidential veto, authorized research, development, and a two-phase demonstration of electric vehicles. As part of phase one, which involved 2,500 vehicles (phase two will involve 5,000 vehicles), extensive questionnaires were sent to potential users of a fleet of electric vehicles. Response thus far exceeds 300 replies.

The technological challenge of electric vehicles and hybrids (combination electric—for short trips—and internal combustion engine vehicles—for long hauls) is in three specific areas: battery (or flywheel), propulsion system, and manufacturing process.

Lighter, more powerful batteries are needed to increase range and reduce recharging time. A better propulsion system is needed for quicker acceleration and fast speeds. And a suitable manufacturing method is needed to produce electrics at a price the general public can afford. ■

Truck Lease-Rental Business Expected to Grow in Next Decade

By Robert J. Franco

Executive Vice President, The Hertz Corp.
General Manager, Hertz Truck Division

During the past decade, truck leasing and renting has more than doubled in terms of units on the road and  has nearly tripled its revenues, outpacing even the record results racked up by the overall truck industry itself in that period.

R. Franco

Over the past 10 years, between 1967 and 1977, our industry has grown at an average annual rate of between 15-16%. By 1977, the latest year for which we have full figures, industry revenues topped $5.9 billion, against just $1.4 billion a decade earlier.

In terms of units on the road, totals jumped from some 432,000 in 1967 to more than 940,000 in 1977, an increase of more than 100%. These advances in both units and revenues are the more impressive when contrasted with the full truck industry itself, where growth has been substantial, but less than lease-rental.

Since 1967, the number of commercial vehicles on the nation's highways has risen a solid 80%, going from approximately 16.5 million units to more than 29.7 million vehicles in service. Commercial units are now taking more than 28% of Detroit's full output, against less than 17% of the total a decade ago. In dollar terms, spending to purchase trucks rose from $5.4 billion on a national basis in 1967 to more than $25.1 billion in 1977.

Despite the striking lease/rental gains, we at Hertz see no evidence of a slackening in demand for our services in the future. In the next 10 years, advances should at least equal those of the *last* decade. Our forecasts show that truck lease-rental industry revenues should exceed the $10 billion mark by 1981 — perhaps even next year if the widely-heralded softening of the economy fails to materialize. Year to year forecasts are more difficult than projecting long-term trend-lines.

There are several reasons for our continuing optimism. First, our favorable forecasts have proved correct in the past. In the 1974-5-6 period, for example, annual lease/rental revenue growth averaged a respectable 12% despite a soft economy in other sectors.

Optimism

But there are more fundamental reasons for our optimism. Perhaps most important, the truck industry itself is generally sound and healthy. Distribution of goods in our country by truck has proved itself an important and viable method of transportation.

True, there are changes being initiated in our transportation system in Washington now. And these may, temporarily, cause disruptions and hardships in some segments of the industry. Furthermore, past vehicle design mandates have added a special burden to truck purchase and operation costs.

But the movement of goods — and people — by truck is still, relatively a fast, flexible and economical system of achieving the nation's transportation needs. Trucks are reliable and becoming more fuel-thrifty. And our interstate highway system is in place.

I am confident that this system will be properly maintained and even expanded, despite some efforts in the public policy area to promote alternative systems of transportation at the expense of the private motor vehicle industry.

Trucks are such a basic part of the fabric of American business life, however, that until a completely new and better system is discovered, alternate transportation methods will not displace motor vehicles.

Of course, we must continue to fight the proposed errors of the inexperienced; we must make sure that changes are improvements and that even the improvements are instituted on an evolutionary basis so that disruptions to any given segments of our industry are minimized.

So, the keystone of my confidence in the lease-rental sector of the industry is the overall health of the industry itself. Another important element in my confidence in truck lease rental growth is the increasing size and complexity — and therefore price — of the trucks of today, paradoxical as that may sound.

The very cost and complexity of trucks helps persuade top management of *other* industries which rely on trucking for their distribution to rely on truck industry experts to help keep these cost increases to a minimum.

Our trucks keep getting costlier to operate and repair as well as to buy, as they get bigger and more complex. Units are being driven more miles each year. And the rising curve of maintenance costs as trucks age, result in these units being sold sooner, thus helping promote a growing market for more newer units.

In addition, licensing, fuel reports and other regulations are proliferating. From specifying and purchasing the truck, to maintaining and repairing it, to selling it as a used unit, all these elements of truck operation now require a high degree of expertise and will require such knowledge in any even greater degree in the future.

High interest rates and insurance premiums are adding to the cost spiral, too.

Our yearly studies show that since 1973 truck operating costs have climbed some 67% — about one-third again as fast as the country's overall inflation rate. Indeed, since trucks are such as integral part of the national economy, the truck cost increases may create a ripple effect and help create more inflation for the nation. Therefore, all of us in the industry must argue strongly against unnecessary regulations and against truck design changes which increase costs at an abnormal rate.

In 1978, the cost of a typical new twin-axle tractor trailer was well above the $55,000 level, compared with less than $34,000 in 1971 and about $37,000 in 1973. In one year alone, though, 1974, the price of an 18-wheeler jumped nearly 23% — or more than $8,400. Such flagrant increases must be curbed in the future.

For an owner-operator who had been out of the market for several years, running older units, the new prices were catastrophic. His charges had not reflected his true depreciation — he had, unknowingly, been under-pricing his services.

More and more shippers turned to leasing and renting to help them solve their dilemma — especially companies whose primary business is in another area, as the cost spiral demonstrated their need for experienced management to control expenses.

Another factor is important to our optimism about the continuing growth of truck leasing and renting: the "market penetration" of truck lease-rental in comparison to passenger car lease-rental's share in that total market.

For example, new *cars* going into lease-rental service in 1977 represented nearly 18% of total new cars sold in the United States; but new *trucks* going into lease/rental use amounted to just a little over 7% of total new trucks sold that year. Admittedly, the ratio of personal-to-non-personal use is different for cars than for trucks; but, counting only vehicles in fleets of 10 units or more, lease rental *cars* account for about 40% of the total; lease-rental trucks (including tractors and trailers) are only about 20% of total new trucks sold.

In short, *the truck lease-rental segment of our business has been only about half as successful in penetrating its part of the market as have our counter-parts in the passenger car lease-rental sector.* We intend to do better.

Much of the real potential also lies in the smaller fleets, those operations running *fewer* than 10 units. Accurate figures are more difficult to assemble in this sector of the business. But statistics from our colleagues in the car side of the business show that they are making solid progress in this section of the market and I believe truck lease-renting can achieve the same sort of success.

Two of the stereotype myths of the entire automotive industry are that new passenger cars are sold primarily for private, personal use and new trucks are sold primarily for commercial service. More than half of all new Detroit-made passenger cars sold each year go into some type of non-personal use (*excluding* commuting). On the other hand, a size-able share of new trucks sold each year are purchased primarily for personal driving.

For this reason Hertz is now expending its rental activities aimed at the casual user. For example, we are now renting smaller trucks — Econoline type vans, pickups and four-wheel drives to private users via our car rental outlets. In the past such units were available only at the Hertz truck locations. In addition, we are currently preparing to expand our _ne-way rental program to additional areas throughout the country.

Our business-oriented users are still our primary market, though. Even our short-term rental fleets — as opposed to our long-term leased units — are geared to serving business organizations — as replacements for leased trucks which are in for maintenance, or for use as additional vehicles required on a seasonal basis.

The rental-unit is an important factor in reducing costs for our lease customers. They can gear their fleet to their minimum needs and use short-term rentals to meet special needs, rather than maintaining a larger fleet of their own.

Beyond a lease company's expertise in specifying, buying and maintaining trucks, a national organization also provides assistance to long-haul operators through the network of company-operated and affiliated outlets across the country. These are tied together with a telephone "SOS" hotline, manned 24-hours a day, seven days a week with truck experts.

Finally, the leasing company can provide advantages in selling the units — determining *when* to sell and how in order to realize the best return. We have taken a page from our Rent A Car Division, retailing selected units, rather than wholesaling them. We now have four separate used truck sales outlets throughout the country and we plan to open five or six more.

We are backing our optimism about the truck lease-rental business future with a $20 million expenditure in new facilities over a two year period, expanding our corporate owned-and-operated sales and service outlets throughout the nation.

The expansion schedule brings to almost 200 our number of Hertz-operated locations throughout the nation. In addition we have some 300 licensee truck outlets plus another 700 affiliated trucks stops — and a total of some 3,000 places around the country at which we can, on short notice, get emergency parts and service for over-the-road truckers.

Our facilities expansion program matches our expansion of our over-the-road business. In 1972, fewer than 10% of Hertz trucks were the heavy-duty, tractor-hauling trailers. Today this ratio of OTR units is close to 30% of our total fleet.

Our new construction program has followed a trend in the trucking industry — getting out of crowded mid-city locations and into larger, more convenient locales on or near inter-state highways and easily accessible to airports.

In summary, we at Hertz see continuing growth for truck transportation, despite the changes in the industry. We see even greater growth for truck lease-rental sector of the industry. We see this lease-rental growth stemming from the growing size, cost and complexity of trucks, the expertise of lease-rental companies and the use of lease-rental by managements as a sophisticated money budgeting and control tool.

We see some potential problems for the trucking industry in the area of public policy changes. We do not fear changes, but we do believe we must be alert to fight against unwarranted changes and against any changes being made too precipitously. We have seen the results of past ill-considered "improvements" imposed on the automotive industry — moves which backfired. We must make sure that the regulators, and de-regulators, completely understand the consequences of changes they propose.

Overall, though, we see the lease-rental segment of the industry continuing, during the 1980s, the same healthy growth pattern it has enjoyed during the current decade.

Harvester's Patrick Kaine Looks at Truck Design of the Future

Following are excerpts from a speech given by J. Patrick Kaine, president of International Harvester's truck group, to a meeting of top management of Ryder Truck Rental, one of the world's largest buyers of trucks:

Inflation and increased operating costs all of us will continue to wrestle with, will demand that we avail ourselves of every opportunity to bring a higher degree of efficiency and sophistication to our operations. One such opportunity for your business is to exercise even greater care in the selection of the equipment you lease or rent. This should be a cooperative venture with your supplier.

And speaking of cooperative ventures, I must cite your company's early work with us on the application of our then-new DT-466 mid-range diesel. I consider this a case book study in cooperation and we are indebted to you for your assistance in proving out our claim for this power plant. For those of you who may not have been involved, in October 1973, you took delivery of the first of nine pre-production DT-466 powered trucks for a joint field test effort. It was leased to NAPA in Milwaukee and was used to deliver auto parts around southern Wisconsin. By May 1976, it had clocked 213,122 without incident. The second unit was put into a known, severe line haul operation between Rocky Mount, N.C. and New York City. By November 1977, it had clocked 149,097 miles.

Of the trial fleet of six trucks with the DT-466, your customers accumulated 1,130,147 miles, for an average of 188,358 miles per truck. The results must have been favorable as you have purchased over 2,000 DT-466 powered trucks since then. Your experience plus additional field results gave us the additional confidence to offer a warranty similar to those on the "big bore" diesel engines, a warranty later adopted by other engine makers. So, we appreciate your assistance in this cooperative venture.

Incidentally, it is a pleasure working with organizations like yours which employ complete and accurate record-keeping systems. I hope that those organizations which have yet to reach your level of sophistication will benefit from the recent story of Ryder's system of specing and maintaining trucks which appeared in a recent issue of *Fleet Maintenance and Specifying Magazine.*

Mid-range diesels

On this subject of product offerings in the mid-range diesel, we have been watching with great amazement, and at times amusement, the claims being made for some European-built mid-range diesels. Many of their ads claimed annual savings in maintenance and fuel costs, based on what they say is a *Commercial Car Journal* article. The amusing feature of this claim is that *Commercial Car Journal*'s source for this data was developed for that magazine by International Trucks. We appreciate their validating our credibility.

Finally, they claim that their class 6 and 7 trucks average about 10¢ a gallon less than unleaded gas. Quite frankly, we don't know of a truck in that class that uses unleaded gas, so the comparison is invalid.

If this appears to be knocking competition, forgive me, but the U.S. truck customer is entitled to the facts. We have been building diesel engines since the early thirties for trucks, construction equipment and agricultural tractors for customers both here and abroad. I believe that somewhat qualifies us an authority on the subject.

Another excellent example of how to work with your supplier to make money with your trucks can be seen in the development of a computer program to help truck owners maximize fuel economy and performance in advance of the purchase. At our Company we call the program TCAPE for Truck Computer Analysis of Performance and Economy. Some of your operations have utilized this service, but with decision-making in ordering trucks becoming extremely complex and with spiralling fuel costs, I would counsel you to take a second look at it. Compare MGP results achievable from the selection of the right combination of engine, transmission, auxiliary transmission, rear axle ratio, tires, fan air deflector and so forth. The system also builds in such considerations as accessory power losses, driveline efficiency, speed restrictions, acceleration, fuel flow in driving cycles, wheel slippage and a host of others.

Obviously, we believe in this system. It is being proven out every day by fleets and individuals across the country. But in a forthcoming issue of *Fleet Owner Magazine,* Jim Bald, senior editor, will report, objectively on its effectiveness.

He compared actual revenue runs against our computer simulation and comes up with a fuel factor difference of just .06 mpg. I believe that whether Ryder pays for the fuel or the lessee does, it can be a significant consideration in your truck specifying. And now, with the development of the portable terminal, access to such program is even more convenient for the customer.

Finally, you asked me to comment on what the truck of the future will be like. I don't intend to fall into the trap of predicting dramatic changes for the sake of being dramatic. The development of the commercial vehicle will continue to be evolutionary, not revolutionary. But the lack of spectacular technological breakthroughs is not the result of unimaginative designers. Truck building is a 75-year-old art and its history is one of steady improvement in performance, reliability, serviceability and longevity. In the U.S., the biggest single advantage we have has been our ability and willingness to vocationalize our offerings. By that, I mean starting with an understanding of the application and designing towards maximum productivity in its given usage. This will continue to be our thrust.

I do not see any other power source replacing the highly efficient diesel engine. I do not see the gas turbine engine as a viable development in trucks. We have a couple of turbine powered trucks on the scrap pile where they have been since we developed and tested them back in the early sixties. Neither do I see trucks floating on a film of air rather than rolling on pavement. And, quite frankly, we don't really see a trend to underslung cabs.

What I do see are continuing advancements in braking systems (if the Department of Transportation lets us get on with our development work). One such project is our program with hydraulic disc brakes. At present, we are testing school bus applications since the benefits are proportional to the number of stops made. But if given the opportunity, future possibilities for the system could be expanded to include additional vocations.

I see remarkable fuel efficiency improvements resulting from sophisticated studies and applications of aerodynamics as well as from refinements to engines and other components. This will not involve a radical change in the basic shape of the commercial vehicles with which all of us are familiar. Many of the trucks traveling the world's highways during the first decade of the 21st century will probably look very much like our trucks today. Indeed, some may well be those very trucks if our reliability predictions are as accurate as we believe they are.

I see further improvements in driver environment — more head room, leg room, belly room, knee room, sleeper room, better heating and air conditioning systems, better visibility and quieter cab interiors. Many of these changes will be effected without a corresponding increase in exterior dimensions due to the use of new and exotic materials in cab construction.

I see improvements in ride quality. In the past few years, there have been tremendous achievements in this area. This will continue through further developments in chassis and suspension areas.

I see a continuation of cab-over configurations in truck design. Contrary to some commonly held ideas, our research indicates that conventional cab trucks generally create more air drag than cab-over units. The cab-over trucks introduced during the 1980s may well match or exceed the driver room afforded by conventional configurations.

All of you are aware of industry efforts to produce quieter, more emission-free and less fuel-consuming models of all sized trucks. But we are working on some less spectacular projects as well. For example, future trucks may include outside configuration designs that afford other vehicles better splash protection in wet weather. Now all of us in this room love trucks but we don't love them quite so much when one passes us in a rainstorm. It's a little thing, perhaps, compared to say, lowering the sound level another 50%, but necessary if trucks and trucking are to gain more favorable public acceptance and thereby reduce the chances of additional regulation.

I see extended maintenance intervals but progress in this area will come through gradual improvements in lubricants, in components, simplified designs and new materials. One area which seems to be making progress is the use of on-board electronics. The technology is available today for diagnostic systems that replace driver decisions in determining road speed in order to achieve optimum fuel efficiency.

I also see the use of automated transmissions becoming more prevalent, not only for medium trucks but for many heavy-duty applications as well.

Of course, better fuel efficiency will come in medium trucks primarily through the increasing use of the mid-range diesel engine. However, radial tires, fan clutches — perhaps even wind deflectors for some vocations — also will become increasingly evident just as they have in heavy trucks. The goal is lower cost of ownership, as fuel costs continue to escalate.

New materials

But if you pinned me down on what I believe will be the most significant contribution to a better product for you, I would say without hesitation, the development of new materials. We are putting considerable dollars and energies into composite materials. We consider composite materials to be the answer to lighter weight, higher strength, longer life and energy efficiency.

It weighs one-third to one-half less than steel and is one-half the weight of aluminum. Its tensile strength is considerably greater than either of these metals or fiberglass. It is impervious to corrosion. Its light weight will increase fuel mileage and it requires half as much energy to produce it compared with steel or aluminum.

For about a year now, we have been proving the feasibility of producing components on a mass production basis at a pilot plant at Midland, Texas. We are highly encouraged with results to date. We see composite materials being applied to cabs, chassis, frame rails, sleeper boxes, bumpers, transmission covers, battery boxes, seat frames, air deflectors and on and on.

To prove the manufacturing processes, we are committed to producing 4,000 International Scout sport-utility vehicles by 1981. What we are learning from this project is completely in tune with our plans for this materials use in medium and heavy duty trucks and you will be hearing and seeing more of composite materials in the days ahead.

Government involvement

So much for tomorrow. Let me close with one thought that I try to include in every public appearance I make. It is an exhortation to anyone who will listen to become intimately involved in our government's activities. Whether it be at city, county, state or federal level, our voices as competent businessmen must be heard, if we are to being realism back into our regulatory and legislative processes. If we are to avoid 121 brake fiascos, we must offer our testimony on every standard being considered. As standards applicable to trucks multiply, you, the users, are having your choices diminish and your costs escalate. . . .

Now, no man in his right mind would argue with the need for safer working conditions and safer vehicles. But the cost/benefit ratio is another matter — what we and the customer get for what we have spent is not necessarily justifiable. Even William Simon, former secretary of the Treasury, is quoted as saying that the burgeoning increase in government regulations is "draining a fortune out of the economy."

And already we have about one-third of our engineering time and talent devoted just to compliance, testing and reporting.

So, is the current situation abating? Are the agencies and is Congress heeding the call from President Carter to slow down? Here are some of the things this industry is wrestling with right now: fuel economy, emissions, ambient air quality, deregulation, noise, operator environment, weight and length, pavement and bridge deterioration, braking and the whole range of safety related issues.

We are just five years away from Orwell's *1984* and I don't say that facetiously. If government wants to design our trucks we should help redesign our government — into an entity reflecting the desires and the needs of the consumer, not the desires of self-styled advocates or of a bureaucrat whose continuing employment depends upon the publishing of rules. They need our guidance.

As Congressman Clarence Brown of Ohio said recently, and I quote, "If a law is going to have a significant job impact on employes, profit impact on stockholders or hurtful impact on our nation's ability to compete abroad, should not the business leaders be expected to advise their employes, customers and stockholders of the situation? As a matter of fact, don't the companies that will be affected have a moral obligation to speak up on the issue?" That was a congressman talking. I like that kind of talk.

Managing Specialized Carriers

Richard D. Eads
Manager
A.T. Kearney, Inc.
Chicago, Ill.

Everyone in trucking needs to understand the specialized carrier segment a little better because of the growth that has taken place in this segment of the industry, and the competitive position of the truckload carriers between private fleets and general commodities carriers. Operators of specialized and irregular route carriers have management problems that are very different from those of general commodities companies. Some of the major differences will be discussed in this article, as well as effective management techniques to improve the specialized carrier's performance.

What is a Specialized Carrier?

How do irregular route and specialized carriers differ from general commodities companies? First of all, the former's franchises from the Interstate Commerce Commission (ICC) consist of **irregular route authority** which gives them the right to serve **regions** rather than specific cities. Additionally the

ICC often limits their rights to hauling specific commodities in contrast to the general commodity carrier's authority to haul general freight. The specific commodities categories include heavy machinery, steel, perishables, liquid and dry bulk commodities, household goods, and commodities which sometimes overlap the general freight list. Often a carrier with general commodities authority will specialize in truckload hauling exclusively by not publishing LTL rates.

Specialized carriers usually serve a small number of shippers. In many cases, a carrier of this type will depend on fewer than a dozen shippers for three-quarters of his revenue while a general freight carrier having the same revenues may rely on several hundred.

Because of these authority differences and the number of shippers served when compared to the general commodity carriers, the rate-making process often becomes a matter of case-by-case review of individual hauling opportunities.

While the general commodity carrier largely depends on tariff bureaus to develop rates for movements between specific cities, the traffic departments of specialized carriers negotiate with individual shippers and develop rates which heavily reflect competitive influences and backhaul opportunities as well as the usual factors, such as length of haul, freight density, equipment requirements and other special-service needs.

Consequently, each carrier plays a large role in his own rate making and may have his own individual tariffs. As a result, the specialized carrier has a unique need to develop costs in terms of the pattern of his own operation.

Role of Terminals

Another major difference between the specialized carrier and the general commodity carrier is the importance of terminals to the operation. This difference has an influence on how to organize a company for the purpose of managing productivity.

To a general commodities carrier, a terminal is where all the action is. It is the focus for sales activity and the focus for controlling labor-intensive platform, and pickup and delivery operations.

Not so with the specialized carrier. The specialized carrier picks up the freight at the shipper's plant and usually runs it to destination with no in-route handling. Of course, there are exceptions to this. For example, LTL shipments of perishables and household goods are sometimes picked up by local fleets and stored.

But the preponderance of movements are shipper-direct-to-consignee with no need for an intermediate handling at a terminal. As a consignee, terminals for these carriers are little more than parking lots rather than important dispatch points.

The different role of the terminal in an irregular route or specialized carrier is reflected in its cost profile. A specialized carrier will spend approximately 10% of his revenue dollar in terminal operations. These costs include the usual building and associated costs as well as dispatching and fleet supervision expenditures.

In contrast, a general freight carrier spends more than 40% of the revenue dollar on terminal-related operations, which include dock work and pickup and delivery. Because of these vastly different terminal cost ratios, it is safe to guess that the management of a specialized carrier is wasting time if it pays as much attention to terminals as their partners in the general commodities business.

Role of Linehaul

But what about the rest of the costs of operating a specialized carrier? Line-haul and related maintenance costs usually absorb at least 75% of the revenue dollar, whereas with general commodities carrier the percentage is nearer to 40%. Allowing 10-15% for overhead for both types of carriers gives us an operating ratio range of 90-95, with the specialized carrier being able to operate comfortably at the higher end due to the generally lower investment required in equipment and property.

In view of the striking contrast between the portions of revenue for the two types of carriers being spent on linehaul, it is suprising that very few specialized carriers have made much progress in tracking linehaul costs and relating the performance of individual managers to productivity of over-the-road operations.

A frequently used method of managing productivity in a specialized carrier has been to copy the terminal profit and loss statement approach used by the general commodity carriers. General freight carriers view the key to success as controlling inbound-outbound balance and terminal costs by tightly managing the terminal. While sound for general commodities carriers, the proposition that a well-run terminal allows linehaul to take care of itself **does not apply** to irregular route carriers.

Why? Because linehaul operations in a specialized carrier are basically different. Each linehaul move made by a specialized carrier is associated with a particular shipper. When the question "What is the operating ratio for a move?" is asked, the answer has to be in terms of freight quality, deadhead miles and shipper-caused delays, and general linehaul productivity, and no terminal P&L approach takes these factors **specifically** into account.

To quickly recap, the elements of a specialized carrier discussed so far can be summarized as follows:

- They serve a limited number of shippers.
- Rate making is often performed on the basis of individual moves.
- Terminals can not be relied upon to be a focus of control because they represent a very small portion of a specialized carrier's cost and activity.
- Linehaul must be closely managed, because it represents the single largest portion of cost and activities often varying with specific shippers.

An Approach to Managing

The classic approach of segregating activities and matching responsibili-

ties to each function can be applied to managing specialized carriers. Underlying this method is the requirement that measures of productivity for each area be developed to "feed back" how well the operation is running.

Kearney has used this approach with several motor carriers and, while the specific results will vary depending on the situation, the following techniques are usually recommended:

- Measure dispatching productivity in terms of volume, freight quality and empty miles.
- Separate linehaul operations from other activities and measure for operational efficiency.
- Relate revenue to costs on a move-by-move basis.
- Control overhead costs.

Gross Margin

To implement these ideas, we have applied a management concept from manufacturing and wholesaling, **gross margin**, to managing specialized carriers. In Industry, **gross margin** is the difference between what an item sells for and what the cost was to make it available.

With specialized carriers, we use

gross margin to show the difference between revenue and the transportation cost of earning that revenue. Driver wages, fuel, depreciation of equipment, as well as other costs are subtracted from revenue to arrive at the gross margin from the operation.

Exhibit I schematically shows how the technique works. The statements shown are the fleet operating statement, the terminal—or region—operation statement, and a summary which capsulizes the results for each operation in the company.

When this approach is implemented, there are many more statements, such as maintenance shop reports and General and Administrative department reports, with much more cost and revenue detail than what is shown. But the diagram will help to communicate the basic idea.

The fleet operating statements are used to separately capture linehaul related costs such as vehicle leasing or depreciation, salaries and wages, fuel, licenses, etc. These charges are shown in detail in Exhibit II.

Estimates of operating costs per mile are used to charge the dispatching unit, which could be a terminal or a regional dispatcher in central dispatch. The dispatching unit is charged for every mile, both loaded and empty, (say at $.65 per mile) required to fulfill his dispatching instructions.

This mileage charge is **credited** to the fleet and **charged** to the terminal or region. The fleet manager's responsibility is to make sure that his tractors operate at no more than $.65 per mile for every mile driven.

The terminal or region statement is

used to evaluate freight quality and dispatching efficiency. Here is where gross margin enters in. Actual billed revenue is credited to the terminal or regions, and the transportation costs are charged. The difference is your gross margin. Excessive empty miles and low-revenue freight will have a negative impact on gross margin.

The basic idea is that dispatching should be constantly cognizant of freight quality and empty miles, and, consequently, should be measured in terms of it. Exhibit III shows a terminal statement with associated terminal costs as well as revenue and charges against margin. A centralized dispatching operation would show only the gross margin section.

Tracking Individual Moves

A useful technique that can be borrowed from the general commodities carriers is **freight profitability analysis**. The major variation for specialized carriers is to match actual revenues for shipments with the actual costs incurred to move them.

With an accurate freight profitability reporting system, the individual movement's revenue, costs and traffic lane can be grouped and analyzed by shipper, commodity, and shipment size to determine where improvements in rates, increased sales penetration or operating plan changes are needed. While the fleet and terminal (region) operating statements guide day-to-day operations, freight profitability reporting offers management of specialized carriers a tool for strategically guiding the entire company.

Activity Measurement

On both Exhibits II and III there are statistics such as total miles, empty mile percent, load factor ratios and revenue per hundred weight, per shipment and per mile. This information is intended to be used for planning purposes and for diagnosing problems.

For example, if a terminal's gross margin is below budget it can be due to fewer than planned shipments, shorter hauls, lower load factors or too much low-rated freight. This capturing and reporting of activity as well as dollar performance allows management to quickly perceive the "whys" behind good or poor financial performance for a terminal or region.

Budgeting

An area related to activity measure-

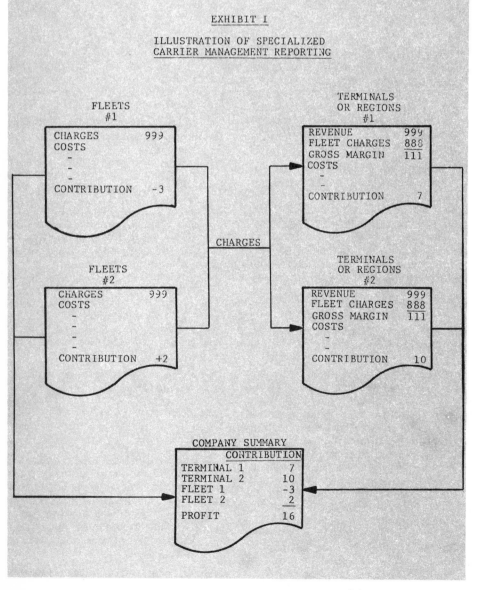

EXHIBIT I

ILLUSTRATION OF SPECIALIZED
CARRIER MANAGEMENT REPORTING

FLEETS
#1

CHARGES	999
COSTS	
-	
-	
-	
CONTRIBUTION	-3

FLEETS
#2

CHARGES	999
COSTS	
-	
-	
-	
CONTRIBUTION	+2

CHARGES

TERMINALS
OR REGIONS
#1

REVENUE	999
FLEET CHARGES	888
GROSS MARGIN	111
COSTS	
-	
-	
CONTRIBUTION	7

TERMINALS
OR REGIONS
#2

REVENUE	999
FLEET CHARGES	888
GROSS MARGIN	111
COSTS	
-	
-	
CONTRIBUTION	10

COMPANY SUMMARY

CONTRIBUTION	
TERMINAL 1	7
TERMINAL 2	10
FLEET 1	-3
FLEET 2	2
PROFIT	16

EXHIBIT II

REPORT ILLUSTRATIONS

FLEET OPERATING STATEMENT
PERIOD 7 - MIDWEST TRACTORS

ITEM	LATEST PERIOD	BUDGET	VARIANCE	PERCENT
REVENUE:				
TRANS. CHARGES	$83,000	$87,500	$- 4,500	- 5.1
OTHER	1,000	0	1,000	100.0
TOTAL	$84,000	$87,500	$- 3,500	- 4.0
COSTS:				
SALARIES AND WAGES	$33,000	$32,000	$- 1,000	- 3.1
FUEL	16,000	17,000	1,000	5.9
MAINTENANCE	8,000	10,000	2,000	20.0
DEPRECIATION	9,000	9,000	0	0.0
PURCHASED TRANS.	11,000	1,000	-10,000	-1000.0
TAXES AND LICENSES	3,000	1,000	- 2,000	- 200.0
OTHER	2,000	1,000	- 1,000	- 100.0
TOTAL COSTS	$82,000	$71,000	$-11,000	- 15.4
TOTAL CONTRIBUTION	2,000	16,500	$-14,500	- 87.9

STATISTICS:

ACTUAL MILES - 134,615		SHIPMENTS - 305
BUDGET MILES - 141,129		LOAD FACTOR - 75%
MILES EMPTY - 22,000		LENGTH OF HAUL - 441
EMPTY PERCENT - 16.3		

action. If fuel costs have risen, the budget should be changed.

Budgeting for fixed costs is performed differently with different implications for variances. Developing a per mile depreciation budget for a tractor, as an example, requires an estimate of the expected miles driven per period.

If the expected miles for a tractor each period is 10,000 miles and the depreciation for a power unit is $450 per month, then the depreciation budget figure developed in this manner is the result of under or over utilization. Each situation may deserve management attention.

Both variable and fixed budgets should be combined and reported on a fleet basis rather than constant tracking of individual units. This avoids spending time running down causes of apparently abnormal occurences which are actually normal parts of the operation.

To illustrate, if a tractor's fuel consumption was high and its utilization was low for a period, the reason might be that it was in the shop for a week with a full load of diesel. Aggregation into fleets and allowing for downtime avoids fishing for red herrings.

Overhead Control

Once linehaul is under control and responsibilities for efficient dispatching are clarified, the last remaining frontier for the specialized carrier is managing overhead. The problem in overhead management is that, inch by inch, these costs can creep out of control by adding just a little bit at a time.

The typical avenue to excessive overhead is to add personnel to the payroll

ment is budgeting. Budget figures can be shown on a per mile basis for both fixed and variable elements of cost and revenues where practical. Budgeting of variable costs, such as fuel, is done by developing what it **should cost** to move a tractor one mile on the aveage. For example, if diesel fuel costs $.50 a gallon and the average expected miles per gallon for a well-operated tractor fleet is 4.5 miles per gallon, then the per mile fuel budget should be $.111. If the reported actual cost per mile is higher, look for efficiency or cost problems.

Efficiency problems arise from low quality maintenance, poor driving habits or even from inaccurate mileage reporting--each requiring management

because of apparent increases in workload without seriously considering alternatives such as redistributing work or improving supervision. Techniques borrowed from the operating side of the business can be applied to budgetary control of General and Administrative areas. Tracking man-hours needed to process freight bills, invoices and claims, and occasionally searching for methods improvements can sometimes shave half a point from the operating ratio. Forcing department managers to plan and live within a budget will help make sure that efficiency does not slip.

Summary

We have taken a look at what makes an irregular route, specialized carrier different from the general commodities carriers. Mainly, rates are often set for specific shippers and the terminal fails to provide a focus for control since the majority of activity occurs outside of a terminal's purview.

Also, we have discussed management reporting techniques designed to specifically control linehaul operations and segregate the impact of dispatching from the issue of linehaul productivity by applying the **gross margin** concept to trucking. Budgeting for operations and overhead was touched on and, in fairness, merits far more space than it was given.

Two comments with respect to the techniques discussed may be appropriate at this point. First, developing fleet statements does not mean that separate fleet managers should be added to the organization. It usually happens that a terminal or regional manager also manages a fleet and he can certainly continue to do so. The development of fleet statements simply means that a terminal manager is **also** a fleet manager and that his dual management responsibilities should be reported separately.

The second comment has to do with owner-operator and company employee fleets. The techniques we reviewed can handle both cases equally well and also encompass situations such as trip leasing, rigging operations, etc. Many, if not all, variations in activities found in specialized carriage can be accommodated within this approach and brought under the umbrella of effective management.

EXHIBIT III

REPORT ILLUSTRATION

TERMINAL OPERATING STATEMENT
PERIOD 7 - ST. LOUIS REGION

ITEM	LATEST PERIOD	BUDGET	VARIANCE	PERCENT
REVENUE	$800,000	$750,000	$ 50,000	6.7
FLEET CHARGES	605,000	530,000	-75,000	-14.2
GROSS MARGIN	$195,000	$220,000	$-25,000	-11.4
CONTROLLABLE COSTS				
SUPERV. SALARIES	$ 2,000	$ 2,000	0	0.0
DISPATCHERS SALARIES	6,500	6,000	- 500	- 8.3
CLERICAL SALARIES	2,000	2,500	500	20.0
COMMUNICATIONS	8,000	9,000	1,000	11.1
RENT	3,000	3,000	0	0.0
DEPRECIATION	500	500	0	0.0
TOTAL	$ 22,000	$ 23,000	$ 1,000	4.3
ALLOCATED COSTS				
G&A	$ 80,000	$ 90,000	$ 10,000	11.1
TOTAL PERIOD COSTS	102,000	113,000	11,000	9.7
TERMINAL PROFIT	93,000	107,000	-14,000	-13.1
OPERATING RATIO	88.4	82.7	- 5.7	6.9

ACTUAL MILES	- 905,000	REV/MILE - $.884	SHIPMENTS - $88
BUDGET MILES	-$820,000	REV SHPT - $810	LOAD FACTOR - 95%
EMPTY MILES	- 81,000	REV/CWT - $2.131	LENGTH OF
EMPTY PERCENT -	9.0%		HAUL - 916

About The Author

A specialist in transportation and distribution, Eads has concentrated on consulting services provided to the motor carrier industry. He has been heavily involved in conducting large scale systems development projects and profitability studies.

Eads, who is 35, has been with Kearney for more than five years. He holds a bachelors degree in mathematics from Ohio State University, and a master of business administration degree from the University of Chicago.

Richard D. Eads has been appointed Manager of Transportation, Consulting Services, in its Eastern Region by A. T. Kearney, Inc., management consultants.

Eads will operate from the firm's offices at 437 Madison Avenue in New York City.

Kearney Management Consultants serves clients in the private and public sectors throughout the world.

Improving Urban Traffic Through Truck-Oriented Measures

by Paul Ross

Introduction

Although our knowledge of automobile traffic is imperfect in most respects, traffic engineering can show some significant accomplishments, and a "science" is beginning to develop. However, only the automobile component of traffic is well understood; the special problems of trucks and buses have not been studied as thoroughly as those of automobiles.

There are reasons for this neglect, with the most important being the question of priorities. "First things first" meant that the historical concern of traffic engineers was to understand the problems of traffic as a whole; when it has been possible to study the components of traffic, the major component—the automobile—has naturally received the major emphasis. Also, separate study of commercial traffic has often been considered unnecessary, because traffic changes which benefit automobiles generally benefit trucks and buses, too.

However, the effects and interests of commercial vehicles are not identical with those of automobiles, and the differences must be studied. The purpose of this article is to urge more interest in the effects of trucks on urban traffic and to locate the most promising returns on short range investments. The emphasis will be on short range improvements to urban traffic in general and not on improvements that specifically benefit goods vehicles. However, it appears that the changes designed to benefit traffic in general also decrease the overall cost of goods movement. Therefore, many of the proposals here are similar to proposals from planners and economists whose primary goal is to improve the goods movement system.

This article will consider only urban traffic, not traffic on rural roads and freeways. The effects of commercial vehicles on traffic on such roads are somewhat different from those considered here. "Commercial vehicle" and "truck" refer to any vehicle engaged in picking up, delivering, or transporting goods or services for other than private use. Pickup trucks and vans used for personal transportation are considered part of the automobile component of traffic.

Commodity Flow Versus Truck Operations

Urban goods movement seems to have two active subfields: *Commodity flow* and *truck operations*. Commodity flow studies generally concentrate on the shipment and transshipment of identifiably different types of goods. It is a broad category; for example, the determination of the optimum point at which to stop shipping energy in the form of coal and, instead, convert it into electricity for further transmission could be considered a commodity flow problem.

Commodity flow is fundamental—at least in the sense that it can be considered the "cause" of the other forms of goods transportation. For example, the flow of wastes "causes" garbage truck trips and the demand for fresh baked goods "causes" bakery truck trips.

Because commodity flow appears causal, the really fundamental changes that are desired in the goods movement system can most effectively be implemented through changes in commodity flow. The belief that such changes will considerably increase the efficiency of the goods movement system or, equivalently, lower the cost of goods delivery is implicit in many studies. (1–8)[1]

Unfortunately, there are no clear-cut results to support this belief. Commodity flow analysis has not had such conspicuous success as traffic engineering. Because of this lack of clear-cut results, there has been little financial support for the field—which, in turn, explains why very little data on commodity flows have been collected.[2]

Trucks represent the visible element of the various commodity flows in urban areas. It may seem that truck operation studies attack the symptoms without understanding the disease but, nevertheless, several studies have been completed and the symptoms have often been ameliorated. (12–21) The cities of Charlotte, N.C., Chicago, Ill., Dallas, Tex., and New York, N.Y., have adopted comprehensive truck regulations. (16–17, 22–23) In Chicago, for example, trucks are prohibited from the downtown loop area except for deliveries; large trucks (over 10 m) may not even make deliveries from the public right-of-way during the day.

Data are not yet complete but a general picture of the truck operations situation is emerging, and a program to improve it can be tentatively outlined. It appears that truck operations are highly constrained (15), but concerted action to relax the constraints may be possible because the interests of private automobile owners and truck operators seem to coincide; more efficient truck operations will improve traffic flow. (24)

Trucks in the Moving Traffic Stream

When considering the effects of goods vehicles on the flow of traffic, two conditions should be identified: (1) Trucks in the moving traffic stream; and (2) trucks which are loading, unloading, or maneuvering in or out of loading spaces.

It appears that *moving* trucks are not substantial contributors to delay in most urban traffic systems. This is contrary to common opinion which is probably influenced by the high visibility of trucks, the unpleasantness of following them closely, and the severity of truck-caused delays when they do occur. Truck trips constitute about 15 percent of central business district (CBD) traffic, but they rarely make up more than 5 to 8 percent of the peak-hour, peak-direction traffic. (23) At peak periods, a large part of the commercial traffic is confined to industrial areas, side streets, or counterflow direction. This reflects the fact that commercial drivers can arrange their itineraries to avoid congestion better than the ordinary commuter. CBD daily cordon counts detect only about 10 to 12 percent trucks. (16, 23)[3] Truck traffic peaks after the morning and well before the evening rush hours. (25)

The above percentages for trucks, although accurate, are not as meaningful as they might appear to be. Truck counts normally include all the vehicles that can be called "trucks"; single unit trucks, semi-trailers, pickup trucks, and camping vans are all lumped together. Some of these "trucks" are actually being used as private vehicles and should not be classed as commercial traffic. Conversely, some of the "private automobiles" are actually used for commercial purposes—for example, small package and pharmaceutical delivery vehicles (fig. 1). The conclusions in this article are nonquantitative and do not depend on exact numbers; it is enough to note that commercial vehicles constitute only a moderate proportion of typical urban traffic.

An upper bound for the maximum possible time saving from any form of truck control in the moving traffic stream can be obtained. The maximum possible time saving to automobiles from controlling truck traffic is certainly less than the time saved if trucks could be totally eliminated from the traffic stream. If trucks constitute 8 percent of the traffic and volumes are half the street capacity, the disappearance of trucks would produce about 4 to 5 percent travel time savings on freeways and 2 to 3 percent on arterials, according to tables compiled by Levinson and Conrad. (23) When traffic is flowing at capacity, much more dramatic time savings are theoretically possible—24 to 28 percent on freeways and 26 to 41 percent on arterial streets—*provided that the trucks are not replaced by automobiles.* This large time savings is due to the fact that when a street is operating near capacity, the removal of any vehicles—even automobiles—has relatively more impact on traffic flow than under other conditions. However, in real, capacity-limited flow, there are always vehicles waiting to use the road which would immediately occupy the spaces relinquished by trucks. In

---

[1] Italic numbers in parentheses identify references on page 97.

[2] Some authors blame lack of results on the paucity of data. (9–11) It probably makes little difference which is the cause and which is the effect.

[3] Truck cordon counts are lower than the corresponding trip distribution, because trucks make more trips that do not cross the cordon lines than do passenger vehicles.

re 1.—*Private automobile being used for commercial purposes.*

pacity flow on level streets, the total elimination of
ck traffic would produce only small improvements in
ffic flow and travel time, but it would allow two or
ee automobiles to replace each truck and, thereby,
mewhat shorten the rush period.

propriate rules for the control of moving trucks follow
gically from these facts. On streets that operate at
preciably less than capacity, restrictions on moving
cks are not likely to produce significant improvements
less there are special circumstances, such as short
ning radii, that affect trucks quite differently than they
ect automobile traffic. On streets that operate near
pacity, each truck will be replaced by several
tomobiles and the question becomes, "Which is more
portant—one truck or three cars?" Generally trucks
at brave the rush hour do so because they are carrying
rgo which has low tolerance for delay; restricting these
cks may have a disproportionately large adverse
onomic impact.

e above rather theoretical analysis is supported by
veral field studies which have also concluded that
lay due to moving trucks in urban areas is not an
portant problem. *(13, 14, 26)*

ere is no general reason for restricting the *movement*
trucks. Only in isolated circumstances, where trucks
counter unusual conditions (such as short, steep
grades or restricted maneuvering space), are there
ffic-related reasons to control truck movements. Truck
utes have been considered and abandoned in London
7), and no logical rules for them were discovered in a
nadian study. *(28)* Of course, there are many
ntraffic-related reasons for controlling moving trucks.

Truck routes may be established to preserve the
character of certain neighborhoods or to protect streets
with substandard pavement. Other legitimate reasons for
restricting trucks include bridge weight limits, safety
considerations, low underpasses, and steep grades.

Loading, Unloading, and Maneuvering

It is generally agreed that trucks have large impacts in
CBD's and other areas where the incidence of curbside
loading is great. *(29)* A poll of major city traffic engineers
reveals that most of them believe that trucks are a
problem only in CBD's. *(15, 30)* Trucks that are double
parked (fig. 2), maneuvering into or out of loading
spaces, or cruising to look for parking spaces are obvious
offenders. Because of this interference, in some cities
the slowest traffic speeds and greatest delays of the day
occur between the traffic peaks, not during the time of
heaviest flow as would be expected. *(13, 14, 31)* In
contrast to the situation with moving trucks, appreciable
improvements in traffic flow are likely if systematic
changes can be made. In the area of loading and
unloading operations, substantial traffic improvements
can be made and research is likely to be most fruitful.

Long term improvements

Long term improvements—those that will require several
years to several decades to implement and become
effective—are the most effective changes that can be
made in loading and unloading operations. Some of the
most often proposed actions are as follows:

1. *Consolidated receiving.* If large commercial buildings
will consolidate receiving and shipping operations for all

Figure 2.—*Double parked mail truck causes through traffic to move to
far left lane.*

39

tenants, instead of having tenants handle their own pickups and deliveries, the truck drivers will avoid searching for individual receivers and shippers, and truck time in the loading zones will be reduced. This will increase the loading zone turnover and decrease double parking. *(19)*

Several methods for achieving consolidated receiving have been proposed; one of the most attractive is to impose a surcharge for individual deliveries. If trucking companies were required to collect surcharges for individual pickups and deliveries, financial pressure would be exerted on building tenants to pool their goods services. However, pressure on building tenants is a devious and inefficient way to force building owners to provide consolidated receiving. Optional surcharges would probably be even less effective because, in the highly competitive trucking industry, carriers would readily waive the fee. Required surcharges may be self-enforcing if competitors complain to the regulatory agency about violations. Municipalities might find surcharges to be an attractive way to raise revenue.

This proposal is justified only by plausibility; data for estimating the benefits do not exist. Such items as the number of separate deliveries and the time involved in each delivery are needed.

2. *Consolidated truck terminals.* In this concept, all goods destined for a given building or city block would be loaded into a single truck at a large suburban terminal. Consolidated terminals would also be used for the outbound flow; pickups would be made by a single truck and returned to the terminal where they would be sorted by destination or carrier. *(4)* Among other benefits, the number of trucks competing for a given curb space would be reduced (fig. 3). The carriers would presumably benefit by decreasing their handling costs while the general public would benefit from reduced traffic impact. However, practical experience with this concept has been discouraging so far: The Newark Freight Terminal of the Port of New York Authority was designed as a consolidated terminal but never actually operated as such due to institutional constraints *(32)*, and a Dallas study concluded that negligible benefits would be gained through this technique because many carriers are so large that they already operate terminals that are, in effect, consolidated. *(16)*

Although United States experience has been discouraging so far, Japan is showing considerable interest in freight consolidation. Intercity trucks are banned from urban areas so carriers are forming cooperative services to consolidate their pickup and delivery operations. The economic benefits realized have not been as great as predicted.

Figure 3.—*This situation could possibly be alleviated by consolidated terminals.*

3. *Improved vehicle design.* Commercial vehicles that could load and unload more rapidly and maneuver more easily in confined areas would obviously decrease traffic interference. The New York City Transportation Administration has proposed the construction and testing of a prototype vehicle.[4] United Parcel Service has evolved standards for their delivery trucks including such items as skylights in the truck body to provide illumination. Evolution will probably continue falteringly in this area.

4. *Offstreet loading.* One effective solution is the removal of the loading and unloading process from the public right-of-way (fig. 4). This can be implemented by zoning restrictions which require adequate offstreet loading facilities. Unfortunately, zoning regulations can only affect new construction; little can be done about existing buildings. Significant improvement cannot be expected in less than the 50- to 60-year lifespan of downtown buildings.

5. *Separation of function.* An ideal solution is to completely separate the goods delivery function from the traffic function. In Chicago, goods delivery was done at one time through a narrow gage railway tunnel that still exists in the loop area—although it is now unusable. *(32)* There are also limited truck tunnel systems in operation in Dallas, Tex., and New Haven, Conn. *(16)* Such solutions are so capital intensive that it is unlikely that they will ever be significant except where existing facilities can be converted.

---

[4] "A Proposal for an Urban Truck Research and Demonstration Project in New York City," by New York City Transportation Administration. Unsolicited proposal submitted to U.S. Department of Transportation, May 1975.

Figure 4.—If offstreet loading were implemented, trucks would not hinder traffic by parking on the curb.

of many carriers to pay fines for standing violations rather than experience the delay inherent in the use of remote loading zones. There is also a security problem inherent in leaving a truck unattended for appreciable periods while walking to the destination. *(23, 33)* For these reasons the effective "search pattern" of most delivery trucks extends only 30 m from their destination—at least, this was the distance observed in Brooklyn, N.Y. *(15)*

Moving loading zones from arterials to side streets is a superficially attractive solution. This would move the conflict from the heavy traffic stream to where the traffic impacts are much less. Unfortunately, truckers are generally very reluctant to use loading zones that are distant from the delivery point, especially because loading zones that are out of sight of the destination

Figure 5.—*Example of regulatory signing.*

More effective enforcement of parking and loading restrictions. Traffic problems would certainly be alleviated if the parking and loading restrictions already in force were better observed (fig. 5). Some of this problem stems from violations by private autos—such as parking in loading zones—and, short of a radical change in public attitude, can only be solved by spending money for more policemen.

The remainder of the enforcement problem stems from violations by truckers. In many Eastern United States cities, a common attitude is that traffic obstructions must be endured for expeditious goods movement. Policemen are often reluctant to ticket drivers whom they regard as doing their jobs as well as they can under difficult circumstances, and many carriers pay fines for standing violations without question. This attitude even extends to State legislatures; in Massachusetts, for example, trucks may double or even triple park to make pickups and deliveries or service calls.

Such attitudes are less common and enforcement is more vigorous in western cities where streets are wider and loading facilities are more adequate. One might speculate that improved enforcement and observance follow improved facilities.

Short term improvements

Short term improvements should concentrate on eliminating double parking and reducing interference due to trucks entering and leaving curbside spaces. Although these measures should include a prohibition against double parking, such a prohibition alone is unlikely to be effective unless an adequate supply of curbside space is available, because it is the tacit policy

41

present severe security problems.[5] Experiments with such side street loading should certainly be tried where they appear feasible, but poor compliance should be expected unless the relocation is accompanied by vigorous enforcement measures.

Off-hours or night delivery is another class of superficially attractive solutions that is likely to be ineffective unless very carefully implemented. The basic difficulty is that off-hours delivery provides a public benefit at a private expense; that is, the general public would undoubtedly benefit from improved traffic flow but the expenses would be borne by the carriers and businesses that would be required to provide night receiving and shipping service. An experimental program in London, "Operation Moondrop," failed for exactly this reason. (35, 36) Incentives, such as subsidized service, could equalize the incurred expenses. In the United States there are institutional constraints which will inhibit such an experiment—principally the fact that many contracts require double time pay for work before 8 a.m. or after 6 p.m. It may be worthwhile to see if these constraints can be relaxed.

Research Opportunities

In view of the foregoing, there are several areas where research appears to have a high potential for improving traffic conditions by controlling trucks without spending large amounts of capital. The Federal Highway Administration has instituted a major research project on Metropolitan Multimodal Traffic Management which is investigating large, areawide traffic analysis and control measures. (37) Within the project, the analysis of truck effects constitutes a major part of one of the tasks, Strategy Development and Testing. Five specific areas have been identified for study:

1. To understand the operations of trucks at curbside and decrease their impact, accurate data and models of the process are needed. Particularly important are well calibrated models that will be able to predict the traffic impact of changes in the system. For example, how much would traffic benefit if curb cuts were made to facilitate the movement of hand carts? Where should these curb cuts be made? Virtually nothing is presently known about the *details* of the loading/unloading process. It is important to examine all of its components so that the good and bad effects of altering one component can be predicted.

2. It is clear that turnover in loading zones would be increased if consolidated receiving were commonly practiced. Increased turnover has a beneficial traffic impact because it decreases the double parking and queueing for loading space. What measures would be most effective for the city in encouraging consolidated receiving operations? Should tariffs be adjusted to favor this kind of operation? This kind of proposal highlights the need for accurate and detailed models of the truck loading and unloading process; such models could be used to predict the decrease in delivery times resulting from consolidated receiving and shipping and the consequent increase in loading zone turnover.

3. One way to reduce the traffic impacts of trucks is to get them to operate at night, or at least during offpeak hours. There has been no research in the United States to see what would be required to get such a program started. Of course there are many obstructions to such a program, but the benefits to be gained are so great that its feasibility deserves careful study; the Federal Highway Administration has such a study underway.

4. Although truck routes are usually chosen for environmental rather than traffic reasons, they should be rationally and consistently chosen. Because very little is known about systematic truck routing, there is considerable need for such research. What reasons are there for truck routes? Where should they be located for the greatest efficiency and the greatest economic benefit? What *is* the current practice throughout the United States with respect to locating truck routes?

5. Because trucks have different acceleration capability from passenger automobiles, the presence of trucks that have to stop and start at signals in traffic streams considerably degrades the local traffic performance. In certain situations, it might be advisable to extend a green display rather than stop a truck. Detectors for this purpose should be easy to produce by modifying bus detectors which have already been developed. More important than the hardware development are other questions: What are the exact effects of trucks in this situation? How much improvement can be expected if trucks are favored by the signals? What is the most effective strategy?

---

[5] Break-in damage to unattended trucks is so prevalent in New York City that at least one carrier has considered making deliveries from Army surplus Patton Tanks. (34)

Summary

This article has discussed the state of the art of what is known about the effects of trucks on urban traffic. It appears that congestion due to trucks loading and unloading at curbside in CBD's is the most severe impact. However, the details of the loading/unloading process are almost unknown, as are most of the other details of the impacts of trucks on traffic. Several areas of research to be investigated under the Metropolitan Multimodal Traffic Management project were outlined.

REFERENCES

(1) Richard Wilson DeNeufville, H. M. Nigel, and Louis Fuertes, "Urban Goods Movement—Consolidation of Urban Goods Movement: A Critical Analysis," Transportation Research Record 496, Transportation Research Board, Washington, D.C., 1974, pp. 16–27.

(2) David S. Gendell et al., "Goods Transportation in Urban Areas: Urban Goods Movement Considerations in Urban Transportation Planning Studies," Federal Highway Administration, Washington, D.C., February 1974. Available from the National Technical Information Service, 5285 Port Royal Rd., Springfield, Va. 22161.

(3) Stanley J. Hille, "Urban Goods Movement Research—A Proposed Approach," Traffic Quarterly, vol. XXV, no. 1, January 1971, pp. 5–38.

(4) Dennis R. McDermott and James F. Robeson, "Urban Goods Movement: The Role of Terminal Consolidation in Urban Goods Movement," Transportation Research Record 496, Transportation Research Board, Washington, D.C., 1974, pp. 36–42.

(5) Arnim H. Meyburg, Walter J. Diewald, and Garrison P. Smith, "Urban Goods Movement Planning Methodology," Transportation Engineering Journal TE4, November 1974, pp. 791–800.

(6) Arnim H. Meyburg and Peter H. Stopher, "Urban Goods Movement: A Framework for the Analysis of Demand for Urban Goods Movement," Transportation Research Record 496, Transportation Research Board, Washington, D.C., 1974, pp. 68–79.

(7) "Urban Commodity Flow: Summary of Conference Findings," Highway Research Board Special Report 110, Highway Research Board, Washington, D.C., 1971, pp. 1–3.

(8) Robert Teas Wood, "Urban Goods Movement: Basic Data Needs for Urban Goods Movement Analysis," Transportation Research Record 496, Transportation Research Board, Washington, D.C., 1974, pp. 101–104.

(9) Frances T. Bolger and H. W. Bruck, "An Overview of Urban Goods Movement Projects and Data Sources," Office of System Analysis and Information, U.S. Department of Transportation, Washington, D.C., March 1973.

(10) Lester A. Hoel, "Urban Commodity Flow: Summary of Conference Proceedings," Highway Research Board Special Report 110, Highway Research Board, Washington, D.C., 1971, pp. 4–10.

(11) Richard D. Leis, "Needs and Opportunities for Innovation in Urban Goods Movement," Research Outlook, vol. 5, No. 1, 1973, pp. 22–27.

(12) Malcolm V. Bates, "Goods Movement by Truck in the Central Areas of Selected Canadian Cities," Canadian Trucking Association, Toronto, Ont., Canada, 1970.

(13) A. W. Christie et al., "Urban Freight Distribution—A Study of Operations in High Street Putney," Report LR 566, Transport and Road Research Laboratory, Crowthorne, England, 1973.

(14) A. W. Christie et al., "Urban Freight Distribution—Studies of Operations in Shopping Streets at Newbury and Camberly," Report LR 603, Transport and Road Research Laboratory, Crowthorne, England, 1973.

(15) K. W. Crowley and P. A. Habib, "Mobility of People and Goods in the Urban Environment: Facilitation of Urban Goods Movement," Office of University Research, U.S. Department of Transportation, Washington, D.C., December 1975. Available from the National Technical Information Service, 5285 Port Royal Rd., Springfield, Va. 22161.

(16) R. W. Holder et al., "Dallas CBD Goods Distribution Project Final Report," Texas Transportation Institute, Texas A&M University, June 1974.

(17) Rodney Kelley, "Improving Goods Movement," APWA Reporter, vol. 43, No. 3, March 1976, pp. 16–17.

(18) R. Kardosh and B. C. Hutchinson, "Truck Trip Generation Characteristics of Manufacturing Industries in Metropolitan Toronto," University of Waterloo, Waterloo, Ont., Canada, 1972.

(19) Norman D. Lea and John R. Hartman, "Urban Goods Movement: Canadian Studies of Urban Goods Movement—A Status Report," Transportation Research Record 496, Transportation Research Board, Washington, D.C., 1974, pp. 93–100.

(20) W. Marconi, "Commercial Vehicles in a Large Central Business District," Traffic Engineering, vol. 41, No. 5, February 1974.

(21) "Trucks at Work in Selected Square Miles of Tri-State Region," Tri-State Transportation Committee, New York, 1968.

(22) "Improvement Plan for Truck Operations," City of Charlotte, N.C., 1951.

(23) Hebert S. Levinson and Paul E. Conrad, "Bus and Truck Roadway Systems and Truck Travel Restrictions," Environmental Design and Control Division, Office of Research, Federal Highway Administration, Washington, D.C., February 1975.

(24) N. Simons et al., "Urban Goods Movement Program Design," Report No. UMTA–INT–RDC–8–71–6, Urban Mass Transportation Administration, Washington, D.C., June 1972. Available from the National Technical Information Service, 5285 Port Royal Rd., Springfield, Va. 22161.

(25) Wilbur Smith and Associates, "Motor Trucks in the Metropolis," Automobile Manufacturer's Association, 1969.

(26) John H. Dupree and Richard H. Pratt, "A Study of Low Cost Alternatives to Increase the Effectiveness of Existing Transportation Facilities—Results of Survey and Analysis of Twenty-One Low Cost Techniques," Office of the Secretary, U.S. Department of Transportation, Washington, D.C., January 1973.

(27) "GLC Drops Lorry Routes," Traffic Engineering and Control, December 1975, p. 567.

(28) E. Hauer, "Truck Route Systems: Survey of Canadian Practice," Joint Program in Transportation, *University of Toronto and York University,* 1972.

(29) "Alternatives for Improving Urban Transportation: A Management Overview," *Implementation Division, National Highway Institute, Federal Highway Administration,* Washington, D.C., November 1975, pp. 10–1/10–6.

(30) Philip Habib and Kenneth Crowley, "Evaluation of Alternative Goods-Movement Programs," *Proceedings, Intersociety Conference on Transportation,* Los Angeles, Calif., July 1976.

(31) "Manhattan Garment Center—Urban Goods Movement Study," *New York City Transportation Administration,* 1974.

(32) Robert Teas Wood, "The Urban Freight System: Why It Doesn't Work Better," *International Physical Distribution Management Conference,* Tokyo, June 1973.

(33) Robert T. Drake, "The Metropolitan Goods Movement Symposium: Metropolitan Goods Movement as Seen by the Long Haul Carrier," *Department of Transportation Planning and Engineering, Polytechnic Institute of Brooklyn,* March 1972, pp. 38–40.

(34) Arnold D. Imperatore, "The Metropolitan Goods Movement Symposium: Frustrations of a Common Carrier," *Department of Transportation Planning and Engineering, Polytechnic Institute of Brooklyn,* March 1972, pp. 41–42.

(35) J. D. C. Churchill, "The Urban Movement of Goods—Operation Moondrop: An Experiment in Out-of-Hours Goods Delivery," *Organization for Economic Cooperation and Development,* Paris, 1970.

(36) C. Kenneth Orski and Wolfgang Jakobsberg, "Urban Commodity Flow: Improvements and Innovations in Urban Goods Movement," Highway Research Board Special Report 110, *Highway Research Board,* Washington, D.C., 1971, pp. 100–109.

(37) William D. Berg and Philip J. Tarnoff, "Research in Urban Traffic Management," Transportation Research Record 603, *Transportation Research Board,* Washington, D.C., 1976, pp. 55–56.

Kenneth C. Clear Receives Award

Mr. Kenneth C. Clear was the recipient of the award in the first annual outstanding paper competition held among the employees of the Federal Highway Administration's (FHWA) Offices of Research and Development. This award covers the documentation of any technical accomplishment which may take the form of a publication, technical paper, report, or package; an innovative engineering concept; instrumentation systems; test procedure; new specification; mathematical model; or unique computer programing. Each eligible candidate is judged on the basis of excellence, creativity, and contribution to the highway community, general public, and the FHWA.

Mr. Clear, a highway research engineer in the Materials Division, Office of Research, received the award for his research report on "Time-To-Corrosion of Reinforcing Steel in Concrete Slabs."

Counterflow bus lanes can obtain greater efficiency from existing facilities. Research is in progress to find methods for safe and effective management.

New Directions for the Federally Coordinated Program of Highway Research and Development

by Charles F. Scheffey

Introduction

The general case for the value of research in modern society hardly needs to be sold. Most people agree that it is necessary in order to keep American industry competitive in world markets, raise our standard of living, conquer disease, improve communications and the entertainment media, and keep our defenses strong. They are less willing to agree that tax money should be spent on research in fields such as transportation. In particular, there is a general assumption that because we now have virtually completed the Interstate Highway System, there is little justification for an ambitious program of highway research. Exactly the opposite is true; there is now a more urgent need for a vigorous program of highway research than at any time since the end of World War II. This is because the highway program itself is now directed toward goals which until now were frequently neglected.

The Need for a Continuing Research Program

In general, the public and some political decisionmakers believe that the highway program is now approaching com-

pletion and there is little need for further research and development (R&D). In some cases, this attitude is due to the idea that the only responsibility of the Federal highway program is the Interstate Highway System. If this were true, we probably could relax, express satisfaction in a job well done, and quietly fade away; however, this is not realistic.

Changing national priorities

The petroleum supply crisis has placed the full weight of the Federal Government behind a move to lighter and more efficient automobiles. This trend has produced a significant change in the composition of the motor vehicle fleet, and in many ways has made a highway system design for 1970 automobiles obsolete. One example is the recognition that our system of guardrails, bridge rails, and median barriers does not provide adequate protection for the new generation of light, small passenger vehicles (fig. 1).

The same energy crisis that is forcing us into smaller automobiles also calls for larger, heavier cargo vehicles. This is not a contradiction. In both cases, fuel economy demands a more favorable tare weight to payload ratio. For

45

Figure 1. — This base for a breakaway sign satisfies present requirements for conventional-sized automobiles, but when struck "side on" by a compact automobile severe damage resulted.

passenger automobiles, this requires reduction of the tare weight as a complement to the efforts to increase payload by the encouragement of carpools. For cargo vehicles, immediate improvement can be obtained by increases in payload; but from both an energy and ton-mile (ton-km) cost standpoint, these benefits are limited by the design and condition of the existing highway network.

Deterioration of the existing system

Another reason further research is needed is the fact that the existing system is wearing out. A major program is already underway to repair, renovate, and restore the system. As the deteriorated state of our pavements and bridges becomes more obvious, the public demand to restore workable levels of service is accelerating. At the same time, the realization that we are not technologically fully prepared to handle this situation is becoming apparent. For example, since 1965 extensive efforts have been made to develop reliable methods to estimate the remaining life expectancy of bridges. These efforts have not produced a solution, but rather a paradox. It has been clearly

demonstrated that the stresses produced in existing bridges are generally well below those anticipated in the design. In fact, the stresses are low enough that even with the greatly expanded level of vehicle traffic, the existing theories of fatigue damage would indicate that in most cases no fatigue fractures should be anticipated. Nevertheless, there are well-documented cases of fatigue failures in highway bridges; some of these failures are on the same structures on which the above-mentioned data on the frequency of various stress levels were collected.

In the past 2 to 3 years, some clues as to the reasons for this paradox have become apparent. However, none of these clues shows that the fatigue problem can be ignored. A parallel program has demonstrated that many of our bridge structures have an enormous reserve of capacity for passing individual heavy loads. One of the bridges tested to ultimate load in Tennessee recently carried 1,250,000 lb (567 Mg) before exhibiting the beginnings of a collapse mechanism — this on a structure designed for HS20 loading![1] As frustrating as these contradictions may be, they point to an attractive opportunity. They indicate that many of our existing structures, provided they are functionally adequate, can be provided with a new lease on life by a knowledgeable program of rehabilitation and repair. However, there is no cut-and-dried set of rules by which this can be done. Bridges are individualistic structures and a competent examination for possible critical details and fatigue damage will require a level of expertise exceeding that which was involved in the original design. Creation of such expertise will require a vigorous continuation of our present research activities to develop understanding of the problem, inspection instrumentation, and methods for analysis and interpretation of conditions discovered in such inspections.

The rehabilitation of pavements finds us in a similar position of running hard to catch up. It is true that rational methods for design of overlays that are more reliable than older empirical methods are now available. However, the investigations that have led to these design methods have also shown that the placement of such an overlay without some method to restore structural continuity in the existing pavement is probably not a good investment. Two or 3 in (51 or 76 mm) of asphaltic concrete overlay should not be

---

[1] Specifically an HS20–44 loading, which would imply a single vehicle of 72,000 lb (32.7 Mg) or a total of 288,000 lb (130.6 Mg) if two vehicles were placed in each lane of the 90-ft (27.4 m) span tested. "Comparison of Measured and Computed Ultimate Strength of Four Highway Bridges," by Burdet and Goodpasture, Highway Research Record No. 382, *Highway Research Board,* Washington, D.C., 1972.

Figure 2.—It looks like a new pavement, but will it give service in proportion to the investment? Should more be spent first on restoration of existing pavement structure?

expected to do a job which 6 or 8 in (152 or 203 mm) failed to accomplish! New approaches to reprocessing, stabilization, or repair in place of the existing layers before resurfacing are essential to economical rehabilitation of the highway system (fig. 2).

There are also major policy problems involved. In both the bridge replacement and rehabilitation program and the pavement restoration activity, we are currently rebuilding a system to a load capacity which economic and technical studies have already shown to be suboptimal. The incremental investment to upgrade the system to obtain greater benefits is modest if it is done in conjunction with the bridge replacement and pavement rehabilitation program. A clear and detailed delineation of costs and benefits of such an improvement must be developed to provide policy guidance.

Environmental, traffic congestion, and safety problems

In addition to these physical aspects of our deteriorating highway system, there are other problems that have been with us for a long time, such as more reliable prediction of the environmental impacts of air pollution, noise, vibration, and runoff water contamination. Beyond mere prediction, better understanding of these problems may lead to an actual reduction of negative impacts. Certain positive environmental effects can be obtained in the design for new or modified highway facilities. Because many future highway projects will involve modification to existing systems, the importance of obtaining meaningful and representative public participation in highway planning and location has increased. Also, managing the existing highway

network, especially in urban areas, in order to achieve maximum efficiency with respect to mobility, energy consumption, and reduction of air pollution is of continuing concern. We have only scratched the surface with respect to what can be done with modern technology in this problem area. Further advances will involve going far beyond the mere control of the traffic signals by a central computer. The next steps for greater efficiency will probably involve information feedback systems to help drivers control their movements to enhance system efficiency and reduce their own travel time. Future improvements may also make use of selective traffic controls that give priorities to high occupancy vehicles and separate cargo movements by route and time as much as possible (fig. 3).

The highway accident problem still consumes enormous resources every year and loss of life and disabling injuries caused by highway accidents rank as one of our major public health problems. The unsolved problems of highway safety would by themselves require a vigorous research program for many years to come. In particular, the new requirements imposed on the system by the shift to lighter, smaller automobiles must be clearly identified and options to satisfy them quickly developed.

Figure 3.—Bypass lanes for carpools is just one of many techniques for encouragement of high occupancy vehicles.

Finally, partial automation of highway vehicles and selected routes is an attractive possibility with enormous benefits in respect to energy conservation and safety (fig. 4). Progress in developing microprocessors has been so rapid that some knowledgeable people in the motor industry predict that by 1985 most new automobiles will contain an onboard microprocessor that will control many of the functions now provided by mechanical linkages and gadgetry. Once a basic microprocessor is available, additional features and capabilities can be provided at very small incremental cost. The possibility for a range of devices in the automobile to assist the driver to carry out his driving task in a safer and more effective manner is very real. The hardware which might be required in the highway system to exploit this capability will undoubtedly be expensive even if it is highly cost effective. Therefore, it would appear prudent to have research programs which would open a wide range of options and alternatives so the most effective system may be selected with full recognition of available capital and expected future benefits.

Figure 4. — Test vehicle used in studies of guidance system for highway automation on the Ohio State University test track.

Keeping the Research Program Responsive

Any complete research program must perform at least four functions: It must solve the urgent and current operating problems, it must provide fundamental insight as to how the system operates and where there are opportunities for improvement, it must identify problems that are developing before they become critical, and it must open viable options for dealing with these problems.

First, the term research must be defined. For the purpose of this article, research includes the broad range of activities from scientific investigations of the basic technologies related to highways to the development of prototype devices for control of construction or traffic operations and the field trials of these devices to show where sufficient performance data exists to permit decisions for appropriate deployment of the device. It includes basic research, applied research, and development, but falls short of "implementation" and "demonstration" which are necessary but separate functions.

Responsiveness of the R&D program to the needs of the Federal Highway Administration (FHWA), the highway community, and the public involves at least five requirements:

● Develop cost-effective technical solutions to major current operation problems.

● Define characteristics of the existing system at an adequate level to provide policy guidelines, to provide factual basis for decisions among available or newly developed alternatives, and to identify emerging problems so development of solutions may begin before the problems become critical.

● Provide a technology base for new functions which are legislatively mandated or established by Department of Transportation policy.

● Compare current design and operating technology with the current research literature of both the highway community and related fields in order to identify elements of technical policy which with revision would exploit technology breakthroughs, thereby permitting more effective or lower cost operations.

● Conduct basic and applied research to open new options for the future.

Those benefiting from a research program may expect some useful technological innovations which provide workable and economical solutions to their problems. In addition, the benefits from the application and deployment of these solutions should demonstrate that the research program is paying its own way.

There are also some things which should not be expected of a research program. The first of these is "instant results." Research by its very nature is future-oriented. Although any well-established research organization must often come up with a quick solution for current operating problems, this is not and should not be its primary function. The bulk of the effort should center on identifying problems in the operating system which are still in the embryonic stage and producing solutions to these problems before they become critical. FHWA's present program in highway research is a mixture of orderly development or options for future action and activities to improve existing operational methods.

A second set of expectations which leads to disappointment is the thought that research studies can provide justification for existing policies. Because of the nature of the research community and because legislative requirements place research results in the public domain, it is possible that carefully conducted studies will show that existing policies are not justified.

Finally, realization of research benefits cannot be expected if the information and insights produced are not applied. The investment of resources in a research program requires parallel commitment by operational elements of the organization to give adequate attention to the results produced and a commitment by top management to deploy innovations and changes in the system where they are cost effective.

In an effort to make FHWA's research program responsive, we now annually engage in a number of formal solicitations in which representatives of operating elements in State highway agencies, city and county traffic departments, highway safety organizations, and the FHWA field offices are asked to identify problems for which research could provide beneficial insights and solutions. The major solicitations are those now managed by the Office of Highway Safety, the Offices of Engineering and Operations, and the National Cooperative Highway Research Program (NCHRP).

It must be stressed, however, that these are not the only channels of communication by which the Office of Research staff becomes aware of operating problems and research priorities. For many years, there have been effective informal channels of communication. First of all, specialists on our staff review every Highway Planning and Research Program (HP&R) research study initiated by a State highway agency. This is perhaps one of the most useful guides to what a State considers important because the initiation of such a study requires commitment of resources by the State agency. These same specialists review every problem statement coming from the States under the NCHRP program.

As a result of these contacts as well as membership in many national organizations related to highway technology, it is rare that the formal solicitations ever turn up problems or approaches to solutions that are totally unknown to our staff. The principal benefit of the formal solicitations is the guidance provided by the operating elements as to the relative importance of the various problems identified.

Changing Directions in the Federally Coordinated Program of Highway Research and Development (FCP)

The impact of the new directions in the highway program and our efforts to improve responsiveness are detailed in figures 5 through 9. A number of new projects have been initiated in the FCP to concentrate research efforts on appropriate objectives. As planned from the initiation of the FCP in 1970, the older projects are being closed out, either because they have successfully reached their objectives or because further extension appeared to have marginal benefits.

In the safety program of Category 1 (Improved Highway Design and Operation for Safety), six new projects have been initiated over the past 4 years. Project 1T, "Advanced Vehicle Protection Systems," is aggressively pursuing the development of the necessary modification of existing traffic barriers and other safety hardware to accommodate the new generation of passenger automobiles and to provide for

Figure 5. — FCP Category 1: Improved Highway Design and Operation for Safety.

Note: The original objectives under Projects 1N, 1M, 1R, and 1S were combined with other projects within the first few years of the program, and these elements were dropped as separate projects. Designation 1M has now been applied to a new project initiated in FY 78.

selective protection for heavy vehicles. Project 1U, "Safety Aspects of Increased Size and Weight of Heavy Vehicles," seeks to obtain well-documented facts on the relationship between traffic accidents involving trucks and their weight classification and to diagnose such accidents and examine the feasibility of countermeasures. The outputs of this project will provide policy guidance for the gathering crises developing over the size and weight issue due to the conflicts between energy conservation, highway maintenance and safety, and other projects in the program which address the technical aspects of bridge and pavement life expectancy.

Figure 6.—FCP Category 2: Reduction of Traffic Congestion, and Improved Operational Efficiency.

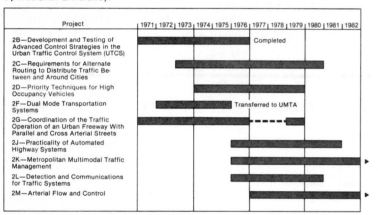

Figure 7.—FCP Category 3: Environmental Considerations in Highway Design, Location, Construction, and Operation.

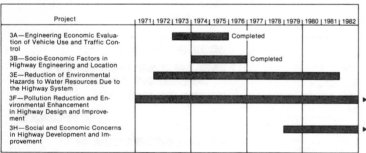

Project 1V, "Roadside Safety Hardware for Nonfreeway Facilities," addresses the critical problem of upgrading older highways and bridges in such a way as to provide concurrent improvements in safety hardware at reasonable cost. When the major project on reduction of skidding accidents was completed, there were still some impediments to effective implementation, resulting in the initiation of Project 1W, "Skid Resistance Inventory Procedures and Equipment." At the request of the Office of Highway Safety, Project 1X, "Highway Safety Program Effectiveness Evaluation," was initiated to develop objective methodology for evaluation and guidance of State highway safety programs. Also at the request of the Office of Highway Safety, Project 1Y, "Traffic Management in Construction and Maintenance Zones," was initiated to provide a major advance in our understanding of driver behavior in such zones and how it may be altered most effectively to provide safe work zones. An additional new project now in the final planning stages will attack the two-lane rural and low volume road safety problems.

In Category 2 (Reduction of Traffic Congestion and Improved Operational Efficiency), four new projects have been initiated. Project 2J, "Practicality of Automated Highway Systems," grew out of earlier HP&R and advanced technology developments. This activity was raised to project status when it became apparent that automated systems were not only technically feasible but also offered significant capacity and safety advantages. The current work stresses resolution of economic, institutional, and human factors problems. Upon completion of Project 2B, "Urban Traffic Control Systems," it was realized that there was a definite upper bound on traffic flow improvements which can be obtained by even the most sophisticated control of signals. Further improvement must involve information feedback to drivers, coordination with public transit, encouragement of high occupancy vehicles, and possible separation in space or time of cargo movements as addressed in Project 2K, "Metropolitan Multimodal Traffic Management." A parallel supporting project—Project 2L, "Detection and Communications for Traffic Systems"—will develop such things as wide area detection methods and methods to exploit effectively the growing number of CB radios in automobiles for both traffic management and safety. The specific problem of arterial highways will receive concentrated attention in Project 2M, "Arterial Flow and Control."

The major projects of Category 3 (Environmental Considerations in Highway Design, Location, Construction, and Operation) are receiving increased resources to address the physical problems of air and water pollution reduction, noise and vibration control, and ecosystem protection. A new effort to develop better approaches to obtaining relevant public participation in highway planning and location

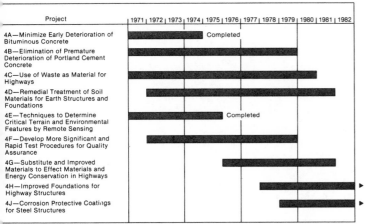

Figure 8.—FCP Category 4: Improved Materials Utilization and Durability.

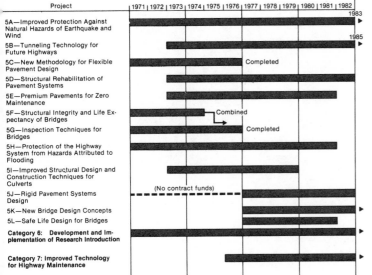

Figure 9.—FCP Categories 5, 6, and 7.

will be launched in FY 1979 as Project 3H, "Social and Economic Concerns in Highway Design and Improvement."

In the traditional research areas involving materials and structures, there is also a new look. In Category 4 (Improved Materials Utilization and Durability) there are three recently initiated projects. Project 4G, "Substitute and Improved Materials to Effect Materials and Energy Conservation in Highways," seeks to reduce dependence on petroleum derived materials for highway construction and repair. There are some exciting developments in the use of sulfur as an engineering material and in activities addressing the problem of shortages of sources of high quality aggregate. The substructure of bridges will get attention in Project 4H, "Improved Foundations for Highway Structures." There is also a new project in the final planning stages aimed at the problem of improved and environmentally acceptable coatings for steel highway structures, which will probably be designated Project 4I. In Category 5 (Improved Design to Reduce Costs, Extend Life Expectancy, and Insure Structural Safety), a national method for design of portland cement pavements will be sought in Project 5J, "Rigid Pavement Systems Design." The problem of bridges will be pursued in two new projects: Project 5K—"New Bridge Design Concepts"—which will include work on bridge repair and strengthening as well as advanced concepts of prefabrication, and Project 5L—"Safe Life Design for Bridges"—which emphasizes the fracture control problem.

The problems of highway maintenance will also get increased attention. However, because the urgent needs in this field appeared to involve mostly improved equipment and management methods, it will be managed by the Office of Development. A series of projects is being developed under Category 7 (Improved Technology for Highway Maintenance) for this purpose.

Conclusion

Experience has shown that it takes 3 to 5 years from the time of commitment of the first significant resources to carry out a major research and development effort from conception to implementation and deployment. Adding the 2-year budget cycle to this, it is apparent that major new thrusts require advance planning and multiyear budgeting. The concern of the FHWA's Associate Administrator for Research and Development must therefore include not only responding to current operational problems, but also insuring that there will be ability and a knowledge base for capable response to requests of future operating leadership. It is his responsibility to recommend a program that provides an effective balance among current concerns, a factual basis for policy guidance, the exploitation of new technology, and a solid base for future options. A program such as this should insure that the necessary highway and transportation research will be accomplished to meet the continuing demands of our changing society.

Chapter 3
Railroads

Where short, fast trains take the freight

By GUS WELTY, Senior Editor

Mile for mile, grade for grade, curve for curve, there is probably not a tougher operating challenge in American railroading today than the one that faces Rio Grande 24 hours of every day. It's a railroad where a 1% grade is regarded as flat country, where anything less than a four- or five-degree curve is pretty straight track, where a skilled locomotive engineer is a craftsman to be prized and praised.

The challenge of operating this railroad and operating it well, however, is only half the story. The second half has to do with the competitive battle Rio Grande must wage, also on a 24-hour, every-day basis. Rio Grande, to put it bluntly, is a railroad that could be run-around with not much difficulty, what with Santa Fe and Southern Pacific to the south of it, and Union Pacific and Burlington Northern to the north of it. It does not stretch credibility too far to suggest that most of the freight routed Rio Grande is moving that way because Rio Grande went out and fought for it—and because a sizeable number of shippers, large and small, appreciate the service-performance record Rio Grande has established and maintained.

As great railroads go, of course, Rio Grande is no giant. It operates just 1,868 miles of lines, of which about 1,000 miles are considered main line. In operating revenues, Rio Grande Industries rests close to the bottom on *Fortune*'s list of the 50 largest transportation companies, tucked in between a couple of regional airlines, North Central and Piedmont.

But when *Fortune* ranks its transportation companies by other measures, things begin to happen. One such measure, a key one, has to do with how much comes down to the bottom line—net income expressed as a percentage of operating revenues. Southern Railway is ranked first. Northwest Airlines is second. Union Pacific is third— in a tie with Rio Grande, each bringing 8.8% of gross down to net. (Rate of return on investment is not one of the numbers Rio Grande people live or die with, but for what it's worth, the rail industry figure last year was 1.26%; Western District roads checked in with 3.73%—and Rio Grande showed 6.54%.)

Admittedly, last year was a record year for Rio Grande—but it is hardly sagging in '78, based upon results thus far. For the first six months., net income climbed by 41% over '77 levels, and on the net-to-gross scale the number was 9.6%.

• **Leading from strength.** What's ahead

for Rio Grande, Railroad and Industries, depends upon a lot of factors, not all of them within management's control. but some observations seem reasonably safe:

—In relative terms, Rio Grande will benefit as much as any road from the boom in western coal. Ten years ago, Rio Grande hauled about 7.6 million tons, but tonnage had more than doubled by last year, when it also accounted for $51.9 million in revenues or about 30% of Rio Grande's total freight revenues. For this year, the forecast looks for movement of 17.5 million tons. For next year, the estimate is in the 20-million-plus range. And the long-range projection sees 35 million tons of coal in 1983, based upon now known plans of producers and users.

—All that coal will be moving over what is essentially a single-track railroad, albeit one with an excellent communications network and with complete ctc coverage on the main line. At this point, Rio Grande operating officers see no real problems with capacity; their answers are going to be line upgrading and installation of ctc on coal-originating branch lines (projects that are already well under way), as well as contingency planning for changes in operating methods and patterns that may someday be needed.

—Coal or no, Rio Grande is not about to allow slippage in its reputation as a service-oriented railroad. It can't afford slippage, not when close to 80% of its freight revenues come from traffic received from or delivered to connections or bridged. The 1977 numbers on revenue: 20.5% local, 19.1% interline received, 24.5% interline forwarded, 35.9% intermediate or bridged.

—Rio Grande will continue to look with interest at possible expansion. On a number of occasions, it has studied a possible hookup with Western Pacific, but Rio Grande thinking now is that WP's proposed new structure should be given a chance to work—with the caveat that Rio Grande would not be happy should another road try to move in on a restructured WP. Today, Rio Grande is looking mostly east, to its proposed acquisition of Rock Island lines from Denver and Colorado Springs to the Missouri River at Kansas City and Omaha, an acquisition that would give Rio Grande a full additional freight-revenue division.

—Rio Grande itself will likely continue to be intriguing as an acquisition.Early in the 1970s, it beat back a takeover attempt by an eastern group, and rumors recur that one or another of its neighbors, separately or together, might like to pluck Rio Grande from the ranks of the indepen-

dents. Rio Grande gives potential suitors no encouragement. Its management sees real hazards in overbigness, and it does not see a day coming when things happening around it will put a real squeeze on Rio Grande's ability to maintain its property and continue to give the kind of service that leads to the claim that Rio Grande is the railroad "where the short, fast train was invented."

—Rio Grande will continue to be something of a maverick in an industry not noted for such. Just one example: Through Industries, Rio Grande is moving ahead with Houston Natural Gas and their jointly-owned subsidiary San Marco Pipeline Co. to develop a working plan for a rail and slurry-pipeline system between Colorado and Texas.

—Rio Grande will also continue to be a road where people, management, and contract employees alike develop rather intense loyalties. Rio Grande has lost a few good men in management (Alfred E. Perlman and John C. Kenefick, to name two), but it has retained a lot more. Among others, Chairman G.B. Aydelott, President and Chief Executive Officer William J. Holtman, and Vice President-Traffic Clarence R. Lennig have never worked for another railroad, though all have had opportunities. Vice President-Finance H.W. Bushacher left Bank of America to join Rio Grande. Chief Engineer E.H. Waring a long time ago gave up New York Central to go west.

If, in fact, there is a soft spot in Rio Grande, it may lie in the fact that a good number of top officers, Bill Holtman excepted, are homing in on retirement age. Management today believes this is a valid concern only in an area or two, and it could well be that Rio Grande will come out as well in the management ranks as it did not so long ago when a lot of veteran locomotive engineers tied up for the last time: Rio Grande put youngsters, relatively speaking, into the right-hand seat, and there was absolutely no falloff in capability or performance.

—For a time, at least, Industries will go on being one of the stranger holding company-conglomerate structures in the railroad industry, with a computer time-sharing company, a land-development company, an amusement park, and a company that builds rides for amusement parks. None of these satellite organizations has been a major contributor to net, and it could well be that one or more could be spun off in the event that Rio Grande or Industries finds a more productive place for capital investment.

—Rio Grande, the railroad, will continue

and run

to be a railroad that spends its money well, as needed and where needed. "We are not tight," one top officer notes. "We're close." And there are reflections all around: Traffic growth demands fixed-plant improvement, and while it has been said that no chief engineer ever had all the money he wanted, Rio Grande's Ed Waring has it this year, to the point where his main concern is getting everything done that he can afford to do before the work season ends. Rio Grande has one of the best locomotive-availability records in the industry, and it has rather consistently poured money into equipment that will be used for off-line loading. Its communications network has few peers, and it's one of not many roads with branch-line ctc and more to come.

But with all this, where *does* Rio Grande go from here? Start with coal.

●**Coal—different, but competitive.**
Coal in Rio Grande territory, Colorado and Utah, is not the coal found on BN in the Powder River Basin that can be easily surface mined. Rio Grande coal comes from both deep mines and surface mines and coal produced from deep mines is more expensive by quite a bit even before it is loaded into railcars. Logically, that cost factor would seem to mitigate against long-distance movement—but it doesn't. Coal originating on Rio Grande is higher in Btu per ton while it is lower in moisture content and ash, and the add-up makes both deep-mined and surface-mined Colorado and Utal coal competitive in the growing market for "compliance" coal. One evidence: A couple of months ago, Rio Grande began originating unit coal trains from Colorado and Utah deep mines for a destination about 2,000 miles distant. Another evidence: Rio Grande is working now on plans for movement of western coal to Florida, in what will likely be a rail-water move.

Harold E. Cash, assistant vice president-fuel traffic, is Rio Grande's man in charge of developing the coal business, and Cash is quietly looking at a boom—but a boom that will come in orderly fashion, and one that will perhaps come more because of electric utility and other industrial conversions than because of new-utility demand for Rio Grande coal. Industrial conversions, Cash says, "are just beginning to surface—but they're going to come rapidly."

Characteristics of Rio Grande-originated coal may better suit the demands of those industries converting to compliance coal: There's less ash to be disposed of; boilers are more attuned to use of high-Btu coal; and the higher output per ton means

A freight train snakes through Royal Gorge in Colorado. On the D&RGW, a 1% grade is regarded as flat country, less than a 4- or 5-degree curve as pretty straight track.

Rio Grande: Performance on-line . . .

	1977	1976	1975	1974	1973
Average gross train load-freight (tons)	3,910	3,842	4,021	3,529	3,661
Average net train load-freight (tons)	2,006	1,935	1,979	1,798	1,806
Gross ton-miles per train-hour	102,528	100,231	104,727	91,634	96,130
Gross ton-miles per transportation employee-hour	4,191	4,037	3,975	3,774	3,895
Cars handled per yard engine-hour	17.9	17.6	17.0	15.7	15.7
Car-miles per serviceable-car-day	105.3	104.0	97.1	96.0	99.0
Net ton-miles per serviceable-car-day	3,672	3,468	3,241	3,115	3,102
Transportation ratio (excluding fuel)	24.8	25.3	25.9	26.7	28.9
Gallons of fuel per locomotive-mile, freight	2.48	2.55	2.53	2.53	2.45
Gallons of fuel per thousand gross ton-miles	2.69	2.73	2.62	2.66	2.64

simply that fewer tons of coal need to be moved, stored, and otherwise handled per unit of energy output.

In the old days, whatever coal production there was in Rio Grande territory came from mines operated by fairly small companies. Today, Cash, along with Gus Aydelott and Bill Holtman, finds encouragement in the number of major producers coming into the territory—names such as Westmoreland, Massey, Consolidation, Island Creek, Amax, and Arco. These and others like them, Harold Cash notes, "don't pick up coal properties for fun. They're companies with the financial, marketing, and technological capabilities to develop mines into top producers." Rio Grande, however, never discounts the smaller companies from yesterday; several of them, such as Energy Fuels Corp., are major producers today.

Right now, Cash is looking at reasonably solid prospects over the next five years—and at least five major projects scheduled for startup in 1983 or beyond. He is also looking at a couple of other things—including a trend on the part of operators of smaller mines to work toward operation of unit trains as a way to improve car supply and utilization, and a trend toward startup of unit-train operations that would serve distribution centers that would in turn serve (by rail or truck) coal users who feed, say, 40,000 or 50,000 tons of coal per year.

How much of this high-Btu coal could Rio Grand tap? Recent estimates put demonstrated reserves in Colorado at 12.4 billion tons of deep-mine coal, 50% recoverable, and 3.8 billion tons of surface-mine coal, 80% to 90% recoverable; for Utah, the numbers are 6.3 billion tons of deep-mine coal and 267 million tons of surface mine coal, with the same percentage recovery figures.

•**Mine it, move it.** The responsibility for getting the coal moved rests basically with J.E. Timberlake, director-unit train operation, and Timberlake is confident that Rio Grande will be ready when whatever volume of coal begins to move.

Timberlake, an ex-Rio Grande switchman as well as another expatriate from New York Central, thinks that Rio Grande can handle whatever coal Harold Cash brings in. Lead times, he believes, will be such that the railroad can make whatever expenditures are necessary for expanding its capabilities ahead of need-time—in ways that don't strain either financial resources or the practicalities of getting work done. At this point, he, like other Rio Grande officers, doesn't see coal gumming up the railroad's other operations—and he, also like other Rio Grande officers, is quick to point out that whatever revenues coal may bring, Rio Grande cannot and could not live without its merchandise revenues.

In running existing unit trains and in planning future ones, Timberlake has to be concerned with track, power, and equipment, maybe in that order, and he is. First, track: The Craig branch may be a good example. It's a part of the old Moffat line that meanders off the main line at Orestod. Not long ago, Jack Timberlake recalls, "I was riding the line and told an engineer that pretty soon he'd have ctc. He said, 'Hell, we don't have signaling now and there's no way there's ever going to be enough traffic on this line for ctc.' Well, much of the Craig line has been upgraded and upgrading of the rest is coming; ctc has been installed on much of the route; and the whole line will be ctc-controlled before long."

Then, consider a line that takes off from the main line at Grand Junction, Colo., runs south to Delta and then east to the Somerset area. That line has had track upgrading, and eventually it is also going to get ctc, once there are enough coal-movement commitments to, as Timberlake puts it, "push the budget button."

In Utah, there is the Pleasant Valley branch out of Colton, near Soldier Summit, a line that came close to abandonment in the late 1960s. It was left in place, however, and in the '70s coal development began. The line was tied and surfaced when it was reactivated; it's in good shape for expansion of traffic now, though it may someday need more heavy rail and ctc.

... equals performance on the bottom line

	1977	1976	1975	1974	1973
Operating revenues	$179,512,000	$168,347,000	$148,310,000	$140,559,000	$118,398,000
Operating income	$28,823,000	$26,984,000	$23,834,000	$25,369,000	$22,109,000
Net income*	$19,780,000	$16,387,000	$14,290,000	$15,503,000	$15,332,000
Capital expenditures	$31,337,000	$7,576,000	$30,241,000	$40,653,000	$14,870,000

*Rio Grande Industries

Outside Helper, Utah, an all-new line may have to be built, to serve coal lands acquired by a California utility. On its so-called Aspen branch, Rio Grande may need track work and a short stretch of ctc. In the old southern Colorado coalfields, something sooner or later may happen, and, in the meantime, Denver-Pueblo trackage is being improved and the Pueblo-Walsenburg line may need upgrading if Rio Grande becomes a coal collector for a slurry pipeline starting at Walsenburg and more ctc seems to be in the works.

•**Facing up to demand.** Most simply put, Rio Grand is getting ready for a lot more coal than it already has. And what about operations, now and then?

In unit coal-train running today, the 100-car train is a neat standard: 100 cars, 10,000 tons, power on the front, and roll it. On Rio Grande, that is not exactly the norm. Rio Grande runs loaded 100-car trains (and 100-car trains of empties) but it also runs a lot of 50-car coal trains and will continue to do so, even though some of those trains, depending upon the circumstances and the route, may run short part of the way and then be combined into longer trains. Helper service? Many roads don't know what the phrase means any

more—but Rio Grande does. In several territories, on the Craig branch, around Moffat Tunnel to the top of Tennessee Pass, and out around Helper, Utah, Rio Grande helps—with a total power requirement of as much as 35,000 hp, 12 units, working on the grade out of Helper, including eight helper units cut in usually about two-thirds of the way back in an 11,200-trailing-ton coal train bound for Kaiser in California.

That train to Kaiser Steel, incidentally, routed Rio Grande-Union Pacific-Santa Fe, has been running for about 10 years—and Chief Transportation Officer D.J. Butters can recall only a few problems. "We've had a couple of broken coupler knuckles in that time," he says. "That's all." That's also one reason why Rio Grande respects its engineers and its road foremen of engines; they run, and run well. (Dee Butters works mostly out of an office in Denver now—but there are those on Rio Grande who still regard him as the best man ever to close his hand over a locomotive throttle).

With Harold Cash forecasting 35 million tons of coal in 1983 and with at least five other major projects expected to come on-line then and later, however, Timberlake

and the rest of Rio Grande have to have problems. But Timberlake and Rio Grande also think they have answers, and the answers come in a number of areas: (1) Rio Grande runs 50-car coal trains where it now thinks it advisable, but it also runs big trains and can combine 50-car units; (2) passing tracks have been and are being extended so that meets can take place just about everywhere they're required; (3) upgrading of track and installation of branch-line ctc, even without new passing tracks, should make it possible for crews to go from origin terminal to mine, load the train, and return within the limits of the present 12-hour hours-of-service law; and (4) operating changes can be made, if and when they become necessary. In that context, for one thing, Rio Grande could use slave units. It doesn't now, but it could go that way, if it should turn out that what is now a hairline decision between helper service and slave units tilts in favor of slaves. It could also make use of alternative routes, on coal moving east. And it could make use of a combination of other alternatives, keeping in mind Rio Grande's traditional ability to move in on alternatives and to make them work.

•**"Practice?" Who needs it?** Rio

With automobile unloading facilities handling GM, Ford, and Chrysler products at Salt Lake City (above) and GM products at Denver, Rio Grande's motor vehicle business is growing. Revenues last year were $19.3 million, about 11% of total freight revenues.

Rio Grande's annual coal tonnage has more than doubled in the past 10 years—and long-range forecasts indicate that it will be hauling almost double this year's tonnage in 1983. In 1977, coal brought in $51.9 million, or about 30% of gross freight revenues.

Grande, not so incidentally, is not about to take on coal traffic at break-even or, worse, at a loss. Almost all of its rates are now at satisfactory levels, and, as Gus Aydelott frequently reminds his people, "We don't need to run trains for practice. We already know how. It's the bottom line that counts."

That brings up another point, regarding who is going to supply the equipment that's going to be used for moving all of the Colorado and Utah coal that's expected to move.

Rio Grande will quote rates on coal to move in railroad-owned cars—standard equipment, that is, not specialized equipment; but, like a number of other western coal haulers, it is expecting that most of the coal will roll in cars furnished by others. Where Rio Grande may differ is in the reasoning behind that expectation. Jack Timberlake, for instance, will agree that in one case or another there is probably merit in railroad arguments having to do with utilities' ability to finance equipment at cheaper rates, shop-capacity problems, and so forth. But he will not go along with the argument that railroads can't afford to acquire the cars themselves: "It gives us an image problem we don't need, and besides, in many cases it's just not so."

Rio Grande's position—one that underlies its refusal to provide special equipment for coal—is that it would be willing to go out and acquire the car types and fleet sizes desired by users *if* the users would bear the risk in the event that changed circumstances (environmental or other bureaucratic decisions, for example) suddenly dried up the need for a whole lot of cars. Mines, Timberlake notes, don't set up for production without firm contracts on what for all practical purposes is a take-or-pay basis—but existing law, apparently, doesn't provide a means for a railroad to protect itself on the provision of equipment.

Motive power is another story. Rio Grande's fleet is adequate, to say the least. It has grown by about one-third over the past five years, and while the road's mechanical and operating people have unkind things to say about the two-dozen-or-so SD45s on the roster, they have nothing but praise for the performance and availability ratings of the SD40T-2 units that have more recently been acquired. Mainline coal operations are designed for six-axle power; the trucks on the 40T-2 models have caused no problems on Rio Grande's many and sharp curves; adhesion factors have been higher than promised—and, while transportation officers appreciate the availability of full tractive effort at lower speeds on upgrades, the real "plus" for SD-type power lies in its additional dynamic-braking capability on downgrades. (For still more braking power, on some captive coal-hauling equipment an extra air line for engineer-controlled setting of retainers has been specified.)

When Gus Aydelott and Bill Holtman sit down to talk about Rio Grande, it's almost like listening to two loving fathers discussing a common offspring: They'll concede that the youngster has a problem or two, but the overriding impression is that they're just damn proud.

Rio Grande is, of course, a relative youngster. The present Denver & Rio Grande Western Railroad Company was born out of a reorganization just 31 years ago, the same year that Holtman signed on as a metallurgist. By that time, Aydelott had been with Rio Grande for 11 years. Fresh from the University of Illinois, he took his BS-Transportation degree west in 1936 and went to work as a welder helper (track) and extra gang laborer.

Today, Gus Aydelott looks back at what Rio Grande was like in the old days: "There was a time when the fence posts looked better than the ties." He looks ahead, and he grumbles: "I wish I were 20 years younger." He expresses a feeling that seems to run all through Rio Grande: "It can be fun to go into a bankrupt property and rebuild it—but it's no fun to go the other way. That's why we're determined: Never again."

• **For the long haul . . .**It's going to be Bill Holtman's job to make sure that it's "never again," and Holtman is ready for the parallel tasks of handling increasing traffic and keeping the railroad in top physical condition: "Most of the decisions we make are long range. We don't trade off for short-range profit. Oh, we could probably ride for two or three years without making any great expenditures—but we also know that if you do that, it's going to get you sooner or later." With its cash flow and its credit rating, it should be noted, Rio Grande has indeed been able to pour money into the property; its bond rating is AA and it has a Triple-A rating on equipment trusts.

One of its problems, though, is that simple geography is beginning to have a stifling effect, which is one reason Rio Grande would very much like Rock Island's lines to the Missouri River. Aydelott and Holtman are constantly aware

G.B. Aydelott

that their road can be bypassed, and that a Rio Grande routing depends in so many cases upon Rio Grande's ability to give superior service and nothing else. They worry, somewhat, too, about the shape of future industrial development in Colorado and Utah, in an environment common in the West in which development is not really encouraged.

At the same time, though, Rio Grande's top managers don't see a breakthrough to the Missouri as essential to survival: "If we don't get it," Gus Aydelott shrugs, "it won't break us, but we do see the eastward extension as a welcome opportunity. If the Rock Island could get the money to fix the line, that would be OK, too. You've got to remember that some things connected with the BN merger hurt us—but we've survived in pretty good shape. And yes, maybe some people see us as hurting if our connections and competitors start getting together, hurting to the point where we won't be able to afford to maintain this railroad the way we want to. Maybe some people see it that way—but we don't."

• **Run, run, run . . .** What does concern Aydelott and Holtman, however, is what Gus Aydelott terms some railroads' "love affair with maximum tonnage—and their reluctance to run extra trains." Productivi-

What Rio Grande's coal operations add up to is efficiency, even with the 50-car trains that other roads might consider too small—and Rio Grande has the numbers to prove just how efficient unit-train operations can be in terms of car supply and equipment utilization. A decade ago, Jack Timberlake recalls, 1,200 cars and 15 to 20 locomotives were needed for pre-unit train movement of coal to U.S. Steel at Geneva, Utah. Now, movement of about the same annual tonnage is

protected with use of just 250 cars and eight units. Coal-to-Kaiser in California is a similar story: A movement that once required a pool of 900 to 1,000 cars is now handled with 200 cars.

• **Safe and good, good and safe.** With traffic increasing and with its tough operating conditions, management is adding items to its top-priority lists—but two that have always been there have to do with accident prevention and track improvement.

Rio Grande's success

W.J. Holtman

ty, Bill Holtman adds, "is a lot more than just getting tonnage. In addition to keeping cars out of terminals, or getting them through terminals as quickly as possible, we just have to run over the road faster than 40 or 50 miles an hour whenever and where-ever we can. Those tonnage trains and slower speeds may be OK where you have no competition, but . . . "

Aydelott raises another point: "A lot of roads don't like to run trains of empty cars. And sure, those trains look terrible when you measure net or even gross ton-miles per train-hour. But who in hell cares? We're supposed to be running railroads, and part of running a railroad is having equipment available for loading where it's needed."

As for problems relating to car shortages and terminal congestion, Bill Holtman is no less direct: "It's poor car movement, as much as anything else, that creates car shortages. And congestion? The best way to get out of a congestion situation is to run short trains—take 40 or 50 cars and run."

Aydelott and Holtman concede that perhaps some of their flexible operating methods might be less readily used on mammoth properties, where standards are more firmly set, management is multi-layered, and communications can bog down. But they don't concede that a measure of flexibility is an impossibility, anywhere.

And they know that you can't operate a railroad in today's competitive environment without it.

For Rio Grande, obviously, it works—and it works without Rio Grande's having to go to a lot of complicated procedures to make it work. Operations control, in effect, comes from a room in Denver, where dispatchers manning four consoles make things happen. Terminal control has been much improved through installation last year of a new monitoring system which gives the Transportation Management Center every-eight-hour updates on yard conditions. The result is that traffic moves—with, traffic officers declare, the transportation department giving its full cooperation in meeting service demands, even if it means dispatching light trains of 2,000 tons or less that would break the heart of tonnage worshippers.

There's even a budget benefit, management points out, from this style of opera-tion: "If you do a lot of blocking for direct delivery to connections, as we do, and if you do everything else possible to minimize yard handling, and if you keep yards clear by running more trains, you get better utilization of power and equipment—and you also avoid having to worry about a lot of yard expansion." The record backs up the observation: Operating statistics are show-ing improvements, and with the exception of replacement of the master retarder a few years ago at Grand Junction and expansion of intermodal facilities, Rio Grande has not had to pour money into yard improvements and expansions.

●**Different—and yet the same.** Today, Gus Aydelott, who became president and chief executive officer of Rio Grande just nine years after it came out of reorganiza-tion, looks warily at his approaching 65th birthday—while Bill Holtman, who became president in mid-1977 and chief executive officer Jan. 1 of this year, is rapid-ly settling in as the man who's going to build upon an already fine record.

They're different men in many ways, but they're twins in at least one respect—in a determination to make a great rail-road greater.

of mileage where it is just not possible for crew members in either locomotive or ca-boose to make visual checks of their train and be able to check the whole train—so the road opted for what amounts to a trip-wire kind of detection system: "We stayed simple and kept our detectors out of the signal system—so we were able to saturate the system with what you might call the economy-model detector. Econo-my, maybe. But it works."

Track? On branches, Rio Grande still has some of the original 85-pound rail that went into track when World War I hadn't yet begun. But that's coming out as tonnages are going up (even though much of it is still in near-perfect condition). And Rio Grande has had track-improve-ment programs that keep getting bigger: In 1976, it was 36 miles of new rail and 192,000 ties; in '77, it was 49.5 miles of rail and 197,000 ties; this year, it was to be 72 miles of new rail (89.5 miles, including relay) and about 250,000 ties, but then in late July Ed Waring got the word that the budget would yield up even a few more miles of rail. About 25% of major lines will get out-of-face surfacing, with another 25% getting spot treatment.

Looking back, Rio Grande's chief engi-neer can recall not so long ago when inser-tion of 150,000 to 175,000 new crossties was regarded as an adequate yearly pro-gram and when track could go 10 years before it needed major surfacing work. Now, Rio Grande is planning for a 1979 rail program similar to this year's; Waring looks at 200,000-plus ties per year as adequate; and he sees a four-to-five-year cycle on sur-facing as probable once coal traffic gets to where it's going in growth terms. Rail programs, however, will likely drop back to about 50 miles per year, after neces-sary upgrading is done.

Almost all rail installed is welded, in-cluding rail laid on curves of up to six degrees, and Ed Waring is planning to test welding on sharper curves next year. One of his minor problems this year was that by the time he knew he was getting additional new rail, his welding plant at Pueblo—a port-able one—had been moved on to another railroad: "Well," said Waring, "you give me the rail—and if necessary, we'll lay it jointed."

Over the years, Rio Grande has been careful in experimenting on track. It tested flame-hardened rail and ran into some problems with deep head separations; it does use CF&I HiSi rail, and, says Ed Waring, "we're very interested" in Chrome-moly. Basic main-line standard for a long time has been 136-pound section for replacement, with 119-pound section go-ing in on other heavy-tonnage lines.

●**Ballast? It's precious.** Over a good part of its routes, Rio Grande is blessed with a solid rock subgrade—and it has been blessed with a good supply of some of the best ballast around—precious-metal slag,

On the prevention side, for example, slide detectors have been installed at every place Rio Grande thinks there's a chance of a slide or rock fall. Including units now scheduled for installation, the road will soon have 33 hot-box detectors sending readouts into the Transportation Management Center in Denver; in moun-tain country where temperatures and train speeds are lower, detectors are spaced 60 to 70 miles apart, but west of Glenwood Springs, where temperatures and speeds

get higher, the spacing is 25 to 30 miles. The big numbers, though, have to do with dragging-equipment detectors. Rio Grande has about 300 of them spread over its 1,800-mile-plus system, all designed to provide a trackside trouble indication and most located to catch a problem before a train reaches a switch or other track element where dragging equipment could trigger a derailment.

As Dee Butters points out, with all its curves and tunnels, Rio Grande has a lot

Rio Grande continues to seek out marketing opportunities in both conventional piggyback and containerization. Its showcase operation: a 30-to-40-car TOFC/COFC train that departs Denver in the evening for arrival in Salt Lake City 15 hours later.

the leftovers from smelters that once refined silver, zinc, and lead ores. Rio Grande has its own pit at Leadville and buys from an outside supplier, but supplies are running low. And, while the road can use and is using steel-mill slag, as Waring observes, precious-metal slag runs 3,400 pounds per cubic yard, mill slag just 2,800 pounds; thus, to conserve remaining supplies, the heavy stuff goes where ballast problems are greatest.

So, Rio grande has the cars, the power, the track, the signaling, the communications, and the people to run. That leaves it up to Clarence Lennig and a lean, hungry traffic department to bring in the freight—and thus far, Lennig and his people have been pretty adept at their job.

They sell service, pure and simple—and it's selling. Examples? Lennig and AVP-Sales Jack D. Key and AVP-Market Development C.D. Brainard and Manager-Marketing Services J.J. Martin have them.

Take, for instance, automobile traffic. First, at a time when you hear a lot of criticism about rail service from the major automobile companies, you don't hear it about Rio Grande—and Rio Grande deals with the Big Three, handling General Motors, Ford, and Chrysler arrivals at Salt Lake City and GM's at Denver, as well as being an intermediate link in the operation of the FordFast train from the East to California. Second, performance is paying off: Transportation equipment brought Rio Grande just $8 million in revenues a decade ago, but last year the total was $19.3 million, or about 11% of gross freight revenues. While revenues have been going up, loss-and-damage claims have stayed low, in large part because Rio Grande doesn't let rack cars sit around long enough for thieves and vandals to do their thing.

Actually, at its unloading points, Rio Grande's aim is to get the racks in, get them unloaded, and get the empties rolling back to the assembly plant the same day. (On that kind of speed, incidentally, Clarence Lennig is somewhat given to musing about the effects of hourly per-diem—mainly because, he notes, with daily per diem there were many, many times when Rio Grande could take foreign cars at one end of the line and run them through to interchange at the other end before a dollar in per diem came due.)

• **TOFC/COFC: Imagination—and growth.** Intermodal traffic is another example of a bit of imagination at work—in both trailer and container traffic.

Rio Grande's piggyback showcase is a 30-to-40-car speedster that leaves Denver each evening and is ready for deramping in Salt Lake City the next morning, 15 hours later. Most of the traffic it is hauling is ex-highway—and performance is keeping the trailers on flat cars. Rio Grande is not all that big in United Parcel Service movements, but on corridors it can protect its performance record for UPS, which, Lennig says, comes in second only to that of Florida East Coast.

Container traffic? With Rio Grande, that's something that's really different, and it all started a few years ago with Rio Grande's making itself a middleman between steamship lines with landbridge containers made empty on the East Coast and forwarders, shipper associations, and shipper agents who could use what would amount to "free" boxes for westbound movement. All Rio Grande can do is to help get the parties together—they route the freight. But it's an idea that has worked, one that other roads have picked up, one that solves problems for both the container lines and consolidators in the East who can use the empties to good advantage—one that's brought decent amounts of new business to Rio Grande.

Rio Grande, though, does have a couple of traffic-related problems. One, shared with other western coal haulers, is the shipper concern that with all that coal moving, other service is bound to suffer. A second is that service performance on so much Rio Grande traffic depends not just on Rio Grande but on roads handling the business before or after or both.

• **"We want you, we need you . . . "** On the first problem, about all Rio Grande—or any road—can do is to be convincing in word and then to back it up with deed. "We continue to convince people that yes, we do want transcontinental business," Joe Martin declares. "We couldn't be a viable railroad without our merchandise traffic."

As for the second problem, involving interline service, when service difficulties do crop up the approach is one that involves both operating and traffic people from the roads involved, most of which are much bigger than Rio Grande. "We're patient," Clarence Lennig says. "But we're also persistent. We hope we're persuasive."

One problem that Rio Grande doesn't have, in traffic, is the loss of key people. As a road that depends so much on business that may be controlled off-line, Rio Grande maintains a far-flung sales force concentrated around 11 regional offices. Sales personnel are in constant contact with customers all over the country, and their work is visible to other railroads—but over the past five or so years, Jack Key can recall only two men who opted to make a career change and leave Rio Grande.

A second problem that it doesn't have is the one that involves the transportation product and what the operating department conceives it to be. Insofar as it is possible, Lennig is convinced, Rio Grande runs for the benefit of traffic and not because it has schedules sunk in cement. Westbound, for instance, there are schedules, to be sure—but as a practical thing, Rio Grande runs off its connections. And eastbound, Grand Junction—the road's only hump yard—does a wide variety of blocking for connections in the way that connections want cuts blocked. Communication? There's that, too. It's standard in Denver, but it seems to work generally. And if a salesman has a particular problem that needs top help, there's no bar to his getting in touch with the chief transportation officer, Dee Butters. "They can," Lennig says, "and they do."

Overall, Rio Grande has the look of health, and the numbers Ward Bushacher keeps indicate that looks aren't deceiving. Total debt, for instance, is about the same as it was 30 years ago, but the mix is a lot different, with equipment debt going up and bonded debt going down. And while there may be large future demands upon cash—for proposed line changes, perhaps, or possibly for acquisition of RI's lines to the Missouri—Rio Grande doesn't really lack for ways to handle those demands.

• **The spirit was willing—and still is.** They tell a story at Rio Grande, a story about a flatlander who came out to take a look, and he took that look at Rio Grande operations, and he came to a conclusion: "Whoever built a railroad here sure wanted to build a railroad awful bad."

Gus Aydelott and Bill Holtman and the rest of Rio Grande today weren't there at the creation, but they're there at least in spirit—wanting "awful bad" to operate a railroad that's awfully good. ∎

Coal: Questions begging for answers

By GUS WELTY, Senior Editor

They've called it "The Great Black Hope."

They've called it "New King Coal."

They've called it "Our Most Abundant Energy Source."

But in stumbling around the fringes of a national energy policy, they—the Executive and Legislative branches of the federal establishment—have mostly succeeded only in confusing and confounding those who want to produce, transport, and use this "most abundant energy source."

Item: Largely because of environmental restrictions on both the mining and the burning of coal, coal operators don't know how far or how fast they should go in developing new mines, even the low-sulphur coal mines of the West.

Item: Railroads are spending hundreds of millions of dollars to improve existing lines and to build new ones to handle coal traffic (with additional millions going for motive power and equipment), but they're finding it less and less easy to predict what annual volume may be even a few years ahead, as government policy remains murky.

Item: Electric utilities, many of them, would just as soon burn coal as any other fuel, but they have little way of knowing what regulations an unregulated Environmental Protection Agency is liable to come up with next, or how the courts may handle disputes over those regulations. (At the same time, a number of utilities are finding that the demand for power is not increasing as fast as earlier projections had indicated it would.)

For more than two years now, the Administration and Congress have gone back and forth over energy policies and, of course, the President came forth with a new one just a few weeks ago. But, it's anybody's guess what Congress may do with this new policy—and in any event, its main concern with coal involved a directive to the Departments of Energy and the Interior and EPA to report in two months on how to increase production and use of this "most abundant energy source."

● **Events take their course.** In the meantime, utility bills keep going up as fuel and other costs rise. Development of nuclear-fueled plants, already under attack, has been seriously wounded by the recent events at Three Mile Island in Pennsylvania. OPEC keeps boosting prices on its members' oil exports. Domestic oil and gas prices are sure to rise, more then they already have. Utilities are warning of the possibility of brownouts (or worse) this summer, especially if nuclear plant operations are curtailed.

In the meantime, too, a lot of coal just sits there. It could be developed quickly, at least by comparison with the time it takes to get a nuke authorized (let alone into operation). It could be moved efficiently, by railroads already in place and under construction. It could be used effectively by utilities and other industries in lieu of scarcer and perhaps more expensive fuels.

For their part and to their credit, railroads are not backing off from their earlier confidence in coal's future—and they're backing up that confidence with money. Some roads may be trimming their forecasts more in line with what's now perceived as reality, but the buildup for coal continues.

Predictably, railroads in the West are especially bullish. Santa Fe, for example, boosted coal volume from 5.7 million tons in 1977 to 9.2 million last year—with the totals expected to climb to 18 million tons this year and to 25 million tons or more by the mid-1980s, and that forecast does not include consideration of possible coal development in the San Juan Basin. Taking a shorter-range view, Rio Grande, which had a 26.5% coal-revenue increase in 1978, looks for gains of as much as 40% in '79. Kansas City Southern's coal traffic also continues to grow, going from a bit more than 1% of revenues to more than 12% in just five years. Missouri Pacific, which moved less than 10 million tons of coal in '78, sees movement of about 15 million tons annually by 1982. And Union Pacific, looking at the possible impact on it of Chicago & North Western's new plan to tap Powder River Basin coal, estimates that this arrangement alone could add as much as 25 million tons a year to UP coal movements by 1985.

Then there's Burlington Northern, which apparently became the nation's largest single coal-originating railroad in 1978—in part because of western coal growth and in part because of the United Mine Workers' strike, which hurt first-quarter '78 production far more in the East than it did in the West. By BN's numbers, it originated 63 million tons of coal last year, and that was almost 10 million tons more than was originated by the carrier ranking second. (On a system basis, BN came in second in '78 to Chessie System's Chesapeake & Ohio, Baltimore & Ohio, and Western Maryland.)

● **Increases, but . . .** BN's 63-million-ton load last year represented a 24% increase from 1977 levels, and BN is anticipating another 24% increase this year, to about 78 million tons. But as one BN officer told a recent Department of Energy coal-train workshop, "I can tell you with great certainty that this rate of tonnage growth will not extend into the 1980s. In the next two to three years, we see a definite slowing in the rate of growth of our coal business. By 1983, we expect that the annual growth in our coal tonnage will be down to a very moderate level." BN's forecast window for the early '80s: 115 million tons likely, 140 million tons possible.

Allan R. Boyce, assistant vice president-executive department, explained the numbers this way: "There are a great many factors which have led us to conclude that many of the early projections of western coal production were overstated. Certainly the best-available-controls-technology provisions of the Clean Air Act will slow down the development of western coal and significantly restrict the scope of its market. Rising energy prices generally have caused many potential western coal users to look at fuel supplies closer to home; a prime example would be the rapid development of Texas lignite that has taken place in recent years. Finally, electric utilities around the country are finding that demand for electricity is increasing at a much lower rate than anticipated; this had led to a rash of cancellations and deferments of plans for new power plants."

One recent study, Boyce noted, points to annual growth of about 4% in consumption of electricity through 1990, down sharply from the historical growth rate of about 7%. At the same time, he said, government forecasts of 1985 coal production have been cut back significantly.

(Uncertainty does not just affect coal producers, railroads, and utilities. Freight car and component manufacturers have to be wondering about how the market will develop, and so do manufacturers of coal-handling equipment. For example, McDowell-Wellman, a major company in that latter category, has been looking long and hard at prospects, and while Vice President-Sales and Marketing John Sheppard describes his company as "enthusiastic" about the market for coal-handling equipment, with a lot of good business shaping up over the short range, he also notes that it's just extremely difficult to chart the long range with any great degree of confidence.)

● **Problems: No shortage.** If you want to go into additional problem areas af-

Railroads are gearing up to meet the demand—but murky government policy makes it hard to forecast its dimensions

levels that reflect true costs and provide a needed return.

Naturally, utilities want to get coal delivered at the lowest possible overall cost. But more than one railroader has found a lack of simple justice in a utility's sitting back with its 10% or 12% rate of return even as it sits upon rail rates that provide a far lower return.

This situation may, however, be in the process of correction, and again, BN may serve as an example. For some time, BN has been working to get questionable coal rates up to compensatory levels, and it has met with some success. Last year, for instance, the Interstate Commerce Commission approved a 30% boost in rates on coal moving to San Antonio, and the road also filed for increases on movements to power plants in Minnesota, Arkansas, and Iowa. This year, BN went for increases ranging from 10% to 56% on certain movements into Minnesota and Wisconsin, and the commission allowed these rates to go into effect subject to investigation and possible refund. One BN officer calls what has happened "solid progress," noting that the ICC "now is beginning to authorize rates that include the current cost of capital and additional investments required to handle new traffic. Moreover, new rate requests are not being suspended, automatically, as in the past."

As for the service problem, it's a stickier one on some roads than on others.

● **Service: Not a rail problem alone.** There were, last year, a host of problems related to getting cars and motive power redistributed when the coal strike finally ended, but the ongoing problem is one of simply maintaining prescribed cycles for unit-train operation—and this is a problem with many causes. The most obvious, of course, have to do with rail operations —not just the effects of derailments or severe weather but also the effects of improvement programs in which line construction and maintenance and installation of new signal systems have to take place under growing volumes of traffic. Less obvious are problems associated with breakdowns at the mine or at the unloading site, but these problems are not less serious when they occur, because a shutdown for even a few hours can have a domino effect stretching out for hundreds of miles.

Then there is the problem of a railroad's getting the right to build new lines to tap new mines, and two examples should suffice here to demonstrate what the carriers are up against.

For Burlington Northern, it all began

fecting coal and its rail-oriented future, consider this quartet: (1) rates, (2) service, (3) the difficulties associated with new-line construction, and (4) the ever-present threat of the coal-slurry pipeline.

First, rates. In the beginning, with not

a lot of experience to draw upon, railroads set some coal rates too low. They've been paying for those mistakes ever since, and it's only been recently that a number of those depressed rates have been jacked up to respectable levels, in 1972 when BN filed application to build 116 miles of new railroad between Gillette and Orin, Wyo. First, the ICC expressed belief that this should be a joint BN—C&NW project (in order to avoid construction of duplicating facilities), so a joint application was worked out, premised upon North Western's upgrading of its existing route through Nebraska. Then there was the environmental impact statement to be developed, and it ran to a number of volumes. Not until 1976 did the commission give the go-ahead to start construction, and at that point an environmental group filed suit. Litigation was not settled until April 1978, but BN did then start building, with the opening of the entire line now scheduled for late this year—more than seven years after the original application was filed.

Santa Fe, meanwhile, hasn't even gotten to the grading stage on the so-called Star Lake Railroad, which would run north from the Santa Fe main line in western New Mexico to serve mines to be developed in the San Juan Basin. Eventually, that new railroad could stretch more than 100 miles—but all Santa Fe can say now is that it hopes the government will approve the environmental impact statement without further delay, delay that already adds up to about three years.

Coal-slurry pipelines? The threat *is* ever present, but pipeline promoters, despite their presumed wealth, power, and influence, have yet to lay a single foot of pipe. They lost a round on eminent domain last year in Washington, they have not been able to snake their way through all of the state legislatures whose sanction would be needed to win the eminent domain fight on a state-by-state basis, and they have yet to come up with acceptable proposals that would allow them to suck in scarce water in semi-arid parts of the West.

While there are many uncertainties about coal production and transportation and use in general, there is little or no uncertainty about the plans of the pipeline promoters: Defeat after defeat, they will be back.

● **Then there is nuclear** . . . In all of these considerations regarding future energy policy and practice, there is one huge imponderable, the future of nuclear power.

Currently, there are six dozen nuclear reactors in existence, with more than 90 under construction and a third as many more planned (the vast majority of these are located east of the Mississippi). Utilities like nukes, one reason being that while they may cost more to build and while they will never achieve their long-ago economic promise (of power so cheap it wouldn't have to be metered), once a

nuclear plant is in place, it's there (or, in view of what happened in Pennsylvania, is it?), and the utility does not have to be concerned about the logistics or the economics of fuel supply.

At least one survey is said to indicate that despite the Three Mile Island inci-

---

A pioneer in unit coal trains now runs seven

Northern Indiana Public Service—NIPSCO—was one of the pioneer utilities in the unit-train business; its first train went into service 14 years ago. Today NIPSCO has seven unit trains in operation, hauling coal from seven mines to four generation stations and piling up about 28 million car-miles a year.

Late last month, the newest addition to the fleet went into service, with 100 100-ton cars (out of a 110-car pool) making the first delivery from a mine in Colorado to a generating station in Gary, Ind., via Rio Grande, Santa Fe, and Elgin, Joliet & Eastern. Like the other cars in the power company's fleet, these cars came from Thrall Car, with new-train cars under lease and a 15-year maintenance agreement with the carbuilder.

While NIPSCO has stayed with one builder for its cars, start-up to today, it has exercised a few options in other areas. There aren't really that many options in the purchase of coal, a NIPSCO officer notes, "because environmental requirements have made it necessary for us to go out west for low-sulphur coal, and about half of the coal we now burn comes from western mines in Colorado, Utah, and Wyoming. . . . There are usually several possible routes that the unit train can take to get to its assigned generating station. Of course, we look at the cost of transportation. But we also have to look at the reliability of the railroad. Our contracts with the mines are mostly long term, so it is important to work with railroad companies that are financially sound and that can be depended upon to provide good service for many years. We work with the top railroad companies in the country."

---

dent, a majority of the population (albeit a slim one) favors continued development of nuclear power for generating electricity —and it could be that inept public relations had as much to do with Three Mile Island antinuke reaction as anything else. Still, as the facts filter out, they present a sobering if not outright terrifying

scenario of what can happen when human errors and equipment malfunctions build upon each other.

Just as sobering, however, is what could be perceived as the "official" attitude toward coal—which is that even though we have coal, here and now—enough coal to see the nation through—"we the people" are going to go to every extreme to avoid using it.

Item: Coal, any coal, is somewhat "dirty" when it's burned. This has always been recognized as a drawback. But lately, there seems to be another drawback cited when increased coal usage is proposed: Coal mining is dangerous. It has always been dangerous, in deep mines —but, some observers wonder, why this new emphasis on "danger" when increasing tonnages of coal are moving from new, safer surface mines in the West?

Item: While all coal is "dirty," low-sulphur coal is a lot cleaner than the bituminous that used to turn day into night over Pittsburgh. Why then talk about requirements for removing 90% of impurities in the burning process, regardless of how pure or impure the coal may be in the first place?

Item: Other sources of energy than nuclear or oil or gas or coal are either available or (probably) technologically feasible. Solar energy is one, and it should be developed. Wind power may be another, and it's probably worth looking into. But coal is here and now—not 10, 20 or 30 years off into the future. And it seems strange, to some at least, to see coal given such brief treatment in what purported to be a major Presidential statement on energy policy, a statement that also included an earnest proposal for tax credits for people using wood stoves.

● **The "syndrome."** Michael M. Donahue, vice president-coal of BN, addressed this aspect of the situation not long ago, referring to an "uncertainty syndrome" so far as national energy policy is concerned. By contrast, Mike Donahue said, "coal is a certainty that offers a refreshing assurance to the American people. Its properties, its value, its safety are all well known. The technology involved in its mining and utilization is well established. Coal's availability is also well established, through railroad transportation, a system that is daily growing stronger."

More narrow, perhaps, but just as important, is the aspect of coal movement that has to do with railroads and other shippers (who may sometimes fear that their service will be lost under an avalanche of coal) BN's Allan Boyce landed hard on that one: "The basic equation is a simple one: More coal traffic equals stronger railroads, which equals better service for all railroad shippers. And that's the future as we see it." ■

13 steps toward a sane transportatio

The importance of rail transportation to this nation cannot be overemphasized. A financially healthy rail system is essential to agricultural and industrial producers if they are to remain competitive in markets across the country. It is equally important to the nation's consumers to enable them to retain access to the widest selection of goods at the lowest possible prices. The rail industry has, however, been hampered in its attempts to maintain its rightful place in the nation's transportation system by the restraints of outmoded and inequitable regulation.

National policy on surface transportation should be revised to reflect the true economic relationships which exist between the various modes of transportation and to better allocate transportation resources to meet the nation's future needs. This can be done by establishing a policy of equitable treatment of the various modes and placing greater reliance on the forces of the free market, rather than by continuing a policy of uneven regulation which has resulted in an unbalanced, subsidized, and, in many cases, inefficient transportation system.

The railroads are today regulated as though they are classic monopolies, which, in fact, they are not. They compete in the transportation market with water, motor, and air carriers. Highway carriers are only partially regulated as a result of the effect of the exempt commodity list which exempts a broad list of agricultural, horticultural, fish, and other items from regulation. Furthermore, agricultural cooperatives are permitted to carry up to 15% of their tonnage in other commodities and for nonmembers without regulation. On the waterways, all commodities shipped in bulk are exempt from regulation, and the nature of traffic carried on the inland waterways results in most water carrier traffic remaining nonregulated. Private carriage by highway or water is also not subject to economic regulation.

Added to the problems of the rail carriers is the inequitable burden of maintaining their rights-of-way while other transportation modes are subsidized. The railroads are privately owned and operate on privately maintained rights-of-way, while highway and water carriers which are also privately owned and operated move on rights-of-way provided and maintained 24 hours a day at government expense.

Government expenditures (including expenditures by state and local govern-

ments) for highways in the period 1921 through 1976 have totalled $457.6 billion and for waterways during the same time have totalled $21.2 billion. During the year 1976, expenditures were $28.1 billion and $1.3 billion respectively.

Government regulatory policy has tended to favor and protect the users of these publicly provided facilities. The operators who use facilities provided by the public receive large subsidies because operating and investment costs are in large part shifted to other taxpayers. The record is unconvincing that these cost benefits result in lower costs to the consumer and suggests instead that inequitable advantages are given to many users of transportation who are fortunate enough to be situated where they can make use of the publicly-provided transportation plant.

The end result of these policies not only is outmoded and inequitable to railroads today, but the regulatory scheme has been taken advantage of by some operators so as to render even limited regulation meaningless.

For example, the agricultural exemption was devised to permit local truckers to carry produce to local market, packing sheds, or grain elevators without economic regulation. It was not contemplated that fruits and vegetables would be moved, for example, from California and Florida to New York, or grains from Nebraska to Galveston, free of regulation, but that is what has happened.

The distortion of the regulatory scheme has further added to the inefficiency of the transportation system. For example, much of the recent public debate over the cost of regulation has centered around highway operations, with great concern about operations over circuitous routes and empty back hauls. In most cases, empty back hauls result from the use of specialized equipment designed for use in commerce where only a one-way haul exists, such as tank trucks, dump trucks, and auto carriers. Also, the agricultural exemption by its nature promotes either empty back hauls or violating the regulations.

It will not correct the inequities now to give an additional advantage to the exempt operators and the private carriers, who are also, of course, exempt from regulation, by giving them unlimited back haul rights and route freedom, while certificated common carriers remain regulated with respect to rates, routes, and commodities and are required to perform service for all on a non-discriminatory basis.

Today's emphasis on deregulation is at the wrong end of the transportation spectrum. Further efforts are needed to loosen archaic restrictions which govern the railroads despite what we thought was Congress's clearly expressed intent to alleviate the railroads' regulatory burden. The emphasis now seems to be on proposals to give even more freedom to other modes, whereas the major effort should be to further loosen the regulatory shackles of the railroads in order to achieve the competitive balance that was envisioned by Congress when it passed the 4R Act.

Nor is unrestricted entry an answer to the country's need for dependable transportation. At the very least new entry must be accompanied by a demonstration of continuing financial responsibility and the payment of fees or user charges adequate to return the public's investment and maintenance charges for the facilities involved.

Surface transportation policy can be changed to eliminate the inequities and provide greater public benefits through the elimination of subsidies and encouragement of competition by greater reliance on the free market for transportation services. Total and immediate deregulation is neither possible nor desirable at this time, but fundamental changes can be made with deregulation as an ultimate goal. A rational and equitable transportation policy requires that all modes of transportation be treated alike. The following recommendations will provide a beneficial restructuring of surface transportation policy:

1. First and foremost, it is necessary to implement the intent of Congress in the Railroad Reorganization and Regulatory Reform Act of 1976 to reduce regulation, not increase it. In this respect the statute's "Declaration of Policy" provides:

"It is the purpose of the Congress in this Act to provide the means to rehabilitate and maintain the physical facilities, improve the operations and structure, and restore the financial stability of the railway system of the United States, and to promote the revitalization of such railway system, so that this mode of transportation will remain viable in the private sector of the economy and will be able to provide energy-efficient, ecologically compatible transportation services with greater efficiency, effectiveness, and economy..."

This declaration then specifies that Congress intended to—

"foster competition among all carriers by

By BENJAMIN F. BIAGGINI
Chairman and President
Southern Pacific

olicy

railroad and other modes of transportation, to promote more adequate and efficient transportation services, and to increase the attractiveness of investing in railroads and rail-service-related enterprises";
and to grant to railroads

"greater freedom to raise or lower rates for rail services in competitive markets." (4-R Act, Section 101)

Despite what would appear to be a clear directive by Congress to the regulators, attempts by the railroads to implement the policies of the 4R Act have not been successful. Instead of less regulation, the new rulings have resulted in more regulation in the pricing and merger areas. I cannot overemphasize the importance of streamlining, simplifying, and pruning the regulatory process if we are going to be able to maintain a viable rail system that is responsive to the needs of the market place.

2. Recognize that rail movement of goods is sound policy from both an environmental and energy efficiency standpoint. Rail transportation enjoys an efficiency advantage of about four to one over highway freight movements. The rail system is in place and has the capacity to handle increased traffic with minor modifications and additions. In the case of coal traffic, for instance, railroad cars and locomotives can be acquired much more quickly than large-capacity mining equipment and much more quickly than new mines can be opened or new generating plants constructed.

3. Recognize that an adequate rate of return is fundamental to a viable transportation organization and consequently permit pricing freedom within limits broad enough to achieve that rate of return and yet protect against any abuse of unequal economic strength. The pricing freedom anticipated by the 4R Act cannot be achieved within the regulations announced by the Interstate Commerce Commission.

4. Eliminate the regulatory agencies' power of suspension and leave as an adequate remedy its present power of investigation and refund for rates found to be unlawful.

5. Declare that mergers and consolidations of transportation companies are in the national interest, and pass legislation expediting consideration and approval of such cases. The tests should primarily be related to financial consider-

ations and the improved public service aspects of the new combinations. They should clarify that the "effect on other carriers" doctrine which has frustrated the rail merger movement in particular is no longer a factor, regardless of the form of the application. Different rules should be developed for consideration of "end-to-end" mergers as contrasted to side-by-side or "parallel" mergers which may present more complicated issues. The present requirements of the Interstate Commerce Commission and the Department of Transportation are unduly complex and are actually obstacles to mergers. End-to-end mergers usually do not present the problems of parallel mergers, and the regulatory agencies should be required to complete action upon them quickly.

6. Common ownership of all modes of transportation should be permitted and encouraged by law. Just as mergers and consolidations of rail carriers can result in improved transportation service, common ownership of all modes of transportation can provide better coordinated service and lower costs to the shipping public.

7. Mandated services, i.e., uneconomic branch lines and passenger service, should be paid for in full by the agency mandating the service or the beneficiaries of that service.

8. User charges should be established for all government provided and maintained transportation facilities. User charges should be applicable to private and for-hire transportation alike.

9. Railroad operating property should be exempted from local property and other taxes. In the event such property produces other revenues, they can be the subject of an equitable tax.

10. Remove economic regulation for bulk commodities and the exempt list commodities when carried by rail, as is now the case when these same commodities are carried by water in one case and by highway in the other.

11. Grade separation structures and automatic grade crossing protection devices should be recognized as parts of the street and highway system, and as such, paid for by the governmental agencies involved.

12. Federal research and development policies and projects have resulted in much benefit to highway, water, and air carriers. The miniscule federal research program for rail equipment and facilities should be expanded.

13. Establish, by statute, shorter periods than now exist, by law or practice, for consideration of all matters requiring approval of regulatory agencies, and expand the concept of temporary authority grants pending investigation.

The prospects and perspectives of the rail industry are and will be affected materially by our labor constraints unless some significant and long-term changes are accomplished. It is absolutely essential that management be given the ability to improve the utilization of labor, which in turn improves the utilization of tools and equipment.

In the collective bargaining now going on, wage increases can be assumed. Unless those increases can be offset by improved productivity through work-rule changes, the industry will slide backward. A 1% increase in wages translates to a $7-million increase in Southern Pacific's labor costs. The work rule changes we want are logical and sensible, and with realistic bargaining they can be implemented without any significant effect on our employees. We need the type of relationship with railroad labor that will allow the industry to take full advantage of present and future technology and further automation of railroad operations.

It took an act of Congress after eight years of effort at the bargaining table to enable us to reduce the force of firemen on diesels. We cannot affort to wait that long for our next major step forward, but we prefer to make this progress at the bargaining table rather than through legislation.

Unfortunately, railroad labor continues to expend its energy and use up its declining political capital in supporting legislation which imposes further restraints on the railroads or which reduces productivity. This is in sharp contrast to many other labor organizations who support legislation designed to aid the industries where the present and future livelihood of their members rest. I would hope that the Congress would welcome coordinated labor-management approaches to the recommendations I have included in this statement, and I invite the cooperation of railroad labor in them. ∎

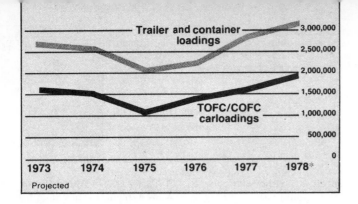

Trailer and container loadings

TOFC/COFC carloadings

	3,000,000
	2,500,000
	2,000,000
	1,500,000
	1,000,000
	500,000
	0

1973 1974 1975 1976 1977 1978*

Projected

Typical of the surge in piggyback traffic is C&NW's

New peaks for piggyback

After reaching record highs in 1973, TOFC/COFC volume fell victim to the 1974-75 recession. But, along with the economy, it pulled out of the slump in '76 and rose to new volume records in 1977, the same year in which TOFC/COFC revenues topped $1 billion for the first time. And 1978? Barring the unforeseen, '78 should see piggyback hitting new highs across-the-board, with trailer/container loadings topping the 3-million mark for the first time.

By FRANK MALONE
Associate Editor

Seldom has the railroad industry stirred itself to such efforts as are now under way in intermodal traffic and operations. With the market tested and found worthy, railroads are moving boldly to improve service, terminals and equipment. Piggyback volume is running far ahead of other rail traffic, much of it moving on trains that operate on passenger-train schedules. The outlook is for more growth as those trains speed between major terminals with improved types of TOFC/COFC cars. One veteran intermodal officer predicts that piggyback traffic, spurred by new technology in terminal and train operations, will grow twice as fast in the next 10 years as it has grown in the last 10 years.

As growth raises hopes, there are fewer doubters raising the standard questions: Are volume increases coming at the expense of other areas of rail traffic? Is there truly enough of a new intermodal market to offset losses in other markets? Is the sharp growth in volume bringing costs that may hinder further growth? Is the growth in revenue producing meaningful growth in profitability?

Such questions, realistic as they may be, reflect an attitude a little too negative for most intermodal boosters, who see the fundamental issue differently. They view intermodal as an area, somewhat less fettered by regulation than most others, where the rail mode can demonstrate its inherent advantage once and for all. They have no doubt that, with the improvements they agree must still come, piggyback can indeed prove profitable and show what railroads can do, given half a chance. They see intermodal as a harbinger of things to come. Above all, they see it as proof that railroads are finally facing up to highway competition by incorporating some of the strengths of that competition.

• **The '78 Scorecard.** The answers to piggyback's basic questions may still be a few years away, but the basis for them is building briskly:

—Despite a four-day strike in the last week of September and severe weather problems in January and February, intermodal carloadings for the first nine months of 1978 were up 11% over 1977, a year in which intermodal revenue topped $1 billion for the first time. Trailers and containers for the first nine months were up 13% over the same period of 1977.

—Several intermodal trains launched in recent years are showing great improvement in backhaul business, which most piggybackers consider the real key to profits, and a couple of new trains this year have gotten off to spectacular starts.

—The roster of designated intermodal trains now includes a federally funded short, fast train in the Chicago-Twin Cities corridor.

—International traffic, both east-west and north-south, is growing to match domestic intermodal traffic in revenue contribution.

—Millions of dollars are going into new and improved intermodal terminals, as the "hub-center" concept spreads.

—Sante Fe's experimental "Ten-Pack" piggyback train has produced greater-than-expected fuel savings after going into Chicago-Los Angeles service in June; Southern Pacific ordered a three-unit articulated double-deck container car; and Trailer Train in late September unveiled a new double-unit car for longer trailers.

—Equipment supply, generally, is keeping up with demand, with Trailer Train adding cars and with both railroads and lessors putting thousands of new trailers into service. The most recent railroad order was from Chessie System for 2,000 hi-cube trailers, and an additional 5,100 new units will be put into service in '79 by the two biggest lessors: Interway, which added 4,438 new and 826 remanufactured trailers to its REALCO fleet this year, will acquire 3,900 and remanufacture 1,200 next year, and Xtra has 2,200 units on order for first-quarter '79 delivery.

• **Fewer skeptics.** Among the boosters is Tom Fante, Southern Pacific assistant vice president-intermodal traffic, who has been involved with piggyback since the primitive days of the 1950s. Fante says there are fewer skeptics within the industry: "In-

66

"Falcon" service, which just added two more westbound trains, set a monthly loading record in September, was headed for another in October.

creasing intermodal traffic and its potential for continued growth obviously have changed the thinking of many industry leaders who, only a few years ago, were less than enthusiastic about intermodal business and particularly wary about handling wheel-less containers."

Sharing that view is Sheldon Landy, director-development planning for Trailer Train, which supplies about 85% of all railroad piggyback cars. Landy says that in his dealings with railroads he has encountered no negativism about piggyback's contribution to profitability. "What we are looking at," Landy says, "are areas where profits can be improved."

The chief executive of a major railroad that came late into intermodal, L. Stanley Crane of Southern, says: "I happen to be very bullish on piggyback."

• **Falcons, Roosters, Rockets, Slingshots.** From Chicago & North Western's well-established Chicago-Nebraska "Falcon" service to Burlington Northern's new Chicago-Northwest "Red Rooster" service, the story is largely one of steady, sometimes spectacular, growth in volume. Showing a 13% increase in nine-month 1978 loadings, "Falcon" service was just expanded with the addition of two more westbound trains. "Falcon" loadings set a new monthly record in September, despite the Clerks' strike, and were heading for another record in October.

Last January, Burlington Northern announced a new intermodal service, the "Red Rooster," leaving Chicago at 1:30 a.m. five days a week for the Pacific Northwest. In early October, BN said the new service had been a major factor in the sharp rebound of its intermodal business after a disappointing first quarter. July-September intermodal revenues were running about 20% ahead of the same months of 1977, BN said. "Red Rooster" first-year

revenues, based on its first seven months of operation, are expected to greatly exceed expectations.

Another success story is in Grand Trunk's Detroit-Chicago intermodal corridor, which has shown a 384% gain in revenue trailers and a 531% gain in containers since September 1975. And this July, GT launched its first dedicated train for the corridor, "Fleet Freight," which runs between two highly automated terminals. The service is expected to produce nearly 60,000 loads this year, compared with 23,620 for the first full pre-dedicated-train year, 1976. Cutoff time at Detroit is 10 p.m. for 9:30 a.m. availability at Chicago; cutoff at Chicago is 9:30 p.m. for 9:30 a.m. Detroit availability. Another Canadian National affiliate, Central Vermont, Sept. 11 started overnight piggyback service known as the "Rocket" between Montreal and Palmer, Mass. Says Phillip Larson, CV general manager: "We foresee a fast-expanding market resulting from cost-saving and energy conservation," for a train which is now being kept short, with a limit of 15 cars.

Southern, too, established a new dedicated train earlier this year to handle growing volumes between Spencer, N.C., and Atlanta. With the new train, traffic from the east arrives at Atlanta for same-day early-morning delivery.

Then, there's a well-established success story, ICG's Chicago-St. Louis cabooseless "Slingshot," which through the first nine months of 1978 had already matched 83% of total 1977 loadings (see p. 26).

• **Real measure, empty miles.** The consensus seems to be that the way to judge piggyback profitability is to look at the loaded/empty-mile ratio. One way to improve that ratio was being demonstrated on Norfolk & Western with rather convincing results until the strike interrupted in

July. The project, known as "common box," involved the use of the largest allowable container on a chassis for both domestic and foreign business. Begun late last year, "common box" was working so well by mid-1978 that June intermodal loadings were almost equal to those of June 1977, although NW had lost its New York market during the year when Delaware & Hudson pulled out of the arrangement. The D&H situation forced NW to discontinue its "Apollo" intermodal service. Despite that, NW had been looking forward to mid-July as the point where 1978 intermodal loadings would surpass 1977's.

"It was proving that we could interchange between domestic and international and reduce empty miles," says R.B. Short, NW director-intermodal sales and service. He adds that for 1978 up to June there had been an overall $800,000 profit improvement despite loss of the New York traffic: "I even had a container line that was interested in furnishing the NW our next equipment purchase on the basis that we would monitor the movement of these containers around the system and guarantee them that they would have containers when they needed them for international business, and we in turn would use them domestically and pay them per diem. It was what I consider a real effort to attack probably one of the last areas where railroads can make improvements, getting rid of empty miles."

Another railroad that attributes intermodal improvement to better backhaul is Rock Island, where the approach has been in rate adjustment to encourage use of empties. The program is supported by a customer-communications system including unit tracing and every-morning monitoring of unit availability. Rock Island notifies shippers as soon as units are empty, to solicit a load for the backhaul.

On the North Western, intermodal officers point to a solid improvement in the "Falcon's" load/empty ratio and an emerging backhaul improvement on the railroad's "Viking" service between Chicago and the Twin Cities. As for the "Falcon," says Jim Ronayne, general manager-intermodal sales, profitability is proven and eastbound business (backhaul) "is improving every month." The story is the same for ICG's "Slingshot," where northbound loadings (backhaul) have also shown sharp increases.

• **Intermodal terminals.** Just as it is hard to find an area of railroading with more activity than intermodal, it's hard to find an area of intermodal with more activity than terminals. The activity is twofold: cut back, build up. Within the near future there will be a definite decrease in the number of piggyback terminals as more railroads move to the "hub center" concept of intermodal operations. Major, strategically located terminals are being drastically strengthened; secondary terminals are being abandoned as short-haul truckers take up the slack. The emphasis is shifting to capitalizing on the rail strength in terminal-to-terminal service.

The emphasis is also shifting to multi-million-dollar improvement of those terminals. One of the biggest programs under way is Southern Pacific's $13-million intermodal-facility improvement program that includes construction of a new 19-acre terminal at Memphis and expansions at Los Angeles, Oakland, San Francisco and Houston. The Memphis facility is expected to be in full operation by the end of this year; the expansions will be completed in about three years. At Houston, site of the biggest expansion, about 35 acres will be added, along with two more overhead cranes. At Oakland, one crane has been added; at San Francisco, a Piggypacker.

Southern is carrying out a $2.2-million addition of piggyback tracks at its relatively new Inman, Ga., Yard, including construction of a double lead over Southern's unique piggyback hump. Completion is expected by the end of the year. Southern is also completing a $750,000 expansion of its Alexandria, Va., intermodal facility.

At Chicago, ICG has undertaken a $1.5-million expansion of its IMX terminal, where two main tracks are being extended and parking space is being greatly increased. Also at Chicago, North Western has completed a $500,000 expansion and streamlining of its Wood Street Yard, improvements that included a new entrance and more parking space. Further C&NW Chicago-area intermodal improvements will include new run-through tracks at

Wood Street and at Proviso Yard. The goal is to reduce switching and truck-tractor time. Terminals, says Roger Gordon, C&NW superintendent-intermodal, represent perhaps the largest single area where railroads can save money in piggyback operations.

Such projects follow several major intermodal expansions elsewhere in the past two years. For example, last year Seaboard Coast Line completed a $1.2-million expansion at Hialeah, Fla., and Louisville & Nashville completed expansions costing more than $5 million at Cincinnati and Louisville. At Detroit and Chicago, Grand Trunk completed terminal improvements costing more than $6 million.

For the most part, terminal improvement includes mechanized loading and unloading, especially side-loading. However, Frisco remains the big exception with its continued reliance on circus loading. Expansion of Frisco's Memphis facility was completed this summer, and a new loading record was reached: 73 trailers in one hour. "We can do it just as fast with circus loading," a Frisco spokesman says.

• **International traffic.** Most intermodal terminal improvements are also aimed at greater container-handling capability, as railroads see international traffic accounting for larger and larger shares of overall intermodal business. Southern Pacific is a good example, as it estimates that it will handle about 110,000 mini-bridge containers this year, compared with about 81,000 last year. "It is significant," says Tom Fante, "that since railbridge service was first introduced in 1972, piggyback has advanced from sixth to second place on the railroads' commodity carloading list." The bridge business, whether land-, mini-, or maxi-, Fante adds, is all new with a virtually untapped potential, and has helped resolve doubts about piggybacking's ability to generate new business for the railroads. The prospect of international business led to SP's experiment with a double-decker container car and to some bold predictions by Fante. He says that by 1985 containers will replace trailers as the primary domestic vehicle between at least one pair of major transcontinental city pairs, and that international traffic in containers will grow faster than domestic intermodal traffic. His one doubt is about railroads' ability to stay ahead of the need for expanded facilities to meet the bridge demand. "I doubt that we will ever lick this problem," Fante says, "since, unlike port developments, we in the railroad business, in connection with facilities, seem to be always after-the-fact and need to go through a great deal of growth pains

and congestion before we can justify the capital expenditures necessary for additional equipment and facilities. In the private-enterprise system within which we operate, capital money for intermodal must compete with capital money for other desirable improvements in railroad plant and facilities."

At the other end of the spectrum of capital investment, on Rock Island, another example of the importance of international business can be found. Though an overall 17% intermodal improvement is seen this year, Rock Island's international business is expected to be up more than 120%. Admitting that it is no match for Santa Fe in service, Rock Island is finding other ways to compete. Under a "one call will do it all" approach, Rock Island is cutting time by cutting paperwork for its customers. Dave Tierney, manager-foreign commerce sales, says that involves not only a tracing system exclusively for containers but delivery of international tariff papers directly to customs offices. "We're trying to make up for the extra day in transit by saving a day in customs," Tierney says. "We're unique in handling IT's in this manner." Rock Island also allows 30 days without detention charges for containers. Don Hansen, Rock Island general manager for intermodal marketing and sales, adds: "We're also becoming more reliable, but we're not making promises that we can't keep." The Rock is looking for a 50% increase in international business in 1979. Although it relies on its good position in relation to the Chicago port, Rock Island is also working out a plan for off-season handling of containers between Chicago and Montreal. "We may not make a lot of money on off-season service, but we'll be helping ourselves in the long run, because customers won't be able to say that we're a seasonal operator only," Tierney explains.

There is another important aspect of the international piggyback market, the north-south intra-continental movement. Here, Missouri Pacific is leading the way with its Canada-Mexico connection, a little more than one year old. At Chicago, MoPac connects with extensions of Canadian National and Canadian Pacific (GTW and Soo Line), and at Laredo, Tex., it connects with National Railways of Mexico. With recent improvements in Mexican customs rules, Missouri Pacific offers through single-line North American transcontinental service (previously, MoPac could deliver to the border, for truck haul into Mexico). At the U.S.-Mexico border, cars are interchanged with NdeM, but that, too, may be changing. "We are discussing possibilities for a runthrough train," says Tom Holzmann, MoPac director-intermodal sales. Also on the way is through piggyback movement into Guatemala via NdeM's new ramp at Ciudad Hidalgo on the Mexico-Guatemala border.

Although reluctant to reveal loading figures, MoPac says its through service is showing a solid increase in volume. "We have experienced a tremendous increase in business to and from Mexico," says Holzmann, "and obviously we feel very good about our early efforts to develop the Mexico-Canada connection. We know the potential is far greater than we can even envision." Overall, MoPac intermodal loadings were up 20% for nine months of 1978.

• **Tip from Conrail.** Regardless of intermodal advances in other parts of the U.S. rail system, piggyback proponents still look to a major part of that system— Conrail— for hints of what really lies ahead. And more and more, it seems, there are some interesting, even hopeful, hints. Growth, says Richard Steiner, Conrail vice

president-marketing, will come through management of equipment as if the railroad were a trucking company, that is, by balancing equipment flows through directional pricing on backhauls. "For the first time," Steiner adds, "we're developing strategies that will team up box cars with intermodal, treating these as complements in the marketplace, rather than as competitors. The strategy will be to approach the market like the irregular route trucker does rather than the traditional rail approach."

And in late September, Conrail announced that it had a new general manager-intermodal operations, James G. Cunningham— previously president of a trucking company, Gateway Transportation of LaCrosse, Wis. He'll have charge of Conrail's 42 piggyback terminals (down from about 70 two years ago) and more than 30 daily piggyback "TrailVan" trains.

• **Pricing.** Conrail's emphasis on pricing to lure backhaul loads, admittedly not an "earthshaking discovery," nevertheless is

further reflection of growing agreement on where the secret of piggyback profitability largely lies. Cost-cutting improvements in train and terminal operations will go a long way in helping railroads offer attractive rates and still improve profitability. But the line is going to be thin for some time, until such improvements can really make an impact. Shippers are already wary of intermodal rate increases and ready to make instant evaluations of piggyback versus all-highway possibilities. As Steiner puts it, "We recognize that long-term growth will not come by increasing rates, although we believe that some commodities are underpriced."

The challenge, then, is going to be to find the right pricing to produce the backhaul essential for profitability—while as soon as possible implementing the technology that will support the tradeoffs necessary for such pricing in the first place. ∎

Mass transport for bulk commodities

By GUS WELTY, Senior Editor

Of all the operational changes that have come to railroading over the past 20 years, those changes related to unit-train operations are having—and will continue to have—the greatest impact.

In theory and in most practical applications, the unit train is a great thing. It's a marketing tool, perhaps an invaluable one. It has an operating simplicity about it that dovetails with the usual perceptions of maximum transportation efficiency, perceptions which have to do with high-volume movements, point-to-point, with minimum intermediate handling.

It shows growth, both in numbers and in commodity scope. In what might be termed their reasonably pure form, unit-train operations actually go back a bit less than two decades, but from the most modest of starts, with coal in Alabama, the unit-train concept has come to span the continent, involving just about every major road and a lot of smaller ones, too. As for the commodities being handled in unit-train fashion, there is coal and there is grain, of course—but there is also a commodity-spread that includes, as of now, petroleum and petroleum products, taconite, ores, phosphate rock and potash, limestone, aggregates, sand and cement, sulphur, gypsum, acids, orange juice, even logs.

Above all, in the unit-train concept, there is potential—the potential for railroads to provide even more of an increasingly essential service, to provide that service at attractive prices and to do the job on bases that result in something more than rock-bottom profit margins.

There are, however, problems, and they could be categorized something like this: rates, competition, maintenance-of-way, maintenance-of-equipment, allocation of resources.

● **Rates, and unanswered questions.** The rate problem could be the most complicated of all. Consider it—as well as the other problems, real and potential—in the context of coal, the No. 1 unit-train commodity.

The first true unit coal train may well have been operated in the eastern half of the country, the old country for coal production, but the major growth in unit-train movements is taking place in the West. Rate structures for coal hauling grew up a long time ago in the East, only recently in the West—and there is just not a whole lot of comparability among the operations being conducted. Too, when brand new unit-coal-train operation did begin out West, railroads were under-

Decade of growth: In 1968 unit trains hauled 27.3% of the 400 million tons of rail-origina

standably short of costing information on which to base their charges. Understandably but unfortunately, in some instances they came up short on the rates, and this has been the kind of shortfall that has come back to haunt—in the sort of haunting experience which piggyback pioneers, some of them, also suffered through because they were going for a new market before they knew fully what it would cost to provide the service to serve the market.

Rate disputes have been the upshot, especially as new rates have been in the processes of negotiation and establishment. And, while no dispute has yet gone to the Supreme Court, one did get to the U.S. Court of Appeals, coming to a decision containing a fair degree of bafflegab.

Most recently, the Interstate Commerce Commission has been more actively doing its thing, looking into western coal rates on an overall basis and wondering whether contract rates—which it once regarded as illegal per se—will be the way to go.

● **Competition: Gaining or losing?** The rate issue, of course, is somewhat related to the competitive issue, an issue mostly related to promoters' efforts to get state and/or federal grants of eminent domain for the construction of coal-slurry pipelines.

On this issue, the pipeline promoters appeared to have a full head of steam a year or two ago. Now, however, some of the steam is gone, for several reasons. One is that railroads have consistently been

Doing what rails do best

The unit train's No. 1 commodity: Coal

al, in 1977 49% of 437 million tons.

	Tons originated	% of tonnage carried in unit trains	Coal as % of: Total rail tonnage originated	Rail gross revenues	% of transported coal moving by rail
1968	400.1 million	27.3%	26.0%	10.9%	75.5%
1969	405.2	30.0	25.6	10.8	74.4
1970	425.9	29.0	26.9	12.0	72.5
1971	380.3	32.2	25.5	10.7	76.2
1972	399.5	34.2	25.6	10.5	74.5
1973	400.3	38.7	24.3	9.8	75.9
1974	415.6	40.0	25.3	11.2	74.8
1975	429.9	43.0	29.1	13.4	73.8
1976	430.0	46.0	28.8	13.2	74.2
1977	437.2	49.0	29.6	13.8	74.2

Sources: ICC, AAR, U.S. Bureau of Mines, actual and estimates

proving what they can do in moving ever-increasing tonnages of western coal over long distances in economical fashion. A second is that more people in power in government have come to realize that westerners mean what they say when they talk about the problems of semi-arid regions with regard to water supplies—supplies already in short supply and supplies which slurry pipelines would presumably have to tap. A third reason is that those people in government, having now been exposed to a number of studies, both industry-sponsored and independent, know more about what railroads can do and are having second thoughts about the common-sense aspects of supporting a new mode of transportation when an existing

mode is already proving it can do the job.

And then you come to the problems that are essentially the railroads' own, problems labeled m/w and m/e.

● **M/W: Needs, being met.** On the maintenance-of-way side, there is no lack of documentation: Track that sees train after train of 100-ton coal cars, all moving loaded in the same direction, may have to be built or rebuilt to new standards, but at the very least that track requires inspection and maintenance far more frequently than track that sees what used to be regarded as a normal mix of traffic. Curves are a special problem. So is new-rail territory, because new rail begins taking the coal-train loads before the rail has had a chance to work-harden. Maintenance costs climb, no doubt about that. But at the same time, there's no doubt about the ability of major coal-hauling roads to do the required m/w job: It's being done.

One western road, for example, will put more than a half-billion dollars into track maintenance and improvement this year, much of it in coal territory. Another western carrier, also coming on strong as a coal-hauler, is taking a page from the past, going back in some areas to maintenance practices of decades ago because those practices can be made to maximize track work while they minimize train delays.

Just as important, along the major coal routes in the West, it's hard to go far without seeing, in addition to stepped-up track maintenance, construction of new passing tracks or extension of existing ones and installation or improvement of ctc—projects

that may be coal-based but will also work to improve service for all traffic moving over the line.

● **M/E and its complexities.** Maintenance of equipment is an area with a few more variables, related to (1) the increasing numbers of user-owned or -leased cars coming into service, (2) the fact that railroad car maintenance and repair shops, with all of the other responsibilities being placed upon them, don't have the capacity to handle all of the new private cars, and (3) the growth of private, contract car-repair shops, which seem to be springing up all across the country.

In theory, a new unit train should be a dream-train. Its cars will usually be built by a single builder, to common specifications, in a single production run, with common components and with construction standards that make the first car like the 100th or the 200th or the 400th. That's theory, and practice doesn't always follow it.

Perhaps more to the point, the unit coal train in particular has brought a whole new generation of car owners or lessors onto the scene—a generation that had no reason to know anything about railcar maintenance, a generation that has sometimes listened to the experts, but with some members that seemed not to. There is, on the one hand, the story—said not to be apocryphal—of the car owner who didn't realize that if he didn't practice preventive or cycle maintenance certain components, such as wheels, might wear out all at once. There are, on the other hand, stories of other private car owners whose preventive-maintenance programs are superb and whose record keeping is the envy of the industry.

One thing is for certain, and it is that railroad shops can't do all or even most of the maintenance job on private cars coming new into the fleet: Railroad shops already are near to full, with normal work and with work associated with governmental requirements to do in addition.

Thus, it's going to remain for contract shops to fill the gap, and this is not a bad situation, generally, because most of the private shops are now being run by people who know what they're doing: They listen to the railroads over whose lines their clients' cars will be running, they spend the money to equip their shops properly, they staff with qualified supervisors and mechanics. Indeed, as one veteran railroader puts it, the real fear now is not that the industry will have to contend with the work of a flock of fly-by-night shops but rather that there will be too many good shops coming along and that some of these shops may not make it in the competitive atmosphere that's developing.

But, whatever happens and however maintenance is handled, the key will have to be prevention—the kind of cycle maintenance that keeps problems from occurring, the kind that keeps equipment in service, the kind that will make it virtually impossible for a unit-train accident to be blamed on equipment failure. To put it another way, railroads will take care of the track—and it will be up to equipment owners/lessors and their contractors to do the same for the cars.

● **Who gets what, and why?** Then, finally, among the actual and potential problems associated with unit trains, there's the thing known as allocation of resources, or, specifically, allocation of freight cars.

With user-owned or -leased equipment, there's no question. But, as a few roads have found out, with railroad-furnished equipment when some of it is assigned to unit-train operations, small shippers are going to holler if they think big shippers are getting the edge in equipment supply.

There are several answers to this challenge, answers that will hold up even against the arguments of those who insist that the definition of a common carrier should be stretched farther than it logically can be. For one thing, in situations where the large-vs-small conflict has come up, there is legal precedent for maintenance of what amounts to two classes of service, one for unit-train users and another for single-car shippers. For another, as one road's study proves, if all railroad-owned coal cars used in unit-train service were taken out of that service and thrown into the pool, small shippers would be worse off than they are now. Reason: The railroad is getting a six-to-eight-day turn on unit-train cars and a turn that ranges from 17 to 25 days on cars moving under single-car provisions—and so pooling would sharply reduce car utilization and car availability.

For the future, as regards unit trains, you have to believe a number of things, based upon the record thus far. One is that the commodity spread may well spread, though coal will no doubt continue to head the list. A second is that railroads will be able to keep pace with whatever the service demand may turn out to be. A third is that track materials and track construction will be improved so that they will handle the new loads better than they do today. A fourth is that unit-train equipment will get better, lighter in tare weight, lower in center of gravity, more durable overall and thus capable of running more with less maintenance. A fifth is that government will agree to establishment of rate schedules that are reasonable to the transportation buyer as well as to the supplier of that transportation. A sixth is that government will have the good sense to turn aside petitions from those whose main interest in the transportation business would appear to be the turning of a guaranteed dollar even if their profit should mean (1) payment of higher prices by other transportation users, especially rail transportation users, and consumers, and (2) reduction in or even elimination of other essential transportation services which might suffer economically if their existence provided the only return from plant investment.

The unit train, as it has evolved, is many things, having many effects.

● **What it is, what it does.** For coal primarily but for other commodities, too, it has changed material-handling concepts, loading and unloading methods as well as transportation. It has done more with less, increasing equipment utilization four-, five-, even six-fold. It has changed concepts of track construction and maintenance and it will change them still further. Its effects on equipment go all the way from metallurgy and basic design to construction methods and concepts of maintenance. It has had political effects, not just in the regulatory area but also in the legislative arena, as government has watched the piling up of a tremendous file of evidence as regards the capabilities of the rail mode.

The unit train has brought change to shippers, to receivers, to railroads, to government and, in ways perhaps somewhat less obvious, to consumers.

Along with the run-through train, it has given an often-beleaguered industry a kind of demonstration project—one that proves the need to renew, not to retire, the old concept of wheel-on-rail.

That is—and will continue to be—impact. Positive impact. ■

How shippers view contract rates

Now that the Interstate Commerce Commission has departed from a years-old policy holding that contract rates made by railroads and shippers fall outside the law, have railroads and shippers deluged the commission with contract-rate proposals? Not really. And a sampling of shippers, those replying to this month's traffic poll, indicates that it may be a while before there's more than a trickle.

Why is this so, or apparently so? For one thing, ICC made its sudden switch only a couple of months ago. The concept is new, and its going to have to be explored. For another, in the current inflationary economic climate, no carrier is going to take a chance on long-term rate agreements without an awful lot of protection. For a third, on sizable volumes of business, business coming under annual-volume provisions, there is already what almost adds up to a contract-type rate. And for a fourth factor, shipper comments regarding railroad slowness to go contract may simply reflect what one top railroad pricing officer sees as an ICC attitude: "They somehow seem to think that once they dispose of an issue, everybody is supposed to drop whatever else he may be doing and rush in. Well, it just doesn't work that way."

In any event, there are a few rail customers who question even the basic concept—among them, T.E. Nast, traffic manager, CF&I Steel Corp., Pueblo, Colo., who observes that contract rates do not appear to differ much from the annual volume rates that have been in effect for a number of bulk commodities. His added thought: "Changing the form from a published basis to a contract basis would seem to open the door for 'under the counter' deals that would afford the opportunity for blatant discrimination."

Just one respondent says he has been approached on the subject, and quite informally. But, says Doyle S. Smith, Continental Oil's manager of traffic, "We have no need for contract rates at this time."

One respondent who says there is a need, D.L. Johnson, director of general traffic and distribution, Emerson Electric, St. Louis, adds: "So far we haven't found any railroad willing to discuss contract rates. Everyone seems afraid of the concept."

The concept was defined by the Interstate Commerce Commission in its change-of-heart statement last December: "A railroad freight rate arrived at through mutual agreement between a railroad (or two or more railroads participating in a through route) and a shipper in which the railroad agrees to provide service for a given price and the shipper agrees to tender a given amount of freight during a fixed period."

QUESTIONS

1. Do you believe that contract rates will provide opportunities for railroads to develop innovative pricing strategies?
   Yes *83%*   No *17%*

2. Do you think the regulatory climate has changed enough to support the intent of contract rate-making, as expressed in Question 1?
   Yes *77%*   No *23%*

3. In what areas do you believe that contract rates could provide benefits for you? Lower transportation costs? Better car supply? Better service? And for what commodities? Please explain.

   (See text)

That definition was part of ICC's announcement that contract rates were not unlawful after all and could be filed under normal procedures. As of Feb. 7, no railroads had filed, but an ICC staff member said, "We've had a number of phone calls from railroads about how to handle this."

Though only one respondent said a railroad had called yet, 83% said they believed contract rates would provide opportunities for railroads to develop innovative pricing strategies, and 77% said they believed that the regulatory climate has changed enough to support that objective.

● **Better service seen.** As for benefits, several respondents say contract rates could lead to more dependable service, in addition to more-widely shared hopes of better car supply and lower rates.

The fullest expression of possible service benefits comes from Walter L. Weart, manager of traffic, Continental Bondware, Palatine, Ill., who says contract rates tied to specific guarantees of service could be a significant breakthrough for both sides. "Commitments known in advance would allow the carrier to plan operational requirements logically, similar to a manufacturer who has a long-term contract," Weart says. "Penalties for nonperformance could give the incentive to revamp service, which would have wide-ranging benefits for many other shippers."

Weart also notes that contract rates could lead to a "total transportation service" in-

73

volving line-haul plus pick-up, delivery, or both: "This would allow a carrier to approach a shipper with a complete program to totally handle the products within a certain geographic area, from shipper's door to customer's door, subcontracting such services as the carrier might not be able to provide."

Greater incentive to improve service when rail rates are lower than truck rates might result from contracts, says another respondent, a Wisconsin general traffic manager who asked not to be identified. "Contracts could be written with fixed rates and service parameters implying car supply so as to move a given tonnage," the respondent says. As for that car supply, "If shippers committed to specific tonnages and railroads to rates and service, innovative pricing opportunities could be explored to motivate greater private ownership of specialized equipment, for innumerable commodities."

Those commodities would be mostly bulk, many respondents said, and in multicar if not unit-train movements. But, according to Allen K. Penttila, vice president-general manager of Evans Products Co.'s transport services division, railroad contract service "could significantly progress the concept of mini-trains, not just the longer unit trains for a few selected bulk commodities." He agrees with other respondents who said contract rates would help railroads retain traffic. For users, he cites this result: "The contract carrier concept would also encourage shippers to better gear themselves to rail shipping in a more and more competitive transportation environment."

Better service from contract rates would be especially likely for regular movement of predictable tonnage between two points, respondents agree. "The characteristics of this kind of tonnage," says J.D. Mitchell, general traffic manager, Coca Cola USA, "encourage the incentive to search out all the opportunities to reduce cost by deciding on the right kind of car, the minimum number of cars required, and to organize a monitoring program which will help to anticipate problems and document a history of the movement."

One factor of improved service under contracts, says Richard Petska, Cedar Rapids, Iowa, Chamber of Commerce transportation bureau manager, would have to be "a stipulation that cars must be available to load at a certain date and unloaded after a certain time delivered at location for unloading."

Service was just one aspect of the Interstate Commerce Commission assessment of contract-rate possibilities: "Anticompetitive effects, if any, may be outweighed by other considerations. Such rates may provide opportunities for railroads to develop innovative pricing strategies. They can result in lower shipping

"Best possibilities: Local moves in shipper equipment"

Although all but one of the shippers responding to this month's traffic poll said they were still waiting to hear from railroads about contract rates, *Railway Age* in early February heard a lot from one major railroad that *is* actively pursuing the contract concept. That carrier's top rate officer, who asked that his company not be identified, said the best possibilities for contract "exploration" seem to be local moves in shipper equipment.

"A single carrier can develop a contract more expeditiously and with less risk of regulatory or antitrust complications than a partnership of several carriers in a joint operation," the officer said. "Because the ICC warned that other avenues of relief are available if contracts develop discrimination in distribution of free-running carrier equipment, it seems that shipper-owned or specially-equipped carrier cars fit the contract potential."

The rate officer said his railroad likes the concept of contract rates because they offer opportunities of mutual benefit for shippers and carriers. When both parties in a negotiation can benefit, he said, there is an opportunity for a successful arrangement: "The carrier makes a commitment covering the primary shipper considerations of equipment, service, and price, and the shipper makes a commitment covering the carrier's primary consideration of known volume and stable price."

The officer pointed out that current volume coal rates, "on the threshold of being contracts," lack permanence beyond one year. "Basically, they rely for any hopes on longevity upon the underlying producer-receiver contract; otherwise, the tariffs are merely year-to-year commitments by both parties. Contract rates on coal, by assuring a more stable time span, would benefit shippers, receivers, and carriers in the areas of capital commitment and long-range planning."

Besides coal, perishable traffic seems to offer a good contract opportunity, the officer said: "A plan using shipper trailers would avoid two pitfalls—equipment distribution and potential allegations of destructive competitive practices, since the business now moves by nonregulated trucks."

He also said contract rate development requires a high degree of accuracy in determining the costs of the movement, because the mutual commitment probably would permit revision only to reflect inflation. Also, all departments of both parties would be required to properly assess the operating characteristics of the movement so that the plans on which costs are based are "reasonably immutable and basically sound."

Though many respondents to this month's traffic poll said contract rates would be good mainly for bulk commodities, the railroad rate officer said nonbulk shippers should not "unilaterally preclude themselves for contract-rate consideration." Shippers of almost any commodity, in any type of equipment in steady movement, should be looking at contract rates, he said:

"The only limitation, aside from legality, is imagination."

costs, better freight-car utilization, increased efficiency, and improved service. They can enhance a railroad's ability to compete with carriers of other modes, and make it possible for both railroads and shippers to make future plans on an informed basis."

● **Some reflections on skepticism.** That all sounds nice on paper, but the realities may be somewhat different, several respondents seemed to be saying in replies tinged with caution, if not outright skepticism. One such reaction came from Vernon J. Haan, director of corporate traffic for International Minerals and Chemical Corp. After explaining how IMC sees contract rates encouraging high-volume movements and "materially increasing" the productivity of basic-product shipments, Haan added:

"I make these assumptions on the basis that the railroads will enter into contract rates in order to encourage investment on

their lines, to recapture competitive bulk traffic and to thus assure future revenues and profits that new and recaptured traffic will produce for them. But, alas, for those captive shippers with sunk investments in existing rail facilities, I do not see any great opportunities for contract rates."

Haan's doubt is directed as much toward the government as the railroads. He believes the "obvious objective" of the Administration's move toward deregulation is to shift the burden of railroad rehabilitation from government subsidy programs to captive rail shippers and "to permit rapacious pricing" for captive traffic. Haan expects railroad pricing managers to sit tight on captive high-volume traffic and wait for the "uncontrolled monopoly advantages being designed and coerced by an Administration that has turned its back on the concept of fair pricing, reasonable rates, guaranteed service, and on a fair arbiter to adjudicate

"Carriers would be able to forecast better, knowing they have a guaranteed traffic base for equipment"

disputes between captive shippers and monopoly railroads."

A briefer reflection of distrust came from E.E. Sears, manager of warehousing and transportation for Lykes Pasco Packing Co., Dade City, Fla.: "We do not think railroads should have the ability to negotiate contract rates. Under these conditions they will haul only what they please."

Ivan Olson, director of traffic, Longview Fibre Co., Longview, Wash., says contract rates would help railroads "tie up" traffic that could go by other modes, but he, too, questioned railroads' sincerity to help shippers, especially in building equipment for hauling basic raw materials. "They hide behind the guise of general increases to selectively hike rates on raw materials," Olson says, "then in turn ask for a much larger portion of the outbound tonnage in relation to the amount of raw material shipped via rail."

Not quite so sure that contract rates would live up to ICC claims for them, R.P. Clinton, traffic manager for Honeywell at Minneapolis, says "perhaps" the rates would provide opportunities for innovative pricing and "perhaps" the regulatory climate has changed enough to support that intent. Such rates might be the only way to get products to market, Clinton observes, adding: "This whole matter of deregulation could be very frightening. It could require that industry take a new look at its transportation needs and try to find some new ways to move its products."

Continental Bondware's Weart says contract rates would lead to innovative pricing only to the extent that rail carriers choose to use their new freedom, but using it would provide opportunities to recapture traffic lost to other modes because volume discount pricing could be used to offset service delays. "In other words, trade time for money," Weart says. However, IMC's Haan believes innovation would still come from the shipper, not the carrier: "These opportunities will not be developed unless initiated by the shipper, as indicated by past history of the railroads' marketing departments."

● **Ready to explore.** Contract rates have really existed, in the form of annual volume rates, for about 10 years, says Dwight D. Long, general traffic manager, ICI Americas, Inc., Wilmington, Del. The only hopeful change he can see is a possible lessening of the "formal and ritualistic trappings" that often are substitutes for substance in ICC proceedings. "This may spur greater use of this pricing mode," Long says, "and if so, we applaud the development. We will explore opportunities to use this pricing technique with our more progressive carriers."

Also apparently ready to explore opportunities is D.C. Warrington, manager-traffic, Amoco Oil Co., Chicago. He says that a commitment by the carrier to price, car supply, and service, for movement of specific commodities under agreed conditions, would be "implicit" in the contract concept. Warrington says he would expect benefits to exceed the common carrier alternative for both shipper and carrier: "The best agreements usually are made when both parties have something to gain."

Equally hopeful, Charles Lynch, general traffic manager, R.R. Donnelly & Sons, Chicago, sees price and service commitments leading to the opening up of problem-solving in a businesslike manner. He thinks application of the concept might lead to development of incentive rates "not now dreamed of," and he sees great opportunity to improve car-movement efficiency through more balanced and heavier loadings: "Best of all, though, might be the conceptual change, and the ability of industry and the railroads to bring new ideas into being."

C.C. Cory, general traffic manager, Firestone Tire & Rubber Co., Akron, joins in the hopefulness—that contract rates could improve all areas involving costs, car supply, and service while assuring the carrier a specified income or at least a commitment that could be used in planning operations and investment. It's his opinion that "there is no limit to commodities that could be considered, so long as a continuing movement is available." But, despite his optimism, Cory adds this: "I have not found a single railroad that is seriously interested, although I have directly questioned many of the large carriers."

● **Better relationships?** Among a number of shippers who see possible improvement in the customer-carrier relationship is James Iwena, assistant general traffic manager-pricing, Kraft, Inc., Chicago: "With a contract situation, there is at least the possibility for us and the carrier to work together. We would guarantee the carrier a certain amount of regular traffic that he could count on—this, of course, contingent upon the carrier's furnishing a regular car supply. This predictability should also result in better service."

E.H. Newman, manager, transportation pricing, Crown Zellerbach, San Francisco, takes a similar slant, seeing contract rates as applicable to at least one of his company's major product lines: "Contract rates based upon high-cube equipment could result in lower transportation costs to both ourselves and the carriers. We would also expect to see improvement in car supply from such a program as well as more reliable service, since carriers would be able

to forecast better, knowing they have a guaranteed traffic base for the equipment."

Robert W. Pettigrew, general traffic manager, Hershey Chocolate Co., Hershey, Pa., would also expect cost and service-efficiency benefits—and he thinks the potential might be wide-ranging: "Most industries have a steady volume moving, either between their plant facilities or to large-buying customers, that would provide many opportunities for the railroads to analyze their costs" and develop contract proposals that would be competitive.

As for George A. Ulam, traffic manager/rail, Inland Containers Corp., Indianapolis, he can even see two-way loaded movement possibilities—pulpboard from the mills to convertors and recyclable material shipped back to the mills in the same cars.

● **Immediate applications.** One respondent, R.J. Mozinski, traffic manager, American Crystal Sugar, Moorhead, Minn., believes there are at least two immediate applications of contract rates for his company: (1) Plan 2 movements to compete with trucks and to reduce transport costs for sugar; and (2) container rates for export beet pulp pellets from North Dakota and Minnesota to the West Coast. Another respondent, Lloyd Philips, traffic manager, Riviana Foods, Inc., Houston, saw possible applications for the movement of rough rice from Arkansas to Houston at lower cost.

"However," Philips said, "contract rates as now planned usually deal with one carrier and for a set amount of freight via one carrier. We need a modification, because rice originates on several lines and we could not ship via one only. If carriers would publish special rates in shipper-leased cars, we could probably lease and assure both carriers and ourselves of benefits. They would move the traffic rather than trucks, and we would have savings plus stability of car supply."

Also specifying a likely commodity was Emerson Electric's Johnson, who said contract rates could bring lower costs and "hopefully" better service for coil steel. J.D. Robins, director of traffic, Caterpillar Tractor, Peoria, Ill., listed machinery and parts for export, plus sand, coal, piggyback, and iron and steel, in high-volume movements "that require less terminal service." And Eugene Smith, manager of corporate traffic Mueller Brass Co., Port Huron, Mich., added scrap copper and brass, at lower transport costs.

As for Phillip T. Catalano, however, the time may have passed. Catalano, manager, transportation services, Steelcase Inc., Grand Rapids, cites a lack of rail interest in furniture traffic that led his company to use of contract motor carriage six years ago. And, he says, "this ICC change of policy . . . we feel has come too late for our company." On the other hand, he concludes, "we will watch the new policy closely, as it is an interesting development." ∎

75

Traffic poll
How shippers view rail mergers

All railroad mergers, acquisitions, and consolidations are not, in fact, created equal —and therein lies the rub, so far as shippers are concerned in (1) assessing past consolidations and (2) coming to a decision as to whether there should be more consolidation and, if so, what kind.

In terms of postconsolidation service, equipment supply and general responsiveness to customer needs, railroads that have been through the process don't get an overall passing grade—though a number of shippers participating in this month's traffic poll make a point of noting that their replies may be colored largely by the Penn Central experience, and that other consolidations appear to have worked out in somewhat better fashion.

In terms of what shippers think should happen next, there is what appears to be a contradiction: Overwhelmingly, users of rail service oppose the creation of regional rail monopoly situations, while four out of five do support development of regional systems in which competition is maintained—but at the same time, more than half look favorably upon formation of a few coast-to-coast roads, even though (1) this would at least imply monopoly, and (2) traffic-flow studies seem to offer little justification for operation of ocean-to-ocean systems. And how about coordinations of routes and facilities that stop short of outright merger? On that one, poll participants come down heavily on the positive side, by a three-to-one margin.

By and large, shippers are very much aware of the excess-plant problem—but they

QUESTIONS

1. In your experience with past rail mergers and consolidations, what happened to:

	Better	Worse	No change
Service?	38%	54%	8%
Equipment supply?	30%	55%	15%
Responsiveness to your needs, overall?	31%	54%	15%

2. Would you favor creation of:

	Yes	No
Three or four coast-to-coast railroads?	58%	42%
Regional systems with one railroad per region?	3%	97%
Regional systems with two-road competition?	80%	20%
Coordination of lines and terminals among competing roads rather than mergers?	75%	25%
Please explain:	*(See text)*	

3. In your opinion:
What are the greatest shipper benefits resulting from rail consolidations? What are the greatest problems? *(See text)*

lean toward coordination as a preferred way of tackling that problem, a way in which carriers may be able to avoid the management and management-labor problems that seem to have come along hand-in-hand with some past mergers.

By and large, too, shippers emphasize the need to keep the industry in the private sector, with a minimum of direct government involvement in whatever consolidation or coordination process may evolve.

● **The cost "Brake."** On the issue of shipper benefits stemming from consolidation, replies range from one shipper's blunt "I don't see any" to an oft-stated observation—sometimes expressed more as a hope than as an observed fact—that consolidation should produce cost reductions that should act as a brake on rate increases and that consolidation should improve both service and car supply.

And always, shippers talk about the

For experienced consolidation-watchers, familiarity breeds

Especially thoughtful views on railroad consolidation came to the poll this month from two Chicago-based shippers, each with broadly based transportation requirements and each with a lot of experience in consolidation watching. One is Vernon J. Haan, director, corporate traffic, International Minerals & Chemical Corp., Mundelein, Ill., the other is Archie Walters, director of transportation, Allied Mills, Inc., Chicago, Among their observations:

IMC's first comment, Vern Haan says, is that there ought to be differentiation between types of mergers—and between shippers with and shippers without transportation alternatives.

IMC, he notes, "is heavily committed to the rail transportation of its products, mainly bulk products from mines and heavy chem-

ical plants—with 85% of the 25 million tons shipped by IMC moving by rail. Much of this product is origin-landlocked, in interior locations served primarily by rail. Thus, our opinions reflect the transportation monopoly environment in which we live. We have had extensive experience with mergers. When the merger was made up of healthy, parallel, competitive lines, the promised sharing of economies never developed." Service, including car supply, diminished, he declares, while existing competitive instincts atrophied and monopolistic tendencies grew.

As for the future, Vern Haan says, IMC "would not resist the creation of four coast-to-coast railroads if rail-to-rail, intramodal competition were maintained in all major markets. IMC would be vigorously opposed to any rail system that developed with one

railroad in a region, such as Conrail now exists in the East. Such a situation is considered by IMC to be a disaster. IMC believes there is more merit to the coordination of lines and particularly of terminals among competing railroads rather than mergers. The difficulty here is protecting the public interests in deciding which of the coordinated lines might ultimately be abandoned to the detriment of the shipping public on that line. IMC believes that the interest of the public on these lines is paramount .... Of course, this opinion of IMC is based on the assumption that the existing traffic was compensatory over both lines considered for consolidation."

As Haan sees it, the only shipper benefit that "can be anticipated from rail consolidations is where the survival of a weaker carrier people problem—the obvious one involved in meshing management and in getting greater efficiency out of the work force, the less obvious one involved in getting everybody pulling in the same direction.

J.D. Mitchell, general traffic manager, Coca-Cola USA, Atlanta, approaches that latter problem directly: The greatest problem in a consolidation, he believes, lies in winning acceptance from all concerned of the fact that there is one new company. Everybody involved, he declares, should work for the betterment of the surviving organization—recognizing that survival was quite likely a major factor in making the merger in the first place.

A similar theme is sounded by a number of other customers. D.C. Garland, manager, traffic department, Zellerbach Paper Co., San Francisco, raises questions regarding the size of a postmerger work force and the labor difficulties involved. B.L. Atkins, traffic assistant, Ashland Oil, Inc., Ashland, Ky., sees poor service resulting from lack of coordination between operating segments, from slippage in morale and from management's inability to get a handle on the larger task confronting it. Dwight Long, general traffic manager, ICI Americas Inc., Wilmington, Del., recalls that earlier mergers in the postwar era "did produce better service. But there have been few if any shipper benefits from the mergers of the '60s, an exception being consolidations undertaken by Southern." Properties, Long says, seem "too large for effective management. There is loss of personal interest and loss of service betterments that flow from intramodal competition. Economies of scale seem to be illusory."

As for the ways in which consolidation might best be carried out, customers—as might be expected—see problems with both parallel and end-to-end consolidation. On the one hand, several note, there can be both cost and service advantages to a pooling of movements over paralleling or overlapping routes—but on the other hand, there can also be a deterioration of service (feared especially by those locked into rail service) resulting from lack of competition. End-to-end consolidation? There, too, there are two hands: On the positive one, there can be gains stemming from the provision of single-line service, bypassing of yards, and so forth, but on the negative hand, the longer-haul railroads resulting from end-to-end consolidation may put most of their emphasis upon solicitation and handling of long-haul traffic, with short-haul business becoming less attractive unless the volume is substantial.

In this context, Zellerbach Paper's Garland, for one, thinks that "facilities should be merged first, particularly yards, before lines are consolidated under one name." What Chesapeake & Ohio-Baltimore & Ohio did, he believes, is "a good example of the right way to do it." G.T. Brewer, corporate director of transportation and distribution, A.O. Smith Corp., Milwaukee, puts it this way: "There should be a combination of mergers and coordinations. Mergers should be of the end-to-end type, with paralleling competing roads stressing joint use of facilities rather than merging. From this, a system will develop."

Meanwhile, Walter L. Weart, division manager of traffic methods and controls, Continental Group Inc., Palatine Ill., likes competition, but with a "but": "Competition is a definite plus in terms of car supply, rate negotiation, service problems, and so forth. Realistically, however, competition requires a substantial amount of tonnage, and this frequently does not exist. There is still too much physical plant in place, particularly in the Midwest and Northeast—and in those cases, both shippers and the railroad industry would be better off with only one carrier, one that had enough tonnage to be a viable, successful operation." ■

wariness

results." And the fear remains that consolidation's main result will be elimination of competition and creation of intramodal monopoly power, to the disadvantage of the shipper who is subject to a rail market dominance.

•"Success . . . is people." Allied Mills' Archie Walters, meanwhile, takes a somewhat broader view:

"You can speak of benefits and problems of rail mergers in the same breath. The benefits are service and equipment—and the problems are lack of service and equipment."

The selling of mergers, Walters believes, may be akin to the "selling of social programs: Results will seldom be even close to expectations."

What matters, he says, is people: "The success of a merger is only remotely related to the joining of property. It is people, managers and managing, that make mergers work. For one thing, you've got to know who is boss before Day 1, and good examples here are the NW and BN consolidations. This leadership has to be capable of hanging in there and making the tough decisions, right now. It has to have continuity."

Merging railroads, Archie Walters concludes, has something to do with progression and regression—and "if you start with two lines that are one-half efficient, you end up with a system that is one-quarter efficient. Merged properties work only when the merged lines have a common goal with good, experienced, knowledgeable, and strong leadership. And that leadership has to be there in the beginning."

Railview

"We have loosed whatever regulatory bonds might have restrained the railroads from competing with the trucking industry for the fresh fruit and vegetable market. We shall watch with interest how the railroads will use their freedom."

By A. DANIEL O'NEAL
Chairman
Interstate Commerce Commission

"A short step down a long trail"

An outsider, unfamiliar with American politics or business, might look at the growing cacophony of voices engaged in the rail regulatory debate and conclude that the debate is bound to bog down in a quagmire of confusion.

Judge Learned Hand may have described the current situation well when he wrote, ". . . right conclusions are more likely to be gathered out of a multitude of tongues, than through any kind of authoritive selectives. To many this is, and always will be, folly; but we have staked upon it our all."

I think it important to spend some time on a deregulation effort of very special interest to the West in general, California most certainly, and the members of the California Grape and Tree Fruit League in particular. I am referring to the ICC's actions on eliminating the regulation of fresh fruits and vegetables moving by rail.

In a move which marks a major milestone in the history of rail transportation, the Interstate Commerce Commission has decided to deregulate transportation of fresh fruits and vegetables. We have loosed whatever regulatory bonds might have restrained the railroads from competing with the trucking industry for the fresh fruit and vegetable market. We shall watch with interest how the railroads will use their freedom. No doubt members of the California Grape and Tree Fruit League—which ships roughly 70% of all fresh grapes and tree fruits transported from California and Arizona—will also watch closely how the railroads seek to use the exemption from regulation.

What could be more clear cut, what could be easier to understand and have fewer snags than taking the regulatory wraps off of that portion of rail traffic?

Of course, as the league's statement before the commission made so clear, there could be some problems. The issues are worth looking at not only because they relate directly to the limited deregulation involved in the fresh fruits and vegetables situation, but perhaps more importantly because they raise some of the basic questions that deserve the atten-

Adapted from an address prepared for the annual meeting of the California Grape and Tree Fruit League at Monterey, Calif., March 21, 1979.

tion of all policy makers engaged in examining the regulation of railroads.

Among the specific concerns is whether deregulation should be tempered by the commission continuing to require through service and joint rates.

We recognize that the interchange of traffic between railroads presents a ticklish problem. An inherent difference between exempt motor carriers and the railroads is the ability of the former to move entirely in single-line service and the necessity for railroads to operate as an

---

"It will take much more than sharp price reductions for the railroads to pick up perishable business. It will take substantial improvements in service and imaginative pricing. . . ."

---

integrated system, which requires joint through service.

The potential for discrimination against connecting lines (particularly against the smaller carriers) in the interchange of traffic and in establishing joint rates is inherent in a deregulated environment. A factor that seems relevant here is that perishable commodities make up a very small percentage (about one percent) of traffic moving by rail.

And as a practical matter, it seems very likely the railroads will rely on existing arrangements and established operating procedures.

Thus, carrier relationships that might impede the flow of commerce or cause unwarranted financial problems for some elements of the system bear watching, but it does not seem for this limited step that the ingredients for a breakdown exist.

Another concern relates to the possibility that railroads could engage in predatory practices at the expense of the trucking industry. In reply, I must acknowledge that the possibility of such practices exists, but not as an immediate threat. As shippers have so often reminded the commission and the railroads, it will take much more than sharp price reductions for the railroads to pick up perishable business. It will take substan-

tial improvements in service and imaginative pricing.

While the commission continues to seek to give the railroads additional flexibility to help them help themselves, we will bear in mind the lessons which led to the creation of the Interstate Commerce Commission.

The commission also will be alert to your concern that widespread shortages of equipment could result from deregulation.

But in the case of fresh fruits and vegetables, we do not anticipate shifts in the existing allocation of cars, since the railroads, with isolated exceptions, are virtually out of the fresh fruit and vegetable market. Re-entry into this market will require investment in new equipment in order to compete effectively. Therefore, we do not foresee new movements of these commodities significantly affecting movement of regulated traffic in the immediate future.

It may well be that in the limited area of perishables many of the statutory provisions covering rail service can be provided through negotiation.

In our fresh fruits and vegetables decision, we indicate that car service, loss and damage, extension of credit, and divisions are areas which may be adaptable to negotiation. Looking at loss and damage will give some insight as to our reasoning. We have been requiring railroads to issue a bill of lading for each shipment, thus relieving claimant shippers using more than one railroad from proving which carrier actually caused any damage. We have eliminated that requirement for the transportation of fresh fruits and vegetables. The railroads have an incentive to provide the most attractive service if they are interested in regaining a portion of the potentially profitable fresh fruit and vegetable market. If the railroads' claims service is not equal to or better than that offered by motor carriers, then shippers will undoubtedly take that into consideration in making their transportation decisions.

Service competition should be an effective replacement for regulation. Mandatory requirements do not seem necessary, since the railroads will have a pecuniary interest in adhering to expedited schedules in order to compete effectively with motor carriers for this traffic. *(Continued)*

In the absence of alternative arrangements made through negotiation, we believe that the railroads will probably include in their rate quotations a reference that some existing tariff provisions will apply. Items such as switching, demurrage, etc., would likely fall into this category. To insure that this alternative is available, we have included in the exemption a statement that all tariffs pertaining to the transportation of fresh fruits and vegetables will be of no further effect, except to the extent adopted by carrier quotations. Of course, antitrust issues will be a consideration.

One of the thorniest problems of exempting fresh fruits and vegetables concerns antitrust immunity. Without such immunity, under the current interpretation of the law by the Justice Department, carriers not in competition may still agree on joint rates without fear of violating the antitrust laws. The situation becomes more complex when connecting carriers, which technically provide end-to-end service, are also in competition with each other for movements of the same traffic. Obviously, aside from actual prosecution for alleged violations, the mere threat of an antitrust suit, with the tremendous political expense, may inhibit railroads from making joint rates.

Since the commission is exempting this traffic from regulation, it seems anomalous to continue a grant of antitrust immunity to allow the railroads to price their services on this traffic on some basis other than in conformity with the antitrust laws. So, despite the factors which I have mentioned, we repealed the exemption. If railroads feel inhibited from making use of the exemption, we will review the situation with a view to making adjustments.

As mentioned earlier, the fresh fruit and vegetable decision might be viewed as a short step down a long trail. The issues generated by the proceeding apply to the general proposition of rail deregulation, but they are not all inclusive. Let me discuss the general philosophy of deregulation under the 4R Act.

Railroad regulation by the Interstate Commerce Commission has existed in one form or another for almost 100 years. For the first several decades of regulation, the trend was toward ever increasing regulation. Gradually, the commission obtained jurisdiction over several facets of regulation—rates, service, entry and exit control, mergers and consolidations, and bankruptcies.

The enactment of the Railroad Revitalization and Regulatory Reform Act of 1976 represented a significant change in approach. For the first time Congress indicated that the railroads' fortunes were such that some lessening of regulation should be tried as one means of resurrecting railroad revenues. The broad aim of the act, as expressed by Congress in its declaration of policy, was to restore, maintain, and revitalize an efficient railway system under private enterprise.

Now, three years after enactment of the 4R Act, we are once again at the crossroads. Many, including the railroads themselves and the Department of Transportation, have concluded that either the 4R Act or the commission's implementation of that act has not worked well enough to revitalize the rail industry.

Our own conclusion is somewhat mixed. I think that the 4R Act has great promise but that the promise has not been fully realized. Despite continuing problems both with the act and with the rail industry itself, many of its fundamental concepts still seem valid and should not be abandoned.

In general, the thrust of the 4R Act was

"The only hope for railroads to improve their revenues is through improving their ability to compete. That will depend on railroads identifying what their customers and prospective customers want. . . ."

---

to maximize rail competition where competition exists, without compromising the rights of shippers and the public where competition does not exist. While further changes may well be warranted, either at the administrative or the legislative level, I have not yet been persuaded that this fundamental premise of the 4R Act should be cast aside.

One example of an area of considerable concern to the commission stems from the wide-ranging ratemaking reforms established in the 4R Act.

The railroads, who must take the initiative under the law to bring about ratemaking reforms, have not done so to the extent hoped. And yet we know—or we think we know—that the only hope for railroads to improve their revenues is through improving their ability to compete. And that will depend on railroads identifying what their customers and prospective customers want, providing the desired service, and pricing it competitively.

Why hasn't this happened as much as seems possible? We're in the midst of a careful review of railroad regulation to try and find some answers.

Another concern: Everyone now claims to be sensitive to the so-called "captive" shipper problem. Some, like DOT, have placed a five-year limit on their sensitivity. Others, such as the "captive" shippers, have a somewhat longer-term sensitivity. Part of the concern, to be sure, is fairness to such shippers. I do not believe that a few shippers should bear more than

a fair share of the burden.

There is also the concern that allowing the railroads to more easily exploit monopoly power will only postpone the day of reckoning a little longer. To the extent it allows railroads to postpone confronting service and marketing problems that hinder the development of competitive acumen, it will disserve carriers, shippers, and the public. We need to look at solutions other than those allowing the railroads to exploit captive markets.

The commission, indeed, has undertaken a number of new initiatives. For example, we recently issued a policy statement approving in principle the concept of railroad contract rates. Currently our Office of Policy and Analysis developed a rail regulatory issues and options paper, which was presented to the commission for discussion in two open meetings, one on Feb. 27 and another on March 6.

The options paper dealt with the entire range of railroad regulatory issues, including maximum rate levels, rate discrimination, common carrier and service obligations, contract rates, encouraging greater use of the 4R Act ratemaking provisions, general rate increases, mergers and industry restructuring, abandonments and entry, intermodal operations, interrailroad relationships, and options for immediate administrative actions. As the options paper made clear, these options are not intended to be mutually exclusive nor are they intended to be exhaustive. Rather, they are intended to bring about an open discussion of relevant possibilities with respect to each subject matter area, and lead to more specific recommendations.

As I indicated at the outset, the rail revitalization puzzle if it is solved will be put together by several participants: the Congress, the Administration, the railroads, the ICC and shippers.

The challenge we face is to make sure that all the parts go in the right place, so that when we see the big picture, it is the right picture. If any of the parties who have parts at their disposal do not contribute to putting this puzzle together, the result will be a disservice to all the other parties. When the puzzle is complete, I expect it will show some easing of regulation as only one of several tools needed to build a healthy, competitive, reliable, and efficient rail system.

I recognize that not all of us who have an interest in the future of the railroad industry will agree on the proper course to pursue, but our differences need not be divisive. Though I, like many others, tend to categorize agreeable people as those who agree with me, I think there is merit in many of the positions put forth by the "multitudinous" voices speaking about rail deregulation. Hopefully, we shall get "right conclusions" and those conclusions will enable us to complete the rail revitalization puzzle. ■

Railview

A new way to measure performance

In this paper, I will introduce what I believe is a new approach to railroad analysis. My approach will enable me to point out some of the strengths and weaknesses in your railroad's performance.

Basically, my new technique is an asset approach based on a rate of return analysis. It supplements conventional analytical tools, but adds a qualitative element by focusing on the interaction of the balance sheet with the income account. The concept is based on formulas designed by E.I. duPont de Nemours many years ago for evaluating new capital projects. We have adopted this rate of return analysis for comparative determination of railroad credit, earnings growth, and, as an end product, the relative investment qualities of rail securities.

The primary objective of management is to improve the return on shareholders' equity and, in turn, the rate of growth in annual earnings. There are many ways of achieving earnings growth, but experience has shown that companies achieving high rates of return on an operating basis, employing suitable financial policies, and having opportunities for profitable reinvestment of earnings, on balance, will produce superior earnings growth. Furthermore, above average earnings growth as measured by return on equity should be translated, in time, to above average market performance of the railroad's common stock.

I recognize that managers working within a regulatory environment do not have complete flexibility with respect to price raising capabilities and asset expansion or contraction, both of which factors have an influence on a railroad's return on assets. However, I am a firm believer that the best-managed companies are those which produce growth in a no-growth industry, and this should be your goal.

In describing my analysis, I intend to walk through a multiplicity of numbers and indicate how a railroad's financial officers may influence the financial

From a paper presented to the annual meeting of the AAR's Treasury Division at Tarpon Springs, Fla., Oct. 4-7, 1978. The rate of return analysis as developed in this paper is based on analytical studies originally made by Faulkner, Dawkins & Sullivan, a firm recently merged into Shearson Hayden Stone Inc.

aspects of railroad operations in order to achieve higher returns. In addition, I intend to focus on two other areas: (1) the perilous path many roads are taking because of dividend policies; and (2) the impact of our rate of return analysis on investors' attitudes towards railroad securities.

•••

There are four principal components or profitability ratios which influence the production of the rate of return on shareholders' equity:

1. The asset turnover ratio.
2. Net profit margin.
3. Net return on assets—the product of the two foregoing ratios.
4. Financial leverage, which is the ratio of the asset base to the equity base.

Finally, the rate of return on shareholders' equity multiplied by the earnings retention rate produces the all-important reinvestment rate which is the implied rate of internal growth.

One of the advantages of the rate of return analysis is that it isolates the operational factors and the financial factors which influence the final result. The operational factors are the asset turnover rate and profit margin; the financial factors are the effective tax rate and financial leverage.

First, let us consider the operational factors. Simply stated, a railroad employs its operating assets that appear on the balance sheet (investment in road and equipment, cash and equivalents, accounts receivables, inventories, etc.) to produce revenues which appear on the income statement. One measure of how well a company is using its assets is the revenue level produced by the investment in the plant; i.e., revenues produced for each dollar of assets. This calculation gives what we call the asset turnover ratio, and the higher that ratio is the greater the operational leverage of a road. But this is only half of the formula. The other half as developed from the income account is how much profit the company is making on its revenues after all expenses and income taxes, namely net profit margin. The product of the two ratios—asset turnover times the net profit margin—produces *net return on assets*. This is the all important key indicator of *economic efficiency* of a railroad.

Briefly stated, the return on asset ratio is a quantified statement of the basic economic character of an industry. In effect, it is the end product of the character of the industry. It reflects a company's competitive position, its product dominance, its production efficiencies, and, finally, management's philosophy and strategies. It expresses the capital

Table I. Return on assets—operational components (1977)

Ranked in order of after-tax return on assets	Operational leverage asset turnover x	Pretax profit margin =	Pretax return on assets*	Tax retention rate† =	After tax return on assets
Missouri Pacific Corp.	.90x	11.6%	10.4%	65.6%	6.9%
Union Pacific Corp.	.73	13.4	9.8	65.7	6.4
Missouri Pacific RR System	.63	10.7	6.7	90.2	6.1‡
Santa Fe Industries	.62	11.8	7.3	72.5	5.3
Rio Grande Industries	.59	12.3	7.3	71.4	5.2
Southern Railway	.49	13.3	6.5	70.8	4.7
Union Pacific RR	.51	13.5	6.9	65.1	4.5
Norfolk & Western Ry.	.47	12.4	5.8	66.8	3.9
Seaboard Coast Line Ind.	.64	5.7	3.6	102.1	3.7
Southern Pac. & Subs.	.56	8.3	4.6	67.3	3.1
Chessie System	.52	6.4	3.3	80.1	2.7
Burlington Nor. & Subs.	.62	3.8	2.4	95.0	2.2

* May not total due to rounding.
† Reciprocal of the effective tax rate.
‡ If a non-recurring tax credit were eliminated from the calculation, MoPac's return on assets in 1977 would have been only 4.8%.

"If rail managers continue
to succumb to dividend pressures,
the railroads will eventually stagnate..."

—and what it shows

By ISABEL H. BENHAM
President
Printon, Kane Research, Inc.

generative capabilities of the company. Obviously, a company generating a 10% return on assets has at least the inherent potential for faster reinvestment and growth than a competitor generating 5% to 6% or less.

In my opinion, the return on asset ratio is a more vital and meaningful ratio than the conventional profit margin ratio which is used so broadly as a comparative measure of operating efficiency. Actually, the profit margin ratio when used alone as a yardstick is one-dimensional in that it encompasses only the limited set of variables included in the income account. By using the return on asset ratio, one may relate the profit margin ratio to other dynamic data determined by corporate planning and change as, for example, management of the asset base.

Table I shows for each of the railroads the components of the operational factors which determine before and after tax return on assets. The companies are ranked in order of the highest after tax returns on assets, the last column on the right.

The most disturbing aspect of the data shown in this table is the low return on assets generated by these quality and investor oriented railroad companies. None of the railroads standing alone has an after-tax return on assets of more than 6%. Moreover, the after-tax return on assets of three of the roads, Burlington Northern, Chessie, and Southern Pacific, in 1977 were below the industry average (after excluding Conrail) of 3.6%. On a pretax basis, five of the 10 companies (excluding Missouri Pacific Corp. and Union Pacific Corp.) have a return of less than 6%. In an environment where long-term interest rates may be at least 8%, the ability of these railroads to raise capital to acquire assets to broaden the revenue base will be limited if asset returns continue to be so low.

Now, let's look at the components of the ratio net return on assets to better understand the cause for these low asset returns. On an overall basis, it is apparent that the roads are turning over their assets too slowly. For the industry as a whole, excluding Conrail, the asset turnover ratio in 1977 was .65x. By comparison, the asset turnover ratio for S&P's 400 industrial companies was more than twice as great (1.33x). In brief, the railroads are not utilizing their assets to the same extent as industrial companies. Though I

am aware of the basic reason for the railroad industry's poor asset utilization, an improving trend in this ratio should be the first goal of a financial officer.

The net return on asset ratio is also a function of profit margins which is a broadly used yardstick for measuring profitability, but as I have previously indicated, tends to be "one-dimensional." One of the advantages of the asset return ratio is that a company having a low profit margin and a high asset turnover ratio can be shown to be economically as efficient as a railroad having a high profit margin and a low asset turnover rate. For example, Norfolk & Western and Southern Railway, with low asset turnover ratios (or operating leverage) have the highest pretax profit margin in this group of railroads. However, MoPac, with a pretax profit margin of 10.7%, almost three percentage points lower than that of Norfolk & Western and Southern Railway, has a substantially higher asset turnover ratio than these other two roads. The result is that the product of the two ratios—asset turnover times pretax profit margin—gives MoPac an economic efficiency factor equal to that of the other two roads. My point is that the conventional yardstick, gross profit margins, does not adequately reflect the overall operating efficiency of a railroad.

Table II shows the impact of the financial components on the ratio net return on

shareholders' equity. The roads are ranked in order of highest returns on equity after taxes.

The financial sources of the rate of return on shareholders' equity are (1) financial leverage (column 2), and (2) the tax retention rate (column 4, which is the reciprocal of effective tax rate). The financial leverage ratio is calculated by dividing average assets by average shareholders' equity. It reflects the extent of "trading on equity." For example, a financial leverage ratio of 2.5x as shown by Chessie means that for each $1.00 of equity, there is an additional $1.50 of non-equity capital on the right hand side of the balance sheet. In effect, the ratio shows how much of a company's assets are financed with stockholders' equity and how much with borrowed funds.

There is no single standard for an appropriate financial leverage ratio. Management style, attitudes of investors, bankers, and the rating services, as well as the quality and stability of revenue flows all play a role in what is acceptable. However, the impact of the financial leverage ratio on the end result—return on equity—can be dramatic. This may be illustrated by a comparison of the pretax return on shareholders' equity of MoPac with that of Union Pacific Railroad. In 1977, both these railroads were fairly comparable in respect to economic efficiency (pretax return on assets). MoPac

Table II. Impact of financial components on return on equity (1977)					
Ranked in order of net return on equity	**Pretax return on assets** x	**Financial leverage** =	**Pretax return on equity**	**Tax retention rate** =	**Net return on equity**
Missouri Pacific	10.4%	3.8x	39.5%	65.6%	26.0%
Missouri Pacific RR System	6.7	3.1	20.9	90.2	18.9
Union Pacific Corp.	9.8	1.7	16.7	65.7	10.9
Southern Railway	6.5	2.3	15.2	70.8	10.9
Rio Grande Industries	7.3	1.8	13.1	71.4	9.4
Santa Fe Industries	7.3	1.7	12.8	72.5	9.3
Norfolk & Western Ry.	5.8	2.4	13.9	66.8	9.3
Seaboard Coast Line Ind.	3.6	2.4	8.6	102.1	8.8
Union Pacific RR	6.9	1.9	13.4	65.1	8.7
Chessie System	3.3	2.5	8.2	80.1	6.6
Southern Pac. & Subs.	4.6	2.0	9.2	67.3	6.2
Burlington Nor. & Subs.	2.4	1.9	4.6	95.0	4.3

Note: May not total due to rounding.

had a return of 6.7% and UP a return of 6.9% (column 1), but because of the difference in the financial leverage ratio, UP earned 13.4% on shareholders' equity before taxes, while MoPac earned over 20%. If MoPac had had the same financial leverage ratio as UP (1.9x), its pretax return on equity would have been reduced to less than 13% before allowing for the reduction in capital expense, or conversely, if UP had had MoPac's financial leverage of 3.1x, its pretax return on equity would have been almost 20% after allowing for the cost of capital.

While leverage is great when business is good, it should not be forgotten that in the event of a sharp decline in business activity and, in turn, in railroad earnings, an earnings decline has a greater adverse impact on the higher fixed cost company and management has less flexibility in cushioning the decline. Thus, highly leveraged companies are not rated qualitywise as highly as more conservatively financed companies.

Table III shows the impact of the dividend payout ratio on the reinvestment rate. In this table, the roads are ranked in order of their reinvestment rate, which is the measure of internal growth (column 3). The reinvestment ratio is influenced by the earnings retention rate, which is

the reciprocal of the more commonly used dividend payout ratio. Actually, the only difference between the rate of return on shareholders' equity and the reinvestment rate is dividend payments.

The reinvestment ratio indicates the ability of a company to grow and managements' perception of opportunities for growth. For example, a company earning 20% on its equity, but

paying out in dividends 75% of its earnings and, consequently, reinvesting at a rate of only 5%, suggests that its management does not consider the company to have a high potential for future growth through reinvestment of its earnings. Thus, it is willing to share its incremental earnings with its stockholders.

For the railroads, this ratio may be interpreted somewhat differently. Ex-

Table III. Impact of dividend payout ratio on reinvestment rate (1977)

Ranked in order of reinvestment rate	Net return on equity	x	Earnings retention rate†	=	Reinvestment rate	Dividend payout ratio*
Missouri Pacific Corp.	26.0%		77.3%		20.1%	22.7%
Missouri Pacific RR System	18.9		80.3		15.2	19.7
Southern Railway	10.9		61.7		6.7	38.3
Union Pacific Corp.	10.9		62.0		6.7	38.0
Seaboard Coast Line Ind.	8.8		70.8		6.2	29.2
Santa Fe Industries	9.3		63.9		5.9	36.1
Rio Grande Industries	9.4		61.2		5.7	38.8
Norfolk & Western Ry.	9.3		45.8		4.3	54.2
Union Pacific RR	8.7		42.3		3.7	57.7
Southern Pac. & Subs.	6.2		46.2		2.9	53.8
Burlington Nor. & Subs.	4.3		68.2		2.9	31.8
Chessie System	6.6		42.5		2.8	57.5

* Includes dividends paid on both preferred and common shares.
† Reciprocal of dividend payout ratio.

Table IV. Earnings and dividends per common share and cash dividend payout ratio

	—Eastern Roads—		— Southern Roads—		Western Roads					
Earnings per com. share	N&W Ry. Co. & Subs.	Chessie System, Inc.	Southern Ry. Sys.	Seaboard Coast Line Ind.	Burlington Nor. Inc.	Missouri Pacific Corp.	Santa Fe Industries	Southern Pacific Co.	Union Pacific Corp.	Rio Grande Industries
1977	$3.31	$4.01	$7.04	$7.02	$5.74	$8.59	$5.92	$4.39	$4.68	$3.69
1976	4.21	5.38	5.85	5.84	5.69	6.86	4.61	4.10	4.02	2.90
1975	2.80	4.59	5.12	3.23	4.12	5.28	4.23	2.81	3.21	2.39
1974	3.61	5.06	5.83	6.73	6.65	4.92	4.67	4.20	2.73	2.68
1973	2.18	3.39	4.47	5.21	4.01	3.40	4.01	3.77	2.81	2.49
Compound growth rate	11.0 %	4.3 %	12.0 %	7.7 %	9.4 %	26.1 %	10.2 %	3.9 %	13.6 %	10.3 %
Earnings per com. share (fully diluted)										
1977	$3.15	$3.77	—	—	$5.31	$8.01	$5.39	—	$4.60	$2.84
1976	3.98	5.19	—	—	5.35	6.17	4.16	—	3.91	2.36
1975	2.68	4.39	—	—	3.95	4.79	3.82	—	3.12	2.06
1974	3.44	4.45	—	—	6.25	4.82	4.20	—	2.64	2.23
1973	2.11	2.93	—	—	3.83	—	3.62	—	2.68	2.13
Cash dividends per com. sh.										
1977	$1.80	$2.32	$2.53	$2.05	$1.60	$1.95	$2.05	$2.36	$1.70	$0.725
1976	1.71⅓	2.155	2.27	1.65	1.30	1.50	1.85	2.24	1.40	0.625
1975	1.66⅔	2.10	2.12	1.60	0.85	1.22½	1.80	2.24	1.40	0.60
1974	1.66⅔	1.875	2.02	1.70	1.60	1.05	1.80	2.20	1.30	0.60
1973	1.66⅔	1.75	1.77	1.05	1.125	0.93	1.65	2.16	1.12	0.60
Compound growth rate	1.9 %	7.3 %	9.3 %	18.2 %	9.2 %	20.3 %	5.6 %	2.2 %	11.0 %	4.8 %
Payout ratio*										
1977	54.2 %	57.5 %	35.9 %	29.2 %	27.6 %	22.7 %	35.8 %	53.8 %	37.9 %	20.4 %
1976	40.5	39.8	38.8	28.3	22.7	22.1	41.4	54.7	36.7	22.4
1975	59.2	45.7	41.4	49.5	20.6	22.5	42.5	79.6	43.7	25.1
1974	45.9	37.0	34.7	25.3	24.1	21.3	38.6	52.3	47.6	22.4
1973	74.6	51.6	39.6	20.1	27.8	46.9	41.3	57.2	39.9	23.6

*Cash dividends % of net income available for common.

cluding MPC and MoPac, whose results are dramatically impacted by both operational and financial leverage, seven of the remaining 10 companies have an internal growth rate of less than 6%. On the other hand, based on after-tax returns on shareholders' equity, which in effect is the rate of growth prior to dividend payments, only half of the companies shown in the table have a growth rate of 9% or more. If the railroads are to offset the impact of inflation which appears to be growing at an annual long-term rate of 6%, they must develop higher returns on equity and higher reinvestment rates. To make possible an improving trend in the reinvestment rate, the dividend payout ratio should be held to a minimum and payments to shareholders not increased commensurately with the growth in earnings.

While all of the preceding charts have been based on the 1977 year, we have found that in working with this technique of rates of return, the level of the rate of return is not as important in the market's evaluation of a company as an improving trend in the ratio.

Now to go back to the problem of the industry's low internal growth rate, what can be done to improve the trend? The first step, as I see it, would be reduce dividend payout ratios, or, conversely, increase earnings retention rates. Unlike industry in general, part of the cause for the railroads having a low reinvestment rate is not because they have no opportunity for developing growth through asset reinvestment, but, rather, because of their need and desire to retain as well as attract equity capital through dividend growth.

Table IV, earnings, dividends, and dividend payout ratio, gives the dividend records of the 10 companies as compared with earnings results. As you can see, all 10 companies paid higher dividends in 1977 than in 1973. Several roads have increased their dividends annually in the last five years; two roads have had dividend increases greater than their growth in earnings per share; and two roads have been erratic in their payments.

In 1977 alone, these 10 companies which we have been discussing earned over one billion dollars and paid out in cash dividends $435 million, a 43% payout ratio. When it is realized that the industry as a whole anticipates annual capital requirements in the next five years of $3-5 billion and Burlington Northern alone anticipates capital needs of $500 million annually, the need for the railroads to retain every dollar of earnings is self-evident.

I realize that rail managements in setting dividend policies are influenced by the emphasis which the marketplace has been giving recently to high-yielding stocks. Then too, there is the popular belief that higher dividends co-relate with higher share prices.

But let's look at the other side of the coin. Management, as well as boards of directors, tends to consider cash dividends as a fixed expense. Once a dividend rate has been announced, management finds it difficult to reduce the rate unless there is a serious reversal in the company's fortunes. As a result, high dividend payout ratios, in general, reduce financial flexibility and over the longer term may endanger the shareholders' investment.

Moreover, and you may not realize this, in the real world, there *are* important investors who prefer higher earnings retention rates to increasing cash dividends. Look for example, at Florida East Coast, which sells around 50 and has paid no dividends since it was reorganized in 1961.

In my opinion, if rail managements continue to succumb to dividend pressures and rail investors insist on squeezing out of meager railroad profits higher dividends, the railroads will eventually stagnate. In brief, if management is doing a poor job in employing its assets, regardless of source, and then dissipates such assets through high dividend payments, everyone sooner or later will be the loser—investor and lender alike. ∎

Amtrak's Boyd: "Congress must make up its mind"

Alan S. Boyd has had a career in transportation that can best be described as checkered. He has served, at one time or another, as general counsel of the Florida Turnpike Authority; chairman of the Florida Railroad and Public Utilities Commission; chairman of the Civil Aeronautics Board; U.S. Secretary of Transportation (the first to occupy that post); and president of Illinois Central Gulf. Last June 1 he became president of Amtrak and—in a sharp departure from his past practice of making himself easily available to the press—Boyd suddenly clammed up. He turned down literally dozens of requests for interviews, explaining that he didn't want to say anything until he felt he had something to say. On Dec. 13 he broke his silence, at a news conference where he presented the "Amtrak Statement of Mission" (see p. 18). A week later he sat down with Luther S. Miller, editor of *Railway Age*, for a candid discussion of Amtrak's future.

RAILWAY AGE: I understand that since you became president of Amtrak seven months ago, you have spent a considerable amount of time traveling around the country, looking at the operation. Have you been surprised at what you have found?

BOYD: The most surprising thing I have found is this: People around headquarters keep telling me how bad morale is at Amtrak. But I have yet to find bad morale in the places I've visited, either at the facilities or on the trains. Most people have bitches, and some of them are very legitimate. But the sense I get is that our people are out there trying, because they believe in Amtrak and want it to be a success. I think we do have bad morale, and I think it's right here in this headquarters. They're asking, what is our future? How long are we going to be in existence? But I don't find that out in the field.

That's not to say that because I think we have generally good morale we have no problems. We do.

I'm less than satisfied with our maintenance efforts on our equipment. Part of the problem is our own doing. We've got a hydra-headed monster of an organization in the mechanical area which I'm confident we are going to straighten out. I have not tried to change it in any major way since I got here because I wanted to find the best mechanical man in the country to take over the operation and set it up right. And I'm happy to tell you we've got him. He is Tom Hackney, assistant vice president-mechanical of the Chessie; subject to board approval, he will become our chief mechanical officer. I'm really pleased. We couldn't have found a better man. And to get a man with his ability and his reputation is an indication to me that there are a lot of people who have some faith in intercity rail passenger ser-

vice and what we are trying to do.

Another thing that was of some concern to me shortly after I arrived was the condition of our food services facilities. Not all of them were in the same shape as mom's kitchen. Some of the problems were really somewhat beyond our control, because of the locations in which we are forced to operate. Others were completely within our control, and I've been on a rampage about that, because I want to be sure that the people who do ride Amtrak are going to get good, sanitary food and courteous service. We are in the process of seeing to that.

I'm not happy with our schedule reliability. I don't want to discriminate: We're not doing any better on the [Northeast] Corridor, which we own, than the contracting railroads are doing elsewhere. That's a bitter disappointment to me, but it's a fact. We're trying to deal with the problem in both areas, our own direct operation in the corridor, and across the country. I'm really unable to assess why we have such unreliable on-time performance.

There's no question in my mind that the chief executives of all the railroads have an intellectual if not an emotional commitment to run our trains on time. Having spent some time in the railroad industry before I got here, I think I have a sense of some of the very real physical problems with which the railroads have to deal, and I appreciate that those problems impact on the service they can provide to Amtrak. I'm not convinced that there is, throughout a lot of companies, the sense of commitment—"By God, we're going to run these trains on time"— that I would like to see. I can't say it's not there; all I can say is that I don't generally see it.

I would speculate that when you get down to the division superintendent and

the trainmaster on these various railroads, you find something of a problem. Their superiors tend to look at them in terms of whether or not they move the freight. Nobody says don't move the passenger trains—but you get your head cut off if you don't move the freight. And that can be pretty persuasive.

I'm not satisfied that either we or the railroads have done an adequate job in outlining the importance of Amtrak service to the various dispatchers, who are really the final word about what happens. I have some sympathy for the dispatchers, even though I'm unhappy about freight-train interference. Those fellows have to make decisions right now to have immediate impact. I'm sure it's very easy for me or anybody else on Monday morning to say, "You know you shouldn't have started that freight that wound up in front of the passenger train," but they have to call it the way they see it.

To sum up my feeling in that area, I would say we're not mad at anybody, though we're disappointed in the quality of service we're getting from some of the railroads and hope they will be able to do better.

I'm not sure that railroads really appreciate the importance of Amtrak to their hopes for a viable future. My own feeling is, and has been, that if the railroads are going to be viable, they've got to have changes in legislation. To win those changes, they've got to have public support. I'm projecting that we'll carry 20 million people this year, many of whom feel very strongly about railroading because they ride the train. And if the Congress is bombarded with complaint letters from passengers about the lousy service they got, whether or not it's the fault of Amtrak internally or poor maintenance levels on the railroads or freight-train interference, those com-

plaint letters are going to impact the minds of the Congress about what the rail industry is.

The rail industry has got a poor public image. I don't know that Amtrak in and of itself can change that public image, but I think it could be a very positive factor and I'm convinced it's terribly important to the industry.

RA: What can you do that you haven't done to try to convince the railroads that this is true?
BOYD: I don't know. We're trying to be cooperative. One of the first statements I made when I came here was that I knew of no institution in the world that had less need for enemies than Amtrak. We want to work with people, we don't want to be in conflict. There are some people here at headquarters who actually feel that we should be out suing railroads for poor performance. I think any such efforts would result in at best a Pyrrhic victory. What I want is better service. I don't want a judgment or a verdict. We are a part of this industry. I don't see us as separate from Conrail or Santa Fe or Burlington Northern or Union Pacific. We're all part of this together.

I think one of the things that is terribly important is for the Administration and the Congress to make up their minds whether Amtrak is here to stay; I have a feeling that some of my colleagues in the freight industry really see Amtrak as just a temporary situation which is going to get out of the way in due course. I would like to see a stabilization, a commitment on the part of our public institutions to intercity rail passenger service, and get the idea out of the minds of freight rail management that we're going to go away. I would hope that we could go from that to the level of somehow persuading people in the railroad industry that we're not

a burden or a bane to their existence but rather an opportunity to serve as a crystal-clear window to the public as to what this industry can be and do.

RA: Aren't the railroads encouraged in this attitude by what they read in the papers and what they hear from the OMB and the DOT?
BOYD: I think so. That's why I think it is terribly important that our policy makers decide whether we are going to survive or whether we are going to be shut down. One thing I don't want is a situation where Congress won't let us die but won't provide us with enough nutrition so that we can be healthy. That's the worst of all possible worlds.

RA: The DOT is coming out early in 1979 with its own restructuring recommendations. Have you any idea what these are going to be?
BOYD: We are working very closely together, and we have a lot of respect for each other's efforts. I think we've seen every combination and permutation that will be involved in any route map that turns up, but I don't think that either we or DOT today are in any position to say, "This is what it's going to be."

RA: Would you like to see Amtrak principally a corridor operation?
BOYD: I'd like to see Amtrak operating over a route structure where it could provide good equipment. I'm concerned about trying to limp along with old equipment, however well we try to rehabilitate it. I read an article the other day about a DC-3 that's still flying somewhere down in Florida. This was written up as an oddity, because the plane was built in 1939. The thought suddenly occurred to me, "Hell, half of our whole fleet are DC-3s." That's a measure of our prob-

lem. We're operating a lot of museum pieces, and no matter what will we have, service is not going to be reliable with that kind of equipment.

RA: Amtrak's capital budget is around $100 million a year. You have said it ought to be $200 million. What do you want the extra money for?
BOYD: We need to buy new equipment, the so-called conventional cars. I'm not interested in seeing Amtrak develop traveling palaces. What we need are cars that are safe, reliable, and simple. I think it's possible to combine those elements.

RA: Have you any realistic hopes of getting that money?
BOYD: "Realistic" is quite a qualifier. I have hope. In fact, I have great hope that the Administration and the Congress are going to come to grips with Amtrak.

RA: When will you have your first Superliner in operation?
BOYD: The latest information is that we'll be able to start service the first of July, with the Empire Builder. Pullman Standard is having difficulty pumping the Superliners through its production line. I'm not really competent to tell you why. I hope to get out to talk to the folks at Pullman Standard and go through their plant in the near future and try to find out for myself what the problem is.

RA: One of Amtrak's problems, in common with every other passenger-carrying railroad, is high labor costs. What is Amtrak's labor ratio—that is, total labor costs as a percentage of revenues?
BOYD: It's in the low 60s. There have got to be some changes in this area.

RA: What can be done?
BOYD: I have for a long time felt that we

had to have changes in work rules and the basis of pay in the industry; I feel that very keenly. I think we have to negotiate those changes on a basis that's fair to everybody. We've got to negotiate changes which protect the individual employee. He is now doing his job as it's outlined and as the terms have been negotiated. To say, "Well, Buster, we don't need you anymore, and goodbye" just doesn't make any sense. I think it's immoral. But I think we should be able to effect changes in a way that will reduce our unit cost and at the same time not penalize the employee in terms of income. I think this is in the best interest of rail labor, and I'm positive it is essential to the future of the rail industry. I'm not just limiting that to Amtrak, although our situation obviously is somewhat different from that of the freight railroads. We've just got to figure some way to create an environment in which both management and labor are able to see this as our mutual problem and then succeed in working out a resolution that effects substantial change.

I have heard a number of my friends in rail labor agree that change is essential, but that agreement is always an abstraction. What I'm hoping is that we can sit down in a nonadversary atmosphere and decide how we can make changes which are going to make it possible for at least Amtrak to provide a greater level of productivity (I hate to use that word: I sometimes think it's seen as a pejorative, and it's not).

I am conscious of the fact that so often in the past those of us in rail management have tended to say "Rail labor's our problem, we've got to change that." Labor, on the other hand, says, with some eloquence and sometimes with obscenity, "You people in management are a bunch of blockheads." I expect we're both right.

I have argued for years that this industry can't keep going the way it has been going, and I think there are all sorts of objective measures to indicate that the way the industry has been going has been wrong. Look at where the industry was 25, 15, or 10 years ago, and look at where it is today. To say that you can mint a medal for the great accomplishments of management is a little bit naive. So I think we in management have got to change, too, and we're trying to change here at Amtrak.

RA: Where do your greatest potential labor savings lie?
BOYD: My guess—and it's only a guess; we haven't tried to price it out—is that it's in the train crew area.

RA: What initiatives have you taken on this with the United Transportation Union?
BOYD: I haven't taken any, the reason being that there's no point in my going to [UTU President] Al Chesser with the message, "Al, we've got to change." I'd better know first what I want, and why, and that's what I'm working on now. I want to be sure that what I want for Amtrak is something that makes sense, not only for Amtrak but for the employees. Now, I can't arrogate myself into the position of saying what is best for the employee, but at least I can make a judgment on what I think is best. We're spending some time on what strikes me as a fairly important aspect of this thing, which is, how do you get the brotherhoods to think and to act in terms of long-term benefit as opposed to short-term benefit, which I think has been one of the banes of both rail management and labor. We have thought in terms of this year's contract and next year's contract, but we haven't looked down the road.

RA: We have recently seen new crew-consist agreements negotiated with the UTU by the Milwaukee Road, by Conrail, and by Canadian National. In the case of CN, which won a better agreement than the other roads, the UTU representative observed that over the long term, the financial success of the railroad was more important to the employees than to anyone else....
BOYD: I should say—based on an article that I read in *Railway Age*—that I was particularly impressed with the CN agreement. The point I have been trying to make, to everybody who would listen to me, is that if we're going to stay in

Amtrak's mission as the directors see it

The following is excerpted from "The Amtrak Mission Statement," by Amtrak's board of directors. It was released at a Dec. 13 news conference in Washington by Amtrak President Alan S. Boyd and Board Chairman Dr. Donald P. Jacobs.

Routes
In Section 4(a) of the Amtrak Improvement Act of 1978, Congress has established the following five criteria to be used in developing route recommendations:
1. Unique characteristics of rail.
2. Energy conservation.
3. Relationship of benefits to cost.
4. Adequacy of alternative modes.
5. Market and population.

The Board has a responsibility to advise the Congress as to what it believes to be the optimum basic network.

Following the congressional establishment of the basic network, the Board believes that Amtrak should be vested with authority to make additions to or deletions from the network and that it should employ as its criteria for such changes the "route criteria" developed by the Board in 1975 and approved by Congress. To the extent that existing Amtrak resources would permit adding service without need for specific further public funding, Amtrak should be empowered to do so. On the other hand, if additional public funding is necessary to commence such service, Amtrak should make explicit request to Congress for further appropriation by route, indicating the reasons for the request and detailing the criteria employed in reaching such conclusion.

All of the above should be done pursuant to the "contractual" approach outlined, *in the following section.*

Financing
There are only two sources of funds: fares and public financing. The Board believes the most effective method of handling public financing is through the establishment of a contractual relationship with Congress. Under such a system, the Board would operate the mandated *basic* system for an agreed-upon grant of funds. The level of funding would be determined taking into account expected costs of providing a quality product through an efficiently managed organization. This new form of contractual relationship would provide clear efficiency incentives to Amtrak and clear indications of management's performance to the Congress.

Productivity
The Board recognizes the public perception that rail labor may be less than fully productive. However, the issue is considerably more complicated than such a simple statement would suggest. In addition to the labor issue, part of the problem has to do with not-yet-entirely-corrected inefficiencies in management.

Some additional problems affecting productivity and cost control are:
1. Amtrak does not negotiate the terms and conditions of employment for the operating *craft* employees. The aim of Amtrak should be to develop a set of uniform terms and conditions for those persons who operate trains, but subject to the operating requirements of the contracting railroads.
2. Amtrak costs are inflated by protec-

business, we've got to have revolution and not evolution. To me the CN-UTU agreement was on the revolutionary side, and I think that's all to the good. They're going to have a stronger railroad, and they're going to provide more employment and better jobs as a result of that agreement. I believe we can do the same thing.

There's got to be some give and take. I can't sit down and dictate what our employees are going to do in terms of working conditions or basis of pay. We've got this mindset—we've got a dual basis of pay; we've got a crew district which is hoary with age and custom and can't be changed; we've got all sorts of things that have been built up over the years which come flooding into everybody's mind when we start talking. And so we say, "How do we ease the yard limits out two more miles, and what do we have to pay for that?" instead of thinking, "What are we trying to accomplish in this business and for this nation, and what's the best way to do it, given the environment within which we operate and the constraints which are imposed on us by law? Why not take a fresh look at the whole thing?"

We need to take a fresh look at a number of things in this industry. Consider what the Rock Island has been doing. They are undertaking to do things which have been considered to be beyond the pale, and as a result they are making a better railroad. Now whether they are going to be able to accomplish enough to make the railroad a candidate for survival, I'm not sure. But they're not saying, "Well, we're in this vise of custom and history and we're just going to have to put our heads down and keep cutting expenses."

That is the family motto of the railroads: Cut expenses. That to me is one of the most deadening things in the world, though I realize it has to be done. I'm mad as hell about some of the things at Amtrak that I've uncovered about expenditures which I don't think have to be made. And I'm going to stop it. But when your mentality just says cut expenses, it makes the possibility of innovation almost nil. The Rock Island is in a state where, literally, they've got nothing to lose. So they're trying to run a railroad the way they think a railroad ought to be run.

RA: Amtrak's operating ratio is around 250%, so labor obviously isn't your only

---

tive guarantees to employees no longer working, as required by contract or law.

3. Productivity may be adversely affected by limited track access.

4. Productivity may be adversely affected by antiquated and restrictive work rules. These rules must be identified and eliminated.

5. Amtrak needs to develop a compensation system that is fair but one that permits efficient performance.

6. Amtrak needs more control over operations and should be a full party to all negotiations affecting Amtrak operations.

Commutation Service
The basic mission of Amtrak is to operate intercity rail passenger service. The provision of commuter service will degrade Amtrak's basic service. Should a public policy decision be made to impose commuter operations on Amtrak, compensation for the full costs must be provided.

Track
Poor Amtrak service is often directly attributable to poor track, usually caused by under maintenance and related slow orders. This problem falls into two broad classifications: (1) track that Amtrak owns; and (2) track belonging to certain contracting railroads.

1. The Northeast Corridor Improvement Project will provide good track, but the program now underway will not be completed for several years. Thus, public policy decisions relative to an important part of Amtrak operations have already been made, but expectations, particularly with regard to the timing of their impact, should be kept realistic. Moreover, additional funding may be required to complete the project.

2. With regard to track under control of contracting railroads, the issue is more difficult. Upgrading of such track requires substantial amounts of money not available to some railroads at this time. Such upgrading is a necessity if Amtrak is to provide effective service.

Equipment
Amtrak, from its inception, has had equipment problems. Much of the passenger equipment it acquired was old and sometimes badly maintained. Widespread shifts in equipment throughout the Amtrak system exacerbated the problem because many of the existing maintenance personnel were unfamiliar with the equipment that they were assigned to work on.

As Amtrak increasingly modernizes and standardizes its fleet, some of the present major maintenance problems will be reduced. Amtrak continues, however, to suffer from uneven quality of its maintenance facilities and, in some cases, poorly trained and inadequately supervised personnel.

A further major problem is the lack of a strong United States railroad passenger equipment supply industry. This places constraints upon Amtrak's ability to acquire new equipment and, more importantly, to develop new technology. Amtrak's equipment situation would be appreciably improved if, as a matter of policy, the government gave better support to the development of new technology in the American industry or if, as a matter of policy, Amtrak was not constrained to buy only from an American supplier.

Obviously, Amtrak will need substantial capital to overcome equipment problems. The organization must develop a well-documented case to support requests for capital funding. Planning will preclude the necessity for frequent small capital requests and will enable both Amtrak management and the various branches of government to better appreciate the Amtrak capital plans in their proper, long-term context.

U.S. Department of Transportation
The Department is in a difficult, if not impossible, position as both a member of the Amtrak Board and as an assigned agency of government exercising public oversight over budgetary and policy decisions. There is strong sentiment on the Board that the Department of Transportation should not occupy a voting seat on the Amtrak Board. Others believe that despite what may be a conflict of interest, the Secretary of Transportation should retain a seat on the Board, as presently provided by law.

Congress
Historical approaches with regard to funding, route structure, levels of service, and the like, have contributed to a most difficult situation for the Congress. Very properly, members of Congress are concerned with both geographic and overall societal concerns. To improve this situation, the Board has made several recommendations under both routes and financing (above). If these recommendations are followed, Amtrak will essentially function as an operating entity with Congress establishing basic structure and financing.

problem. Are there any other areas where you think you can reduce cost?

BOYD: As I indicated earlier, I think we can be more efficient in our maintenance of equipment. I have some real concern about the number and location of our mechanical facilities. I'm particularly concerned about our turbotrain facilities, which are probably the best we have, and I think the people in those facilities are doing a fine job. The problem is we don't have enough trains to run through them to bring the overhead down. I'm counting on our new chief mechanical officer to give me an assessment of what can be done in the mechanical area.

RA: The Northeast Corridor Improvement Project has been getting some bad publicity. What is the corridor situation?

BOYD: Structurally, we've got some very real problems. The organization, with the Federal Railroad Administration, Amtrak, and De Leuw Cather all involved, is not a textbook approach. I wouldn't say the organization problem has been resolved, but our working relationships have improved substantially. Northeast Corridor service will deteriorate somewhat in 1979—it will be our worst year from the standpoint of operations. We will suffer more delays because of construction. It's a trade-off situation: How much delay can you put up with and maintain the bulk of your passengers while you are trying to improve the service for them in the future? By the end of the third quarter we should begin to get the benefit of some of the improvements we've made.

RA: What reaction have you had to your recent statement on Amtrak's mission?

BOYD: There is a great deal of interest in the contract concept. We have not spelled out what we mean—we're not yet in a position to do so in specific detail—but the idea of creating some sort of stability which hopefully will minimize political interference and permit some intelligent long-range planning seems to have struck a responsive chord.

RA: How do you feel about this job after seven months? Are you sorry you came?

BOYD: No, sir. I'm delighted, I'm having the time of my life. I'm working with a lot of fine people. I feel that Amtrak is making some progress—to some degree because of my efforts, but it's really because there are a lot of people here who are interested in Amtrak and who are reacting very favorably to what I hope is some leadership as to where we're going and how we're going to get there. ∎

Chapter 4
Air Carriers

New Dimensions In Air Cargo Traffic

By Fred H. McCusker

Although it may come as a surprise, airlines have actually been using a form of containerization for about 30 years. The concept of pre-loaded services began in the late 1940s and early 1950s as a means of expediting the shipment of freight by air and limiting the amount of time aircraft had to sit on the ground while being loaded or unloaded.

The very first airline containerization efforts consisted of skids loaded with cargo conforming to the contour of the aircraft.

The forerunner of today's intermodal container arrived on the scene exactly 20 years ago, in 1958 - and American Airlines was the innovator. Called the "Paul Bunyan" box, this was the first unit load container designed for air freight.

The Paul Bunyan container was constructed of light-weight aluminum and was rectangular in shape, measuring 84 inches wide, 63 inches deep, and 42 inches high. Each Bunyan box had a capacity of more than a ton of cargo. The units were moved on and off the aircraft with a forklift truck. A DC-6 freighter could handle as many as ten of these containers.

The value of such a container was recognized even at that early date. The *New York Times* reported that *"the containers are expected to speed freight handling and eliminate excessive packaging costs."* This was one occasion where predictions of a rosy future proved to be right on target.

The Paul Bunyan box was also significant because it established the principle which provides for free tare for air carrier defined containers.

The next development was pallets with cargo built up on top of them and secured by nets. These required careful, time consuming manpower in loading and rearranging to meet fuselage clearances. This challenge was faced when American Airlines intro-

duced the *Igloo*, the first container designed specifically for use in jetfreighters.

The units were called "Igloos" because their shape was contoured to fit the interior of a 707 freighter, and they eliminated "template" loading difficulties. The earliest igloos were open on two sides and secured by nets. Later, improved structural versions came complete with locking doors.

Although the Igloo did what it was supposed to do - speeding up ground time and expediting loading and unloading of aircraft, it remained essentially an airport-to-airport unit because it was not efficient for over-the-road use. And the same limitation applied to various "Lower Deck" (LD) containers designed to move in aircraft bellies.

Arrival of the 747

It was not until the arrival of the 747 freighter in the early 1970s that the industry was able to break away from this limitation and containerization really gained momentum.

Introduction of a freighter version of the giant 747 made a unitized system of handling air cargo not merely desir-

Mr. McCusker is vice president-freight marketing, American Airlines.

able but essential. There was simply no other practical way of getting over 100 tons of freight on and off an aircraft in little more than an hour of time.

The first container designed specifically for the 747 freighter measured 8x8x10 feet. It looked like a squared off igloo, but because of its shape, it offered 605 cubic feet of capacity, a considerable increase over the 365 ft. of cubic capacity offered by the igloo.

At the same time, this ten-foot long container which we call the M-1, offered shippers a net weight of 13,950 pounds. It was compatible with the ground equipment already in use to handle the igloo, providing a big plus in keeping costs down. However, it still had the aircraft pallet base requiring specialized support equipment.

Intermodal Container

The next step was development of an 8x8x20 ft. container. This unit has 1,125 cubic feet of capacity and a gross weight of 25,000 pounds, providing the user with almost 23,000 pounds of capacity, and it has a structural base.

Even more important from an intermodal standpoint, it provides a perfect fit between surface modes and the 747 freighter. This unit can move on a worldwide standard ISO chassis and can be stacked.

As the number of 747 freighters in operation grows, so will the need for more intermodal containers. According to recent reports by Boeing, some 95 main deck cargo carrying 747 aircraft have been delivered to various airlines to-date and are serving most of the world. 25 more will be delivered each year well into the 1980s.

Demand For Smaller Vans

The arrival of the intermodal container does not mean, however, that the igloo and other contoured containers are about to become obsolete. To the contrary, contoured containers are likely to survive well into the future for a number of reasons.

For one thing, there is a continuing demand for smaller size containers offering from 150 to 230 cubic feet of capacity, and this need can best be met by smaller contoured containers that fit in the lower deck of either passenger or cargo aircraft.

Although these smaller containers come in a variety of sizes and shapes, they have one thing in common- they offer an efficient and fast means of moving products for the shipper and airline alike.

The smaller belly containers will continue to play an important role in the overall development of air freight.

The Air Transport Association of America recently estimated that belly capacity in passenger aircraft accounted for 11.9 billion of the total 17 billion available ton miles in the U.S. domestic air freight industry last year. A similar ratio undoubtedly existed world wide. Given this sort of capacity we have only scratched the surface of the potential market.

The standard igloo will also continue to have a role in air freight, particularly in markets served by the 707 and DC-8 freighters that do not have sufficient volume for 747 freighter service.

Intermodal Air-Truck-Sea-Partnership

However, as far as high-volume markets are concerned, the intermodal container is quickly becoming the common denominator. Because the intermodal unit can be transferred so easily by truck, we can expect a big increase in trucking services operated by airlines linking key hub cities where the 747 freighter operates with other cities located up to several hundred miles away.

Intermodal containers open a whole new vista of partnerships with the trucking industry and the steamship industry as well. They conform to all requirements of the International Standards Organization, are made of light-weight aluminum construction for efficient movement by air, and have both top and bottom corner fittings making them compatible for top lifting on ocean vessels or transfer to truck.

The Future: Container Pools

Now that the intermodal container is here and the support equipment is available, airlines must be alert to the opportunities and shipper benefits of joint procedures through joint marketing efforts.

One hopeful first step in the development of a standard industry program has been undertaken by CTI-Container Transport International. This company, a major force in leasing containers in the marine industry, is working to establish a pool of intermodal containers using a type of container that conforms to all ISO requirements.

Any carrier joining the pool would lease containers and the units would be interchangeable among all participating modes. A computer system would keep track of the airline container equipment and provide pool members with accurate activity reports and monthly billings.

American Airlines has been leasing containers from CTI since last summer. We began with an initial order for 25 units, but acceptance by customers was so strong that we recently ordered an additional 67 containers. Although no other airline has joined the pool to-date, CTI tells us that a number of carriers are studying entry very seriously, and we hope that our successful experience will cause others to move ahead.

From our point of view, the pool offers an ideal opportunity for airlines to get out from under all the heavy administrative work involved in owning and operating a fleet of containers and it also removes from our shoulders the burden of positioning equipment involved in interchanges. In short, it would take the worry out of interchange and permit a freer flow of the units worldwide, including interline exchanges.

As things stand now, the relatively limited number of intermodal containers in circulation has hindered the development of the container traffic that is in the marketplace.

Sea-Air Moves

Free interchange of containers would eliminate the need for breakbulk between modes that remains a major deterrent to sea-air programs and it would make international door-to-door container service an everyday occurrence.

Although sea-air moves have been growing, particularly between the Far East and the eastern half of the United States, the potential market has been held back by the fact that once containers move across the Pacific by ship, freight must be transferred into an air container at the port of entry before continuing to its eventual destination. This is because the additional tare weight of the sea container reduces the shipper's payload in the air. Once there are enough intermodal containers in circulation to permit their use in these sea-air moves, the breakbulk problem will be eliminated.

The freight move will originate in an air container, which will move from land to water to air and finally back to land as it moves from continent to continent. To do this efficiently, air containers must be part of worldwide container pools and air carriers must participate in these container pools.

Handling Equipment

There are two pieces of equipment used to transfer intermodal containers between modes. One is the main deck loader, which is used when a rollerized trailer is involved. In these cases, the container is simply rolled off the trailer onto the main deck loader and then lifted to the height of the waiting 747, so it can be rolled into the aircraft's main deck.

For cases where the container arrives on a non-rollerized trailer, we have located straddle carriers at all 747 freighter cities. This giant piece of handling equipment, while common to the marine and railroad industries, is new to airline operations. It can lift up to 64,000 pounds at one time, far in excess of the 25,000-pound gross weight of an intermodal container.

The combination of advanced ground handling equipment, intermodal containers and large freighters is all designed to provide the shipper with everything needed to ship by air with a minimum of investment because it is compatible with the present operation of his warehouse or terminal. When these various elements are brought together in sufficient quantities, we have a service that can only become more attractive as manufacturers recognize the additional pipeline time they gain by shipping by air. No one needs to be involved with unnecessary warehousing as the cost of money continues to increase, and use of air freight can play a major role in reducing inventory.

The faster the product gets into the consumer's hands the faster money flows back to the manufacturer. In short, the old adage that time is money is truer than ever before. Air freight buys the time the shipper needs to make a profit.

The industry is constantly in search of opportunities to work with shippers in developing container programs for mutual benefit. New equipment and handling systems introduced in the past several years have brought about dramatic advances in the state of the art, making it particularly timely for shippers to review their own needs and examine how air freight might fit in the picture. Greater profits are awaiting those who make containerization part of their distribution program now. □

Michael B. Basch
Senior Vice President
Southern Division
FEDERAL EXPRESS is interviewed

Federal Express, the largest single venture capital start-up in the history of American business, specializes at this time in overnight, door-to-door transportation of small packages.

It has grown from six packages and one aircraft on its first day of operation to more than 18,000 packages daily, a fleet of 32 fanjet aircraft and now a fleet of 727s.

Now operating 75 terminals throughout the United States, Federal Express is providing daily service to 130 major U.S. cities and more than 10,000 smaller communities from coast to coast.

In contrast to air freight forwarders, Federal Express owns and operates its own airplanes. The company also operates more than 500 radio-dispatched courier vans, which pick up and deliver shipments.

The privately-owned corporation was founded in mid-1972 by Frederick W. Smith, who was 28 years old at the time. The company has been operating profitably since June 1975.

Given this background, PartsBank is just what you would expect from a company like Federal Express. Recognizing that manufacturers of computers,

electronic instruments and other high technology goods were having serious problems in getting time sensitive parts to their customers, Federal Express combined its nationwide air transportation network with a warehousing service and several years ago, began to create a new concept in physical distribution management.

In effect, PartsBank works much like any other public warehouse, but it is a highly specialized one. The shipper stores a selected inventory at PartsBank, and any person authorized by the shipper can place an order there at any hour of the day or week. Three levels of service allow the PartsBank user to choose response times ranging from six hours to two days.

Michael B. Basch, Senior Vice President of FEC's Southern Division, is the man responsible for the development of the PartsBank Division. Pacific Traffic appreciates the time he devoted to this interview, and believes that you will find many exciting and useful ideas in it.

Kortum: *What is your background in this industry?*

Basch· Initially I was with United Parcel Service for some eight years, then

four years as a distribution consultant with A. T. Kearney and Rapistan's Technics Group. This involved physical distribution in the sense of inventory, transportation and warehousing. I joined Federal Express prior to the start-up of service in 1973, and put together the planning and the implementation of the pick-up and delivery system throughout the country. I then moved into a corporate development function as senior vice president. That involved things like controls and the development of measurement indicators for a new business. Then I initiated the Industrial Relations Department, and developed PartsBank in 1974.

I was actively involved in PartsBank, until last May. I am now Senior Vice President and General Manager of the Southern Division of Federal Express. I'm responsible for ten states in the Southern United States, our Memphis sorting Hub operation and for PartsBank.

Kortum: *Is PartsBank still continuing to grow as fast as it has for the past few years?*

Basch: No, but that's going to change during this coming fiscal year, starting in April.

92

We have several things in mind for PartsBank. One is to automate it, in terms of order entry and inventory control systems. Presently, PartsBank operates on a strictly manual basis. That was done for a purpose: so that we could get our feet on the ground and know what the customer's needs are. Now I think we are mature enough to automate. We have, up to now, de-emphasized PartsBank. After April we're going to promote it pretty heavily.

Kortum: *What are some of the other things you're planning?*

Basch: Well, we want to move from distribution to inventory management as a philosophy. Of course, that means a lot of things to a lot of people, but what I mean is that, right now, we simply take orders, process the inventory and the order, and send it out. That, to me, is distribution. The customer tells you how quickly he needs to get it there, you give him the options, he says he wants it there immediately, and you tell him how soon he can get it. That's good information, but it's just distribution.

Computerization will be the first step. What we now want to begin moving to, as the second step, is inventory management. In other words, the capability of allowing the small-to-medium size high technology company to manage their inventory assets. In other words, how much inventory should they have at each location in order to optimize between service, transportation and inventory. We'll have software that will allow the customer to develop an entire system; to track what inventory there is; where it is; to determine the proper stocking levels to meet service demands; and to order against stocking levels. In other words, an entire system that allows them to provide the best possible service at minimum cost.

Kortum: *Would you, in effect, be taking over the customer's whole warehouse function?*

Basch: That's the intent: to take over his distribution function by showing him that we can manage his inventory much better than he can. Not only because we have the transportation and warehousing facilities, which we do, but because we have the inventory management expertise, software and information systems that surpass what he could economically provide for himself.

Kortum: *Can you handle all of that out of Memphis, or are you planning on establishing other warehouses?*

Basch: We have one Hub now at Federal Express, in Memphis, but we're going to four Hubs. We haven't determined the exact cities, but they will be in the New York metropolitan area, the Chicago area and probably the Denver area, which would serve the Western United States.

Kortum: *Will you have a PartsBank at each of these Hubs?*

Basch: Yes, but the central stocking facility will probably be in Chicago. This will allow a PartsBank customer the same benefits that he has now from Federal Express' central stocking facility, with the added benefit of having more scheduled airlines out of Chicago.

Kortum: *Does PartsBank utilize the scheduled airlines, in addition to Federal Express?*

Basch: Yes. We have three levels of service. The first level, which is called Urgent Service, meets a same day need.

Federal Express has daytime flights, but for Urgent Service we'll schedule the next flight out, and the shipment could go on American Airlines, or Delta, or whoever, just so that it leaves Memphis and gets to the customer as quickly as possible. The second option utilizes overnight Federal Express Service, which is less expensive, and under the third option, which is the least expensive, we may use Federal Express or UPS, and we'll get it there in two days.

As we move into other Hubs, the Urgent Service out of Chicago will become, of course, quicker, because of the tremendous number of daytime passenger flights. So the customer would have the option of centralization that he has now, with a quicker response in the daytime. He would also have the option of going to a regional system with the traditional fast-moving items. Regionally he would have very quick response, and be able to cut his inventory in local areas, as well as a central system for slow-moving high value items, and really cut inventory down to the bone.

Kortum: *At this point, though, what is the service level that most people are selecting?*

Basch: Generally speaking, overnight service runs about 50 percent; Urgent Service runs about 40 percent, and second day service has been accounting for about 10 percent. Urgent Service is a convenience to the customer, and somewhat less profitable, but it's a vital part of the overall service.

Kortum: *Is UPS the only surface carrier that PartsBank uses?*

Basch: Yes, and its only used within about a 300 mile radius. In other words, we'd use UPS to increase our options within that radius, because we can count on reliable service there. Otherwise, we ship by air.

Of course, if a customer comes in and requests a certain carrier to be used, we'll

pacific traffic about - -

PartsBank

certainly honor his request. But so far, the customers have accepted our routing options.

Kortum: *Do you have any customers who are storing their entire inventory with you now?*

Basch: We have one customer, Intertel, which is doing 94 percent of its distribution from PartsBank. That doesn't mean that they have all of their inventory at PartsBank, but rather that their working inventory is with us. From there, our customer's use goes down to the point where you have some customers handling only one part for a specific emergency need.

Kortum: *Approximately what percentage of Federal Express' profits come from PartsBank?*

Basch: About one percent. But eventually PartsBank probably will become part of a company that will be separate from Federal Express. We may have a name like "Federal Express Supply". That company would have three functions: the first is basically what we're doing now; the second is to be the supply arm of Federal Express for our own operations, and third, we may get into the business of buying and selling critical inventories. By that I mean, for example, aircraft parts. We'd offer a service to fixed-base operators where we'd carry a stock of various parts and supplies for aircraft, and allow them to call an 800 number and order against that stock.

We're going through the planning for this right now, and so we haven't set a profit objective on that basis; that's about six to twelve months away. Right now we're deciding what inventories apply to this concept; what's the financial potential of selling those inventories; what's the risk, etc. There are a lot of variables that we have to consider in this planning stage before we establish a profit objective.

Kortum: *How many shipments are you presently making from PartsBank?*

Basch: We're making about 75 shipments per day.

Kortum: *What special storage facilities does the PartsBank warehouse offer?*

Basch: We have refrigerated storage, high-security storage and regular shelf storage. It's a very clean facility, but there's nothing special other than that.

Kortum: *Will you expand the Memphis PartsBank warehouse, or just branch out into the other Hubs?*

Basch: We're now at 22,500 square feet, but in March we'll be moving to 95,000 square feet. The space available to PartsBank will effectively double, since Federal Express will also supply their own operations from that facility.

Kortum: *Federal Express' claims rate is one of the lowest in the industry. Is this true for PartsBank too?*

Basch: Yes. In fact, our problems with the warehousing operation in this area are practically zero. That part of the system works extremely well.

As for our service level, we measure service by getting there within an hour of when we told the customer we'd be there; having the right part in the right quantity, and in right condition. That service level has been consistently over 99 percent.

The problems we do have are schedule problems as opposed to any kind of packaging or quality problem. In other words, a scheduled airline might not make it there on time, as opposed to our shipping the wrong quantity or the wrong part in poor condition.

Kortum: *Is packaging part of the PartsBank service?*

Basch: We provide a packaging service for those customers who desire it. However, we recommend that customers with high-value, time-sensitive items prepackage them. For example, pacemakers, printed circuit boards and other high value items are usually prepackaged.

The decision to prepackage or not depends on the individual customer, of course. For example, if a customer such a Raytheon decides to use us for most of his distribution needs, there will be multiple pieces going on the same shipment, and we would then really need to do the packaging. But if the customer uses PartsBank for emergencies only, he could prepackage.

Kortum: *Do you pick up parts from the consignee as well?*

Basch: One of our options is a "Return & Repair" option. Traditionally, the computer industry has had a very significant problem in inventory getting to the consignee (field engineer) and never coming back. Most high technology equipment is repaired these days by exchanging high value components (subassemblies). For example, a $1,000 circuit board would be exchanged if an 85 cent transitor has failed. But what often happens is that the engineer, because he doesn't trust the system, begins stockpiling these boards and may try to fix them himself. As a result, control is lost and repairs are frequently inefficient.

So the option of "R & R" simply says that if we deliver the replacement to that engineer we're going to hang onto it until he gives us the repairable. We'll open the box, pull out the good part, hand it to the engineer, and put the bad one back in the same package. The return airbill is already made out, so all the Federal Express Courier has to do is put it in the box, and the package will automatically go back to PartsBank or back to the customer's repair facility.

Kortum: *How widely is "R & R" being used?*

Basch: Many customers are using it; approximately 12 or 13 out of our 60 customers are using it actively. It's somewhat expensive, in that you're paying for air freight both ways, but the control and lower inventory may justify it.

Kortum: *It still seems like a good way to keep control over expensive components.*

Basch: That's right. People also use it when they have a problem engineer, or a problem part that may be very scarce.

Kortum: *Do you get involved in substituting one part for another?*

Basch: We have not developed that capability, mainly because of the industry's lack of standardization. Each company has to determine on its own, based on experience and technical knowledge, what to substitute.

Kortum: *They should know what they are stocking at PartsBank anyway.*

Basch: Yes. We provide a weekly report that tells each customer basically what he has there. Also, the customer can call up on the phone and order a part, and if we don't have it we'll let him know what is available within seconds.

Kortum: *You can do that even though you're not yet automated?*

Basch: Other than Xerox, which stocks about 10,000 parts, most customers are in the 100's, with some up to about 2,000 parts. So we use a specially designed inventory record system that allows us to find the parts within seconds. As part of the order, we always tell the customer whether we have the part or we don't, so that he can be assured that the part's on its way.

Kortum: *Can the consignee order direct from PartsBank?*

Basch: We allow the customer to authorize whomever he wants to. Each customer submits lists in writing to us, and the authorized people get a plastic, numbered "credit card". When one of them calls PartsBank, he gives his number, which is checked against the list of names. These people could be consignees, field engineers, or whoever the customer authorizes to have a number.

It's also possible to have extra security restrictions. For example, a lot of companies don't want engineers to be able to order a $25,000 part directly, and so it's possible for a company to authorize only certain people to have access to only certain parts. Orders for high value or scarce parts have to come out of corporate headquarters, for example.

That's one reason why we stayed as long as we did on the manual system. It's added a lot of flexibility in terms of individual customers.

That's going to be one of the drawbacks of automating the order entry function. We can computerize quite well, but even so, the customers may lose some individual flexibility.

Kortum: *How can international shipments be handled in PartsBank?*

Basch: We have the capability of delivering on an overnight basis (late the next day) to 14 major cities in Europe out of PartsBank. In other words, an order received by 3:00 p.m. in the afternoon will arrive at the airport in any one of the major 14 cities, except for London, by 3:00 p.m. the next afternoon. That's pretty good service. This does not, however, include customs clearance time.

What we do is use the Federal Express system to Boston, and Swissair handles it from Boston via their parcel center in Zurich.

Other than that, we serve Toronto, Canada directly.

Kortum: *Are Federal Express sales representatives promoting PartsBank?*

Basch: No. That is one reason why we're not growing. At this point, the customer has to approach us, and PartsBank's Operating Manager, Claudia Betzner, would make the sales call.

Kortum: *How will this change after May?*

Basch: During the next fiscal year, we intend to do three things to get PartsBank growing: Automate to provide a faster and more complete service to our customers; develop an audio visual presentation for PartsBank's introduction by Federal Express salespeople; add an inventory management sales/consultant to our PartsBank staff.

Kortum: *How has deregulation affected the operations of PartsBank and Federal Express?*

Basch: Federal Express, of course, will be operating larger airplanes and will have to file tariffs under regulatory requirements. We've bought seven 727s and have options for six more. The first 727 went into operation between Memphis and Los Angeles. Incredibly, it's been full both ways.

As we begin to add 727s its bound to affect our ground operations, as well as how we operate in the field. The second one will go in on April 5th, out of San Francisco. It will also make a stop in Denver to pick up packages from Salt Lake City, Seattle, Portland, etc.

Kortum: *The 727 also eliminates a lot of hand loading.*

Basch: Actually, we're still loading by hand, but we're able to load all day. For example, during the Memphis sort, the container is loaded from 12:30 to 2:30, and then when the plane is loaded, it takes ten more minutes. But with a Falcon, you have to load containers which are then taken out to the plane. We're also finished loading at 2:30, but it takes another hour to load the airplane, because the packages have to be bulk loaded onto the airplane. With the 727 you can be loading all night long and simply load the container on the plane. It's much more efficient.

Kortum: *Would you say that most PartsBank customers are computer or electronics manufacturers?*

Basch: The majority are. However, Union Carbide just came in. They are stocking parts for blood analyzer equipment. We also have several pacemaker companies. Medical electronics involves small high technology and high value type materials. We have one resin manufacturer who stocks chemicals in refrigerated storage. The resin compounds are used in plastic dies. When you get a crack or some other problem in one of the dies, you need the resin and you need it quickly, because it holds up the manufacturing process.

Other than that, Xerox stores copier parts; mainly slow moving items. Very slow moving; once a year type usage.

Kortum: *What types of future business are you looking for?*

Basch: We'll zero in on the traditional market of mid to small electronic companies. In electronics, we believe the big market potential is in inventory management. In other words, if we can show the medium to small electronic's companies that we can do an effective job in managing their inventory dollars, while providing better service, we think that's still our prime market.

Secondarily, we'll go after medical very aggressively. There are also some markets where the total inventory can be captured, but that's downstream.

For example, optical frames, for eyeglasses: I believe that we can put together a system that would drastically reduce inventories in this area. It's an intriguing thing all by itself, but there are substantial savings that a centralized distribution system can provide in that kind of operation.

However, that's a departure from the basic PartsBank concept, in the sense that you're dealing with the consolidation of all of the inventory in the industry, as opposed to the traditional, high value individual component parts.

Kortum: *Who are some of your West Coast customers?*

Basch: We have a lot of customers in the "Silicon Valley" area, including Four-Phase Systems, Beckman Instruments, Data Pathing, Stromburg, Data Graphix, Finnegan, General Automation, and Lear Siegler.

Kortum: *What are the advantages of PartsBank to the Western shipper?*

Basch: I believe that PartsBank can be especially advantageous to Western shippers, for several reasons. One is that the floor tax out there is high, so the more inventory a company can store in PartsBank the better off it is, because there is no floor tax in Memphis. Secondly, there is the time zone problem. There are early departing flights so that an order placed at close of business (say 5:00 p.m.) will miss planes going to most U.S. cities and, therefore, arrive two days later rather than overnight. Thirdly, service at the perimeter of the United States just isn't close to what is available out of the central cities. For example, it's very difficult to get from San Francisco to Little Rock, Arkansas, because of the number of transfers that have to be made. For a passenger, it's difficult enough, but for a package, the chances of getting lost somewhere are quite high. Perimeter cities also don't get as many flights as interior cities. For example, Chicago has the biggest airport because it's an interior city. Flights pass through it, as opposed to a perimeter city, which is either the origin or destination for all but intercontinental flights.

Road?

Within one year of their deregulation, domestic air cargo carriers—as well as freight forwarders now able to take to the air—show they have the potential to be much more competitive with surface carriers.

Consider the following:

• Despite raising some airfreight tariffs an average 16% since their deregulation from Civil Aeronautics Board rate and route control, major domestic airfreight carriers now post rates on some commodities that are less than double the ICC tariffs charged by over-road haulers (see box #1)

"And," says one insider, "many air-industry experts foresee cargo rate price-cutting, especially as more and smaller airfreighters get airborne."

Thus, for example, BN Air Freight, the airfreight forwarder subsidiary of Burlington Northern railroad, has gone airborne, operating a charter cargo air fleet of its own. Over short haul under 500-mile routes, airfreighters can be expected to cut prices, if only to inch toward competitiveness with truckers over the same hauls.

Says a trucker who still champions ICC tariff regulation for trucking, "Here on the ground we're as regulated as ever. Overhead, the potential competition is literally free as a bird."

• While many airfreighters are rapidly expanding their pickup/delivery fleets, most say they have no in-

tention of becoming directly competitive with highway carriers, either over the long haul or short.

Airfreight's buzz-word is "time-sensitive."

Says an airfreight executive, "To ship by air rather than by road, time must still be more valuable to a shipper than the cost of transport."

Yet there are signs that air is indeed honing its road competitiveness.

Typically, Federal Express, once strictly a small package handler, now dispatches some 1,000 delivery trucks in 140 cities and has the capacity, now that it flies a sizable fleet of planes, to carry larger loads—something it had wanted to do previously but had been prohibited by the CAB.

Apparently more contradictory is Flying Tiger Line, the free-world's largest airfreight carrier. Part of the contradiction stems from a corporate structure which finds the airfreight carrier (Flying Tiger Line) outwardly less road-ambitious than its holding company (Tiger International), which boldly declares its highway intent.

"Our program," William M. Caldwell, Flying Tiger Line's vice-president of marketing, told *GO*, "is not designed to get us into the trucking business."

Yet Tiger International's dynamic, aggressive chairman and chief executive (who is likewise chairman of Flying Tiger Line), Wayne M. Hoffman, in a recent and widely publicized speech (see box #2) before industrial traffic managers, declared his big air-cargo line ready "to compete head-to-head for surface traffic" with motor carriers.

Hoffman is no new hand at trucking. A lawyer and former executive vice-president of New York Central, he also ran the railroad's truck line. Moreover, a recent issue of Fortune (June 19, 1978), analyzing Hoffman's and Flying Tigers' post-deregulation dreams, sees visions of trucks . . . a lot of them.

(Continued on next page)

HOW COMPETITIVE ARE TRUCK AND AIR RATES?

Despite airfreight's deregulation and Flying Tigers' own new, significantly lower door-to-door tariffs, air's general commodity rates to air-haul most "time-sensitive" shipments are still flying high—hardly "price competitive" with trucking. But the cost gap is narrowing. Charted here is the air vs. road tariff differential for moving so prosaic a shipment as *100 lbs. of toothpaste, Los Angeles to New York,* and handling it door-to-door:

Flying Tigers	(by air)	
Airport-to-airport (LA to NY) charge		$55.00
5% Federal "airport tax"		2.75
Delivery time: total P&D charges		-3.00
2nd day		
Total airfreight cost		$60.75
Transcontinental trucker	**(by highway)**	
Terminal-to-terminal (LA to NY) charge:		$33.01
min. delivery charge (NY)		3.03
Delivery time: Total over-road cost		$36.04
7 days		

(Continued from preceding page)

According to Fortune, as *both* trucker and air-cargo carrier, Flying Tigers would serve its shippers from assembly line to ultimate customer—warehousing, computer controlling inventory, then transporting the cargo by truck or plane (sometimes by both).

"But," concludes the Fortune analysis, "the profitable development of this system depends on whether Tigers is permitted to use trucks." To become, in a word, a highway common carrier as well as air-cargo carrier.

• Apace with these contradictions loom others, almost all of them coming in the aftermath of airfreight's deregulation.

Foremost are a rash of airfreight innovations which, although they mean new conveniences to air shippers and cost reductions, still fail significantly to bring airfreight rates down to road level.

Among the innovations: new "door-to-door" pickup/delivery service, which in some instances reduces ground-service costs to shippers by up to 90 percent; new container rates which give shippers the incentive to ship more weight in air-cargo containers at lower cost per pound; consolidation of a shipper's former 3-part airfreight bill (ground pickup, air-haulage charge, ground delivery) into a single, precisely calculable billing (something not previously always the case).

One result (simplified here because air-cargo tariffs are nearly as complex as road tariffs) has been a contradiction in itself: for while reducing the door-to-door (meaning pickup/delivery) charges to small shippers (for shipments, say, of under 200 lbs.), airport-to-airport rates have actually been increased.

To reduce the complex to the simple, some airfreighters—led by Flying Tigers—have eliminated the ever-increasing "zone" pickup/delivery charge—the ground charges that increase the farther from an airport a pickup is made and the farther from an airport the shipment is delivered.

Flying Tigers, for example, now charges a flat $1.50, typically, for pickup and delivery—far lower than previous pickup/delivery charges for a small, 100-lb. shipment. Yet while P&D "ground" charges have been substantially *reduced,* "airport-to-airport" tariffs—air transport fees—have been *raised.* Despite higher transport tariffs between such major metropolitan markets as Los Angeles and New York, a small shipper's total air bill has been reduced 15%.

Here's how it works:

100-LB. SHIPMENT, LOS ANGELES TO NEW YORK

Pre-deregulation	
Airport-to-airport transport	$51.10
Federal airport excise tax—5%	2.56
Pickup charge, Los Angeles	8.10
Delivery charge, New York	9.70
Total airbill/100-lb. shipment	*$71.46*
Post-deregulation	
Airport-to-airport transport	$55.00
Federal airport excise tax—5%	2.75
Pickup and delivery ($1.50 *each*)	3.00
Total airbill/100-lb. shipment	*$60.75*

Or consider the same package air-cargoed between Cincinnati and Houston:

100-LB. SHIPMENT, CINCINNATI TO HOUSTON

Pre-deregulation	
Airport-to-airport transport	$36.35
Federal airport excise tax—5%	1.82
Pickup charge, Cincinnati	11.40
Delivery charge, Houston	11.00
Total airbill/100-lb. shipment	*$60.57*
Post-deregulation	
Airport-to-airport transport	$42.00
Federal airport excise tax—5%	2.10
Pickup and delivery ($1.50 *each*)	3.00
Total airbill/100-lb. shipment	*$47.10*

The total airbill down-pricing in this case? An even more sizable 22.2%.

Certainly, as any over-road hauler recognizes, the reduction of P&D charges encourages the shipper with 100 lbs. of freight (marginally "time-sensitive") to go air rather than going highway. And yet, an airfreighter *earns more while in the air*—precisely where its costs are highest.

As Flying Tigers' marketing vice-president Caldwell explained in announcing Tigers' new consolidated P&D rates in door-to-door service:

"Flying Tigers will increase shipper incentives to use our door-to-door services. . . . We are taking the *lowest* pickup and delivery rates for any P&D zone in each of our markets and letting that rate apply to the *entire market area.*"

"This," he continued, "will mean generally lower door-to-door rates for all shipment sizes because currently the farther you get from an airport or central business area, the higher the pickup and delivery rates."

From this ground/air rate manipulation evolves a final—and for truckers—perhaps a critical contradic-

HEAD-TO-HEAD COMPETITION WITH TRUCKING

While executives of the air-cargo arm of Tiger International (Flying Tiger Line) declare the air-freight-carrier has no intention of competing directly with road-haulers, Tiger International chairman Wayne M. Hoffman recently said otherwise—dramatically.

On November 21, addressing 900 National Industrial Traffic League delegates at their annual convention in Bal Harbour, Florida, Hoffman declared airfreighters are ready to challenge any intermodal segment of transport. And, particularly trucking.

Said Hoffman, "We should be free to enter the motor carrier industry both as an adjunct to the air-cargo business as well as to compete head-to-head for surface traffic."

"Intermodal restrictions," insisted Hoffman, "are outdated."

"It is particularly inconsistent," he continued, championing airfreight's and his own Flying Tigers' view, "to fence out air carriers from operation or control of over-the-road truckers when the course of regulation and the realities of day-to-day business concerns have not placed similar restraints on the foray of over-the-road carriers into other modes."

tion: airfreight's immediate need is to make such door-to-door P&D work; and to extend, if not totally eliminate the so-called "ICC exempt zone"—now a 25-mile radius from major air terminals but scheduled in May to extend to 35 miles plus (*GO—March*).

While elimination of ICC "exempt zones" would not immediately nor necessarily put major airfreighters "into the trucking business," it would come close to it, at least on short, near-airport P&D routes.

In fact, however, many airfreighters seem to be "doing P&D business as usual"—meaning leasing or contracting their exempt-zone P&D service, rather than buying, operating or maintaining trucks.

Thus, despite Flying Tigers' own post-deregulation expansion into eight new domestic terminal cities (Anchorage, Atlanta, Charlotte, Dallas, Fort Worth, Houston, San Juan and Cincinnati), and its aim, within five years, to service the U.S.'s 50 largest market cities, it has not become "a trucker."

Quite the contrary.

"We aren't buying trucks," explains Robert L. Husk, senior operations supervisor, distribution services, at Flying Tigers' big Los Angeles airfreight terminal, "We're doing pretty much what we've always done— leasing or contracting with truckers for P&D—but on a larger scale."

Currently, 11 of 17 Flying Tigers' P&D rigs operating from Los Angeles International are leased. Six are contracted from owner-drivers. All carry Flying Tigers' colors (as do their uniformed drivers), but the big airfreighter (although dispatching the rigs) leaves the driving, the ownership, the maintenance, the insurance . . . and the headaches to others. Three years ago, Flying Tigers operated only ten leased rigs from LAX. Should it install lease fleets at all of its new terminals, its fleet total—in terms of bigtime trucking—would still be modest.

Nonetheless, Tigers' LAX fleet manager, having carefully studied the advantages/disadvantages of truck ownership, shrugs. "It's a toss up," he concludes.

How the ball eventually bounces insofar as Flying Tigers' and other airfreighters' excursion into trucking may well depend on how far the present "exempt zone" is stretched (if it is not eliminated altogether) . . . on how fast deregulated air-cargo carriers expand to major U.S. market cities . . . and when or whether, as airfreight tariffs become closer to those of surface carriers, aircargo's top management decides it has become expedient to "compete head-to-head with surface traffic."

DEREGULATED: AIRFREIGHT TAKES OFF

While highway carriers and ICC debate the when, if and whether of over-road deregulation, domestic airfreight—deregulated on Jan. 9, 1978 from Civil Aeronautics Board route and rate control—has become what one insider calls "transport's casebook example of deregulation in action."

The "action" during airfreight's first deregulated year has been fast, furious—and for highway carriers, watching from the sidelines, potentially formidable:

• Airfreight rates, far from falling to a wildfire of price-cutting (as with domestic airfares), have actually risen—by an average 8% during deregulation's first year, with further rate hikes due before this article sees print (airfreight rates were set to rise an average 7.9% in February, for an inflation-pacing overall average 16% rise during air deregulation's first two years).

• All-cargo air fleet capacity, declining by 20.9% between 1970 and 1977, jumped 14.6% during deregulation's first six months. And load-factors increased even more dramatically.

• As airfreighters expanded to cities from which the CAB had previously restricted them, the scramble for aircraft—notably the stretched DC-8 and the 747, the only two U.S.-built cargo planes most airfreighters consider "profitable"— grew frantic. Used DC-8s (Douglas no longer builds the plane) were all but unobtainable. New Boeing 747 freighters, tagged about $60 million each, were price-escalating, some sources said, by as much as half a million dollars a month. In desperation—to keep pace with booming airfreight expansion plans—airfreight's biggies scrounged the overseas market (thus on Feb. 1, Tiger International, Flying Tigers' holding company, entered into negotiations with Singapore Airlines to buy, for upwards of $250 million, seven of that carrier's used Boeing 747s.

• For some, as for all-cargo Flying Tigers, deregulation's impact was unprecedented. Flying Tigers domestic traffic increased 83% during deregulation's first 9 months, due in part to its rapid post-deregulation expansion to 18 major U.S. freight markets, a near doubling of the ten markets the CAB had permitted it to serve pre-deregulation. Overall, industry-wide airfreight traffic increased some 13% over the same 1978 deregulated period . . . a figure significantly lower than the Tigers', say insiders, because other deregulated airfreighters were slower to grasp their new opportunities.

• For others, deregulation's first year was less than upbeat. Big TWA, for one, decided to end its all-cargo service (lack of economic-to-fly cargo planes, rather than competition, was the primary reason for TWA dropping all-cargo flights, say some insiders).

Summed up Flying Tiger board chairman Wayne M. Hoffman, ". . . deregulation permits free entry but also free exit."

On October 26, 1958, a Pan American Boeing 707 departed New York for Paris, marking the initial flight of an American-built jetliner in commercial service. The U.S. had arrived late on the jet transport scene; the British Comet, French Caravelle and Soviet Tupolev 104 had all preceded the 707 in passenger carrying operations. But by virtue of technological superiority, the latecomer American plane builders swiftly achieved dominance of the commercial transport market and held it through two decades; today, 85 percent of the jetliners flying the world's airways are of U.S manufacture.

As we commemorate the 20th anniversary of U.S.-built jet service, American manufacturers face a new threat to their traditional lead in transport sales. The technology gap has narrowed and foreign competitors are mounting their strongest-ever challenge. The commercial transport segment of the U.S. aerospace industry is responding with plans to introduce a new family of advanced technology jetliners. Here is a report on the competitive situation and the types of airplanes and engines on which the U.S. is counting to maintain its leadership, an important factor in the U.S. economy as a whole and the international trade balance in particular.

The summer of '78 witnessed a number of major developments in the world of air transport production:

• Early in July, having received a substantial number of orders, the French/German consortium called Airbus Industrie formally committed itself to development of the A310, an advanced technology version of its Airbus twin-engine transport.

• Only a week later, while aviation observers were still digesting the significance of this new threat to U.S. air transport dominance, Boeing Commercial Airplane Co. threw a counterpunch. On the basis of an order from United Airlines, the largest commercial transport order in aviation history,

Boeing launched development of its new 767 widebody twinjet.

• In August, Lockheed Aircraft Corp. announced plans for an advanced technology, flexible-range version of its L-1011 TriStar called the Dash 400.

• At the end of August, Boeing announced still another new development: the twinjet standard body 757, a companion to the 767 aimed at a different segment of the market. Orders for 40 757s from Eastern Airlines and British Airways provided the production base which enabled formal start of hardware development.

These airplanes, along with the earlier launched McDonnell Douglas DC-9 Super 80, are the advance members of a new generation of jetliners which will begin airline service in the early 1980s. Several other models, on both sides of the Atlantic, are waiting in the wings; years of research have produced firm designs, but transport builders cannot afford to lay out heavy development money—in some cases more than a billion dollars—until airline customers sign contracts.

There will be a great many orders. The airlines, financially pressed for several years, deferred orders for new airplanes to replace older, noisier and less efficient transports. Now that they are regaining financial health, they must not only replace older planes, they must also acquire additional capacity to meet rapidly-mounting demand; although airline traffic is already at record levels, estimates indicate that it will almost double between now and 1990. Thus, the greatest air transport production boom in history is forecast. Estimates of airline purchases over the next decade range upward from $60 billion and the figure could reach $100 billion.

The competition among aircraft builders will be—and already is—intense. European manufacturers have long thirsted for a greater share of the market and they are working hard to get it. American plane builders are equally determined to maintain their market dominance. The international struggle is far more than a battle among manufacturers—it has strong effect on the economies and the peo-

1. *Pratt & Whitney JT8D Dash 209.* The metal, sculpture-like fixture in the Dash 209's tailpipe is an exhaust mixer which reduces jet engine roar, one of the major causes of aircraft noise. In the turbofan type of engine, there are two separate streams of air. One flows through the combustion chamber, is mixed with fuel and burned; the other bypasses the combustor and is ducted—to the rear of the engine. The mixer combines the high velocity stream of exhaust gas with the slower bypass air stream to create a uniform-speed exhaust; the result is lower noise and lower fuel consumption. Noise and fuel burn of the Dash 209 are further reduced by internal design techniques. This engine, which will make its service debut on the McDonnell Douglas DC-9 Super 80, features lower levels of objectionable exhaust emissions in addition to sharply reduced noise and fuel expenditure.

2. *McDonnell Douglas DC-9 Super 80.* Scheduled for operational use in 1980, the Super 80 will be the first of the new generation of U.S. jetliners to enter airline service. It looks very much like earlier members of the DC-9 family, but it contains a number of advanced technology features. Principal among them are new turbofan engines which combine reduced fuel consumption with lower levels of noise and exhaust emissions, and a substantially larger wing which further contributes to fuel savings. The Super 80 is 43½ feet longer than the original DC-9 and—depending on customer's choice of seating arrangements—carries roughly twice the passenger load (137 to 172 passengers). The airplane will operate for the most part on routes of less than 1,000 miles, but its designers built in additional range capability to make it suitable for medium-range flights of about 2,000 miles with full passenger load.

ple of the various nations involved.

Of paramount importance is the international trade balance. The U.S. is already staggering under the impact of huge trade deficits which have caused an alarming decline in the value of the dollar and increased inflation at home. The nation can ill afford any reduction of transport sales abroad, which has been one of the bright areas of a generally gloomy export-import picture. In fact, a national aim is to increase exports; highly-valued high technology products, such as jetliners, offer the best opportunity for improving the nation's export posture.

New jetliner orders also mean new jobs, a particularly important matter at a time of high unemployment in the U.S. Tens of thousands of jobs are involved in the international competition; one indicator is a labor union estimate that a single United Air Lines order to Boeing may generate as many as 15,000 new jobs.

Elements of the Competition

One might assume that, having dominated the jet transport scene for two decades, U.S. manufacturers would be favorites in the new round of international competition. That's true to some degree, but there have been a number of changes in 20 years, changes that have considerably eroded the American competitive position. Still, U.S. industry retains some of its traditional advantages.

One of them is technology. Although foreign plane and engine builders have substantially improved their technological capability, the U.S. is still Number One. Another edge is the continuity factor. Most of the world's airlines are now flying American-built equipment. Operators know that U.S. planes perform well and that they are designed with utmost attention to operator profitability; they know, too, that they can count on effective post-sale support from U.S. producers. Like the home consumer pondering purchase of a new TV, airlines tend to favor manufacturers who have served them well—unless there are compelling reasons to change.

Still another advantage is the broader American product line. it must be remembered that the competition is not confined to the new generation of airplanes; there is a steady flow of orders for transports already in production, such as the Boeing 707, 727, 737, 747, Lockheed's L-1011 TriStar and the McDonnell Douglas DC-9 and DC-10. The U.S. offers current or new aircraft across the entire spectrum of airline needs with the single exception of the supersonic transport, which plays little part in the competition for the 1980s.

These American plus factors make it necessary for Number Two—foreign competitors collectively—to try harder. They are doing so, and they have one major advantage over U.S. manufacturers: the strong backing of their governments.

Recognizing the economic value of technology advancement, foreign nations have made increasingly large investments in research and development, especially in commercial transport technology; by contrast, the U.S. R&D growth rate has declined. Foreign R&D investments are paying off in greater technological capability, evidenced by the growing number of foreign-built aircraft entering the world inventory.

Foreign government support goes well beyond R&D; it has several other influences in the current competition, one of them "directed procurement." Most foreign airlines are wholly or partially government-owned; this creates a situation whereby the government may tell its airline what type of airplane to buy, without regard for technological merit.

Foreign competitors have a big edge in government subsidization of commercial transport development programs. U.S. plane builders must raise development money from private sources. But most foreign manufacturing companies are either nationalized or government controlled. Thus, foreign governments are often participants in jetliner programs, absorbing most of the heavy financial risks and putting up 50 to 90 percent of the costs of launching a new program.

Foreigners charge in rebuttal that U.S. manufacturers are similarly subsidized by NASA technology develop-

Air Transports:
The New Generation

BY JAMES J. HAGGERTY
Associate Editor, Aerospace Magazine

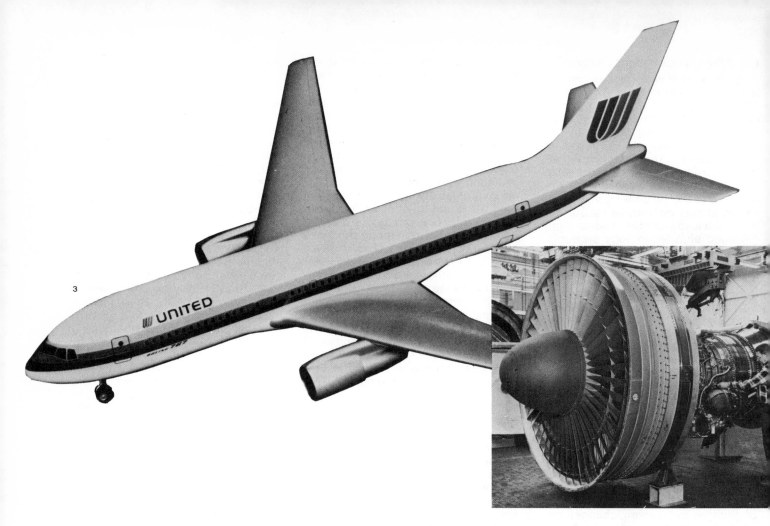

3

ment and by commercially-applicable fallout from military aircraft programs. It is not a valid argument. NASA research does make a contribution, but it is modest in relation to overall transport development requirements. As for the military fallout benefit, the argument suffers from outdated information. There was a time when commercial plane builders got a developmental headstart by applying some technology earlier developed for military aircraft. But in the last 20 years, there has been sharp divergence of military and commercial emphasis; today there is little fallout from government-sponsored programs. In fact, it sometimes works the other way. The recent military purchase of McDonnell Douglas DC-10s as transport-tankers is a case where the government got the fallout benefit, since the development costs had already been paid by private enterprise.

Additionally, government backing with regard to financing airplane sales make it possible for a foreign competitor to offer a prospective customer a better deal. In recent instances, foreign manufacturers have won important airplane and engine sales by providing—with government help—extremely generous loan terms, such as long-term, full-purchase-price guaranteed loans with no down payment. Such terms are in violation of an exist-

ing international agreement and would not have been possible had the airlines opted for American equipment.

Foreign government assistance takes other forms. A recent case in point was a competition involving the U.S. McDonnell Douglas DC-10 and the French/German Airbus; the customer was China Airlines of Taiwan. The Airbus won the order—but, some observers say, only because the French government sweetened the deal by throwing into the package landing lights in Paris for the Taiwan airline. This deal, another apparent violation of the international rules, drew the ire of Rep. Mark Hannaford of California, who protested vigorously and said he would pursue "a legislative solution to this kind of predatory competition."

So, in addition to improved technological posture, foreign competitors have a lot of advantages not shared by their American counterparts. The latter find themselves competing not only with foreign producers but with foreign governments as well. U.S. industry officials have sharply criticized unfair foreign competitive techniques and called for U.S. government action to correct the trend or to provide similar assistance to American airplane and engine manufacturers.

Areas of Competition
Excluding very short-haul commuter

airliners, but including planes currently in production which will be flying throughout the 1980s, there may be more than a score of commercial jetliner types competing for sales.

Not counting the airlines of the communist world, there are some 4,800 jetliners in service today. About one-fourth of them are more than 10 years old; they constitute the replacement market, estimated at about 40 percent of the total market for deliveries in the eighties; the rest of the market lies in the need for additional capacity. Most of the aging aircraft to be replaced are in the medium-range, medium-capacity class. In addition, studies of projected traffic growth indicate that the greatest need for additional capacity will also be in the medium-range, medium-capacity category. The differing route structures and other requirements of the various airlines make it difficult to define this category precisely. For simplicity, industry marketing people are calling it the 200-seat class; actually, seating plans accommodate from 180 to 230 passengers.

There is also large market potential for new airplanes of lesser capacity, for use on short-haul routes or on certain medium-range trips where passenger demand does not require the higher-density of the "200-seat" jetliner. In this category are new generation airplanes ranging from feeder

5

liners with fewer than 100 seats to relatively large twinjets accommodating up to 180.

In the large airplane category—those seating upwards of 230 and having transcontinental or longer range—all currently operating jetliners are products of the last decade and do not figure in replacement plans. However, the demands of additional capacity for future traffic growth indicate that substantial new orders will be forthcoming. In this class, the U.S. has clear edge with its family of long-range, high-capacity widebody jetliners.

To give themselves widest sales latitude, manufacturers are designing jetliners to accommodate an airline's choice of different engine types. Engines are in themselves high-value, labor-intensive products, hence they play an important part in the competition with respect to the national economy benefits involved. The engine situation is complicated by the fact that a foreign-built airplane may be powered by U.S.-built engines, or vice versa; primary powerplant for the Airbus, for example, is a General Electric engine and at least one Airbus model will have Pratt & Whitney engines.

The national economy potential of jetliner sales is further complicated by a trend toward increasing international joint ventures. U.S. manufacturers already have, or are working on, a num-

3. *Boeing 767.* A \$1.2 billion United Airlines order in July launched full-scale development and production of the Boeing 767, first new Boeing jetliner since the 747 start of 1966. United's 767s will be powered by two Pratt & Whitney JT8D-7R engines; customers may opt for either of two other advanced technology engines. The 767 is aimed at the "200-seat" market, a convenient designation for medium-range aircraft accommodating from 180 to 230 passengers; the 767 seats about 200 in typical mixed-class configuration. Its design makes use of a number of advanced technologies to combat rising airline operating costs. Fuel burned per passenger seat, the company says, is 35 percent less than earlier medium-range jetliners; a 10-airplane replacement fleet could save an operator \$14 million a year in fuel costs. Other design achievements include the two-aisle passenger cabin pioneered in the 747, use of new structural materials for weight saving and longer airframe life, reduced noise and emission levels, and a number of advanced airplane systems. First delivery is scheduled for mid-1982.

4. *Pratt & Whitney JT9D-7R,* selected by United Airlines as the powerplant for its Boeing 767 widebody twinjets. A high bypass turbofan, the Dash 7R develops 44,300 pounds of thrust. The "R" stands for "rerated," meaning that the engine is designed to operate at less than maximum design thrust; this permits use of less complex turbine hardware, reducing engine weight, fuel consumption and maintenance costs. Pratt & Whitney's JT9D family consists of six models spanning the thrust range from 39,000 to 56,000 pounds; they are applicable to a variety of airplanes from the new medium-size twinjets like the 767 to the big, long-ranging transports powered by three or four engines. Pratt & Whitney is also developing a new, advanced technology turbofan specifically aimed at the new medium-range trijets; designated JT10D-132, it develops 32,000 pounds thrust and is scheduled for certification late in 1981. The company is studying other versions of the JT10D which would cover a thrust range from 25,000 to 35,000 pounds.

5. *Lockheed L-1011 Dash 400 TriStar.* Lockheed's new generation jetliner is an advanced technology version of the company's trijet which will have the same fuselage diameter but will be 20 feet shorter. The smaller airplane will accommodate 200-230 passengers, compared with up to 400 in earlier models of the TriStar. Thus, Lockheed is focusing on the upper end of the "200-seat" market and offering flexibility with regard to range—medium distance, transcontinental flight or, with an optional change, a nonstop full-load range of more than 5,000 miles; this would allow an airline to use a single type of 200-seater on a wide variety of routes, for substantial savings in crew training and spare parts costs. The Dash 400 is designed for the operator's choice of three advanced technology engine types in the 42,000 pound thrust class. Other advanced technology features include active controls which contribute to reduced drag, hence lower fuel consumption; additional fuel savings through an automatic engine control system which provides maximum fuel efficiency throughout a flight; a digital autopilot with five times greater reliability; and an automatic takeoff thrust control system for considerably longer engine life and reduced maintenance costs. Assuming a 1981 production start, the Dash 400 could be delivered in 1981.

6. *General Electric CF6.* This family of high bypass turbofans powers twin-engine (Airbus), three-engine (DC-10) and four-engine (747) jetliners. The CF6 is built in two basic models: the CF6-6 in the 40,000 pounds thrust class, and the CF6-50 with 50,000 pounds thrust or more. The family includes nine production models and three new models in development; among the latter is the CF6-32, which extends the thrust ratings of the CF6 family into a new area—30,000 to 36,000 pounds. This engine, to be certified in 1981, has the basic CF6-6 core but has a smaller fan and a number of other refinements; it is a candidate for powering medium twinjets and trijets of the new generation. Like other engine manufacturers, GE has focused developmental effort on reducing fuel consumption; the company says its CF6 engines have a specific fuel consumption level 25 percent below that of earlier turbofans. GE has been able to get an appreciable reduction of noise in the CF6 engines by means of a number of innovations, including changes in the fan design and new sound absorption materials in engine inlet and exhaust areas. Additionally, an advanced combustor design contributes to smokeless engine operation and substantially reduced pollutant emissions.

ber of arrangements whereby foreign companies participate on a cost-and-work-sharing basis in production of a U.S. airplane or engine. This reduces the financing need for a new development program and gives the U.S. teammate access to a foreign market that might otherwise be denied by the foreign practice of directed procurement. Although jobs and profits are divided, there is still substantial benefit to the U.S. economy in such arrangements.

The New Generation

Some may have expected the new family of jetliners to be dramatically different in appearance from their predecessors. They are not, for the reason that they are still subsonic airplanes operating in the same flight regime—500-600 miles per hour and 30,000-40,000 feet altitude—as the planes they will supersede. The dictates of aerodynamic science make all airplanes of similar flight performance more or less similar in basic design. So, with variations in wing shape, fuselage width and engine mounting, the members of the new family resemble their forebears, and they also bear considerable resemblance to each other.

Nonetheless, they are new airplanes, incorporating advanced technology developed over the last decade. For the most part they are "derivative" airplanes, derived from earlier designs; this is hardly surprising, because it makes design sense to use a proven technology that is still applicable. All of the new generation, however, have advanced technology features aimed at reducing airline operating costs, lowering maintenance requirements and improving environmental characteristics. The degree of advanced technology varies, but generally the jetliners of the new generation will offer some or all of these improvements:

• Dramatically improved engine performance with regard to fuel consumption, a particularly important factor in light of still-rising prices for fuel, a major contributor to total airline operating costs.

• Significantly lower engine noise levels and a reduction in objectionable exhaust emissions.

• Design innovations which allow longer engine life and reduced maintenance.

• Advanced technology aerodynamic improvements, particularly new wings, which contribute to lower rates of fuel consumption by easing the engines' workload.

• Advanced structures for extending airframe life.

• New flight and engine control systems and digital autopilots with substantially improved reliablity.

• Interior improvements for greater passenger comfort, such as new seating arrangements, lower levels of cabin

7. *Boeing 757.* The twin-engine 757 is a short-to-medium range jetliner which combines the fuselage width of Boeing's 727/737 airplanes with an advanced technology wing and new engines. The new plane has certain features of both its predecessors and certain performance advantages, particularly in the important matter of fuel consumption: 40 percent less, Boeing says, than the airplanes the 757 will displace. Powerplants are two 33,500-pound-thrust engines; the customer may choose one of three optional types, and with any of the engine types the 757 would have lower noise and emission levels. Eastern Airlines and British Airways, first purchasers of the 757, both selected the Rolls-Royce RB211 Dash 535 engine.

8. *McDonnell Douglas DC-10.* The airplane shown is the Series 30 model of the McDonnell Douglas trijet, already in airline service. The company is planning a "stretched" higher-capacity version of the intercontinental DC-10. It would be an advanced technology airplane incorporating new engines for reduced fuel consumption and a variety of advanced avionics equipment. McDonnell Douglas is also working on an all-freight DC-10.

9. *General Electric/SNECMA CFM56 turbofan.* The CFM56 is under development by the Paris-based CFM International, a company jointly owned by General Electric Co. and the French engine manufacturer SNECMA. The CFM56 is an advanced technology engine featuring improvements in fuel consumption rates along with reduced levels of noise and emissions. The engine is scheduled for certification late in 1979; initial versions will produce 24,000 pounds thrust but growth to more than 27,000 pounds is planned. The CFM56 is intended for use on short to medium-range transports, such as the European JET 1 and JET 2, and for re-engining some older planes, such as the Boeing 707 and the McDonnell Douglas DC-8.

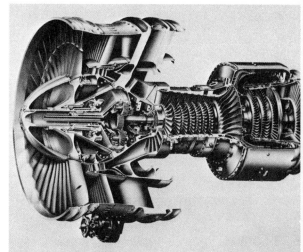

10. *McDonnell Douglas ATMR.* The projected Advanced Technology Medium Range twinjet is aimed primarily at airline regional routes. Its design is based on an advanced supercritical wing and the airplane would also have the latest in propulsion systems for reduced fuel consumption and lower exhaust emissions. In various seating configurations, it could accommodate from 166 to 200 passengers.

11. *Avco Lycoming ALF 502H Turbofan.* A new but already certificated version of Lycoming's moderate thrust engine family, the ALF 502H will power the British Aerospace 146 four-engine feederliner, expected to debut in 1982. The ALF 502H produces 6,700 pounds of thrust in the feederliner installation, but more powerful versions have been developed. The engine offers exceptional fuel efficiency and extremely low noise levels; it is considerably quieter than turboprop engines now operating in short-haul aircraft. A simply-designed engine, it also features smokeless exhaust with minimal undesirable emissions.

noise and better pressurization/air conditioning systems.

New U.S. Transport Family

Among the new generation of U.S. jetliners already in development or projected are these:

• *Boeing 767,* in development with first deliveries scheduled for 1982. The 767 is a new twinjet widebody design intended for the 200-seat, medium-range market. It will be built in two versions: the 767-200, carrying about 200 passengers, and the 767-100 with 180 seats.

• *Boeing 777,* a three-engine companion to the 767 which would carry 210 passengers on longer-ranging and overwater routes.

• *Boeing 757,* a standard body twinjet targeted for the lower density market; it accommodates 174 in a typical mixed class configuration. First deliveries are scheduled for 1983.

• *Lockheed L-1011 Dash 400,* a shortened, reduced-capacity version of the company's TriStar aimed at the higher end of the "200-seat" market with accommodations for 220-233. If airline orders are forthcoming in 1978, the plane could be delivered in 1981.

• *McDonnell Douglas DC-10.* The company is planning an advanced technology, higher-capacity version of its trijet.

• *McDonnell Douglas ATMR,* or Advanced Technology Medium Range jetliner, a projected twinjet transport designed for the lower end of the 200-seat class (166-200 passengers).

Foreign-built Competitors

Lined up against the American jets are several new planes to be built in Europe, all of them multinational risk-sharing projects, some of them involving extensive American participation. They include:

• *The Airbus Industrie A 310 Airbus,* a twinjet transport already in develop-

ment and slated for initial deliveries in 1982. The 310 is an advanced technology, scaled-down version of the Airbus types now in production; it has a capacity of 200 passengers, compared with 220-345 in earlier models of the airplane. The 310 has been ordered by four foreign airlines and others, including one American carrier, have options for future orders. Airbus Industrie is a European consortium controlled largely by French and German interests, with lesser degrees of participation by The Netherlands and Spain.

• *The Joint European Transport (JET),* which is actually two airplanes —Jet 1 and Jet 2—in the short-to-medium range category. The JETs are relatively small twin-engine airliners; JET 1 has 130 seats and JET 2 accommodates 160. The proposed JETs would be built by the Airbus team, possibly with British participation.

• *The British Aerospace 146,* approved for development and scheduled for first deliveries in 1982. A feederliner for airlines serving small cities and towns, the 146 is essentially a short-haul airplane but it is capable of a maximum range of more than 1,000 miles. Powered by four American-built low-noise turbofans, the plane will carry 71 to 109 passengers. Avco Corp.'s Lycoming Division will supply the engines and negotiations are under way whereby Avco would also produce the jetliner's wings. Similar negotiations are being conducted for Swedish and Italian participation.

U.S. ENGINES

Among the major American-built engine types that figure prominently in the international competition are these:

• *Avco Lycoming ALF 502H turbofan,* powerplant for the British Aerospace 146. Rated at 6,700 pounds thrust and featuring exceptionally low noise levels, the 502H is an advanced

model of the engine family used to power a number of executive transports.

• *General Electric CF6-45B,* turbofan powerplant for the Airbus 310, with 46,500 pounds of thrust; a companion version of the engine is designed to power special performance models of the Boeing 747. GE is producing several other models of the CF6 engine family with thrust ratings ranging from 40,000 to 52,500 pounds of thrust; three new CF-6 models, incorporating further gains in fuel savings and other improvements, are in development.

• *General Electric/SNECMA CFM-56,* a 24,000 pound thrust turbofan being developed for certification in 1979. To be marked and manufactured by DFM International, a company jointly owned by GE and the French engine firm SNECMA, the CFM-56 is applicable to short-medium range members of the new jetliner generation, or for re-engining some of the older transports such as the Boeing 707 and the McDonnell Douglas DC-8.

• *Pratt & Whitney Dash 209,* newest member of the JT8D family of engines, the most widely used commercial powerplants. The Dash 209 is the powerplant for the McDonnell Douglas DC-9 Super 80.

• *Pratt & Whitney JT9D-7R,* turbofan powerplant for the Boeing 767, which covers a thrust range from 39,000 to 46,000 pounds; other members of the JT9D family fit airplane needs from 46,000 to 56,000 pounds thrust.

• *Pratt & Whitney JT10D Dash 132,* a new turbofan development expected to be certified for airline use by the end of 1981. Rated at 32,000 pounds thrust, the Dash 132 is specially aimed at Boeing's 777 trijet; other models of the JT10D have thrust outputs ranging from 25,000 to 35,000 pounds and are applicable to twin-engine designs in the medium-size category.

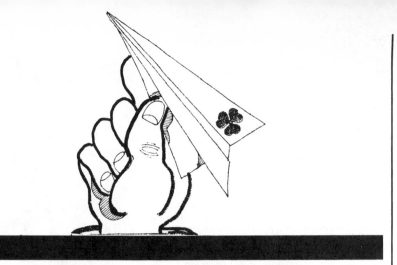

365 DAYS AFTER DEREGULATION

By Frank Kortum

What did air cargo deregulation accomplish during its first year? According to many shippers, the benefits have been obscured by rate increases that the carriers feel were kept artificially low under the CAB regime. But even if shippers and forwarders are dissatisfied with the higher rates, they are keeping the cargo space filled. One air freight marketing executive contacted by Pacific Traffic was not exaggerating very much when he said that his airline could double its cargo capacity and still not satisfy demand.

Air cargo deregulation was originally supposed to be a "test case" for deregulation of the rest of the industry. The theory was that air cargo would be given a chance to perform under a deregulated environment for a while, after which the implications of removing controls on the entire industry could be analyzed. That this theory was largely a smokescreen could be seen in the emphasis the Carter administration put on passenger deregulation almost as soon as the next session of Congress convened.

Now, of course, deregulation is a fact of life for the entire industry, and since passenger service still "calls the shots" for most airlines, it's going to be hard to be sure of the effect of passenger deregulation on air cargo. The line of airline company representatives that waited for literally days outside of the Civil Aeronautics Board offices in Washington, D.C. until President Carter finally signed the new law exemplifies the relative importance the carriers attach to passenger routes. We won't know immediately what will happen to the route structure that existed before deregulation. Although unused routes (those for which the airlines had authority but were not serving) were opened up on a first come-first serve basis, so that theoretically, routes could be taken away from established carriers and given to new operators, the "establishment" wasn't caught napping; United Airlines made sure it was first in line at the CAB window. In addition, the airlines got about 45 days to decide how they wanted to use their new authority, so we won't know immediately what, if any, changes to expect in this area.

IMPACT ON CARGO SERVICE

But any changes in the passenger route structure will have a substantial impact on cargo service, simply due to the role played by belly cargo space. For most of the more than 500 cities that now have scheduled airline service, airline deregulation will bring changing patterns of travel, and, as a result, changing patterns of air cargo service.

Industry observers predict that some small cities probably will lose airline service, while the airlines add service at already saturated metropolitan airports.

For the smaller and medium-size cities, deregulation will mean fewer long-distance flights. With airlines free to fly where they want, the trend toward hub-and-spoke route systems is expected to accelerate. Airlines will concentrate their efforts on routes where they have the greatest opportunity to fill their planes. This means that there will be more and more flights from small cities to regional hubs, where passengers (and freight) will have to change planes for distant destinations. It also means that airport operators and city officials will now have to work harder to keep the schedules they already have and to attract additional airline service.

Civil Aeronautics Board member Elizabeth E. Bailey says the problem of small and medium-size communities "is going to become worse before it becomes better." Scheduled airlines cannot economically operate large jet airliners into most small cities, and past CAB policies have discouraged design of planes with 30 to 60 seats by requiring that unregulated commuter airlines must operate planes with 30 or fewer seats. Therefore, according to Bailey, the "scarcity of such planes means service to smaller communities may not be as good as we might wish in the short run." But the CAB is lifting the small-plane restriction, and Bailey says that "the joint effect of our rule-making and the new legislation should be to encourage commuter services and also to encourage the smaller trunk and local-service carriers to develop new connecting hubs at terminals that now receive only limited service." The new law permits subsidies to commuter airlines, so no city should lose all air service.

NEW OPPORTUNITIES

Saturation at such hubs as Atlanta will create opportunities for some cities. Memphis, for example, already is developing into a secondary Southeastern hub, benefiting from crowding at Atlanta. United Airlines plans a sharp increase in its service through Memphis, adding 16 daily flights. Similarly, PSA, Allegheny, Braniff, Frontier, Hughes Airwest, Northwest, Texas International and Ozark have already expressed interest in serving Oakland International Airport.

WHERE ARE THE FREIGHTERS?

All of this passenger-oriented activity tends to overshadow the role of the new all-cargo carrier, who had been relied on to bring rates down after the grandfather provisions expired.

This may be because there probably won't be that many new entries. Of course, there has been some expansion of existing service, the most notable example being the move by Federal Express into Boeing 727s, but this seems to be

(Continued from page 26)

more of a natural extension of the carrier's small package role; Federal is not going after a different kind of freight with the new plane as yet. For its part, Flying Tigers made a dramatic move into the Sunbelt in one of the biggest service expansions in its history, encountering some growing pains in the process. Several airlines and forwarders have moved freighters into the Seattle/Portland/Los Angeles corridor.

But for the time being there is no indication that there is going to be the flood of new entries that CAB Chairman Alfred Kahn and others had counted on to keep rates down. Few, if any, combination carriers that were not already operating freighters put any on order in advance of total deregulation, and at press time, spokesmen for Boeing and McDonnell-Douglas said there were no orders for freighters from "new" companies. This is hardly surprising, since the high initial and operating costs of this sophisticated equipment puts it out of reach of most new operators. Where will these new entries get their planes? Perhaps from a company such as American Jet Industries, in Van Nuys, California, a company whose activities include, among other things, the conversion of passenger aircraft.

NO INVENTORY

But at the present time a customer can't just come in off the street and pick up a cargo airplane, because there's no inventory. Such planes are "snapped up" quickly, according to William Boone, Director of Marketing. His company is "extremely busy converting older passenger airplanes into freighters. It's gotten to be a big business, and we've got backlogs like you wouldn't believe."

In fact, AJI can't even find any more Lockheed Electras to convert, and so it recently purchased 16 of TWA's fleet of Convair 880s, with options on another eight. When contacted by Pacific Traffic, the company was in the process of converting the first of them to a cargo configuration. But it already had received "lots of inquiries" about the planes, even though they hadn't been advertised yet. And if past experience is any guide, the planes will probably be sold before they get out of the hangar door. There have even been instances where American Jet had orders for freighter conversions before they were able to get the planes released from their former owners. However, this kind of activity was going on before deregulation. "For the last four years, anything that we put a cargo door in, we sold," Boone said.

"15 CENTS PER TON MILE"

Even though the 880 is now obsolete as a passenger plane, it can still make money in cargo service, and can move freight for less than 15 cents per ton mile. As a freighter, the 880 can carry an increased payload: 50,000 pounds for 1,800 nautical miles, with reserves, at an operating cost of about $1,800 per hour. A used Convair 880, "in reasonably good condition," painted in the customer's paint scheme, and ready to haul cargo, will have a base price of about $1.5 million.

A Lockheed Electra (if available) costs about the same. It can carry a 36,000 pound payload for 1,500 miles, and it can't move as fast as the 880. But it can operate in and out of airports with 5,000 foot runways, while the Convair requires an international-size airport.

About 1/3 of American Jet's sales at its Van Nuys facility come from freighter conversions, although this activity uses, by far, the majority of the company's employees. "It's very labor-intensive," Boone said, noting that AJI is certified as an unlimited airframe repair station. "We literally gut the plane, right down to bare metal. Of course, in the process of the conversion, we bring the airplane up to snuff mechanically. We give it a searching inspection; it's the ideal time to do it, because it's all apart. It looks like a new airplane when it rolls out of the shop." The company installs a cargo tie-down track system, and the customer supplies his own roller conveyor system, which he can install in a few hours.

THE NOISE PROBLEM

What about federally-mandated noise standards, which some consider to be a gun pointed at prime-time all-cargo operations? Well, the Convair 880 won't meet them. But an airplane that will, costs about $6 million. "The operator is going to have to realize that he's buying a low cost airplane," Boone said. "He's got about six years to operate it before it will have to be written off." A Convair could be re-engined, but Boone doubts whether it would be economically feasible to do so. Electras, of course, "will be around forever," because they meet the noise standards.

Where are AJI's converted freighters sold? Boone estimates that it's about a 50/50 split between domestic and foreign operators. In domestic service, the planes are going mostly to contract carriers. For example, Fleming International, which has purchased four planes from American Jet, regularly picks up a load of electronic components in Los Angeles and flies it to San Juan, Puerto Rico, where the components are assembled into CB radios. On the return trip, Fleming drops the radios off at distribution centers across the country on the way back to Los Angeles to pick up another load of parts. And from where Boone sits, contract air carriers are growing even faster than common carriers. Other contract carriers that AJI has dealt with include Great Northern Airlines (based in Alaska) and Hawaiian Airlines.

Hawaiian's air cargo division presently has five Electras in service, flying automotive parts from Detroit to various markets throughout the country. Four more Electras are on order, with three of the planes scheduled for delivery by the end of November and the final aircraft due shortly after. Some of the planes were purchased with cargo doors and some had to be converted.

CONTRACT CARRIAGE IS FIRST

"The common carriers," Boone explained, "generally operate newer equipment. They can afford to operate stretched DC8-63Fs at $11 million each. It's the little guy that buys the older cargo equipment. He can compete with the common carrier in that he doesn't leave until he's full. He doesn't have a schedule to maintain whether he's got cargo on board or not. He's got a contract to move a certain amount of cargo, and he goes out at gross weight every time. So even though his equipment may be a little more expensive to operate, he's got two things going for him: it didn't cost him much to acquire it, compared to the common carrier, and he's got a 100 percent load factor each time."

Boone also hopes to take advantage of the burgeoning growth of the small package carriers. He predicts that as they get bigger, they'll begin to encounter freight "that they can't get in the door," at which time they'll decide that they need one of his cargo airplanes, with a bigger door. He points out that these operators also tend to use older equipment, because it doesn't cost them much to get it. "But the small package operator, after he's established, and starts giving good service, will find that shippers will want to give him more and bigger pieces of freight."

The process Boone is describing, however, will not happen overnight, and this means that even though air cargo is now open to everyone, many shippers will have to wait for the lower rates that come with increased competition among the air common carriers. Unfortunately, Alfred Kahn, who was so confident in predicting lower air cargo rates under total deregulation, has gone on to other things. While we hope he is successful in his attempts to control inflation for President Carter, it's too bad that he's not around to see the consequences, for better or worse, of what he has helped accomplish. ✈

Deregulation Sparks Criticism

Loss of service to small and medium-sized cities draws anguished cries, but congressional amendment unlikely

By Michael Feazel

Washington—Little congressional sentiment to amend the Airline Deregulation Act of 1978 is surfacing, despite mounting criticism because of the proliferation of lost airline service to small and medium-sized cities.

A Civil Aeronautics Board study indicates 34 hub and 281 nonhub airports received less airline service Feb. 1, 1979, than a year earlier. An AVIATION WEEK & SPACE TECHNOLOGY survey indicates airlines either have cut or have announced plans to cut service to at least 60 airports since Feb. 1.

Despite the service cutbacks to some cities, nationwide air service was up 8.4% in the past year, according to the CAB study. The increases were in all regions of the country and in cities of all sizes, the CAB said.

The service cutbacks have provoked cries of outrage from local civic officials and legislators. Among the leading congressional critics have been Sens. Jennings Randolph (D.) and Robert Byrd (D.) of West Virginia, George McGovern (D.-S. D.), John Stennis (D.-Miss.) and Rep. G. V. "Sonny" Montgomery (D.-Miss.).

West Virginia's capital, Charleston, is losing 50% of its airline service as a result of United Airlines cutbacks. Eight Mississippi cities have experienced service cutbacks, and South Dakota is facing the possibility of major cutbacks if the Western-Continental merger is approved.

But those legislators as well as those from two of the biggest service losers, Alaska and California, have indicated little interest in legislation to make it more difficult for airlines to 'leave markets. Instead, they are focusing most of their efforts on the airlines and the CAB in an effort to stop or delay the service cutbacks or find replacement carriers.

Some legislators are refraining from supporting legislation blocking exits because they believe their hands are tied by their votes in favor of the deregulation act. The only exception to date is Sen. McGovern, who is considering legislation to limit market exits.

"The senator has not committed himself to anything, he is just considering options," one aide said. "He has a whole laundry list of ideas, but we haven't got anything down for drafting."

Sen. Howard W. Cannon (D.-Nev.), chairman of the Senate Committee on Commerce, Science and Transportation, has scheduled aviation subcommittee hearings on airline deregulation for Apr. 25. The oversight hearings will focus on changes in service levels.

The hearings are not a result of any pressure to amend the deregulation act, staff members said. They are mainly to provide a forum for spokesmen both for and against amendments to "blow off steam," they added.

Service at small, nonhub airports has actually increased 5.2% in the past year, according to the CAB report. The only cutbacks have been in service from nonhub to nonhub, a drop of 1.4%. But service from nonhubs to small hubs was up 3.7%, to medium hubs up 13.1%, and to large hubs up 9.2%. Service in all other types of markets increased.

Nationwide, scheduled service was up 8.4% since February, 1978. Total departures were up or stayed the same at 117 hub airports and decreased an average of 6.9% at 34 hubs. Departures increased or remained constant at 459 nonhub airports and declined an average of 21.2% at the remaining 281, according to the study.

The CAB says that even though service between nonhubs decreased, overall service has improved under deregulation because the increase in flights to hubs makes it easier for passengers to get from small cities to where they want to go.

But some small cities have experienced severe cutbacks, the study admits. Among them are Catskills/Sullivan Co., N. Y.; Hot Springs, Va.; Jamestown, N. D.; London-Corbin, Ky.; McAlester, Okla.; Merced, Calif.; Ponca City, Okla., and Astoria/Seaside, Ore., which are all experiencing or expecting complete elimination of service current since February, 1978.

Such cutbacks cannot necessarily be attributed to deregulation, according to Mimi Cutler, director of the aviation consumer action project.

"The loss in flights in many cases is just an adjustment to a free industry environment," she said. "It is not unique to a less-regulated market place; it has been happening all along." Supporters of deregulation also point out that such cutbacks did happen before, and that prior to deregulation in many cases the airlines did not even have to give public notice before pulling out of a market.

"Right now, any service change in the country is being blamed on deregulation, when in many cases it has nothing to do with deregulation," one legislative staff member said. "There is no denying there are some losers, but 99% are winners."

Some of the biggest losers among states were Alaska, with 72 airports showing service losses in the past year, California with 19, Mississippi and Alabama with eight each and Texas with seven.

A spokesman for Sen. Ted Stevens (R.-Alaska) said he does get complaints on service losses "on sort of a regular basis" but the number of complaints does not seem to have increased under deregulation. Hearings are scheduled in Alaska later this year to determine essential air service levels.

Some changes in the deregulation act that have been considered as a result of the wave of service cutbacks include:

■ Making it more difficult for carriers to leave markets.

■ A better definition of essential air service.

■ A "fix" for slotting problems at airports like Washington National. If an air carrier with slots at Washington National pulls out of a community, the commuter airline that replaces it may not be able to get slots at National, forcing a significant change in airline service.

Service changes since Feb. 1 include:

■ **Allegheny**—Discontinued service to Utica, N. Y., Feb. 6. Added service from

---

Brazilian Charges

Brazil has increased its airways charges by 1,000%, raising Pan American World Airways' fees in that category from 1978's $186,000 to nearly $2 million this year.

Brazil informed Pan American that the increase was necessary to defray costs of improved VOR/DME and nondirectional beacon systems. Airways charges are higher in a sector that includes Rio de Janiero, Sao Paulo and Brasilia. Brazil adopted the Eurocontrol method of computing the airways charges, which, according to Pan American, forces international carriers to pay six times the rate paid by domestic carriers.

The new airways charges went into effect in January along with higher landing fees.

Braniff International also is affected, but to a lesser extent, having fewer flights to Brazil. Both the State Dept. and the Transportation Dept. were reported to be investigating the increases to determine whether the inequities in price structures were illegal.

Western to Keep Network, Stress Utilization

Los Angeles—Western Airlines' decision not to seek major expansion of its route network following deregulation of the airline industry was based on the carrier's dedication to maintaining its previous high aircraft utilization rates and load factors.

Western represents one pole of deregulation strategy as contrasted with Braniff's expansion policy.

Western chose not to apply for any route under dormant authority provisions, and the carrier has added only two new segments since deregulation—one as its automatic entry selection and the other under an exemption.

"In our situation, we felt we had to play the game in accordance with our situation and not be influenced by other carriers," James L. Mitchell, Western's senior vice president of corporate planning, told AVIATION WEEK & SPACE TECHNOLOGY. "We feel we are unique, and simply because other airlines ran out and acquired a great deal of new route authority doesn't particularly mean that is wrong for those airlines."

The major factors that have put Western in this unique position are its high fleet utilization and high load factors, Mitchell said. Western's utilization has continued to improve in recent years, and the carrier last year reached an average daily fleet utilization of 8 hr. 37 min. Its 1978 load factor average of 63.4%—up from an average of 57.4% attained the previous year—was the highest of any U.S. trunkline, carrier officials said.

"We believe we use our equipment—in fact our total utilization is as well, if not better, than any other carrier," Mitchell said. "Additionally, we carry our passengers over an average mile at a lower rate per mile than most other carriers."

Without the immediate addition of aircraft, Western could not find the means to undertake any significant expansion, Mitchell said.

The service instituted this year tied together cities already served by Western, eliminating the need to establish new airport stations and other facilities. The carrier began Salt Lake City-Phoenix service in March under an exemption and it will start flying between Seattle/Tacoma and Reno on Apr. 29 as its automatic market entry selection.

Mitchell said the airline expects some of the competition created by the recent entry of other carriers on its route structure will be eliminated as the competitors are forced to pull out of their new markets.

As an example, Mitchell cited the startup—and subsequent planned suspension—of competitive service by Hughes Airwest between Denver and Great Falls, Mont.

"Here is an indication—and there are many of them—of what probably will be repeated on many routes. The initial competition may have hurt us a little, but the other carriers are finding out they can't support some of the service," Mitchell said. "The startup and reduction of competitive service means there will be a significant waste of resources in the air transport industry."

Western's conservation in route expansion is borne out by the carrier's modest 5% increase in available seat miles during the first two months of this year, compared to the double digit increases of some other airlines.

Cleveland to Phoenix and Pittsburgh to Raleigh-Durham, N.C. Seeking permission to fly from New Orleans to Cleveland and Pittsburgh.

■ **American**—Suspended service to Providence, R. I., and plans to suspend to Charleston, W. Va., the end of May. Has added 20 new routes and eight new cities.

■ **Continental**—No deregulation-related cutbacks.

■ **Delta**—Terminated service to Asheville, N. C., and plans to terminate Beaumont/Port Arthur, Tex.; Meridian, Miss.; Paducah, Ky.; Presque Isle/Holten, Me. and Springfield, Mo. Also cutting service between New Orleans and Venezuela.

■ **Eastern**—Withdrew from Macon, Ga.; Chattanooga, Tenn., and Canton/Akron, Ohio. Planning withdrawals from Huntsville, Ala.; Cincinnati, and Ponce, Puerto Rico. Has added service to Austin, Tex., from Atlanta; to Savannah, Atlanta and Miami from San Francisco; Salt Lake City from St. Louis, and New York City from Albany.

■ **Frontier**—Terminated service to Kearney, Hastings, McCook and Columbus, all in Nebraska. All were picked up by Pioneer Airways of Denver. Plans to terminate Alamogordo and Silver City, N. M. Adding service to Detroit; Redding, Calif.; Shreveport, La., and Jackson, Miss.

■ **Hughes Airwest**—Deleted service to Santa Maria, Bakersfield and El Centro, Calif.; Medford, Ore.; Yuma, Ariz., and Guadalajara and Guaymas, Mexico. Added service to Burbank, Oakland, Ontario and Redding, Calif.; Eugene and Klaman Falls, Ore.; Spokane and Seattle, Wash.; Taxco and Mazatlan, Mexico; Calgary, Canada; Denver, and Phoenix. Cut frequency of service to Eureka, Chico, San Diego, San Francisco and Sacramento, Calif.; Las Vegas and Reno, Nev.; Boise, Idaho; Kalispell, Mont.; Portland, Ore.; Puerto Vallerta, Mexico; Salt Lake City, Utah, and Tucson, Ariz.

■ **National**—Eliminated service to Providence, Boston, Philadelphia, Charleston, S. C., Panama City and Daytona Beach, Fla. Made significant service reductions to Norfolk, Va., and Savannah, Ga., and significant increases to Houston, New Orleans, Seattle/Tacoma and San Juan, Puerto Rico.

■ **North Central**—No significant cutbacks. Added service from Chicago to Houston and Detroit to Houston.

■ **Northwest**—No reductions.

■ **Ozark**—To delete Ottumwa, Iowa, May 15. Added service to Houston.

■ **Piedmont**—No major cutbacks. Adding Tampa, Fla., and Charlotte, N. C.

■ **Southern**—Suspended service to Columbia and Charleston, S. C., and Columbus, Ga.

■ **Texas International**—Suspended service between Albuquerque and Roswell, N. M.; Shreveport La., and Dallas; Hot Springs, Ark.; and Dallas, and Texarkana, Tex., and Dallas. Adding service Apr. 1 between Houston and St. Louis, both Houston and Dallas and Baltimore/Washington International, and Apr. 6, between Houston and Cozumel, Mexico.

■ **Trans World**—Cutting Albuquerque-Columbus eastbound, Albuquerque-Pittsburgh eastbound, Reno-Albuquerque eastbound, Columbus-Indianapolis and Columbus-Tucson westbound, Cincinnati-Oklahoma City westbound, Hartford-Denver westbound, Los Angeles-Harrisburg eastbound, Harrisburg-Phoenix westbound, Harrisburg-Wichita westbound, Indianapolis-Las Vegas westbound, Indianapolis-Phoenix in both directions, Kansas City-Reno westbound, Las Vegas-Oklahoma City in both directions, New York-Oklahoma City in both directions, Palm Springs-St. Louis eastbound, Amarillo-Columbus eastbound, Amarillo-Washington, D. C., westbound, Cleveland-Oklahoma City westbound, Oklahoma City-Hartford eastbound, Wichita-Hartford eastbound, and Indianapolis-Reno westbound. All changes are effective Apr. 29.

■ **United**—Suspending Asheville, N. C.; Chattanooga, Tenn.; New Orleans, and Marced and Visalia, Calif., effective June 8. Reducing service to Charleston, W. Va. Adding service from Ft. Lauderdale to Chicago and Pittsburgh to Las Vegas.

■ **Western**—No suspensions. Adding service from Seattle to Reno and Reno to San Diego Apr. 29.

How To Schedule An Airline

by
Marsha D. Banovetz
Manager-Cargo Marketing Development-Western Region
United Airlines

*H*ow do you take over 300 planes of various types and configurations and maximize their utilization? That's the scheduling problem United Airlines solved recently.

I will describe for you three areas of scheduling. First, how to schedule an airline; second, how to change a simple flight; and third, how to evaluate a regular schedule change—i.e., 4/29 daylight time change and summer flying times.

United Airlines thought it was doing an excellent job of scheduling its fleet until the results of 1976 rolled in and we proceeded to look at the top 10 airlines.

Compared to the other nine airlines, United's unit cost for selling/servicing was among the *lowest* in the industry, but costs relating to other areas showed United Airlines ranked:

#8 Flight
#8 Maintenance
#9 Ownership
#10 Inflight
#10 Aircraft Utilization
#10 Breakeven Load Factor

The last two items are not costs. Aircraft Utilization affects unit costs. Breakeven Load Factor *derives* from costs, among other things. All of this together ranked United Airlines as #9 in terms of ROI.

How did this happen?

Well, to be successful in the airline business you can

1) Drive down your Breakeven Load Factor and be satisfied with an actual load factor which exceeds your breakeven comfortably, even though it is low in industry terms. That's what Northwest has done. Or, you can

2) Maximize segment load factor by compromising aircraft utilization.

United chose to follow the second method. For example, we were prepared to hold a DC-8 arrival at EWR at 8:00 PM until 4:00 PM the next day for a preferred departure time (combining the passenger and cargo loads), or

We would take a 737 from ORD-GRR and hold it and its crews on the ground for several hours to make connections in Chicago.

This kept the load factor the highest in the industry but also put our breakeven load factor the highest in the industry. It also makes for lousy aircraft utilization. We lost sight of our real profit center—the aircraft. At that point, our President, Dick Ferris stated:

1) That we now had a major corporate goal: United would be

among the top *three* carriers in terms of ROI by 1980. Remember, we were currently 9th.

2) He "suggested" to us that it might be a good idea if we tried to build a schedule that increased utilization of our aircraft, and was efficient in crew, inflight and ownership terms.

Scheduling's first attempt was to fly the hell out of every plane we owned and the result was a MONSTER: an airline in production terms the size of United, Western and Continental combined! We had developed an airline that was 40% larger!

So we started again, this time with a clean sheet of paper. We asked ourselves the following questions:

■ Could better aircraft utilization (hours flown/day) allow us to:
   1) More efficiently use our crews?
   2) Could it turn crew penalty time into productive flying?
   3) Could it fly the schedule with fewer aircraft and reduce own-ship costs?
■ Should we change our connecting bank scheduling concept to:
   1) A no banking concept (i.e., forget about cross-connections),
   2) A revised banking concept (i.e., ORD, CLE and DEN equal size), or should we
   3) Continue our current hub and spoke concept (i.e. maximize cross-connections and feed traffic from smaller cities through larger cities).

A special task force was set up with some basic rules. We arrayed all passenger and cargo markets on the basis of United's revenue potential in 1978. We assigned aircraft to markets on the basis of *local* market revenue and aircraft mission (that is, DC-8's flew like DC-8's and 737's flew like 737's. We used local traffic *until* we flowed the traffic through the hubs: and then, of course, the laminated traffic demanded different numbers and gauges of aircraft. We worked with *utilization* rules and rules which were built to guard *crew* efficiency. *Inflight* efficiency was reviewed when it involved a passenger plane.

We decided that we'd try to schedule for our present market coverage, with much greater efficiency, and let the number of aircraft be a fallout. Figure it out for yourselves; present market coverage, much busier airplanes, and you're going to need fewer aircraft. And if you're going to need fewer aircraft, then it follows you're going to need fewer crews. We then decided we'd show senior management *two* schedules.

First, the one described; present market coverage; busy airplanes; busy crews.

Second, a schedule which would describe new, profitable market opportunities to use our surplus resources, both aircraft and crews.

Basic to any schedule and normally implicit in it, has to be a plan for each of the markets. You don't assign aircraft randomly. It isn't by good luck that B747s fly to Hawaii and bad luck that B737s fly to Muskegon.

We ranked all markets in terms of their November 1978 revenue potential and determined what aircraft and how many of them each market could support in economic terms. That isn't difficult to do, but when you impose the rule that *each aircraft must meet utilization goals,* (flying hours/day) then it gets more difficult!

Schedule 1 used 264 aircraft year-round and used an additional 5 aircraft during the summer months. These 4 additional aircraft were assigned as maintenance aircraft for the other nine months. In other words, we essentially flew our present market coverage with 42 fewer aircraft—42 aircraft which were available for new opportunities.

Schedule II: We still had 42 aircraft to use on productive endeavors. They turned out to be B727-100's because, being our remaining least efficient aircraft, they tended to drop out to the bottom. But they were productive aircraft and there were crews to go with them. So, we got involved in designing productive, new opportunities in which to use them.

Last June, we expanded our available seat miles and available ton miles substantially. We flew not only our regular schedule but also new additional schedules in both current markets and new markets. In September we increased our freighter flying 20% with the same number of aircraft.

The nice thing is that we still have not used all the planes. We sold some and can use the "surplus" planes for further expansion.

Did all this work of rescheduling work? It certainly did! By the end of 1978 United Airlines ranked #3 in the top 10 airlines in terms of ROI...two years ahead of our goal.

Now let's zero in on an individual flight. What do we do in order to change a flight based upon an individual request?

For example, a customer asks us if we can retime a DC-8F trip 35 minutes later, which would increase volumes by 15,000 lbs./trip. Let's assume this trip is flying SFO ORD JFK, and is a prime time departure.

First we review this with the local station:

1. ■ How does this affect your peak traffic time?
   ■ Do you have the space for it?
   ■ Is it better traffic than what you are now carrying?
   ■ Can it go on another trip? Is it time sensitive?

Let's assume SFO's current departures are at: 2200, 2230 and 2300.

The 2200 trip is to be operated 35 minutes later, now at 2235. We now have one departure at 2230, one at 2235 and one at 2300. Does this increase the manpower needed to build up the trips? No, the peaking is okay.

2. Now we have to check ORD for the through time. This trip currently arrives at 0350 and departs at 0500. Now it would arrive 0425 and depart 0535. Can ORD handle it manpowerwise? Yes.

■ Does it misconnect any trips currently connecting to it? Yes. What stations and customers are involved?

■ Are you losing that transfer business or can it be saved or rerouted?

■ Will your new added 15,000 lbs. simply be a replacement for the transfer traffic lost? Is it a plus or status quo?

■ What does this retiming do to the parking areas at ORD for the peak banking period? For example, do we now have five planes on the ground instead of four and only four parking spaces; or does ORD have five parking spaces?

■ What about the slot problem? United Airlines, like other carriers, is allowed only 'X' number of landings and takeoffs at ORD during various times of the day. Is this trip within the slot limit for that period of time?

OK. We seem to have no problems with manpower, transfers, parking or slots.

Now let's go to JFK and review their situation. This trip currently arrives at 0754 and now will arrive at 0829.

Again we go through some of the same questions as we did with ORD. Are there any manpower, peaking or parking problems? Is there any international traffic onboard whose connection will be affected?

EVERYTHING IS OKAY—OR IS IT?

What about the delivery trucks? The trucks leave the docks at 0845 now. This means the new 0829 arrival will miss the truck. Will another truck with a later departure be acceptable to the shippers and consignees? Will we lose some business we are now carrying? After checking all these items out, we find that with some give and take it looks like the proposed schedule change is workable from an operations standpoint.

The next step is to review this proposal with flight operations to see if we can fly it.

Does this timing change the crew pairing? Originally this trip had a SFO crew flying SFO ORD and an ORD crew picking it up in ORD to fly to JFK. The ORD crew, when it gets to JFK, turns around and flies a daylight freighter out of JFK to DEN. The later departure and arrival of 35 minutes now makes them illegal for the JFK—DEN trip. This means an additional crew is needed to fly this trip. We probably will have to deadhead the original crew back to ORD, pay them, and not be able to reassign them, *PLUS* bear the added costs of more crew hours.

Let me divert from this SFO ORD JFK trip for just a moment to show you how this type of crew problem can also work in reverse. Say a SFO crew is flying a passenger DC-8 SFO LAX round trip. This is a 2 hour flying trip. The pilot's contract calls for a minimum of 4-½ hours pay.

■ The 2 hours flying is referred to as "Hard Hours".

■ The 2-½ hours non flying is referred to as "Soft or Penalty Hours".

At times like this we can evaluate the markets to see if there is some short haul DC8F flying needed. For example, could we extend a freighter from the east that terminates in SFO to LAX? Using part of that 2-½ hours of soft time gives us a "free" trip. This could allow the eastcoast city another outlet as well as help SFO.

Back to the original flight SFO ORD JFK. Now that the needs are known, we estimate new volumes on the SFO and ORD flights plus any other stations' connecting traffic at ORD to see if the package prices out better both on a revenue and profit basis. Any manpower costs or savings will be added to this to determine the worth of the change.

If the package is marginal we determine what the potential of this customer and/or others will be by this change; what customers will be affected, and what the competitive picture looks like. The decision is then made.

Now let's take a look at a normal schedule review, due to daylight time changes or seasonal changes.

In a normal schedule review of the entire schedule pattern, we know how many crew hours by fleet type we have available.

A schedule draft is developed with advance marketing recommendations taken into consideration. A preliminary crew pairing is made by computer which determines how the proposed schedule fits the available crew hours. Invariably we have more schedule than crew hours. For example, let's say we have 52 hours a day more proposed flying than we have crew hours. This usually is broken down by fleet type which complicates the problem.

The schedule draft is then sent to the field to review the ground times, the peak periods of inbound/outbound timing, ground equipment needs, competitive schedules and connection trips.

The division works with field stations throughout this process and with headquarters' scheduling to solve as many problems as possible while at the same time reducing the crew hour overages and implementing marketing recommendations.

This final process of manual massage usually requires a multitude of minor changes including revised timings, turn times and equipment gauge to try to zero out each type of equipment.

It can have a snowball effect. Once you get the DC-10s zeroed out this could increase the hours you are over in the other fleets. You can get into situations like changing a DC-8 to a 727 in a segment. That's one reason why you may see a passenger trip that was a SFO ORD PHL trip become SFO ORD BAL—the short haul portion of the trip can be changed easier. Sometimes a five minute change in a schedule can save four hours of crew time. Hard to believe? But it's really true.

Confused yet? Well there is one more basic item that we still haven't confronted and that is maintenance requirements.

For example, United must have 40 planes of various types into SFO by 2100 every day, available for maintenance between 2100 and 0900. Other major stations that do maintenance checks have similar but smaller requirements. What does this mean?

Let's assume Washington wants a trip to SFO to leave at 6:45 PM. This would give them the best departure time. Their SFO arrival is 9:35 PM. That's fine, except that this plane is one that has to be in SFO for maintenance by 9:00 PM.

So, you see, there are many requirements and problems to scheduling, even for a single departure.

And, you can also see that scheduling is a complicated operation, particularly if you have over 300 planes of various fleets. We also have 74 more planes on order: DC-10s, 727-200s and the new 767s. We also have an option for 79 additional planes.

During the next few years it will become even more intriguing to schedule the airline as we have the opportunity through deregulation to fly into new cities and enlarge our route system.

Access Looms as Critical Problem for U.S. Airports

Deregulated airlines soon will be able to fly almost anywhere; the question is whether or not they can land, park and take off again

By Joan M. Feldman

Ah for the good old days when it was easy to pinpoint an airport's trouble spots. Most of them, at least at large hubs, involved noise.

Today's airport world is much more complicated, especially in the light of last year's record everything: traffic, profits, new-plane launches, aircraft orders. And at the big hubs, the noise problem has now been joined by concerns over such matters as congestion, allocation of landing slots, the demand for space by new airline entrants, and a changing competitive environment that does not necessarily guarantee that the same carriers will be around to produce airport revenues year after year.

In other words, today's big problem is access. As the Federal Aviation Administration's chief counsel, Clark Onstad, puts it, "airport access is where the action is."

And the conflicts are already building. The U.S. government is insisting upon access for all publicly certificated interstate companies to all airports receiving public funds, even when the airports maintain they have no room. At the same time, the issue of federal and/or state preemption over local airport operators is popping up regularly.

How far the federal government eventually will intrude into the so-called "cozy relationships" between airport operator and airline is still unknown. But there are signs that the Civil Aeronautics Board, and to a lesser extent FAA, are becoming more and more aggressive.

Meanwhile, the old bugaboo of aircraft noise continues to head the list of airport problems. While, in the words of one official, "95% of the airports are looking for noise (new business)," major airports around the world are confronted by noise problems that should have been solved yesterday.

In the U.S., the Noise Control Act of 1972 gives FAA the authority to regulate aircraft noise at its source. To achieve lower noise levels, the agency has set a series of deadlines by which various models of aircraft must meet new noise standards. By 1985, all aircraft are supposed to be quieted.

Shared Responsibility

Ultimately, new-technology airplanes and modern land-use policies will take care of the problem. But now, airport operators are contending with lawsuits and are seeking short-term solutions by imposing their own noise standards on airlines. The carriers, in turn, keep trying to get FAA to preempt the regulation of noise, but the agency has been sidestepping that action because preemption means liability—and liability could mean paying damages to noise-impacted citizens.

FAA so far has contended that it will take care of noise at the source but that reduction of airport noise is a shared responsibility. It has opposed airport regulations that it feels are discriminatory or that it thinks create an undue burden on interstate commerce. But it has agreed that airport operators are within their rights to seek to reduce noise.

The lines have been drawn clearly by the federal government in the case of the San Diego Unified Port District versus the State of California's Department of Transportation (Caltrans). In an *amicus curiae* brief which reportedly received the approval of government officials up to and including President Carter, the Department of Justice told a federal appeals court that Caltrans' insistence on a longer curfew at San Diego was strictly a matter between the airport operator and the state agency.

In another matter involving San Diego, however, FAA took off its seldom-used gloves because it felt discrimination was involved. In this instance the airport, in an effort to meet Caltrans' noise standards, declared that it would impose a one-year moratorium on the entry of new airlines.

FAA thereupon told the airport that its action was a violation of the Federal Aviation Act's prohibition against the granting of "exclusive rights" by airports receiving federal funds. What made matters worse, FAA said, was that San Diego was permitting incumbent airlines to increase flight frequencies (noise). In the face of threatened penalties, the airport withdrew its moratorium.

FAA also charged discrimination when San Francisco attempted to hold down entry by new airlines through the passage of a resolution banning new operations by aircraft not meeting noise standards established by Part 36 of the Federal Aviation Regulations. FAA pointed out that airplanes operated by incumbent airlines at San Francisco often don't meet the Part 36 limitations.

It thus appears that FAA is more than willing to help CAB enforce the Airline Deregulation Act of 1978. But FAA is showing signs of backing away from its own Part 36 noise deadlines.

For the past several years, the airlines have come up each year with a new reason why they can't or shouldn't comply with the deadlines. FAA administrator Langhorne Bond supposedly has told both airlines and airport operators that he won't countenance any extension of the deadlines, but suddenly there is talk of giving "well-designed waivers," perhaps to airports rather than airlines.

As one top FAA official told *ATW*, "We need to be flexible," particularly since there are major airlines (TWA, Eastern and Allegheny, to name three) that will have difficulty meeting the deadlines. The airports

they serve will be the ones under pressure, this official feels.

"Flexibility" may be an understatement in view of the fact that the first deadline, applying to two-engine and three-engine airplanes, comes up on Jan. 1, 1981. There is very little retrofit activity in progress, and political support for some type of relief is building.

So federal noise policy remains confused, and additional pressure is created by the Deregulation Act and the limits on airport access which noise creates. And like FAA, the present CAB is not reluctant to go to court over access.

Running Out of Space

CAB general counsel Philip Bakes, who helped write the Deregulation Act, states flatly, "The (competitive) policy in the Act won't work if there are 40 or 50 different answers" from state and local authorities. "It's a very important interstate commerce principle involved here," he adds.

But someone has to find space for new airline entrants. Throughout the world, airports are running out of landing slots, gates, terminal space, parking spots for airplanes, room for automobiles.

And the answer is not a simple matter of dividing an airport's capacity by the number of airlines or flights. The situation is complicated by the way airports are financed.

At major U.S. airports, federal funds are a minor source of financing, and one that might even be eliminated if some of the proposed revisions in the Airport Development Aid Program (ADAP) come to pass. Revenue bonds guaranteed by airline fees provide the bulk of the money. And airport operators, a conservative bunch, often tie airlines up with contracts running as long as 30 years, using these contracts to back bank loans.

The implications of these policies are clear. The long-term incumbent airlines don't want new guys to come in who haven't paid for the facilities (they would not be so crass as to say they don't want competition). This is a problem that doubtless will come up during hearings this year on renewal of ADAP, which expires on Sept. 30, 1980.

Airports also are faced with the complexities of providing space to airlines in a service environment which CAB calls "dynamic." If deregulators' dreams come true, airlines will be entering and leaving markets on a continuing basis. CAB, in fact, thinks the situation will be so fluid that allocations will have to take place *monthly*. And how, then, does an airport operator calculate revenues on any coherent basis?

CAB is not happy with the present system of dividing up space and slots, but it has not yet come up with a better answer. To Bakes, the principle is the same that applies to seaport allocation of use of piers.

One possibility is a move in the U.S. to the European system wherein no airline has dedicated gates. There, carriers contribute financially to the entire gate system and then pull up to whatever space is available.

Bakes says the financing question boils down to whether "the long-term contract satisfies the requirements of the community. Congress decided that communities should vote with their pocketbooks (through the marketplace). But if the ballot box is closed (new entrants are shut out), they can't vote."

Ultimately, Bakes concedes, the U.S. government is supposed to stay out of such decision-making. That was what the Deregulation Act was all about. But he insists that in the transition there are difficulties that the government may have to resolve.

Yet another problem is the allocation of

One proposal for coping with airport congestion involves elimination of dedicated gate complexes like this and establishment of a first-come, first-served system.

Airlines with long-term commitments on airport space are reluctant to make room for new entrants who haven't helped to pay for the basic facilities.

Airport Access

scarce landing slots at congested airports. Most airports have not yet reached their capacities, but four major U.S. airports have been operating under a slot system for several years.

In the early 1970s, CAB allowed the airlines to establish scheduling committees to parcel out the slots. But now the Board is investigating all airline agreements and questioning whether they should be allowed to continue with antitrust immunity.

The slot system has worked, but Bakes

questions, "What is 'worked'? True the airlines are not fighting each other in the streets. But is it the best way, given the more competitive, flexible environment?"

CAB and FAA are looking at alternatives, and they even have contracted for a computer model that will spit out varieties of access solutions, considering classes of carriers, bid systems, connection requirements, peak/off-peak pricing, community participation, monthly auctions and other factors. If no new scheme proves workable, says Bakes, the current method may continue.

Included in the study is the question of

who should conduct the allocation. Is it the right of the airport operator? Should the community itself, which will be determining which airline service succeeds, become involved? This question of "proprietor's rights" could provide the basis for a substantial debate this year.

FAA, quietly but firmly, is urging CAB to proceed with caution. FAA definitely does *not* want to be in charge, and it even is finding the exploration of alternatives painful. "It's the toughest question we have here," says Onstad.

And another FAA official told us, "There isn't sufficient pressure on the system that (allocation) can't be handled by the airline scheduling committees." The agency apparently disagrees with CAB that the present setup is a "cozy relationship" between airline and airport operator.

However, Bakes is emphatic in his belief that communities should not be in charge of any hypothethical new allocation system. "Congress didn't want to substitute states and local jurisdictions, or the larger communities, for the federal government," he declares.

And the airports don't seem to want the task either. "We don't want to become mini-CABs," an industry official told *ATW*.

Landing slots, of course, are not the only ground problem facing the major airports. Getting passengers to and from the airport also ranks high on the problem list. Airports like Los Angeles International ran out of space for automobiles long ago. And with a few exceptions like Cleveland, grand schemes for rapid transit links between city and airport have never come to fruition because of the cost. One often-discussed solution is to pour a lot more money into reliever and satellite airports, but airlines historically have resisted moves away from the hubs.

Land-use planning also is a potential solution, and the new ADAP program likely will include money for this purpose. Planners hope the day will come when protection of airports against encroachment by residential areas will help to cushion both airports and airlines against protests.

And one airline industry official, at least, makes the rather radical suggestion that some of the airports' problems can be relieved without spending money. New types of air service, he says, can create new hubs in cities like Denver, St. Louis, Houston or Kansas City. It is not necessary for every airline to schedule its connections at Chicago's O'Hare, he says, noting that United, the airline with the biggest presence at O'Hare, has already begun shifting some operations to Denver and Cleveland.

Big new complexes will be necessary in the future if traffic continues to grow as it has. But, this official says, some measures can be taken now to avoid the inconvenience of airports like Montreal's Mirabel or Tokyo's Narita.

As Onstad says, airport access is today's big subject of debate. And the relationships between airports and airlines, cozy or not, are bound to change.

Court Cases Related to Proprietor's Rights and/or Preemption

Allegheny Airlines v. Village of Cedarhurst. U.S. Circuit Court, Second Circuit, 1956. Upheld injunction against a village ban on flights under a certain altitude.

Griggs v. Allegheny County. U.S. Supreme Court, 1962. Held that airport proprietor is financially liable for damage from aircraft noise.

American Airlines v. Town of Hempstead. U.S. Circuit Court, Second Circuit, 1968. Held unconstitutional a town ordinance banning use of certain flight paths.

City of Burbank v. Lockheed Air Terminal. U.S. Supreme Court, 1973. Established rights of proprietors to set noise rules on a nondiscriminatory basis. Held city could not use police powers to establish airport rules.

Air Transport Association v. Crotti. U.S. District Court, 1975. Held that Congress did not preempt the entire field of airport noise regulation. Proprietor's right to control use of airport exempted from federal preemption.

National Aviation v. City of Hayward. U.S. District Court, 1976. Allowed City of Hayward, Calif., as proprietor, to set a curfew.

British Airways v. Port Authority of New York. U.S. Circuit Court, 1977. Overturned a lower court ruling that the airport operator could not ban Concorde. Held that operator can formulate "reasonable regulations to establish acceptable noise levels for the airfield and its environs."

San Diego Unified Port District v. Gianturco. U.S. District Court, 1978. Held that a state agency which is not a proprietor cannot dictate a curfew extension. Now on appeal.

114

Chapter 5
Pipelines and Domestic Water Carriers

Pipelines energize America

As the energy-conscious decade of the 1970's draws closer to an end, pipelines have come to gain their just share of public attention. The awareness probably stems from publicity surrounding the Alaska pipeline. Yet for many years oil and natural gas have moved more efficiently and economically by pipeline than by any other means.

One reason is the energy needed to move energy. Transportation by pipeline enjoys the lowest cost of all modes. With no packaging or circuitous routing or deadheading, continuous, high-volume pipeline movement delivers energy with little wasted energy.

Measured in ton-miles, pipelines transport about 60 percent of the nation's petroleum (transport by water is next with 35 percent, followed by transport by rail and truck, which combined account for 5 percent). In 1976 petroleum pipelines moved 24 percent of all intercity freight. Rails moved 36 percent, truck, 24 percent, and water, 16 percent.

Pipelines can transport a variety of products, everything from liquids to solids such as coal (in the form of a slurry, that is, ground up and mixed with water to form a sludge). With coal slurry pipeline technology perfected, several lines are proposed, one of the largest being a 900-mile slurry pipeline from the Rocky Mountains to the Texas Gulf Coast.

Though most pipelines run underground, engineers know how to pipe products under water, from offshore oil and gas wells to refineries along the coast. A section of a submarine pipeline was recently laid in the North Sea in water 1,260 ft. deep.

Sections of pipe were welded together end-to-end on shore. A tug pulled the pipe into the sea as sections of pipe were welded to the end of the line on shore. After final positioning of the line in a 12-foot trench dug into the sea bottom, it was pressurized and ready for business.

Triumph in Alaska. Against tremendous ecological, geographical, and economical barriers, the Trans-Alaska Pipeline went into operation in June 1977. The maiden voyage of North Slope crude had to overcome sabotage, a pump-house explosion, and minor leaks. Yet after only short delay, the *Arco Juneau* was filled and set sail with its first load of Alaskan crude.

When fully operational, the pipeline should contribute just under 10 percent of total barrel miles of petroleum traffic moving through pipelines in the United States. Its hugely inflated cost, though, more

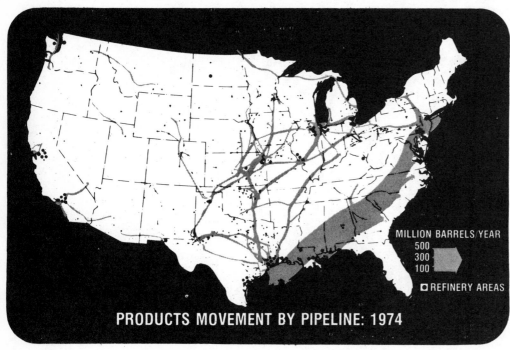

MILLION BARRELS/YEAR
500
300
100

□ REFINERY AREAS

PRODUCTS MOVEMENT BY PIPELINE: 1974

Products pipelines flow from refining areas, mostly along the Gulf Coast in Texas and Louisiana, to consumer areas mainly along the East Coast and in the Midwest. Products lines are largest at refining areas and get progressively smaller as products are dropped off at terminals or metropolitan areas along the route. Small stub lines serve individual refineries. Refined products, being crude oil, require lines with smaller diameters, averaging about 10 inches. The lines transport anywhere from 25,000 barrels to 1,800,000 barrels a day.

than doubled U.S. petroleum pipeline investment.

The next step is to get the black gold from oil-glutted California to the hungry buyers in the industrial Midwest and Northeast, where it's most needed. Standard Oil of Ohio (Sohio) recently received approval from the Federal Energy Regulatory Commission to convert a natural gas line.

Actually, the decision allowed the El Paso Natural Gas Co to abandon a 669-mile gas line from Ehrenberg, Arizona to Jal, New Mexico. That decision sets the stage for Sohio to convert the line for oil, reverse the flow, and complete the 1,012-mile link between Long Beach to Midland, Texas, where the oil will be switched into existing lines running to the Midwest.

President Carter has recently signed a joint Congressional resolution approving the Alcan gas line, American-Canadian natural-gas pipeline to carry North Slope gas from Alaska. The line, to cost perhaps $10 billion, will be the biggest construction job ever undertaken. It will start at Prudhoe Bay, follow the Trans-Alaska oil pipeline, and branch off through Canada to its destination in the Lower Forty-Eight, 2,700 miles away.

The line will follow the oil pipeline to a point just south of Fairbanks. Then it will parallel the Alaska (Alcan) Highway through eastern Alaska into the Yukon Territory to Caroline Junction in southern Alberta. The line then will split. The west leg will go to northern Idaho, where it will loop in with an existing gas line. The east leg will go through Saskatchewan to Montana, South Dakota, Iowa, and Illinois, and will end near Chicago.

In other pipeline developments, Samarco Mineracoa, a South American company, recently completed a 250-mile iron-ore slurry pipeline. The line transports hematite ore, a first. Other lines have transported only magnatite ore, which is half as corrosive and abrasive.

Mobile has agreed to design, build, and manage a 48-inch, 750-mile oil pipeline in Saudi Arabia. The pipeline will carry 2.3 million barrels of oil a day from the Persian Gulf to the Red Sea.

Train in a tube. Technology is at a point now where pipelines can carry more than just liquids, gasses, or slurrified solids. Tubexpress Systems of Houston has developed pipeline transportation for dry, solid cargo. Freight moves in vehicles that ride a stream of pressurized air—much like a train in a tube.

Vehicles loaded at one end of the closed-loop, two-way system ride the air current through the tube and are tipped at the end, dumping the load. The vehicles then enter the return tube for another load.

One possible use for Tubexpress is in transporting coal. The system can complement railroads (and maybe slurry lines) in achieving President Carter's goal of increased coal production. ■

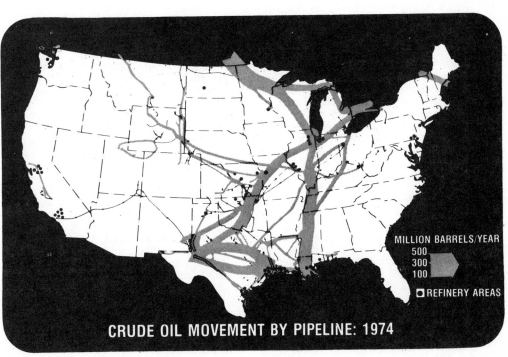

Crude oil pipelines flow from producing areas to refining areas. Small gathering lines (4-8 inches in diameter) transport oil from individual wells to larger trunk lines (10-20 inches), which increase in size (22-48 inches) as they pick up additional crude production.

Since crude oil is heavier and more viscous than refined products, crude lines must be larger in diameter than products lines to transport the same volume. Crude lines can handle anywhere from 50,000 barrels to over a million barrels of crude a day. Average diameter of crude lines is about 16 inches.

MILLION BARRELS/YEAR
500
300
100

☐ REFINERY AREAS

CRUDE OIL MOVEMENT BY PIPELINE: 1974

West Coast Crude Oil Pipeline Systems:

Projects and Problems

by Donald B. Bright, Vice-President
EFS (Environmental Feasibility Studies), Los Angeles

Since the completion and placing in service of the Trans-Alaska Pipeline System (TAPS), a surplus of oil has developed on the west coast, and while a west-to-east pipeline system would provide a much-needed outlet for this surplus oil, construction of such a pipeline system has not gone beyond the wishful-thinking stage.

The major existing crude oil pipeline systems serving the midwest and southwest were described, and proposals for moving the oil from west coast terminals to midwestern and southwestern destinations by pipeline, by rail or by water were delineated in a presentation at the annual meeting, last August in Pittsburgh, of the American Society of Traffic and Transportation, by Dr. Donald B. Bright, who at that time was director of commerce for the Port of Long Beach, Calif. Dr. Bright left the Port of Long Beach commerce directorship at the end of October to become vice-president of EFS (T.W., Nov. 6, p. 10).

The information given by Dr. Bright at the AST & T meeting about oil pipelines, present and proposed, in the United States gave evidence of extensive research by Dr. Bright on this subject and was regarded by the editor of this magazine as material of special interest to Traffic World *readers.*

Since his graduation from the University of Southern California with a bachelor's degree in zoology, in 1952, Dr. Bright (who received his Ph. D. in zoology from U.S.C. in 1962), has had uniquely diversified experience as an educator and researcher in scientific fields, in the U.S.A. and in many foreign lands. He began his career as an officer in the U.S. Army Medical Service Corps in 1952. Three years later he became a teaching assistant at U.S.C. In 1956 and 1957 he was a research assistant at Cedars of Lebanon Hospital in Los Angeles. In 1959 and 1960 he was a lecturer in the U.S.C. department of biology and, also, docent in the Los Angeles County Museum of Natural History. For the next eight year he was an instructor in the Division of Life Sciences at Fullerton (Calif.) Junior college. In the years that followed, until he became director of commerce at the Port of Long Beach, he was chairman and later professor in the department of biological science at California State University in Fullerton. In each of the years 1967 to 1971 he was a lecturer on fundamentals of tropical zoology in the Organization for Tropical Studies at the University of Costa Rica.

In the years since 1956 Dr. Bright has received nine research grants, including one from the U.S. Fish and Wildlife Service, two from the American Philosophical Society, and one from the National Geographic Society.—Editor.

When oil was discovered on the North Slope of Alaska, it was heralded as one of the greatest "energy finds" in recent American history. This discovery came at a time when available sources of crude oil and natural gas in the continental U.S. were declining. With all the accolades about how the North Slope reserves would solve our American energy problem, we immediately should have been suspicious, because in today's world, new oil production/transportation systems can not evolve without full exposure in a "crucible" composed of economic, regulatory, political and public review. Also, unlike most other projects, the production and pipeline facilities for the Alaskan oil delivery system were approved before it was clearly determined where the supply of oil would be delivered. Thus, at the outset, a cloud of confusion settled around the need for, use and delivery of North Slope crude oil.

When the Trans-Alaska Pipeline System (TAPS) was approved, it was determined that all of the Alaskan oil could be used at the three major refinery centers on the west coast: Puget Sound, San Francisco, and southern California. We now know that was false, for today there is a surplus of oil on the west coast. How could such a position have evolved?

The major crude oil pipeline systems supporting the U.S. oil industry originate in the central U.S. (Figure 1). These crude oil pipeline systems have been continually modified in response to the long-range needs of the refining industry. Additionally, these systems are reasonably flexible and can be adapted to meet most changing crude oil supply conditions. The one exception to this is the essentially isolated west coast area, which is part of the Petroleum Administration Defense District (PADD). This area has been isolated due to the availability of local production, particularly in California, together with the importation of certain kinds of foreign crude oil, in particular low sulfur crude oil from Indonesia.

Thus, when Alaskan oil became available on the west coast, the heretofore isolated west coast area, even after "backing out" certain foreign deliveries, had a supply of oil far exceeding present demand. However, that surplus of oil is not due simply to the increased flow of oil from Alaska, but it also is due to: (1) The continued dependence on low sulfur foreign oil for use in environmentally sensitive areas (to reduce air quality impacts), and (2) the fact that much of California's indigenous production is high in sulfur and low in specific gravity, and thus of limited use in California without major refinery modifications. *All* of these conditions have produced an excess of oil on the west coast. The opening of the Elk Hills Naval Reserve also will exacerbate this situation. Since there are no existing west to east crude oil pipeline systems, the problem already has reached extreme proportions. Why has no definitive action been taken to efficiently resolve this problem?

Until 1960, the United States was essentially independent of foreign oil supplies, producing and consuming more oil than any other country in the world. Yet, in 1970, as production from other fields peaked and new exploration and development diminished, primarily because of less expensive imported oil, domestic petroleum production began to decline. This declining supply, combined with an average 4-per-cent annual growth in consumption, resulted in our increasing reliance on imported oil. Import dependence grew from 18 per cent in 1960 to 45 per cent in 1977.

Aside from the oil supply issue, the rise in imports and related increase in the price of oil placed severe burdens upon America's balance of payments for energy. In 1970, the U.S. paid about $3 billion for foreign oil as compared to about $45 billion in 1977. Also, simultaneously our vulnerability to a foreign oil embargo continued to rise.

During the extensive Congressional hearings and debates in the early 1970s on the construction of the Trans-Alaskan Pipeline System (TAPS), the suspicion was expressed that Alaskan oil would be sold to Japan. Oil-industry and federal government spokesman gave extensive assurances that this would not occur, and that all the Alaskan oil would be needed on the west coast. Thus, Congress, based on these assurances, essentially barred the exporting of North Slope oil. Standard Oil, Ohio, generally called SOHIO, a major participant in the TAPS project, did not believe that all the North Slope crude would be used on the west coast. Based on their studies, they tried to convince others that a west to east pipeline system would be needed to deliver Alaskan crude oil to energy deficient areas in the Gulf Coast and midwest, areas which previously had indigenous supplies of oil as well as related crude oil transmission systems. Hardly anyone agreed with SOHIO, so their efforts were not taken seriously.

In 1973, the foreign oil embargo resulted in extensive revision to various

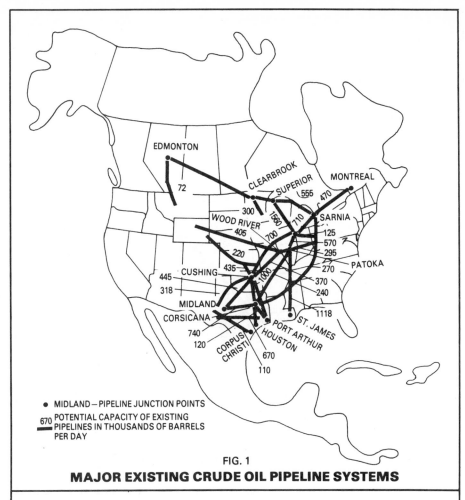

FIG. 1
MAJOR EXISTING CRUDE OIL PIPELINE SYSTEMS

- ● MIDLAND – PIPELINE JUNCTION POINTS
- 670 POTENTIAL CAPACITY OF EXISTING PIPELINES IN THOUSANDS OF BARRELS PER DAY

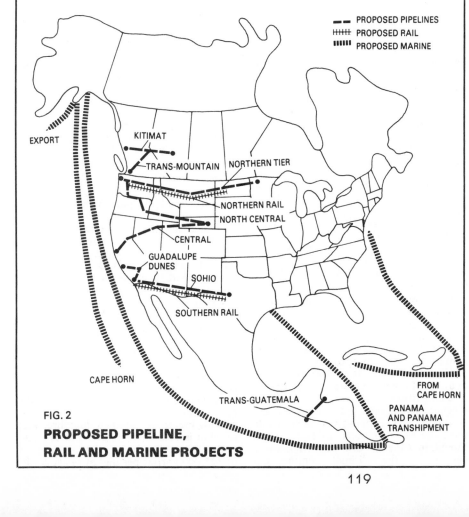

- ▬ ▬ PROPOSED PIPELINES
- ┼┼┼┼ PROPOSED RAIL
- ▥▥▥ PROPOSED MARINE

FIG. 2
PROPOSED PIPELINE, RAIL AND MARINE PROJECTS

energy supply and demand forecasts, so that gradually it was recognized that there could be a surplus on the west coast when Alaskan crude oil entered the market. Additionally, new environmental regulations, such as those related to the use of low sulfur fuel to reduce air emissions, and changes in consumer-use patterns reduced the demands on the west coast for crude oil. Thus, in 1973, no real planning had taken place to deal with surplus, and although the embargo focused the need for state and federal energy plans, bureaucratic and political processes moved very, very slowly.

Once the need for solving the surplus problem was recognized it became clear that the availability of North Slope crude oil would result in two problems for any given existing U.S. pipeline system: Firstly, it is a large incremental volume which has to be moved, and, secondly, its absorption into the refinery systems involves the displacement of both foreign and domestic crude oil within the same or other pipeline systems. Such incremental movements also could result in "capacity imbalances" in the pipeline network.

Several potential problems have already been identified and analyzed with respect to the capability of existing pipeline systems. For example, a recent Department of Energy study indicates that Montana and eastern Washington are the only Northern Tier areas (states along the Canadian border) likely to suffer from acute crude oil shortages. It is projected that in 1979, having exhausted all existing transportation alternatives and lacking Canadian exchanges in oil, Montana will experience a short fall of about 28,000 barrels per day in petroleum products. That translates into the loss of approximately $303 million in real income for the state. Obviously that short fall would increase in future years. Similarly, eastern Washington, which receives petroleum products by barge from western Washington, and by pipeline from the Salt Lake City area and Montana would have the possibility of shortages on the order of 9,600 barrels per day in 1979, escalating to 13,000 barrels per day in 1980. Ironically, indigenous Montana crude is adequate to serve the state's needs, but Montana's eastern and central oil producing regions don't have pipeline links. Other Northern Tier states shouldn't have any shortages through 1980. For example, Michigan should have sufficient supply, although pipelines into the southern part of the state will have no spare capacity. Wisconsin's product shipments into the state will need to be increased from 253,000 to about 290,000 barrels a day in 1980 as the state's refinery utilization slips from 63 per cent to 32 per cent due to the lack of proper feed stock.

One significant recent modification is the looping of part of the Williams Pipeline Co. Oklahoma-to-Minnesota products pipeline system. This looping facilitates the shipment of Prudhoe crude to Twin Cities refiners, provided the crude oil is delivered to the Gulf Coast. Therein lies the crux of the problem, i.e., a means of delivering the oil that is surplus on the west coast to crude deficient areas. The absence of a west to east pipeline system represents the crucial link in completing the crude oil transmission systems of the United States.

A number of pipeline projects have been proposed for the movement of surplus oil from the west coast to the central United States (Figure 3). At one time or another, eight separate pipeline projects have been moving forward, declining, gaining renewed interest, winding their way through the regulatory processes, etc. These pipeline projects are: 1. Kitimat Pipeline from Kitimat, British Columbia to Edmonton, Alberta; 2. Trans-mountain Pipeline Partial Reversal from Cherry Point, Washington, to Edmonton, Alberta; 3. Northern Tier Pipeline from Puget Sound, Washington to Clearbrook, Minnesota; 4. North Central Pipeline from Puget Sound, Washington to Sidney, Nebraska; 5. Central Pipeline from Moss Landing, California to Sidney, Nebraska; 6. Guadalupe Dunes Pipeline from San Luis Obispo Bay, California to Midland, Texas; 7. SOHIO Pipeline from Long Beach, California to Midland, Texas; 8. Trans-Guatemala form Buena Vista on the Pacific Coast to Gulfo de Honduras in the Caribbean. In addition to these eight pipeline projects, there are three other possible transport routes: (1) Movement by rail of North Slope oil in the Northern Tier (Washington, Idaho, Montana, N. Dakota and Minnesota) and/or the Southern Tier (southern California); (2) Panama Canal and/or the Panama Canal pipelines; and (3) movement on very large crude carriers around Cape Horn for delivery into the Gulf of Mexico.

From October, 1977, through May 1, 1978, 315 tankers transited the Panama Canal carrying 6,849,077 long tons of Alaskan oil and paying $8,419,291 in tolls. The average cost per transit was $29,880 laden and $23,515 in ballast. A simple comparison of the total transportation costs for each of the key pipeline routes as contrasted with the use of the Panama Canal illustrates that Panama Canal costs are something on the order of 75¢ to $1.25 more for transport to either of the key market destinations—Chicago or Houston. Therefore, there is great incentive on the part of the various oil companies to develop an east to west pipeline system or systems. The Department of Energy has strongly supported the need for both a Northern Tier system and a Southern Tier system. The Northern Tier system being either Kitimat or the Northern Tier or the Trans-mountain Pipeline partial reversal. The Southern Tier system is represented by SOHIO's project. The Trans-Guatemala pipeline generally is not considered to be a primary option since it would not be a total American system.

The characteristics of the major proposed pipeline projects are:

Kitimat Pipeline Project:

The proposed Kitimat pipeline will run 753 miles from a crude oil receiving terminal in the town of Kitimat on the Kitimat arm of Douglas Channel in British Columbia to Edmonton, Alberta.

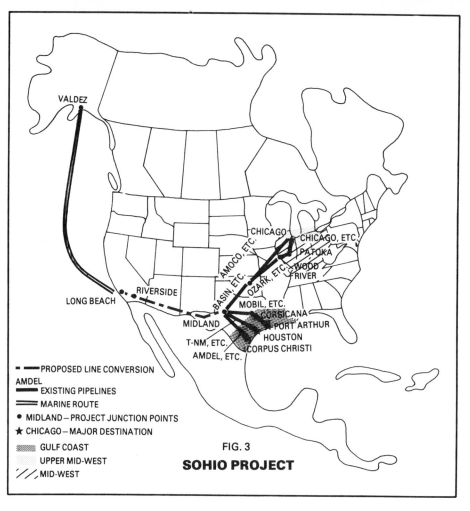

FIG. 3
SOHIO PROJECT

- ▄ ▄ ▬ PROPOSED LINE CONVERSION
- ▬▬▬ EXISTING PIPELINES
- ═══ MARINE ROUTE
- ● MIDLAND — PROJECT JUNCTION POINTS
- ★ CHICAGO — MAJOR DESTINATION
- ▓ GULF COAST
- ░ UPPER MID-WEST
- ╱╱╱ MID-WEST

The pipeline is basically a joint-venture between Koch Industries, Ashland Oil Canada, Murphy Oil, Hudson's Bay Oil and Gas, Inter-provincial Pipeline, and Farmers Union Central Exchange. The system is designed to feed both imported and Alaskan crude oil into the Inter-provincial system at Edmonton. It is designed to serve Northern Tier refiners, to make use of spare capacity in the Inter-provincial pipeline system serving markets in the upper Midwest and Eastern Canada, and to provide a means of alleviating the PADD V surplus of Alaskan crude oil. The pipeline also could eventually serve other Canadian refiners through additional inter-connections at Edmonton, Prince George, and Valemount. The Prince George inter-connection could be used to deliver North Slope Crude to Vancouver and potentially to the Puget Sound refiners via the existing Kamloops system.

This pipeline system is designed for a maximum capacity of 650,000 barrels a day. The pipeline will be constructed of 30-inch diameter pipeline except for about an 80-mile section which will be 36 inches in diameter. Since this project would serve markets in the Northern Tier and upper midwest of the United States, it is directly in competition with two other proposed pipeline systems: the Trans-mountain and Northern Tier Proposals, which would serve the same markets. In fact, Trans-Mountain Pipeline Co. was originally a partner in the Kitimat venture but

withdrew prior to the time of initiating permit applications in Canada.

The Kitimat proposal has met strong resistance from environmentalists and also from the provincial government. The key issues center around air quality impacts at Kitimat, pipeline construction impacts in critical habitat areas, and Canadian energy policy issues.

The vitality of the Kitimat proposal has waxed and waned. There still is no clear indication of whether the project is dead or soon to revive.

Trans-mountain Pipeline Project:

Trans-mountain Pipeline Company has a 24-inch crude oil pipeline system running east to west, from Edmonton, Alberta, which supplies sweet Canadian crude to Vancouver and Puget Sound refineries on the west coast, a distance of some 625 miles. Due to the declining availability of sweet Canadian crude, it was proposed that the flow of this line could be partially reversed to permit west to east flow of Alaskan crude oil from Puget Sound to Edmonton. Atlantic Richfield Co. and the Trans-mountain Pipeline Co. jointly announced an agreement to seek an approval to install a second berth at ARCO's existing Cherry Point refinery to construct a pumping station and pipeline inter-connection facilities within the state of Washington. This would allow for the existing line to operate in a dual direction or what is often been referred to as "yo-yo" fashion. This means that an average of 125,000 barrels per day of sweet crude

120

could be moved westward and during the remainder of the time flow could be reversed and the line would carry about 165,000 barrels per day of Alaskan crude to Edmonton.

The problems with respect to expanding the ARCO Cherry Point refinery, the nature of the ARCO vs Ray decision, (see Northern Tier Discussion), and a recent amendment to the Marine Mammal Act basically have precluded the Transmountain Pipeline Project from being seriously considered.

Northern Tier Pipeline Project:

The Northern Tier Pipeline Project contains a number of sponsoring companies such as Butler Associates Incorporated, Cowan Oil U.S. Steel, MAPCO Inc., Amoco, and so forth. The purpose of the Northern Tier Pipeline Project is to transport crude oil from the Port Angeles area, Puget Sound to Clearbrook, Minnesota. The project has been conceived as a common carrier line to supply crude oil to the refineries in Puget Sound and the Northern Tier states and to deliver additional volumes of imported and North Slope crude oil to the existing Lakehead and Minnesota pipeline systems. The initial design of the system calls for the delivery of 600,000 barrels per day of crude oil to Clearbrook, Minnesota. The bulk of the main pipeline is to be 40" in diameter so as to allow for the ultimate expansion to deliver 800,000 barrels per day to Clearbrook, Minnesota as well as to allow for the delivery of additional crude oil to supply the Puget Sound refineries. To accomodate all these potentialities, it was proposed to install a 42" diameter pipeline over the 183 miles from Port Angeles to North Bend a spur line would then be installed to serve the needs of the Puget Sound refineries.

The problems related to the construction and operation of the Northern Tier pipeline are complex. The ARCO vs Ray decision, based on the challenge of the state-established 125,000 DWT ship restrictions in Puget Sound, established that the federal government would set tanker standards and limits with respect to the operational characteristics of tankers, while on the other hand the state still has the prerogative of establishing certain criteria for tanker operations provided they are not contrary to existing federal jurisdictions. Additionally, the state of Washington has indicated that if a major crude oil receiving facility is to be built in Port Angeles that it should be sized to service all the Puget Sound refineries thereby eliminating extensive tanker traffic in the inner portions of Puget Sound. Also, there are doubts as to whether there is sufficient land at the proposed Port Angeles site to accommodate enough berths to take care of all of the projected oil uses for this area. Furthermore, the option of using single point moorings in the straits of San Juan de Fuca is not attractive due to the weather conditions and heavy shipping using this congested waterway. Thus, the viable options are not that attractive.

The Northern Tier Project has suffered from an absence of definitive action. The environmental problems will necessitate extensive mitigations due to the character of the terrain over which much of the pipeline route is to be constructed. There also will be high construction costs, and the limitations on operations in Puget Sound will be difficult to overcome economically.

SOHIO Pipeline Project:

In 1970, the Standard Oil Company of Ohio (SOHIO) became, through its agreements with British Petroleum Company, the major producer of Prudhoe Bay oil. Based on oil in place, SOHIO estimates that they will be entitled to an excess of 54% of Prudhoe Bay production. That represented approximately 325,000 barrels per day at the start-up of the TAPS pipeline and approximately 650,000 barrels per day at the present. Faced with limited markets on the west coast, SOHIO considered several options for disposing the surplus North Slope crude oil to the crude deficient Midwest and Gulf Coast refining areas. In 1975, SOHIO reached an agreement with El Paso Natural Gas Company to lease and convert for oil service an idle natural gas pipeline, which runs from the Colorado River in Arizona to Jal, New Mexico. Further, within California, the project would use an underutilized Southern California Gas Company Natural Gas Pipeline. Thus the basic project consists of: A marine transport operation from Valdez to Long Beach using 11 dedicated vessels; a 500,000 barrel per day marine terminal in the city of Long Beach; and a pipeline system from Long Beach California to Midland, Texas, where connection to existing pipelines can be accomplished. SOHIO's pipeline will be approximately 1,027 miles long but almost 800 miles of that pipeline is already in place as part of the existing El Paso Gas Company and Southern California Gas Company natural gas pipeline systems.

Although the SOHIO project represents, in an overall way, the least environmentally damaging of all the proposed west to east pipeline systems, basically because of the use of existing natural gas lines, it will produce large amounts of air emissions into the already exacerbated non-attainment areas of southern California. However, all of the impacts can be mitigated, including those related to the air emissions. A total of 715 permits are required to authorize construction of the SOHIO project. To date, over 90% of those permits have been received. The three remaining hurdles relate to the approvals of the air quality agencies in California, California Coastal Commission, and the Army Corp of Engineers. Among these three approval by the air quality agencies is the most difficult and problematic; for even though SOHIO has agreed to provide $55-85 million to retrofit existing facilities to reduce air emissions, the debate is far from over.

Trans-Guatemala Pipeline Project:

This project has been proposed by the Central American Pipeline Co. (CAPICO). As proposed (Figure 8) the pipeline would initially be sized at 1.2 million barrels per day and would carry not only Alaskan North Slope crude, but also other crudes such as those from Indonesia and the Persian Gulf to the U.S Gulf Coast and the Caribbean. Jones Act vessels would be required to move Alaskan oil via this pipeline. However, since this project involves the "export" of Alaskan crude, which currently is not permitted, legal hurdles would have to be cleared in the U.S. and serious issues of national security are anticipated. However, U.S. federal government approval is not required for construction of the project; financing may prove difficult unless firm commitments can be obtained from U.S. companies willing and able to use the line for the transit of Alaskan crude oil.

The proposed pipeline route starts at Buena Vista which is close to the Guatemala-El Salvador border and ends in the Gulfo de Honduras in the Caribbean, a distance of 225 miles. It is proposed to use a 42-inch pipeline to move the 1.2 million barrels per day. There is some indication that by the addition of more pumping capacity and some looping, the throughput could be increased to 1.5 million barrels per day.

A detailed route for the line has not been selected although a preliminary pipeline profile has been prepared. It appears that the proposed pipeline route would traverse some rather severe mountainous terrain for the first 85 miles and then would traverse typical tropical lowland areas (farms, swamps, mangroves, etc.) Because of the problem of locating single point moorings on the Pacific Ocean side, the project involves the construction of two fixed berth facilities capable of serving 200,000 DWT tankers. An additional problem is the long distance required to reach deep water suitable for SPM's on the Caribbean side. Until such time as the LOOP superport is constructed there will be a limitation of 100,000 DWT tankers on the Caribbean side of the project.

The transit through the mountain terrain and through the lowland areas will create a number of environmental impacts. However, the regulatory agency processes in Guatemala are such that even though the impacts might be substantial there is very little likelihood that extreme mitigations would be required.

Conclusions

From the above discussion on all the proposed projects, it is clear that SOHIO is the furthest along in obtaining the necessary approvals. The likelihood of the SOHIO project being approved during the first quarter of 1979 is very high. However, the SOHIO project alone, because the California regulatory agencies already have limited the maximum throughput to 500,000 barrels per day, will not solve the total west coast surplus problem. Therefore, and as repeatedly pointed out by the Department of Energy, it will be necessary to develop a second system. That second system could be either Kitimat, Trans-mountain or the Northern Tier. For the reasons noted above it seems most likely that the Northern Tier proposal would be the most acceptable and feasible considering overall economic, engineering and environmental impacts.

Recognizing that a west to east pipeline system is necessary, why has it taken so long to approve such a pipeline system? There are many reasons for the delay in authorizing the construction of any of the proposed systems. Almost anyone who has helped to develop the necessary documentation for one of the proposed projects can provide a list of reasons. The reasons will differ from project to project, but there are at least six basic reasons:

1. The Lack of National and Individual State Energy Policies:

This will continue to plague us until such time as we experience a true energy shortage. Until the public is acutely aware that there is an energy shortage there will not be any attempt to pinch and save to protect the future nor any attempt to make major shifts to other energy sources. Thus to only criticize government for its failure to respond is to be remiss, for preparing to meet future energy crises will take a strong joint effort between government, business and the public to decrease our energy use and provide realistic alternative energy sources.

2. Lack of Public Understanding of Oil Transportation Procedures and Processes:

To the average citizen, an oil company is a giant monster with one goal in mind: *make money at all costs.* In addition, the average citizen believes that oil is simply taken out of the ground, transferred to a refinery, broken down into usable products and the products made available for public use. Further there is a common belief that because a large quantity of oil is available the demand will naturally increase for the products produced from that oil. In point of fact, none of these three common views are correct. The pro-

cesses of marketing, transporting and refining oil are complex and interrelated with the problems of availability, regulatory processes, equipment and economics; and demand for products is based on need, not the availabilty of crude oil. There is no simple answer, and thus there is little public understanding.

3. The Absence of Clear-Cut Enforced Tanker operation Rules and Procedures:

The awareness of impacts from oil spills began in 1967 with the rupture of the *Torrey Canyon* and it continues to-day. Public concerns will continue with respect to this problem because there is an absence of historical data, an absence of well defined tanker operational procedures, unloading procedures, and an absence of adequately trained ship personnel, particularly with respect to the efficient use of various safety devices. It however, would be remiss to totally blame the tanker operator, for at the center of this problem are the thorny issues of jurisdiction, that is, who has control local, state or federal government, and what procedures are best for safe, efficient operation.

4. The Absence of Well-Defined Procedures to Comply with State and Federal Environmental Laws:

This can be illustrated by the SOHIO project. It falls under the jurisdiction of at least six states and the federal government, so say nothing of the numerous special districts and local governments. Therefore, questions were never ending and complex. Such as: What jurisdictions apply in coastal waters? Can an individual coastal state require that all oil tankers install air monitoring/control equipment? What technology is "best" to control various impacts and what agency makes that determination? If mitigations are the same, should national interests supercede local and state interests? and on and on. . . .

5. Federal and State Political Gamesmanship:

For any of the pipeline proposals there are two significant aspects to this problem: a) the unwillingness of the federal government to immediately, specifically support one or more of the proposed projects; and b) the maneuvering of the various regulatory agencies at both the federal and state level to protect their territorial imperative and/or extend their jurisdiction. With respect to the SOHIO project, the title of one agency report illustrates this point well: "The Proposed El Paso Abandonment: Should California Fight or Switch."

6. Participation of the Public in the Decision Process:

Although the degree of participation varies from one part of the country to another, public participation in the decision process has increased in recent years. The primary results of public participation had been that: a) environmental considerations have become a requirement for development in most parts of the country; b) additional bureaucratic layers have been added to the process, often times these layers are extremely complex; and c) public access to the process has been greatly increased and therefore there is stronger public interest/participation.

In conclusion, it is clear that there is a need for west to east pipelines to reduce the excess of oil on the west coast and to deliver that oil to the crude-deficient areas of the Gulf coast and the midwest. Further, it is clear that such a system needs to be in place as soon as possible. Yet, the absence of strong direction from the various concerned state and federal agencies, continued political "gamesmanship" between local, state and federal individuals, and the absence of a clear energy crisis in the daily lives of every citizen, do not bode well for immediate resolution of the west coast surplus oil problems.

Board Marker Buffy Omey posts Pillsbury Company's 150% offer on a shipment for which Illinois Grain Company hoped to get a rate of 125%. Ms. Julie Mogester, a trader with Pillsbury, and Tim Tegeler, a broker with Don Walker Company, watch posting and communicate with principals, who must decide whether to revise bids and/or offers.

BEGAN AUGUST 1

St. Louis Grain Merchants Create Bid Competition On Barge Delivery Of Export Grain To New Orleans

Other commodities may be added later; try to "keep it simple" by limiting bid sessions to export grain movements initially; bargemen reluctant at first but begin to show greater interest in sessions as experience is gained; is compared to Baltic Exchange in London, though committee which developed procedures in St. Louis had no knowledge of world shipping exchange in London.

Daily bidding for grain barge freight began on the trading floor of the Merchants Exchange of St. Louis August 1 on a cautious note, as grain merchandisers and barge company representatives sought to determine the impact the new call-sessions would have on the grain market.

Initially, bidding will be limited to export grain movements from river points to loading terminals on the Lower Mississippi in and around New Orleans. If this proves successful, call sessions may later be broadened to cover other commodities moving in both directions.

Although only one trade was consummated during the first daily session, exchange officials said they were satisfied with both the initial turnout and long-term outlook of grain barge trading.

"Things look optimistic; I'm very pleased with the turnout today," exchange president William D. McDevitt said. "I was very pleased to see a trade on the first day, but the real story will be how this works out over a period of time."

Jay Vroom, executive vice president of the exchange, agreed. "The next six months or so will tell the story," he said. "It's bound to have some effects (on grain barge transportation). If it becomes a trend setter, then we'll have been successful."

The opening session was attended by more than 100 exchange members and invited guests, including representatives of Federal Barge Lines and SCNO Barge Lines of St. Louis; Riverway, Inc., Minneapolis; Twin City Barge & Towing Company of St. Paul; Peavey Company and Alton Barge Service of Alton, Ill.; Gateway Barge & Grain Company, Clayton, Mo.; Flowers Transportation, Inc., of Greenville, Miss.; and Continental Grain Company, New York.

Riverway, which transports grain barges throughout the inland waterway system, joined the exchange after participating in the development of a trading guidebook for the exchange, Vroom said. He said he anticipates several other large barge and towing companies that handle a large amount of grain traffic may also join the exchange in the near future.

Only exchange members may participate in the call sessions, Vroom said.

The First Trade. The sole trade completed during the initial floor session was offered by Midwestern Grain Company, which contracted with Peavey for the transportation of two bargeloads of grain from Peru, Ill., on the Illinois Waterway to New Orleans. The barges were to be moved during the

123

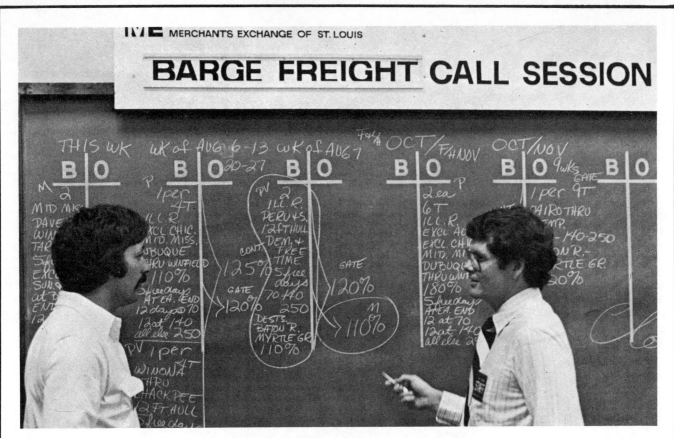

MERCHANTS EXCHANGE OF ST. LOUIS

BARGE FREIGHT CALL SESSION

The First Trade: How To Read It

Jay Vroom (r), executive vice president of the St. Louis Merchants Exchange, explains the first completed transaction on the Exchange to Allen Toberman (l), a merchandiser with Toberman Grain Company of St. Louis.

The cargo to be moved is detailed in the circled area under the "B" or bid column of the call session board. The "O" side represents the offers made by the barge operators.

Date of Move: The cargo was to be moved during the week of August 7, represented on the board by the terms "wk of Aug 7" at the top of the column.

The Cargo: Peavey Company of Alton, Illinois (PV), will have two bargeloads of grain at Peru on the Illinois River for shipment in standard barges. Free time allowed is five days with demurrage at $70 per day for the first 12

days, $140 per day for the next 12 days and $250 per day afterwards. Destination is Baton Rouge, and Peavey will accept a bid at 110% of the benchmark tariff developed by the Merchants Exchange to provide a uniform bidding system. (**See details of bid system on Page 20.**)

Barge Offers: Gateway Barge and Grain Company made the initial offer on the Peavey movement at a rate of 120% of the tariff table. Midwestern Grain Company's trader on the floor then came forth with an offer at 110%, which was what Peavey hoped to get, and the trade was completed.

By the third day of trading, when the cover photograph for *American Shipper* was taken, the Exchange had developed a more uniform method of posting Barge Freight bids and offers. This accounts for the more consistent style of markings used by Ms. Buffy Omey in the cover photo.

week of August 7 at 110% of the tariff rate schedule adopted by the exchange as a baseline for trading activities.

The only major problems encountered during trading resulted from the lack of standard abbreviations for many contract terms, leading to a confusing array of bids and offers being placed on the trading board when compared to other grain call sessions.

Vroom said he hoped that many of the terms would be simplified or abbreviated as exchange members became more familiar with the terms used in the barge freight sessions.

At mid-August, trading activity was still slow, but Exchange members were

becoming "more at ease" with the call sessions and commercial barge operators were showing more interest, Vroom reported.

During a call session, members of the exchange may post bids and offers for barge freight service, specifying terms such as shipment dates, number of barges, origin points, demurrage rates and price. When the terms of a bid and offer match, a trade is consummated.

The concept of call sessions for barge freight was first discussed at an open meeting hosted by the exchange in St. Louis and attended by both exchange members and nonmember representatives of barge and towing industry

companies. A "Standard Contract Trading Terms" guideline was then developed by a 10-member advisory committee in cooperation with the exchange call session committee.

Oldest Exchange in U.S. Dating back for more than 140 years, the St. Louis Merchants Exchange is the oldest grain exchange in the United States. Its cash grain call sessions, begun in 1971, are now the largest in the country, according to exchange officials. The barge freight call sessions are the first of their kind ever to be held in the U.S., Vroom said.

Regular grain call-session trading averaged nearly one million bushels per day in 1977, and is presently running 30 to 40 percent ahead of year-ago volumes, exchange officials said.

40 Qualified to Participate. Forty companies, all members of the exchange, have fulfilled requirements for participating in the call sessions including grain interests, barge and towing companies, financial analysts and brokerage firms.

The daily trade sessions for barge freight begin at 10:45 a.m. CDT. A market record, which includes a complete rundown of each bid placed on the board for trade, is sent to members of the exchange after every session.

Vroom told *American Shipper* the call session for barge freight was conceived by grain merchants in order to create a competitive element in the movement of export grain to New Orleans. Because of this, some barge lines have been reluctant to participate in the call sessions and much of the activity during the first half of August was confined to offers and bids by grain companies which have their own fleets of river barges. After an initial "wait and see" period, however, the bargemen began to display more interest in the exchange.

Similarity to Baltic Exchange. The Barge Freight Call Sessions initiated by the St. Louis Merchants Exchange bear many similarities to the Baltic Mercantile and Shipping Exchange in London—

better known in the shipping world as The Baltic Exchange or, more simply, "The Baltic."

This similarity between the two exchanges is purely coincidental, however, attributable only to the fact that both were formed to meet a similar need. Vroom had never heard of The Baltic Exchange in London until asked by *American Shipper* and said that to the best of his knowledge none of the committeemen who developed procedures for the St. Louis Merchants Exchange had any knowledge of The Baltic. While export grain specialists with such firms as Continental Grain, Cargill and Illinois Grain certainly know of The Baltic, none were involved at St. Louis, Vroom said.

The Baltic Exchange in London traces its origin to coffee houses where trading merchants gathered for refreshment and to transact business during the first half of the 18th Century. Trading at one such coffee house centered on grain and other products from the American colonies and seaboard states of the Baltic Sea. In 1744, the place came to be known as The Virginia and Baltic Exchange. Later this was contracted to The Baltic and the exchange is now officially known as The Baltic Mercantile and Shipping Exchange.

The Baltic Exchange many years ago became the recognized world center of shipping.

On the floor of The Baltic Exchange,

brokers representing cargo vessel owners from around the world meet with other brokers or agents representing grain, coal and other commodity shippers with goods to be moved. The Baltic has specialists in various trades, thus assuring an order to the process.

Brokers on The Baltic Exchange negotiate charters which need only to be confirmed by their principals before being "fixed." Virtually all transactions are verbal, and the word of the Exchange member is literally his bond until the charter can be translated into documents—a procedure which requires time.

In recent years, The Baltic Exchange has become a center for charter of aircraft and many other types of activity in the transportation field.

All charters fixed through The Baltic Exchange are on standard contracts and terms of the charter agreements are posted, providing an immediate public record which enables merchants and vessel owners alike to know the exact status of the market and its trends.

The Future? Whether the St. Louis Merchants Exchange will emerge as a center of charter activity in the United States comparable to The Baltic Exchange in London remains to be determined. Its birth was similar, however, and considering the size of the American trade, a vigorous growth can be expected.

BARGE FREIGHT CALL SESSION
STANDARD CONTRACT TRADING TERMS

1. Purpose: The purpose of the Merchants Exchange of St. Louis Barge Freight Call Session is to further competition in barge freight by making available to Exchange members an open auction market in which barge freight service can be competitively traded.

2. Time: Barge freight trading will begin each weekday (Monday through Friday except on official Exchange holidays) at 10:45 A.M. The call Session will be open for at least 5 minutes (until 10:50 A.M.) and no longer than 44 minutes (until 11:29 A.M.).

3. Shipment Date(s): At the discretion of each trader and is to be stated at the beginning of each bid or offer. Shipment dates may be confined to any time period, i.e. within a month, week, day, etc.

4. Contract Quantities: The standard contract quantity will be in barge units and the barge size for trading purposes is assumed to be 200/195 ft. by 35 ft. unless otherwise specified by each trader.

5. Minimum Loading: For contract trading purposes bids and offers are assumed to be 1,300 tons rake/1,500 tons a box.

6. Points of Origin: For Call Session trading purposes, points of origin will include eight distinct regions defined as follows:

1. Illinois River (Chicago through Alton)
2. Mid Mississippi River (McGregor, Iowa through Winfield, Missouri)
3. Twin Cities (all inclusive from one mile above McGregor, Iowa through head of navigation)
4. Mississippi (Granite City through Cairo)
5. Lower Mississippi (South of Cairo)
6. Ohio River
7. Arkansas River
8. Missouri River

The trader shall specify in his bid/offer a specific point on the river **or** a region.

7. Point of Destination: For contract trading purposes, destination shall be assumed to be the Mississippi River—Baton Rouge, Louisiana through Myrtle Grove, Louisiana.

8. Method of Bidding: In order to facilitate Call Session trading, bids and offers may be stated as a percentage of the Merchants Exchange Benchmark Rate for the involved haul or traders may bid or offer a flat, cash per-short ton price.

9. Products to Carry: It is understood that bids and offers made during the Call Session are for transportation of grain and soybeans only, unless otherwise stated.

10. Insurance: Cargo Bills of Lading for barge transportation traded in the Call Session will be fully insured per National Grain and Feed Association Rules.

11. Demurrage: Origin and destination demurrage shall be as specified in each bid and offer.

12. Failure to Perform: Settlement of failure to perform situations arising from Call Session trades shall be settled between the parties involved in the transaction and the Exchange shall only be involved when such situation is in dispute and brought to the Exchange for arbitration.

13. Payment Terms: Arrangement to be established between parties involved in the trade. Payment is due carrier within 5 days of receipt of invoice accompanied by proof of delivery (bill of lading) and weight certificate.

14. Alteration of Bids/Offers. Once a bid or offer is placed on the chalkboard, the trader can only alter that bid or offer by "improving" it—i.e., offer barge transportation for a **lower** rate, or bid for barge transportation at a **higher** rate. The only other alternative to a trader is to CANCEL a bid or offer which automatically makes him liable for Call Session charges normally assessed to **both** parties involved in a trade ($10 per barge).

15. Additional Terms: Other terms may be specified at the discretion of the trader in the bid or offer.

16. Charges: Each side of a Call Session trade of barge freight (buyer and seller) will be charged $5.00 per contract (barge) traded. These charges are established by the Board of Directors as authorized in paragraph 901 of the Exchange Articles of Association, By-Laws, and Rules.

17. Operation: Paragraph 900 and 901 of the Merchants Exchange Articles of Association, By-Laws and Rules and applicable Board of Directors resolutions will govern operation of the Barge Freight Rate Call Session.

BARGE FREIGHT RATE CALL SESSION BASIS TRADING BENCHMARKS - JUNE 1978
(Benchmarks in Cents Per Ton)

TO: (Baton Rouge, Destrehan, Myrtle Grove, New Orleans & Reserve) FROM:						
ARKANSAS		Dallas City	508	South Chicago	578	Louisville	446	Napoleon	648

FROM	¢		¢		¢		¢		¢
		Dallas City	508	South Chicago	578	Louisville	446	Napoleon	648
		E. St. Louis	399	Spring Valley	507	Owensboro	404	New Madrid	380
		Florence	464	Warsaw	508			St. Joseph	718
		Frederick	464			**MINNESOTA**		St. Louis	399
		Fults	399	**INDIANA**		Minneapolis	619	Waverly	648
		Hardin	464	Evansville	399	Red Wing	619	Winfield	484
		Havana	464	Mount Vernon	399	St. Paul	619		
		Hennepin	507			Shakopee	619	**NEBRASKA**	
ARKANSAS		Henry	507	**IOWA**		Winona	619	Blair	828
Barfield Landing	351	Joliet	524	Burlington	508			Brownville	796
Cracraft Landing	229	Joppa	382	Clinton	532	**MISSISSIPPI**		Nebraska City	796
Dardanelle-Russellville	415	Keithsburg	532	Council Bluffs	796	Greenville	229	Omaha	796
De Soto Landing	247	Kingston Mines	481	Davenport	532	Mayerville	229	Plattsmouth	796
Fort Smith	472	Lacon	507	Dubuque	600	Natchez	229	Rock Bluff	796
Grand Lake	229	La Salle	507	Greenbay Landing	508	Perthshire	267		
Helena	299	Lockport	531	Guttenberg	600	Vicksburg	229	**OHIO**	
Huffman	351	Meredosia	464	McGregor	600			Cincinnati	469
Lake Village	229	Meyer Light	508	Meeker's Landing	508	**MISSOURI**			
Little Rock	364	Morris	524	Montrose	508	Birds Point	380	**OKLAHOMA**	
Osceola	351	Naples	464	Muscatine	532	Brunswick	648	Catoosa	564
Pine Bluff	313	Nauvoo	508	Sioux City	925	Cape Girardeau	399	Muskogee	526
Yellow Bend	247	New Boston	532			Caruthersville	354		
		Oquawka	508	**KANSAS**		Glasgow	648	**TENNESSEE**	
ILLINOIS		Ottawa	507	Atchison	718	Gregory	508	Boothspoint	354
Albany	**532**	Ottawa	507	Kansas City	648	Hannibal	484	Cottonwood Point	354
Iton	399	Pekin	481	Leavenworth	718	Jefferson City	605	Gold Dust	351
Beardstown	464	Peoria	481	White Cloud	796	Kansas City	648	Hale Point	351
Cairo	380	Peru	507	Wolcott	660	La Grange	484	Heloise	354
Chester	399	Quincy	484			Lexington	648	Memphis	314
Chicago	578	Rock Island	532	**KENTUCKY**		Linda	380		
Chillicothe	507	Seneca	524	Henderson	399	Louisiana	484	**WISCONSIN**	
Creve Coeur	481	Shawneetown	399	Hickman	380	Miami	648	La Crosse	619

Iowa Department of Transportation
5268 N.W. 2nd Avenue
Des Moines, Iowa 50313
515/281-4292

COMPARE

CARGO CAPACITY

LARGE SEMI
25 TON
875 BUSHELS
7,560 GALLONS

100 CAR UNIT TRAIN (GRAIN)
10,000 TON
350,000 BUSHELS
3,024,000 GALLONS

JUMBO HOPPER CAR
100 TON
3,500 BUSHELS
30,240 GALLONS

15 BARGE TOW
22,500 TON
787,500 BUSHELS
6,804,000 GALLONS

BARGE
1500 TON
52,500 BUSHELS
453,600 GALLONS

EQUIVALENT UNITS

60 TRUCKS

900 TRUCKS

=

=

2¼ UNIT TRAINS

15 JUMBO HOPPERS

=

=

1 TOW

1 BARGE

EQUIVALENT LENGTHS

36 MILES
ASSUMING 150 FT.
BETWEEN TRUCKS

2¾ MILES
2¼ UNIT TRAINS

¼ MILE
15 BARGE TOW

Prepared by:
Planning and Research Division
Iowa Department of Transportation

127

The Coast Guard Board of Inquiry and the Lake Carriers' Association have opposite views into the sinking of the Edmund Fitzgerald—and the corrective measures which should be taken depend upon the viewpoint.

Here, in summary, is what each believes happened—why it happened— and what can be done to minimize the risk of future tragedies.

The Fitzgerald Sinking: Two Views

THE COAST GUARD POSITION

A Coast Guard Board of Inquiry has reported its findings into the cause of the 1975 sinking of the *Edmund Fitzgerald*. The Coast Guard Marine Board of Inspection cited a loss of buoyancy as the probable cause for the sinking of the Oglebay-Norton operated vessel. The buoyancy loss was attributable to possible ineffective hatch covers and damaged vents, according to the report.

Admiral Owen W. Siler, Commandant of the Coast Guard, cited his intention of proposing a number of regulations designed to prevent similar disasters, including the installation of watertight bulkheads between cargo holds, a highly expensive proposition, especially for self-unloading vessels.

A second measure being considered by The Coast Guard is on-the-spot repair of damaged hatch covers. Hatch coamings are sometimes dented during loading or unloading processes with minor repairs normally put off until winter lay-ups. Because even a minor dent precludes a watertight fit, the Coast Guard is considering a requirement that all dents be repaired on the spot.

The use of covered life boats, survival suits and self-launching rafts were also suggested as possible new safety measures. The *Fitzgerald* sank on November 10, 1975, with a loss of all 29 members of the crew. The Board said the ship sank probably because of massive flooding in the cargo hold. While admitting it could not positively determine the cause, the Board indicated the flooding of the cargo hold took place through ineffective hatch closures.

"The flooding which began early on the 10th of November, progressed under worsening weather and sea conditions and increased in volume," the report said, "finally resulting in such a loss of buoyancy and stability that the vessel plunged into the heavy seas."

The *Fitzgerald*, broken, lies in 530 ft. of water near Whitefish Bay.

[See page 129]

THE LAKE CARRIERS' POSITION

T he Lake Carriers' Association has rejected the findings of the Coast Guard's Board of Inquiry into causes for the sinking of the *Edmund Fitzgerald*, and points to shoaling rather than poor hatch closures as the cause of the Whitefish Bay disaster.

In a report filed with the National Transportation Safety Board (NTSB), the Association took strong exception to the Coast Guard position regarding "ineffective hatch closures" and pointed to other safety measures which might be taken to help alleviate similar sinkings.

The Lake Carriers' (LCA) is an organization established by 15 domestic bulk shipping companies in the Great Lakes / Seaway system and includes over 135 vessels with a registered gross tonnage of nearly 1.4 million.

"It is important to note that the spar deck inspection of the *Fitzgerald*, conducted ten days before the sinking by the Coast Guard OCMI at Toledo and the American Bureau of Shipping, the classification society relied upon by the Coast Guard, revealed no significant damage of the hatch coamings or closure fittings," the LCA noted in its report.

"We call attention to almost forty years' experience with the current type of hatch covers...If ineffective closings exist, as alleged by the Coast Guard, surely during the forty years operating experience there would have been watery cargo to unload...this not only would have been readily apparent, but also a costly problem that vessel and cargo owners would not tolerate."

"Water could be handled." It should be emphasized that minutes after passing Six Fathom Shoal the *Fitzgerald* reported a list . . . both ballast tank vents had been carried away and two ballast pumps were in use. "Capacity of the two pumps was 14,000 gallons per minute. Each vent opening in the deck would be eight

[See page 129]

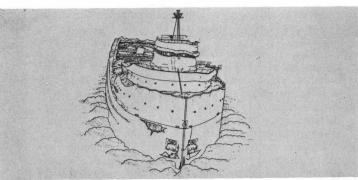

Sketch from Coast Guard report shows bow damage, severence from midsection and stern.

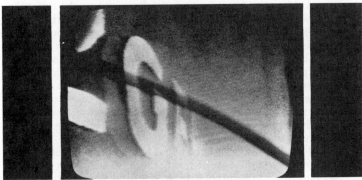

Underwater TV camera shows letters Z...G...E...R.. from stern section, which lies upside down on Lake Superior bottom.

THE COAST GUARD POSITION

The bow of the vessel is upright with the stern upside down at a 50° angle and the midsection scattered on the lake floor (see SEAWAY REVIEW Vol. 6 No. 1, page 34).

The *Fitzgerald* was sailing from Superior, Wisconsin to Detroit with a cargo of taconite. Enroute, the ship encountered 10 ft. seas in a bad November storm. James A. Wilson, chief of the Marine Safety Division of the Coast Guard's Ninth District at Cleveland, and a member of the investigating board, reconstructed the last hours of the *Fitzgerald*, noting that waves apparently washed over the deck, causing added damage to hatch covers that were already worn by regular use.

Apparently between two swells, "the ship's bow did not recover its buoyancy, dived into a wall of water and the ship went to the bottom." Before going down, the Board stated, the *Fitzgerald* had noted a list and some damage, including the loss of two vents and deck railings, as well as difficulties with radar.

The *Fitzgerald* had asked a nearby vessel, the *Anderson*, to provide navigational information and apparently had slowed down to allow the *Anderson* to catch up. The report noted that "this action might have been taken because the master of the *Fitzgerald* (Capt. Ernest M. McSorley) knew or sensed that his problems were of a more severe nature than reported (to the *Anderson*)." □

THE LAKE CARRIERS' POSITION

inches in diameter, so the amount of water entering two eight-inch vents could readily have been handled by the ballast pumps," the report state.

"With the two pumps operating there should have been no list from this source of water, particularly in as short of time as 10 to 15 minutes. Captain Cooper of the *Anderson* testified that 'he took that list which seemed to be real fast'.

"Within the time frame involved, such a list can only be readily explained by holing of the vessel's ballast tanks, caused by striking Six Fathom Shoals."

There was no indication water was entering the holds from topside other than the small amount coming through the two openings. It should be kept in mind that the hatch covers are on coamings raised two feet above the main deck, LCA noted.

"Had the water causing the list (of the *Fitzgerald*) been entering the cargo hold from topside, the amount of water passing aft to the cargo hold section would have been insufficient to support even one ballast pump. It is also questionable whether water in the cargo hold would have resulted in a list since it would not have been restricted to one side of the vessel."

The damage, LCA contends, had to be on the bottom and, since there was no indication of any structural failure, it must have been caused by an external force such as shoaling.

After the initial damage caused by shoaling, LCA theorizes that the vessel labored in heavy quartering seas for over three hours, proceeding towards Whitefish Point.

"As the vessel filled up gradually from the bottom to the point where its buoyancy was marginal, a large wave or series of heavy waves could have raised the stern, starting the bow's dive underwater, never to recover," the report stated.

Uncharted Shoal. A hydrographic survey of the Caribou Island shoal waters conducted by Canadian Hydrographic Service, at the request of the Coast Guard Marine Board looking into the *Fitzgerald* sinking, identifies a shoal less than six fathoms deep more than one mile farther east than any in the Six Fathom Shoal cluster depicted on the latest navigation charts.

"This verified shoal", LCA notes, "was in the track of the *Fitzgerald*, as observed by the *Anderson*, thus making shoaling even more certain as the start of the fateful events leading to the sinking."

Moving into areas of safety, LCA told the NTSB that "Some background may be helpful to counter the thinking that lake vessels have no watertight compartments and are merely one large bathtub.

"Great Lakes vessels are designed with segregated ballast tanks. This means that the ship has tanks designed exclusively for water ballast and it is not necessary to utilize the cargo hold for water ballast when in the light condition. These tanks provide a double shell over the entire bottom of the cargo hold and vertically up the sides to about the loaded water line on most ships.

"Tunnels under the weather deck have watertight doors and afford watertight integrity several feet above the main deck...The typical Great Lakes bulk vessel has six to nine ballast tanks on each side, with each tank divided port and starboard by a watertight center vertical keelson and fore and aft by a watertight bulkhead.

"Additionally, the ship is divided into complete watertight compartments by the collision bulkhead forward and the engine room bulkhead aft."

These watertight subdivisions, LCA notes, along with the ballast tanks, afford a substantial margin of safety in case the shell of the vessel is penetrated, allowing water to flood one or more of these compartments.

In House Merchant Marine and Fisheries Committee Coast Guard oversight hearings at Sault Ste. Marie last year, LCA listed a number of safety recommendations under consideration by government and industry. They included:

Hull monitoring: the development of a hull monitoring system with an appropriate pilothouse readout to interpret hull actions in all weather situations and to alert the vessel's master that trouble is developing. *Seaway Review* has learned that a MarAd contract is in process to develop and test such a monitoring system on a lake vessel.

Develop an all-weather capsule: a change in Coast Guard regulations to permit development and use of survival equipment other than traditional life rafts and lifeboats.

(Since recommending development of a "survival capsule" for shipboard use, interest has been expressed by several firms in this country. In Norway, government, shipping and classifications society authorities have developed a 36-man capsule that can be ejected from a ship's deck.)

Survival suits: after considerable study, the Coast Guard in August approved two survival suits for shipboard use.

Improved weather forecasting: weather buoys, the assignment of marine forecasters, more vessels reporting weather data, looking at the lakes as a weather system for marine purposes and better communications are under consideration or in process. This, together with improved meteorological training of deck officers, LCA believes, will further enhance safety of lake shipping.

Position keeping on the lake: two changes are underway that will improve lake navigation in the future. One will be especially helpful: as part of the national navigation plan, Loran-C coverage for the lakes is to be provided by the Coast Guard by 1980. This remarkably accurate position finding system is not affected by visibility, sea return or other weather conditions. It will be the principal means of navigation, complementing radar, and will obsolete radio beacons on the lakes. Consequently, completion of the Loran-C coverage should be expedited.

The other change is a requirement for fathometers on lake vessels. The bottom characteristic of the lakes and the limited bottom information shown on charts will limit the usefulness of this equipment, but it may be of some help in special situations.

And finally, the uncharted shoal less than six fathoms deep over one mile east of Six Fathom Shoal, north of Caribou Island, will be shown on future navigation charts of eastern Lake Superior. □

The All-Season Seaway Draws Closer

Each year, about December 15, one of the largest transportation systems in North America, a system that in 1977 moved more than 63 million tons of wheat, soybeans, iron ore, coal, steel, machinery, chemicals, fertilizers and containership loads of every imaginable kind of general merchandise, starts literally to grind to a halt.

The system is the St. Lawrence Seaway and the grinding is that of ice. Ice builds on the walls of canal locks, making them too narrow for large ships. It lodges in the lock gate recesses so that often gates cannot be opened. If the gates can be opened, a ship may push so much ice into the lock that the ship itself cannot enter and the ice must first be locked through as though it were another ship.

As the great winter storm systems swings Arctic air south, a race to escape the ice and exit the Seaway begins among the general cargo-carrying "salties" or oceangoing ships that provide the Great Lakes ports with their highest revenues and largest source of employment. In late summer, an official Seaway closing date, based on long range weather predictions, river flows, icebreaker availability and other factors is announced by the U.S. and Canadian Seaway authorities (see box). But that date is not a guarantee that all ships will clear the Seaway. The closing date is rather "a commitment," says the U.S. St. Lawrence Development Corporation, "that every reasonable effort will be made to move out all of the ships that are in line at the designated call-in point by closing time." In 1977, the closing date, midnight December, 15, arrived with 83 outbound ocean ships plowing their way through the brash ice to the St. Lawrence River call-in point at Whaleback Shoal, just east of Alexandria Bay. By working crews day and night, and aided by a week of unusually mild temperatures, the U.S. and Canadian Coast Guard equipment and pilots managed to clear the last latecomer by December 26.

When the last ship has pulled away from the St. Lambert and Beauharnois Locks, the Seaway settles in for its traditional three-and-a-half months of winter hibernation. On the Upper Great Lakes, linked by the Sault Ste. Marie (Soo) Locks, bulk carriers may continue to operate as late as February if the winter is mild, and in recent years, under a congressionally-authorized demonstration program, some ships have continued to operate throughout the four lower lakes for the entire winter. In the St. Lawrence River section, ice breakers may keep channels open long after the official closing date. But the artery to the sea is closed by ice in all its forms—brash (broken), frazil (a jelly-like mixture of ice and water), open pack, close pack, compact and consolidated.

Seaway Revises Closing Procedures for 1978

The St. Lawrence Seaway Development Corporation announced in August that it is revising its closing procedures for this year's navigation season to ease some of the problems encountered in recent winters. Upbound vessels transiting into the Great Lakes, and wishing to return downbound through the St. Lambert Lock will be accepted at the Welland Canal calling-in point (CIP) up to 2400 hours on December 6, 1978. Downbound vessels will be accepted for transit at CIP Crossover Island up to 2400 hours, December 15. Upbound vessels will be accepted at Cap St. Michel up to 2400 hours, December, 15. Vessel captains not reporting to the designated call-in points may be allowed to transit, but will be assessed a surcharge of $20,000 for reporting December 1, $40,000 for reporting December 17, $60,000 for December 18, and $80,000 for December 19 and thereafter. The agency has also revised certain dimension, draft and horsepower restrictions for the St. Lambert-Iroquois segment of the Seaway to reduce the problems caused by ships operating in ice. These restrictions will become effective December 7, with more stringent restrictions coming into effect after December 12.

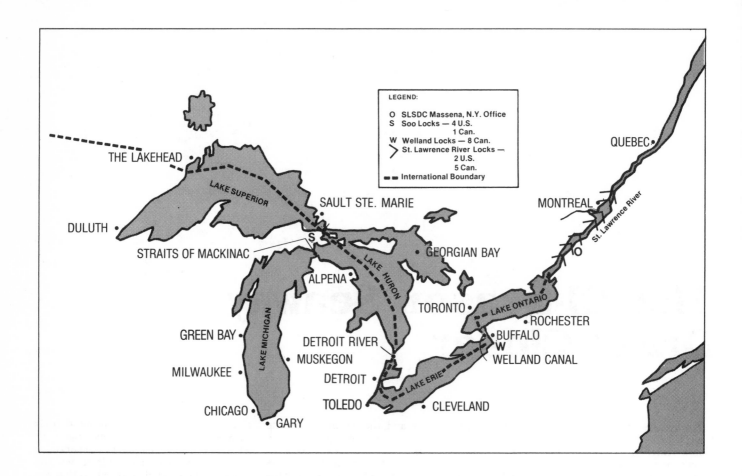

Abbreviated Selected Tariff Definitions

Bulk Cargo — goods transported loose or in mass, i.e., coke, cement, domestic package freight, liquids, ores and minerals, pig iron, pulpwood, raw sugar and woodpulp.

Containerized Cargo — any general cargo shipped in an enclosed, permanent, reusable, nondisposable, weathertight, shipping conveyance having a cubic capacity of 640 feet or more and fitted with a minimum of one hinged door.

General Cargo — non-bulk and non-Government aid cargo which includes packaged, processed and manufactured products.

Grain — all major food and feed grains, including wheat, rye, corn, barley, soybeans, rapeseed, grain screenings, buckwheat, and dried beans and peas.

Government Aid Cargo — processed food products donated or purchased by the Federal governments of the U.S. or Canada for the purposes of foreign aid or disaster relief, i.e., U.S. Public Law 480, Title II cargo.

NOTE: For complete tariff and transit rules, write to: Saint Lawrence Seaway Development Corporation, Office of Communications, P.O. Box 520; Massena, New York 13662.

For the Lakes ports on what is often called "America's fourth seacoast," it is a costly closing. A Department of Commerce study of 11 of the 19 states comprising the Great Lakes Economic Region found that a 12-month shipping season would add $382 million constant 1967 dollars to those states' labor earnings by 1980 and almost $1 billion by the year 2020. The Port of Toledo estimates in a recent study that for every two days the navigation season in the Lakes can be extended, Toledo would receive $1 million from the economic benefits of port-related goods and services. An earlier study of firms shipping through the Port of Cleveland indicated that even a 10-month season would mean a 22-per-cent increase in the port's traffic and a year-round season would increase traffic by at least 33 per cent. On the Canadian side, the Port of

Toronto estimates that an extended shipping season would increase overseas tonnage into the port by 20 to 30 per cent.

The prime beneficiaries of an extended Seaway navigation season would of course be the Great Lakes region shippers who must now, like corporate Cinderellas, change their entire pattern of operations at midnight December 15. Exports that for eight-and-a-half months of the year have taken the all-water route now must be shipped overland to Gulf or east coast ports. Users of bulk commodities are forced to stockpile vast quantities of materials to maintain production during the freeze. Ships and equipment that must be paid for over the entire year now fall idle, and utilization is distorted into an extreme "peak and valley" pattern that causes much economically obsolete capital equipment

to be retained to handle the rush of the high season.

With the benefits of an all-year Seaway obvious to all (though not, perhaps, to competing railroads), it's not suprising that reports and studies of the feasibility and cost benefits of breaking through the winter ice plug have been circulating since shortly after the Seaway was opened to deep-draft navigation in 1959. In 1972, Congress authorized a five-year demonstration project that recently culminated in a report concluding that "the practicability of navigation season extension on the Great Lakes-St. Lawrence Seaway system has been successfully demonstrated." The demonstration project was directed by the Winter Navigation Board, the coordinating body for a multitude of participating agencies that includes the Corps of Engineers, the

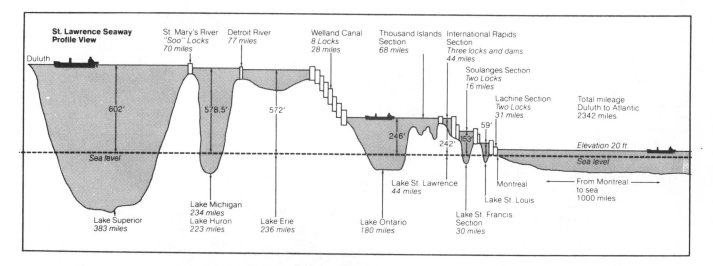

St. Lawrence Seaway
Profile View

Duluth

St. Mary's River
"Soo" Locks
70 miles

Detroit River
77 miles

Welland Canal
8 Locks
28 miles

Thousand Islands
Section
68 miles

International Rapids
Section
Three locks and dams
44 miles

Soulanges Section
Two Locks
16 miles

Lachine Section
Two Locks
31 miles

Total mileage
Duluth to Atlantic
2342 miles

Elevation 20 ft.

602'   578.5'   572'   246'   242'   153'   59'   Sea level

Sea level

Lake St. Lawrence
44 miles

Montreal

From Montreal
to sea
1000 miles

Lake St. Louis

Lake Superior
383 miles

Lake Michigan
234 miles
Lake Huron
223 miles

Lake Erie
236 miles

Lake Ontario
180 miles

Lake St. Francis
Section
30 miles

Icefloes pile up at the entrances to locks so that the ice must often be locked through before the ship can enter. Ice also lodges in lock gate recesses and builds up on lock walls, making the lock too narrow for large ships to enter.

Coast Guard, the Maritime Administration, the Federal Energy Regulatory Commission, the Department of the Interior, the National Oceanic and Atmospheric Administration and the Environmental Protection Agency as well as the entities directly concerned with Seaway and Great Lakes, such as the Great Lakes Commission and the St. Lawrence Seaway Development Corporation.

In the words of the *Seaway Review,* the Winter Navigation Board's report proclaims that the extension of the winter navigation season on the Great Lakes is "an event that's trying to happen," feasible from both an engineering and an economic viewpoint. The program showed for example, that suitably designed ice booms permit ships to navigate through gaps between them *without* churning the ice cover of the whole channel into vast jams. (Surprisingly, for those who think in terms of simply smashing a way through, one of the major problems in keeping the Seaway open during the winter months is that of maintaining a stable ice cover in the rivers and connecting channels between the Lakes. Beneath the ice sheet, the water continues to flow, but once the sheet is broken, ice floes drift together, piling up into massive dams 30 to 40 feet thick that cause flooding in the spring thaws. Broken ice can also block the turbine inlets to the important hydro electric plants that are scattered throughout the Seaway.)

Air bubbler systems, which move the warmer bottom water to the surface to prevent ice forming, and bubbler-flushers, which use air bubbles to create currents that flush ice away from lock gates and docks, are also highly successful additions to the ice-fighting arsenal, according to the Winter Navigation Board's report. Bubblers work on the same principle as a child blowing warm breath through a straw in a glass of iced lemonade. They can be fitted to the hulls of ships as well as installed on lake and channel bottoms. Aboard ship, the air jets "lubricate" the hull with a layer of air so that it easily slides through the ice-covered water.

Inevitably, computers have been called into the many research and development projects that have branched out from the main winter navigation programs. The Department of Naval Architecture and Marine Engineering in the University of Michigan's College of Engineering, under contracts with the Maritime Administration, has developed an Extended Season Program (ESP) for simulating on the computer the operations of "a vessel of any reasonable characteristics, in any feasible commodity movement on the Lakes over any length of navigational season." The program designs the vessel, computes its capital and operating costs, predicts its performance in various ice conditions and produces measures of economic return for its owners, according to a description published in *The Winter Navigator*, which reports the activities of the multi-agency Board. A later development of the program called ESP2 includes ice data for the St. Lawrence River thus making it possible to choose computer-designed routes between the Great Lakes and the Gulf of St. Lawrence ports for the computer-designed ship.

Computers also figure largely in a number of other projects. In mid-1976, the Seaway corporation awarded a contract to Arctec, Inc., a consulting firm specializing in the problems of shipping in arctic conditions, for mathematical and hydraulic ice modeling of portions of the International Rapids section. In addition to the computer "models" of figures and formulas, Arctec was commissioned to construct an actual 422-foot-long replica of a 13-mile stretch of the St. Lawernce River between Stillwell Point and Red Mlls, one of the most difficult reaches of the river with many power company ice booms across the navigation channel.

This model, housed in a large building built for the purpose near Baltimore, Md., makes use of a variety of ingenious devices to recreate in miniature the river ice conditions and their effects on ice booms (*see box*). Based on tests being made with the model, modifications to the actual booms will be made during the coming winter to "improve winter navigation while maintaining or improving the stability of the ice cover and the hydraulic integrity of the River," according to the Seaway corporation's 1977 annual report.

The U.S. Army Corps of Engineers, at its new Cold Regions Research and Engineering Laboratory (CRREL) in Hannover, N. H., is also modeling stretches of the Seaway as part of a general attack on the problems of ice on

Two ice booms spanning the navigation channel at Ogdenburg-Prescott and Galop Island in the International Rapids section of the St. Lawrence River will be modified for the 1978-79 navigation season to allow a limited number of ship transits through them. The booms are made up of 30-foot long Douglas fir timbers connected to a steel cable by lengths of chain and anchored to the river bottom. Pictures above show the Arctec 422-foot-long hydraulic ice model used in ice engineering research, and the building housing the model at the Howard County Fairgrounds, Md. Wax-like chemicals approximating the properties of ice are used to simulate the ice cover.

the Nation's waterways. The Corps' ice engineering laboratory is a two-story building with a test basin and a "flume room" where all the stages of ice formation can be studied through underwater windows. The flume, which measures two by four feet in cross section and 120 feet long, can be tilted to produce various strengths of water flow, and has a refrigerated bottom so that "the river" can be frozen from the bottom up. This reverses the natural process of river ice formation and allows the investigators in effect to turn the ice sheet upside down and examine its underside. Other problems being studied include the damage that ice can do to bridges, shorelines and harbor

facilities and the effects of ice on drainage.

But if year-long navigation on the Seaway is ever to become something more than a matter of models, the engineers all agree that brute-force ice breaking will still have to play a major part. In 1976, the Maritime Administration joined with a group of seven Great Lakes shipping companies in sponsoring a $230,000 contract, again to Arctec, Inc., to find out if the bows of Great Lakes bulk carriers could be modified, without loss of cargo capacity, so as in effect to turn them into ice breakers. A tug barge was fitted out for a series of ice impact load tests, and the results together with data from other shipboard tests, have been used by Arctec to develop a mathematical (or predictor) model to help designers predict the ice impact forces on various bow forms.

The ice also stresses ships' hulls, of course, and various programs are being conducted to provide design information to combat these stresses. Because of their extreme length, the Great Lakes bulk carriers tend to "spring" or flex up and down in rough weather and this tendency may be aggravated by the impact of ice. MarAd and the U.S. Coast Guard have combined funds and expertise to examine this problem and MarAd has also joined the American Bureau of Shipping in sponsoring ship-springing research at the University of Michigan.

The true icebreakers, however, remain the focus of the agency concern and research effort. The U.S. Coast Guard icebreaker fleet has only one ship specifically designed for Lakes icebreaking and that was built in 1942. The rest of the fleet is made up of five converted harbor tugs, five buoy tenders with some ice breaking capacity and a renovated wartime polar icebreaker that sometimes has to be rescued, when stuck, by the Lakes icebreaker. The Coast Guard iteself describes this heterogenous collection of vessels as "overaged" and "obsolete" and there has been considerable debate in Congress and elsewhere as to what to do about it. In the early years of the winter navigation demonstration project, MarAd awarded a half-million dollar contract to a Finnish firm, OY Wartsila, for research into ice-breaking bow designs for Lakes ore carriers, and to buy Finnish icebreakers has been proposed as the quickest method to improve the ice breaking fleet. But the Coast Guard has showed a marked reluctance to buy Finnish, despite estimates that it would take five years for U.S. shipbuilders to design and build equivalent icebreakers. The odds are good that at least one Finnish icebreaker will be bought, however. Representative John M. Murphy (D-N.Y.), chairman of the House Merchant Marine and Fisheries Committee, recently returned from a visit to Finland convinced that the Finns make the world's most efficient icebreakers; and Representative James L. Oberstar (D-Minn.), chairman of the Great Lakes Conference of Congressmen has introduced a bill calling for a $55 million appropriation to buy an icebreaker—"preferably," reported the *Seaway Review*, "a Finnish one."

The Canadian Coast Guard also has a important interest in extending the St. Lawrence Seaway shipping season—and by a happy economy, in extending the Arctic shipping season. In winter, its fleet of 22 icebreakers operates on the Great Lakes and the Seaway ap-

SAINT LAWRENCE SEAWAY JOINT TARIFF OF TOLLS

Comparison of 1977 tolls with those to be assessed from 1978-81

Per Metric Ton

CARGO TOLLS/ COMMERCIAL VESSEL CHARGES	1977	1978	1979	1980/81
Combined Sections (full Transit of Montreal-Lake Ontario (Mo-Lo) & Welland Canal Sections)				
Bulk	.44	.70	.86	.99
Containers	.99	.99	.99	.99
Government Aid Cargoes	.44/.99*	.61	.65	.72
Grain	.44	.61	.65	.72
General	.99	1.55	1.88	2.15
Vessel charge, per gross registered ton	.04	.14	.14	.14
Vessel charge for 8 locks	800.00	none	none	none
Montreal-Lake Ontario Section (full transit)				
Bulk	$ .44	$ .50	$ .62	$ .68
Containers	.99	.68	.68	.68
Government Aid Cargoes	.44/.99*	.41	.41	.41
Grain	.44	.41	.41	.41
General	.99	1.27	1.49	1.65
Vessel charge, per gross registered ton	.04	.07	.07	.07
Welland Canal Section (full transit)				
Bulk	none	.20	.24	.31
Containers	none	.31	.31	.31
Government Aid Cargoes	none	.20	.24	.31
Grain	none	.20	.24	.31
General	none	.28	.39	.50
Vessel charge, per gross registered ton	none	.07	.07	.07
Vessel charge for 8 locks	800.00	none	none	none

*Government aid cargo includes cargoes currently classed in both the bulk and general cargoes.

OTHER CHARGES

1. Partial transit by commercial vessel (1978-81):
   - Mo-Lo section — 15% per lock of applicable toll (same as 1977).
   - Welland Canal section — 13% per lock of applicable toll (new charge).

	1977		1978-81	
	Mo-Lo	Welland	Mo-Lo	Welland
2. Per paid-fare passenger	$3.50	None	$5.25	$6.00
3. Pleasure craft (minimum charge)	2.00/lock	$3.00/lock	4.00/lock	4.00/lock
4. Other vessels (minimum charge)	4.00/lock	5.00/lock	8.00/lock	8.00/lock

proaches; in summer the fleet heads north to the Canadian Arctic to escort ships and supply remote settlements. The Canadians talk of icebreakers so massive that eventually Arctic shipping as well as that on the Lakes will be conducted for 12 months of the year.

The Canadians have reported 1975 tests that show air cushion vehicles (ACV's) have the unexpected ability to break ice up to two feet thick while speeding along at 20 knots, and much thicker ice at lower speeds. In collaboration with the Canadian subsidiary of a Texas firm called Arctic

Engineers and Constructors, the Canadian Coast Guard has held some impressive demonstrations at Thunder Bay with an ACV icebreaker called "Iceater." Members of the U.S. Seaway corporation who observed the demonstrations were reported to be examining the ACV's potential for similar applications in the U.S. sections of the St. Lawrence River.

On some of the other problems of achieving the all-season Seaway, however, Canadian and U.S. viewpoints have shown signs of diverging. The Canadians favor a step-by-step ap-

An important part of the season extension research and development program is directed to improving hull designs so that bulk carriers may be their own ice breakers.

proach. Paul Normandeau, president of Canada's St. Lawrence Seaway Authority, said recently that the Canadians wanted first to "add another 15 days to the season and a full month later on." For the time being "we don't want to speculate on an 11-and 12-month navigation season," he said. A tentative policy of the Canadian Seaway authorities contemplates extending the navigation season in the four upper Great Lakes to January 31 over the next three to five years and to the same date in the lower St. Lawrence over the next five to seven years. Another Canadian proposal calls for a three-phase program to open the Lake Ontario-Welland Canal section one month earlier than the traditional opening date of April 1. But, says the *Seaway Review*, Canada "is lagging considerably behind (the U.S.) in its zeal for year-round navigation."

On the U.S. side, Seaway authorities talk wistfully of a crash program similar to the man-on-the-moon project, but concede many problems still to be solved, not the least of which is money. "We are not stretching the state of the engineering art a lot to achieve year-round navigation," says Gen. Robert L. Moore, the former chairman of the Great Lakes Navigation Board. "The question is: What price do you have to pay, and what benefit do you achieve with the price you pay." In an interim report recommending an extension of the navigation season on the upper four Great Lakes to January 31, General Moore's own Corps of Engineers estimates the average annual savings for year round navigation on the entire system would come to more than $200 million with annual costs of $33.8 million — a benefit/cost ratio of six to one. But the Canadians see most of those benefits going to the U.S. while a sizable share of the costs — those of winterizing the Welland Canal-Lake Ontario-St. Lawrence exit to the sea, for example, would be theirs. Year-long navigation would almost certainly require "twinning" locks in this section so that annual maintenance work, at present performed in the closed season, could be carried out. Estimates of the costs of *that* project would give even the U.S. Treasury pause. But, say the U.S. agencies, until the Canadians see their way to making the more of a commitment to a 12-month shipping season on the Seaway, all the cost/benefit analyses will remain academic exercises. In 1977, the Winter Navigation Board asked the State Department to see what could be done to improve cooperation with the Canadians in current winter navigation projects. For the moment, however, "there is no official policy for any further winterizing of Canadian navigation facilities along the inland seas," according to reports in the *Seaway Review*.

The Seaway, opposed by powerful interests from its inception, has represented as much a triumph of political engineering as of the marine variety. With most of the technical problems of transiting the winter ice now solved, the focus shifts to attitudes and events in the U.S. Congress and the Canadian Parliament. One problem that yielded to a little indirect political persuasion was that of high insurance premiums on ships navigating the Lakes in the winter months. A 1972 MarAd study of insurance rates on Lakes vessels found that these rates went up so steeply during the winter months as to be "an inhibiting factor" on extending the shipping season beyond its traditional limits of April through November — to the point that the federal government might have to subsidize winter insurance. Prompted by congressmen from Seaway states, MarAd called a series of conferences of ship operators and insurance companies to enlighten both parties on what the new ice engineering could do to limit risk of damage. The result was that by 1976 Robert J. Blackwell, Assistant Secretary of Commerce for Maritime Affairs was able to tell Representative Phillip E. Ruppe (R-Mich.) that rates for winter shipping on the St. Lawrence River have been lowered generally and that government-subsidized insurance for Lakes shipping wouldn't be needed.

But government sponsorship, at least, is a necessity if the winter navigation programs and projects are to continue and budgetary consciousness was becoming acute among the various entities of the Winter Navigation Board as fiscal year 1978 drew to a close. "Understand," said a recent report from the board, "that when the current demonstration program ends, our ability to support navigation during the winter months diminishes until Congress approves our feasibility report and we move to the advanced engineering and design phase."

Environmentalists, particularly in the State of New York, have had strong reservations about the winter navigation program from its beginning. New York has little to gain economically from the program, since its section of the Seaway has no ports, and its environmental lobby fears it has something to lose. Dr. James Geis, project manager for the New York Environmental Assessment Project and a professor at the state university in Syracuse, said that the probable impacts of the program are disruption of habitats, damage by wave action, potential release of pollutants, flooding and reduced hydroelectric power production because of ice jamming.

But environmentalist opposition has also been raised in Michigan, where the Michigan United Conservation Club (MUCC) has criticized both the costs of the program and its risk of oil and chemical spills. David Robb, director of comprehensive planning for the St. Lawrence Seaway Development Corp., has replied to MUCC assertions that industry will be the only beneficiary of extending the winter navigation season by charging that environmentalists are "fuzzing the issues." Anything that can be done to cut transportation costs benefits the country as a whole, says Mr. Robb, adding: "We're talking about a one year demonstration . . . that we can shut down any, time (it) looks environmentally unstable. . . "

According to George Gribenow, coordinator of the Environmental Assessment Program on the Great Lakes and St. Lawrence Seaway, the issue is the need to keep the Great Lakes in competition with the other areas of the United States without losing its environmental advantages. "We feel (winter navigation) can be accomplished in a safe and environmentally acceptable manner . . . however, it is linked to greater problems, namely, the enhancement of the quality of life on the Great Lakes . . . We must develop a constructive compromise."

In search of such a compromise, the Corps of Engineers is presently conducting workshops throughout the Great Lakes region to inform the public of the findings of the program to date and to answer questions. The Corps has also published its "Preliminary Draft Feasability Report" and the associated "Environmental Plan of Action." (A list of the workshop locations, and copies of both publications are available from: Department of the Army, Detroit District, Corps of Engineers, Box 1027, Detroit, Mich. 48231.)

All indications are that Congress will approve the Board's preliminary feasability report for extending the season to January 31 and the environmental and engineering studies will continue. By the end of fiscal year 1980, the board expects to submit its final feasability report to Congress. Almost certainly, barring a recession in the meantime, that report will propose that the Seaway, all 2,340 miles of it, from Duluth to the Gulf of the St. Lawrence be open through the winter's ice.

Chapter 6
International Transportation

THE PORT OF JIDDA, SAUDI ARABIA

Middle East distribution— no Arabian nightmare

By PATRICK GALLAGHER, *associate editor*

One successful international freight forwarder favors "total logistics transportation" to meet the challenge of keeping products moving in Saudi Arabia.

To say that Saudi Arabia is a unique place to do business understates the point. The train of civilization is on a jetstreak in the desert kingdom and all is transformed by its passage. Glance away for a minute and rows of ancient mud houses crumble to be replaced by high concrete and glass towers.

Two years ago, every Mideast port was so clogged with ships, four-month delays were common. Cargo wasted in holds and expenses multiplied out of sight. Conditions would remain this way for at least a decade, declared the experts. Today, congestion in Persian Gulf and Red Sea ports is nonexistent. In two more years, the region probably will have an overabundance of container-handling facilities.

But Saudi Arabia is still a nation blinking the sleep of centuries from its eyes. Changes have been erratic. The society may appear totally westernized in some respects, while in other ways it remains a static culture dominated by the Islamic religion. As a result, what is an ordinary business practice in Frankfurt or Philadelphia may prove an absolute disaster in Dammam.

138

Yet despite the hectic conditions and the wide cultural gap, business is obviously being conducted, and U.S. companies are getting their share. The United States has maintained its position as Saudi Arabia's leading supplier in the face of heavy competition. But success has required some adapting, especially in transportation and distribution.

A biased opinion. Jon Thad Stephens believes that an American company exporting regularly to Saudi Arabia would be wise to turn the transportation job over to a freight forwarder, preferably one experienced in the Arabian world and physically on-site to deal with whatever difficulties might arise.

Not that Mr. Stephens is completely impartial. He is president and cofounder of Interconex, an international transportation company and freight forwarder that has made a mark for itself in the Middle East by giving shippers just the kind of service he describes. Without disparaging the competition, Interconex believes that it offers a premium service especially well-suited to developing areas like Saudi Arabia.

In discussing Interconex's experience in the Middle East, Mr. Stephens, Interconex chairman Lionel W. Achuck, and their staff offered us numerous insights into the convolutions of culture, customs, and distribution in the newly-rich desert nations. Several Interconex customers added details.

Interconex's specialty is handling large shipments of European and American materials bound for projects in the Middle East. Customers buy a premium service: total logistics control. An Interconex distribution package could include packing, documentation, transportation, customs brokerage, delivery to the site, and more.

"I think we're more marketable in difficult areas," says Mr. Stephens. "Someone going to Europe will not be as receptive to our particular type of service as someone building a hospital in Pakistan."

Interconex does handle shipments to Europe, but underdeveloped areas and ongoing projects requiring constant attention are its main business. "We're not consolidators," stresses Mr. Stephens, "although we are handling some consumer items, like electronic equipment for Radio Shack and videotapes for MGM. But these are regular shipments in container-size lots."

Development in Saudi Arabia is still at an early enough stage that most of the inbound freight is construction material or capital equipment, much of it moving breakbulk or ro/ro. The flow of consumer goods is growing through, and Interconex is positioning itself to capture a portion of it.

The boom goes on

Ten years ago, as the United States prepared for and then succeeded in landing a man on the moon, it became popular with the media to speculate on the prospects for lunar colonies. Incredible futuristic cities would spring up and flourish on the arid moonscape. Space was the final frontier.

The moon will have to wait. What is happening in the oil-rich deserts of the Middle East—most spectacularly in Saudi Arabia—is enough to boggle the 20th century mind.

The Saudi Arabian government is currently at the midway point of a five-year development plan unprecedented in world history. The plan will pour $142 billion into internal development and should transform the Kingdom of Saudi Arabia into a modern state with a complete social and industrial infrastructure based on petroleum and natural gas.

The massive expenditures have stimulated the already strong private developers of such supporting services as catering, transportation, education, and housing. Although urban consumers in Saudi Arabia now number only about 3 million, plus another million foreigners stationed there, the spending power of these two groups makes the consumer goods market very worthwhile too. Into the 1980's and 1990's,

the Saudi government is likely to provide incentives to greatly increase the population.

The point here is, if your company is not now doing business in Saudi Arabia, it may soon be. And if your company has already established a beachhead, your involvement is almost certain to be a long-lived and expanding one. The United States has historically supplied 25 percent of all Saudi Arabia's imports, a share that is expected to grow.

American companies enjoy a vast advantage in Saudi Arabia. "All else being equal, a Saudi will generally prefer the American product," says Riad El-Azem, deputy director of the U.S.-Arab Chamber of Commerce in New York. However, he believes that American companies are not making the most of the opportunity. "They could do much better."

The oil companies and a handful of big construction companies were the first to penetrate the Saudi market, and they have capitalized on their early ties. But domination by the few and the large is a thing of the past.

"I see a great future for smaller companies from this point on," say Roger McCauley, deputy director of the Action Group for the Near East at the Department of Commerce. "The number of services that the Saudis will require is almost endless. It's an exaggeration to say that only large companies have broken into the Middle East market. Many firms who never even thought of themselves as exporters are over there—and not just large companies."

For example, the government of Iraq is considering flying plant maintenance teams into the country once a month to service new power plants, says Mr. McCauley. And in another deal a Mideast country was negotiating with a major U.S. food chain to set up a nationwide food distribution system.

What if the sun should somehow set on the glory of the petrodollar? Even if the highly unlikely should come to pass, it would not leave Saudi Arabia a shamble of sandswept ruins. The country's rulers are intent on diversifiying the economy to meet the uncertainties of the future, and no one doubts that Saudi Arabia will remain a force to be reckoned with well into the next century. ■

Photo by Richard Burns

Meeting a demand. Interconex got into the materials freight forwarding business as an afterthought. Jon Stephens and Lionel Achuck formed Interconex in 1968 as an international mover of household goods for corporate accounts, with an empasis on premium service.

"While we were perfecting door-to-door household goods moving, our customers began to ask for the same door-to-door service for their general commodities," says Mr. Achuck. "We decided that there would be a real demand for the door-to-door shipping of material to a rapidly growing Middle East."

Interconex's first office in the area was in Teheran, Iran. Two more followed in Jidda and Dammam. "It took two years of hard work over there to get set up with the people we wanted. We invested and we learned our lessons." says Mr. Stephens.

"The biggest problem you have is that you cannot rely on people to do things in Saudi Arabia," he continues. "The only way to insure that things get done is to have our own people to enforce our requirements. Every day we talk with Saudi Arabia by telephone and then confirm and get the details by Telex. This keeps us and customers up to date."

"One of the reasons doing business in Saudi Arabia is so difficult is the social structure," says Michael Courtemanche, Interconex vice president, and a frequent traveler to the Middle East. "No one ever wants to say no. Ask a question, and you'll get an answer that is pleasing to you and seems to take care of everything, when in fact nothing is going to happen. The attitude in the culture is that everything will take care of itself, so don't get upset. The Arabian word 'Inshallah' covers it. Basically, it means 'If Allah wills it.' "

Strange customs. Many of Interconex's clients are veteran Middle East shippers who, nonetheless, depend on the company's expertise in packaging, forwarding, document preparation, and customs brokerage.

"Unless the consignee specifies that he will have his own people at port to accept delivery of a shipment, it is very important to have someone there to handle documentation and to arrange for transportation to the actual site," says Bill Nolan, purchasing agent and export traffic manager for Construction Equipment and Supply International (CESI) of New York. CESI, a major supplier of construction projects throughout the Middle East, has used Interconex for several years to accept materials shipped to Iran and Saudi Arabia from the United States and Europe.

"Conditions in the Middle East countries have improved tremendously," says Mr. Nolan, "but it is still frustrating dealing with the bureaucracy. We are constantly hassled on tariff assessments. Scaffolding which should be assessed at 3 or 4 percent gets a 20 percent rate slapped on it because the customs agent assesses the whole shipment at the rate for one rivet that is actually a part of the scaffolding.

"It happens constantly. And because we are foreigners, we usually have to bite our tongues."

Interconex has no all-purpose way to avoid arbitrary tariff assessments. Proper documentation, however, is critical. Says Mr. Courtemanche: "You must break down your commercial invoices to the values of all the different cargos in a container, or you pay duty based on the highest dutiable item in the container (for example, Mr. Nolan's rivet). We saved a client $50,000 once by redoing the invoices almost on the spot and avoiding a $65,000 tariff.

"But you can be overscrupulous," says Armand Lecompte, Interconex director of marketing. "If you use too technical a term to describe an item, there may not be an Arabic word for it, and the official might construe it as something else. You end up paying a higher duty.

"One of the golden rules of Saudi Arabian customs regulation," he continues, "is that if an official is uncertain about the proper tariff, he will assess the shipment at the highest rate possible. He won't be wrong, because that's their law. The mechanism exists for you to recover duties that were overpaid, but it's an ordeal. I just came back after two years over there, and I've been through it."

Customs regulations are not static, either. The rapid diversification of Saudi Arabia's industrial base brings new protective tariffs with little notice. Say the usual duty on imported PVC pipe is 3 percent. A plant manufacturing PVC pipe is built in Dammam, and to protect the new domestic industry, the government raises the duty to 20 percent.

You're buying PVC pipe in Pittsburgh and shipping it from Philadelphia to Dammam for a project in Riyadh. Communications being what they are in Saudi Arabia, you may not hear about that 20 percent duty back in the States for several expensive months. Meanwhile, your agent continues to process your PVC pipe through customs according to your original instructions. Had you known about the change, you might have been able to make some new purchasing or shipping arrangements.

Double coverage. Another thing a company like Interconex can provide its customers is alternatives, says Mr. Courtemanche. "You might have a shipment set up to go to Riyadh via the port of Dammam. Many times you'll find that after the cargo has been loaded, the carrier cancels Dammam as a port of call. Because we have our own people in the country, we have the ability to discharge that cargo in Jidda instead and deliver to Riyadh just as fast.

"This is a real problem. You have your documents waiting in Dammam and your cargo sitting in Jidda. It happens so often that now we always prepare two sets of documents, one for Dammam and one for Jidda. Just in case."

Some of its biggest customers employ Interconex only for moving people and their household goods. Other customers, like CESI, the construction materials supplier, employ Interconex to handle documentation at the ports of origin and arrival, and for subsequent transportation to the final site. That last leg of the trip can be critical. A Middle East specialist from the Commerce Dept. told us of one company which does 40 percent of its business in the

Middle East repairing equipment damaged in transit.

Grove Construction, another Interconex customer, has been working in Saudi Arabia for 14 years and maintains staffed offices in Jidda and Riyadh. Grove takes care of its own inland transportation, but employs Interconex to handle the paperwork. Interconex makes certain the bill of lading is properly prepared and all other necessary documents are legal, correct and confirmed with the Saudis.

Bob Tighe, Grove's director of purchasing, is responsible for making all shipping arrangements for Saudi Arabia-bound cargo. However, on a new road project in Oman, Interconex is selecting the shipping line for each individual Grove shipment.

Still other customers call on Interconex to help them prepare bids on projects. Interconex is able to provide them with reliable transportation figures. Once a bid is accepted, the forwarder helps on such matters as whether to ship in containers or export boxes, and on which ship lines.

Mr. Stephens tells of one job where Interconex recommended wooden export boxes to a shipper instead of standard containers because the shipment was bound for a little island in the Persian Gulf. Interconex knew that a serious excess of containers on the island would make it expensive to bring more containers in. The wooden boxes could be constructed for less, and furthermore, they would bring a nice return on the island, where wood was in very short supply.

In the wilderness. "Unlike many forwarders who may never have actually been to the Middle East, we have someone over there at least every month to coordinate with our people in the country," says Mr. Achuck. Interconex, like everyone else, has difficulty finding and keeping good people.

"That face to face contact is important," says Mr. Lecompte. "There's got to be a feeling of continuity. You're over there and you're all alone."

One factor that has helped U.S. penetration of the Saudi Arabian market is the high number of young Saudis who were schooled at American colleges and universities. Interconex is making its own small (and self-serving) contribution to this trend.

While we were visiting at Interconex's New York offices, we met Mohamed Hamdaoui, a young Algerian who was just completing a six-month crash course in distribution management under the tutelage of Interconex. He was soon to return to Algeria to work for Sonelec, the Algerian national electronics company.

No doubt, Interconex will be handling some of the Sonelec traffic. Having someone like Mr. Hamdaoui working the one end may make the lonely Saharan wilderness seem less threatening. ∎

STRATEGY TWO:
A Freight Forwarder Offensive

For the shipper just getting started in exporting, and even for
the experienced international shipper, using a forwarder to handle
your European freight can save you time, money—and mistakes

A freight forwarder is "an outside export department for a shipper," according to one New York forwarder's definition of his own kind. Shippers interviewed by DISTRIBUTION WORLDWIDE agree enthusiastically with the forwarder's definition.

Any shipment that leaves the country carries with it skeins of paperwork peculiar to export. The burden of knowing which documents must be used in each situation, of filling out those documents properly and of getting them in the right hands at the right time is often too much of a chore for the U.S. shipper.

For the company which sends relatively small amounts of goods overseas, the export paperwork often proves intimidating. And even for the large company which ships in volume, the rigors of getting all the documents in order is a noticeable burden.

That's why there are some 1700 licensed forwarders in the U.S., many of them with branch offices in several cities.

International Harvester, a large company by all measures, expects to ship a total of 18 million pounds of cargo to Europe this year. The farm equipment maker ships breakbulk, by container—more than 225 this year—and Ro/Ro. It used to try to do the job of the forwarder, but gave up on it.

"We have found in the past that it's to our economic benefit to have forwarders do all the documentation rather than do it ourselves," says Jerry Pridemore, international transportation analyst for IH. "We used to have an office in New York and

one in New Orleans where we did all of our own documentation. We just found that we were better off using a forwarder."

In addition to the blessing of getting all of that costly paper shuffling out of the corporate structure, Pridemore notes, the forwarders also proved useful because "they have a broader experience than we would have."

IH's consignments to Europe include trucks, grading and road building equipment and agricultural equipment—as well as parts for all those pieces of equipment. The company also ships gas turbines and turbine equipment to Western Europe, but all of those goods leave from the West Coast.

"We ship mainly to ourselves," explains Pridemore. The company ships to its facilities in Germany, France and Great Britain. "We have distribution centers as well as assembly facilities there," Pridemore continues. "We build tractors, grading and road building equipment and engines in Europe." Some of the products built there are later shipped to the U.S. for sale.

IH's use of its forwarder varies, depending on the size of shipment and the product being shipped. Pridemore explains: "We make our own bookings, except on less-than-carload shipments. Most of those are handled by a forwarder.

"We make all the bookings on any kind of volume. The forwarder offers that service, but we feel we have better control and we keep a better handle on it by doing it ourselves."

On the LCL shipments, the company doesn't bother to have a

forwarder or NVOCC containerize shipments. Instead, it collects LCL shipments at a New Jersey location and combines lots "into something larger than the minimum bill of lading," Pridemore explains.

"We may have two or three different shipments moving to the pier which will move out under one bill of lading," he adds.

When IH has containers to ship, it does call on its forwarder for some help with the paperwork. Pridemore notes, "We supply the forwarder with the inland bill of lading and the commercial invoices. The forwarder will make any other special invoices or export documents."

Once the containers for shipment from IH are packed, the company consigns them to the vessel at the pier. It asks the people at the pier to notify their forwarder of the arrival of the shipment. "The forwarder keeps a check on things to be sure that the material arrives at the pier in time for the vessel," Pridemore says.

Though IH doesn't make use of all the services offered by their forwarder all of the time, Pridemore points out that "the forwarder comes into play on every shipment we make—whether they do the booking or not. There's just some variation in just how much service they do provide on different types of shipments."

Like nearly all of the U.S. forwarders, the forwarder which serves IH finds that its duties end abruptly when the ship carrying
Continued

143

Forwarder CONTINUED

export goods lands in the foreign port. From there on out, the material is in the hands of the consignee, who has its own broker in Europe to handle the movement from the pier to their premises.

If a big company like International Harvester can save administrative costs and problems with a forwarder, then the savings are that much more apparent for a smaller company like Findlay Adhesives Inc. in Milwaukee.

"We use forwarders because our business is not big enough where our shipping department is set up to handle the export paperwork," says company general manager David Wells. "There are many extra things you have to go through [in export] as opposed to shipping domestically."

Findlay Adhesives sends some 2 million pounds of hot melt adhesives to the European packaging industry annually. All of the shipments are made in containers, a flow of about 50 containers from the company to Western Europe eacy year. Findlay sends its product to two public warehouses where it rents space—one in Rotterdam and another near Cologne, West Germany.

The company relies on its forwarder. "They know the ropes and the paperwork and they've got good contacts with shippers and with foreign shippers," he says. "They arrange the shipping schedule, log the space on the ship and handle the paperwork needed for compliance with regulations."

There's another important service offered by the forwarder which Findlay Adhesives often uses. That is the quick tracing of shipped merchandise. Wells notes that he recently was asked by a client in Saudi Arabia to pinpoint a shipment was en route. The company's forwarder soon located it.

This service, Wells emphasizes, "is quite important to us."

Findlay Adhesives also relies on its forwarder to have containers shipped to its plant in Milwaukee. The company's own work force loads the containers before they are sent back to the docks. Shipments leave from Milwaukee or Chicago and pass through the Great Lakes to Europe.

Once the shipment has arrived at its European port, the customer or a representative from the overseas warehouse sees to its pickup.

Findlay Adhesives is loyal to its forwarders—and for their own good reasons. "We stay pretty much with one forwarder," Wells says. "We really vacillate between two forwarders, but one of them gets most of our business. We tried a couple of forwarders and we settled on this one."

Why this particular forwarder? Wells is brief: "He knows what the hell he's doing. We have confidence in him."

Confidence and loyalty play a large part in the Toro Company's choice of forwarder. The Minneapolis lawn care equipment maker not only sticks with its New York forwarder, but it politely insists that its European customers stay with the forwarder, too.

"We chose a forwarder that we were comfortable with many, many years ago," explains Keith Clark, Toro's General traffic manager. "Despite the fact that the customer is paying for his fee, we tell our customers, 'We'd like you to use our choice of forwarder.'

"We're telling the customer that the forwarder knows our people and our products," Clark continues. "We're also telling our customers that this forwarder's charges are very compatible with the marketplace."

It's therefore not too surprising that all of Toro's customers use the same forwarder. Clark sums up the forwarder's service to Toro: "He arranges for the handling of all the paperwork in-

Continued

The Growing Role of the NVOCC

"A forwarder is the guy who does the documents, while the NVOCC is the non-vessel ocean carrier who has tariff rights to certain destinations." That is one shipper's succinct—and possibly oversimplified—way of separating freight forwarders from non-vessel operating common carriers (NVOCCs).

There are 475 NVOCCs operating in the United States, according to the Federal Maritime Commission. The FMC has regulatory authority over the NVOCCs, who are subject to the Shipping Act of 1916.

Roland Murphy, an FMC examiner, explains that NVOCCs have a dual personality. "To the steamship line, the NVOCC is the shipper," Murphy notes. "But to his own customer, he's a carrier."

NVOCCs must file their tariffs with the FMC, Murphy continues, "just as if they were a regular carrier. They have to do the same things, primarily, and do the regular carriers. The only things they do not have is the equipment—they don't have any steamships."

While a freight forwarder will prepare a shipper's bill of lading, an NVOCC prepares its own bill of lading and takes responsibility for the shipment. "A forwarder handles paper," says Murphy, "but an NVOCC takes it a step beyond that."

The NVOCC's services can include picking up export goods at the shipper's dock, combining it with other LCL shipments from other customers, filling a container with the various customers goods, and shipping it overseas. The NVOCC takes responsibility for getting the goods from the shipper's warehouse to his customer's premises.

NVOCCs do not own ships, but rely on steamship lines in the same way that a forwarder relies on a common carrier. The NVOCC's responsibilities include coordinating movement of the shipper's goods from the shipper's warehouse to the port of embarkation.

In the U.S. the NVOCC sees to the stuffing of a container and getting it to the dock for loading. Abroad, the NVOCC handles the unpacking of the container and delivering or rerouting to its destination.

The NVOCC collects through charges, provides handling services, routes and traces shipments, settles claims, performs transfer services, and actively seeks business for its container-filling system.

volved. He goes through the currency exchange program and actually helps us with the bookings. He also makes sure the containers don't get hung up in the port city. He just presides over the whole ceremony," Clark concludes.

Clearly, the forwarder is involved in distribution services and not so much in actual moving of goods. This is where the non-vessel owning common carrier (NVOCC) differs from the forwarder (see box).

An NVOCC handles goods, and—importantly—takes legal responsibility for goods during their journey to their destination. Some forwarders are NVOCCs, some are not.

Tony VanDerWielen, administrative manager of the international division of Rexnord's Fluid Power Group in Racine, Wis., gives an example of what his company *could* do. The example graphically shows the differences between forwarders and NVOCCs.

"I could use an NVOCC and have an independent forwarder," VanDerWielen says. "The forwarder would send my commercial invoices. He would cut the export declarations, make the bookings with the ocean company, and so on.

"The NVOCC would take my goods right at my door in a truck. He would have a tariff to a destination and he would have his own ocean tariffs. He would containerize the export goods and put them on the vessels."

VanDerWielen uses a forwarder who is also an NVOCC, and this saves Rexnord money. "We ship from 25,000 to 35,000 pounds a month to eight or nine destinations scattered through Western Europe," he says. "That's part of the reason we use the NVOCC—to take advantage of his containerizing service." The NVOCC cuts the bill by using his own containers because he has enough product from all of his customers to economically fill containers for

each destination in Western Europe.

Rexnord sends its export goods to the forwarder's warehouse. The forwarder takes the freight and puts it in the appropriate containers. "He can offer, in most cases, a more attractive tariff depending on where his rights go to," VanDerWielen explains.

The savings Rexnord realizes can be dramatic. VanDerWielen gives an example that shows how inland costs are slashed by an NVOCC. "If I would put my goods on a regular truck line and send them from Racine to Chicago and from Chicago to Baltimore, I might wind up paying about $15 per hundred pounds.

"But the NVOCC is licensed to different points, depending on his tariff. If I used an NVOCC who had rights to Baltimore, I might be able to move my goods for, say, $5 a hundred pounds.

"Where we're located, we find

that an NVOCC can cut an ocean bill [if] he has rights out of Chicago. This saves us a lot of money. Obviously, we're only paying trucking from Racine to Chicago. At that point, our NVOCC would cut us an ocean bill that states the [route] from Chicago to Rotterdam, for instance. I pay one rate from Chicago to Rotterdam. The inland rate is a lot less because Chicago is only 60 miles from Racine, while Balitmore is 1200 miles away.

VanDerWielen admits that if his shipments were big enough, Rexnord might be able to containerize at its own dock for one destination. Then it might be cheaper for the company to load the container and use a forwarder.

"But our 25,000 to 35,000 pound may be spread out and the NVOCC has enough freight going to each destination that he can put ours in their container and save us on the rate," he says. ∎

"We'd rather ship it ourselves"

Many European buyers of U.S. goods prefer to buy FOB factory and arrange the transportation themselves. While this is often done for financial reasons, the Europeans usually buy FOB simply because they lack confidence in the U.S. manufacturers' ability to ship the goods properly.

"We never allow our U.S. suppliers to route their own freight to us," said W. van den Berg, a traffic manager for DAF in Holland.

"These shippers apparently lack the knowledge or the interest to do their exporting properly," said the TM for the Dutch truck manufacturer. "We have found that something always goes wrong if we let the U.S. exporter handle the shipment. Now we just make it a matter of policy to route the freight from this end using our forwarder to handle the arrangements.

"The main problem is with the paperwork," said van den Berg. "On the few occasions we have had shipments routed from the U.S. we have had to telex back to the shipper to get more complete information for the customs and banking people. Usually this means we have to be the bank guarantor, which can mean an unnecessary expense for us.

"We rarely have problems now that we have our forwarder (Van Gend & Loos) handle all these shipments from the U.S.," said van den Berg. "The forwarder has offices in the U.S., and he sends us a telex every time a shipment is sent identifying the contents, carrier and so on. Invoices are air mailed to us the same day.

"We chose Van Gend & Loos as our forwarder because it is a large and influential one here in Europe, it has offices in the U.S. and it has a joint NVO operation with a U.S. forwarder (Emery Ocean Freight)," van den Berg explained.

"A big forwarder can be very helpful when you need special services from ocean or air carriers," van den Berg continued. "During the dock strike, VGL was able to arrange air charters for us when most shippers had trouble getting any air freight moved. Having an NVO capability is also becoming more important in keeping down the cost of LCL shipments. But probably the biggest advantage to using a forwarder like VGL is that all our shipments from the U.S. can be handled by one entity. We now have a pipeline for this freight, not 30 trickles."

Hub of International Commerce . . .

EXPERT MIDDLEMAN

The Customs Broker Is a Vital Link in the Movement Of Import Goods via the New York-New Jersey Port

Importation of goods into the United States has been governed since 1789 by one cardinal stipulation: that a fee shall be paid to the government on every item of foreign origin brought into this country. Today, in service of this apparently simple regulation, the United States Customs Service and a myriad of other agencies exist to process imports from origin to consignee. Principal among them is a vital middleman — the customs broker — whose job it is to attend to the forest of regulations and procedures by which his client's goods will be processed into the country and shipped to him with all due speed. Over 60 percent of the nation's 1,700 licensed customs brokers are headquartered in Lower Manhattan to handle the huge volume of imports processed into the New York-New Jersey Port.

Primarily the customs broker's function is to verify papers on shipments entering the U.S. to make sure they are in order. He must then see to the payment of duties and collect freight charges and make arrangements for the movement of cargo from piers or airports to consignees.

In theory, any importer can handle his own import processing. In practice, more than 90 percent of all imports are handled through customs brokers for the very good reason that the increased complexity of importing goods now requires the time and expertise that most shippers cannot afford to acquire.

Because it is a business which depends so much upon daily experience and acquisition of a familiarity with directives, import goods, governmental regulations, modes of transport, and the individual people involved in the process all along the line, customs brokerage is not truly a business that can be learned in the classroom. Despite the fact that good courses are now offered at schools like Pace University, New York University, the World Trade Institute and the Connecticut Institute of International Traffic, to name a few, most brokers learn their business on the job. There is no set period of apprenticeship, but the average broker has upwards of 10 to 15 years experience, and many of the larger firms employ experts with at least twice that amount.

According to Vincent Bruno, executive vice president of the Manhattan-based National Customs Brokers & Forwarders Association of America, there are 23 local brokerage associations across the country, the majority located in the nation's major ports, as would be expected. Though customs brokers must register every three years with the federal government, the current best estimate of their number is about 1,700 individual brokers working in more than 800 broker/freight forwarder firms. Most work as officers, partners, or employees of firms rather than as independents. The companies vary in size — from a large, long-established house such as Daniel F. Young, Inc., to a 10-man company, which is the average staff of a small firm.

Brokerage firms customarily provide dual services. Often, they are ocean freight forwarders licensed by the Federal Maritime Commission. They also act as air freight sales agents for airlines and some are international air freight consolidators authorized by the Civil Aeronautics Board to act as indirect carriers for shipping goods by air. There are brokers at the New York-New Jersey Port who act as local truckmen, warehousemen, packers, coopers, weighers, vessel agents

Left: *Bustle and paperwork seen here in offices of Leading Forwarders, Inc., New York, are typical of customs brokers' offices everywhere.* **Right:** *Computerization of the myriad documents for customs broker's thousands of annual transactions is a must.*

146

Left: *"Difficult" shipments, like luxury yachts from Taiwan, are specialty of brokers at Leading Forwarders, Inc.* **Right:** *Firm's president, Leonard Shayne, seen here overseeing the morning's correspondence, is a veteran broker and chairman of the National Customs Brokers & Forwarders Association.*

and even act as travel agents for some of their clients.

There is a high degree of specialization among customs brokers. Some handle only airborne shipments, others only small inventory, simple cargoes offering little complexity but a high rate of turnover. Still others specialize in what might be termed the "difficult case," the cargo or shipment which, by virtue of its makeup — large inventory, limited quota items, high perishability factors, high value/high risk items, etc. — will be shunned by smaller or newer firms. In recent years, with more and more items deemed perishable — a term brokers use to describe any commodity which will lose its value if too much time is spent transporting it, a factor common to foodstuffs, high fashion goods, and even certain jewelry items — there has come to be a greater demand for this type of firm's services. It is no surprise to find the largest number of these specialists in the New York-New Jersey Port, the import center for the fashion, jewelry and gourmet food industries in the U.S.

Generally speaking a customs broker is the "opposite number" to a freight forwarder. As the forwarder is principally the agent for the exporter, the customs broker is chiefly the importer's agent. It is he who will prepare documentation on incoming cargoes, see to its processing through Customs, have it prepared for shipping, and arrange for its transportation to whatever locale the importer specifies . . . and all within as short a time as possible.

The process usually begins with a call or correspondence from an importer/client to a broker informing him of an incoming shipment. If the client is an inexperienced importer, he may have no idea of the myriad details the broker must undertake. Most likely, he is primarily concerned about the duty he will have to pay. What he may not know, but the broker must, is that the physical characteristics of the item to be imported will determine the rate of duty. In addition, the broker must know whether there is an importation quota on the item and whether or not the item can be brought in under that quota at the desired moment.

He must also be familiar with countervailing duties, licensing requirements, trade mark restrictions, Department of Agriculture controls, special marking requirements and other considerations beyond the ken of most importers. The broker will also advise his importer/client about new restrictions which may not yet be in effect but which may apply at the time of importation.

Beyond this, he will refer his client to the proper Customs or government agency official and help to interpret the language of directives, regulations, and laws so that his client's cargo may be brought in as smoothly and quickly as possible. Often, the knowledge of whom to contact and where can be as important in facilitating cargo movement as a knowledge of regulations. In a business where urgency is a constant demand, the time spent on each transaction is so crucial that there can be no loss allowed for research into names and telephone numbers. And only experience can teach a broker how to balance the personalities of those with whom he must deal in order to get his client's cargo moved as fast as possible.

Finally, he pays duties, often out of his own resources in anticipation of reimbursement by his client to prevent delay in processing. And he keeps his client apprised of how he may protest duties he deems unfair.

For all of this, he charges his client a service fee and whatever out-of-pocket expenses may have been incurred along the way: as, the aforementioned duties or, perhaps, warehousing charges run up during time a cargo was awaiting clearance.

As one experienced broker put it, it's "a business that ought to be simple but simply is not." Today, with over 400 federal laws and regulations enforced by the Customs Service upon goods entering the U.S., and with more than 40 percent of the value of the entire nation's imports coming in through the nation's premier port of New York and New Jersey, it is easy to see why one of the busiest and most important keystones in international commerce is the customs broker.

The Essentials of Export Documentation

Paperwork required for shipping to Western Europe is relatively simple—eight basic documents, six of which the shipper can have his forwarder fill out. However, in completing all forms, shippers must make sure they are talking the same language as their carriers and customers.

There's a story making the rounds at the Port of New York about a customs inspector who looked in an export shipment and was seriously hurt by dangerous fumes. He didn't know the box was loaded with something that could hurt him. He didn't know because the documents weren't filled out properly.

Paperwork isn't always a life or death matter in exporting, but it is always a matter of importance. Red tape follows every cargo from the shipper's loading dock all the way to the consignee's warehouse abroad. Every foul-up with the forms can—and does—cost time and money.

Luckily for shippers either in or looking at the Western European market, the paperwork they must complete is relatively simple.

"Western Europe is probably the easiest part of the world to ship to as far as documents are concerned," says Steven Schneider, vice president of Arncam Shipping Co., Inc., a New York City freight forwarder.

Indeed, the basic documentation for shipping to any point in Western Europe looks deceptively simple. In general, the shipper has from six to eight basic forms to fill out:

Continued

Documentation CONTINUED

Marks Make the Difference

Putting too much information on a package for shipment is almost as bad as putting the wrong address on the box.

According to the National Committee on International Trade Documentation, "study has shown that in some instances marks have become so lengthy and detailed as to tax the capability of the sides of the packages to hold them."

The anxious shipper who puts in more information, more detail, more spelled-out words than necessary may think he is improving the chances that a package will make its way to its destination quickly and accurately.

Just the opposite is the case. "The very purpose of package markings—that of simple and quick identification and movement of goods—has now been largely defeated because of application costs and difficulties of interpretation," says NCITD.

An additional problem—in terms of extra costs and chances for greater error—is that every complex box marking must be transposed, exactly, to all shipping documents.

NCITD suggest the following for simpler, speedier, more accurate markings and shipments:

Do

1. Do keep markings concise.

2. Do mark packages on two sides only.

3. Do place markings in the best viewing area on sides of packages or pallets.

4. Do use durable non-fading paint or waterproof ink when marking packages.

5. Do use stencils when marking packages.

6. Do limit color coding to simple shapes and sizes.

7. Do mark packages suitably for the mode of transportation.

8. Do remember every character you eliminate saves you time and money.

9. Do relate the size of stencil characters to the size of the package.

10. Do relate use of package numbers to shipping documents.

Don't

1. Don't accept tradition and habit as an excuse for continuing past practices.

2. Don't apply marks to reusable containers until all old markings are removed or covered over.

3. Don't allow excessive marks to interfere with the safe, timely delivery of your cargo.

4. Don't mark areas which will be covered by straps or bands.

5. Don't use hand markings unless absolutely necessary. Avoid using script.

6. Don't ask for letter sizes larger than 1¾" tall.

7. Don't use difficult configurations to mark cases, such as stars, lightning bolts, etc.

8. Don't add anything to the mark that will defeat the purpose of a mark.

9. Don't use marking materials of questionable durability.

First, the commercial invoice. This familiar document serves as the shipper's bill to the consignee. In Western Europe, it also serves the important function of letting the consignee prove to his country's customs officials the value of the shipment. Without the commercial invoice, the consignee cannot pick up the goods and get them through customs.

Second, the packing list. This document details the goods sent in one shipment by listing package contents, markings, weights and dimensions.

Third, delivery instructions. This form lists the name of the shipper and his forwarder. It also specifies the domestic routing of the goods and lists their point and country of origin. It states which pier or airport the goods are to be delivered to, names the exporting carrier, designates the port of loading and port of discharge, and notes the destinations for transshipments. In addition to telling each party what to do with the goods, it tells them how to identify the goods. The form shows the marks and numbers of the cargo, the number of packages in the shipment, a description of packages and contents, their gross weight and measurement.

Fourth, dock receipt. This important document carries the same information as the delivery instructions, above. Additional information is filled in by the dock master to show who delivered the goods, when they arrived, when they were unloaded, who checked the goods against the receipt and where the goods were put—on the dock or in the vessel. This form, signed by the dock master, can be a negotiable document, says Arncam's Schneider. That is, it can be presented for payment at a bank since it proves that a service has been rendered—for example, that the carrier has delivered the goods to the pier.

Fifth, the bill of lading. This

Continued

Documentation CONTINUED

document serves as the contract between the shipper and the steamship company for the transport of goods. It carries all of the information listed on both the delivery instructions and the dock receipt. In addition, it specifies the consignee by name and lists a party to be notified of delivery or of problems. It also specifies the place of delivery. Perhaps the most important legal feature of the bill of lading is that, with it, the steamship line takes responsibility for the cargo from the time it receives the goods until the time it delivers them, as specified on the document.

Sixth, the shipper's export declaration. This form carries all of the information which appears on the bill of lading. Its purpose is to tell U.S. Customs what products are leaving the country and how they are departing. The information is confidential, and is used primarily for statistical compilations by the government.

Seventh, certificate of origin. This document is required by some countries, and may be required by consignees. It carries the same information that appears on the bill of lading. The form, if required, must be notarized by a recognized Chamber of Commerce. Its purpose is to document the country of origin of the goods shipped.

Eighth, a bank draft which might be required by the shipper's bank if the shipment is not made on an open account.

Of these documents, the shipper must fill out the first two—the commercial invoice and the packing list. The remaining documents may be prepared by the shipper's freight forwarder.

A brief look at these documents would leave any observer convinced that they are easy to fill out. They are. What's difficult is to fill them out properly and then get them into the right hands.

"It's not so much the paper, it's
Continued

Shipper's Glossary

One hazard of international trade and documentation lies in the definition of terms of shipment. In short, the U.S. shipper must be positive that his foreign consignee and he agree on exactly what the terms used in documents mean.

Following is a brief explanation of some commonly-used export terms. Shippers who must make use of these terms are advised to seek professional help from forwarders or lawyers to insure that the terms they use apply to their particular shipments and agreements.

EX WORKS (ex factory, ex mill, ex warehouse, etc.)—Shipper must supply goods according to contract of sale. Under this term, the price quoted applies only at the point of origin and the seller agrees to place goods at disposal of buyer at the agreed place and on the agreed date. Buyer pays export taxes, other export fees and costs of obtaining documents needed for export.

FOR (free on rail) and *FOT* (free on truck)—Seller must order proper car or truck for right time and load car or truck properly. With LCL load, shipper must deliver goods to railway or trucker at appropriate time; provide packing of goods; and notify buyer that goods have been delivered to railway.

FAS (free alongside ship)—Shipper must deliver good alongside vessel at loading berth named by buyer, at the specified port and in manner customary at port; notify buyer that goods have been delivered to port; provide packing of goods; provide at own expense customary clean document in proof of delivery of the goods alongside the named vessel.

CIF (cost, insurance, freight)—Shipper must contract and pay for carriage of goods to agreed port of destination; pay freight charges and charges for unloading at port of discharge; obtain export license or other governmental authorization needed for export of goods; load goods at own expense on board vessel at port of shipment and notify buyer that this has been done; procure a transferrable policy of marine insurance against risks of carriage; bear risks of shipment until goods have passed ship's rail at port of shipment; provide buyer clean negotiable bill of lading and invoice of goods shipped as well as insurance policy; provide packing of goods; pay dues and taxes incurred by goods up to time of loading.

EX SHIP—Shipper must place goods effectively at disposal of buyer on board vessel; bear risks and expense of goods until they have been effectively placed at disposal of buyer; provide packing; pay checking costs; notify buyer of expected date of arrival and provide buyer in due time with the bill of lading or delivery order and any documents enabling buyer to take delivery of the goods.

EX QUAY—Shipper must place goods at disposal of buyer on the wharf or quay at the agreed upon port and at the time provided in contract; bear expense and provide import license and pay import duties or taxes including customs clearance; provide packaging, pay costs of checking; bear all risks and expense of goods until they have been effectively placed at disposal of buyer.

FOB (free on board)—Shipper must deliver goods on board the vessel named by buyer at named port of shipment on date specified; notify buyer that goods have been delivered on board; obtain any export license or other governmental authorization needed for export; bear all costs and risks of goods until they have effectively passed the ship's rail; provide customary packing; pay costs of checking operations.

C&F (cost and freight)—Shipper must contract for carriage of goods to agreed port of destination; pay freight charges and any charges for unloading at the port of discharge which may be levied by regular shipping lines; load goods at his own expense on board the vessel at the port and notify buyer that this has been done; furnish buyer clean negotiable bill of lading and invoice of goods shipped.

Note: A clean bill of lading is one which bears no superimposed clauses expressly declaring a defective condition of the goods or packaging.

Documentation CONTINUED

the knowledge of what to do with it," notes Schneider.

For example, some countries—none in Europe, however—require that the documents be filled out in a language other than English. The person filling out the documents must know which language to use in filling in the blanks.

Another example is that the person who fills out the documents must know whether or not a letter of credit exists that applies to the shipment. He must know what a letter of credit can do, and what it cannot do.

Furthermore, some countries—again, none in Western Europe—require additional documents which must be secured from the consulate of the destination country. The trick here is knowing what is required, where to get the forms, and how to fill them out.

The maze of paper complexities here is what leads most companies to turn to the forwarder. Schneider estimates that forwarders fill out these forms for U.S. shippers in nearly every case.

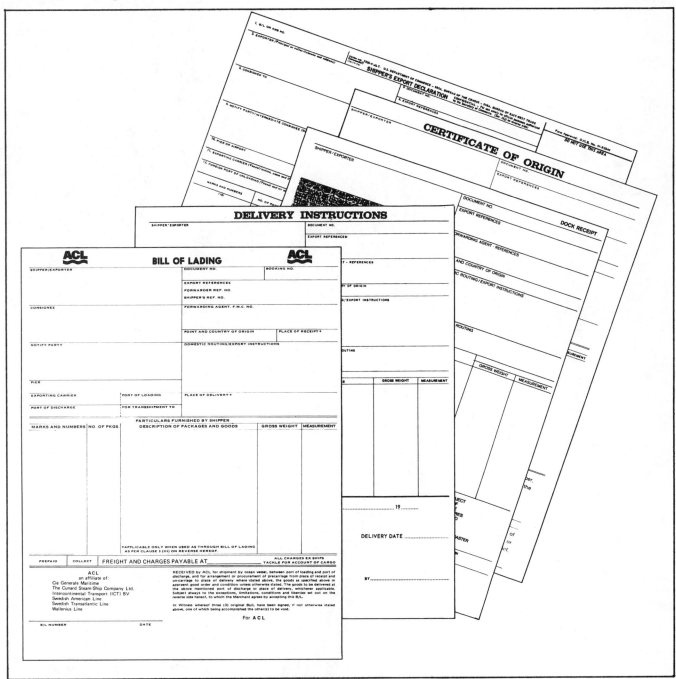

Basic export documents which either the shipper or forwarder prepares are the bill of lading, delivery instructions, certificate of origin, shipper's export declaration and dock receipt.

INTERNATIONAL AIR POLICY

—BETWEEN THE LINES

By Brock Adams
U.S. Secretary of Transportation

On August 21, President Carter unveiled a formal statement of the United States international aviation policy, designed to provide guidance for U.S. delegations in negotiating new air transportation agreements with other nations. The policy marks a fundamental rethinking of the role of international aviation—and the international air transport community—in our national affairs. This new initiative is important, I think, not only to the airline industry but to anyone else who deals in international trade.

Although the policy statement was released formally in late August, the principles embodied in it have been guiding our negotiations for several months prior to its announcement. We have gained nearly a year's experience with the results of the policy, and they are mostly good.

Last year was a good year for the world's airlines. Passenger traffic was up by eight percent; revenue by 12 percent. More significantly, after several years of surplus capacity, airlines added more passenge

152

than seats. Load factors—the industry's term for the percentage of seats that are filled—reach a ten-year high of 58 percent.

As a consequence, U.S. airlines ended the year with very welcome profits.

But 1978, under the Administration's new policy, was even better. During the first six months of the year, a period that does not include the peak summer travel months, air traffic between the United States and Europe increased 11.3 percent over the same period last year. More important, earnings increased also. America's two major international airlines—*Pan Am* and *TWA* —nearly doubled their earnings during that period—from $44 million in 1977 to $94.5 million in 1978.

Not surprisingly, load factors also increased, offsetting the substantial fare cuts that nearly every international carrier instituted in 1978. During August, a peak travel month, *Pan Am* operated with a load factor of 73.2 percent.

Because the North Atlantic is where our new international aviation policy has been most effective, that is where the results can be seen most clearly. It will be seen even more clearly, I believe, in the coming years, for we are still in the process of negotiating a number of significant major air transport agreements. As this is written, we are in various stages of talks with about 25 separate nations. Each of these agreements, when it is reached, will further affect the air transport market. And, to the extent that these agreements reflect the principles embodied in our policy, the effect on the air transport industry will be positive.

What is that policy?

In our international negotiations today we are seeking a competitive system of air transportation, and we have several specific objectives:

• **Innovative pricing and fare flexibility.** Different consumers have different needs, and no single fare structure will satisfy everyone. Business travelers and tourists, for example, require different levels of service, and neither should have to pay for service he doesn't need—or isn't receiving.

• **Liberalized charter rules.** Charters are an important competitive spur to scheduled carriers and ought to have great flexibility.

• **A reduction or elimination of artificial restrictions** on the number of passengers airlines can carry.

• **Elimination of discriminatory competitive practices.**

• **Permission for the United States to designate multiple competitors in international markets.**

• **Greater access to international markets.** We want to obtain more non-stop service in international markets and better integration of domestic and international routes.

Because we are committed to a competitive international air transport system, we are not seeking advantages at the expense of other nations. We believe in competitive equity—the right of all competitors to have equal competitive opportunities.

Negotiation, of course, is the art of compromise, and concessions are inevitable. We believe in reciprocity. Our strategy, however, is to trade competitive opportunities rather than restrictions, and to make concessions only in return for progress toward a fairer marketplace.

The U.S. policy has been criticized by those nations who do not share our pro-competitive commitment. Many countries view their international airlines less as carriers of passengers and freight than as instruments of foreign policy. They prefer to negotiate on the basis of their foreign policy interests rather than their transport interests.

Certainly, foreign policy is a factor in international aviation, but it is foolhardy to make it the dominant factor.

I doubt that any government can afford to pour endless capital into an enterprise that, when properly managed and developed, could support itself. No prudent nation would do so, even if it could. The world's airlines will need an estimated $60 to $70 billion through 1985, a capital demand of enormous proportions.

All governments are hard-pressed to find enough resources to cover their expenses, and none should be allocating scarce economic resources to their airlines on this scale. In the long run, we believe, other nations will realize that they have the same interest in the prosperity and self-sufficiency of their airlines that we have in ours. They can hardly do otherwise.

That interest is best served by a policy that permits an airline management to expand and grow by responding to the needs of its customers.

This is the policy we are pursuing with, I believe, notable success. There may be dangers ahead of which we are unaware, but surely they can be no worse than the stagnation that the air transport industry experienced during the last decade.

It is more likely that, by offering increased service to the public, the international air transport industry will stimulate traffic growth, generate new markets and produce increased revenues—not only for their airlines but for such related industries as tourism. We have seen it happen in the United States, in the domestic air transport industry, and the international potential is even greater.

If there is a message between the lines of our international air transport policy, it is this: centuries of experimentation and tinkering have failed to develop an adequate or efficient substitute for the marketplace. We should let it work.

IB

Singapore Emphasizing Cabin Service on

By Robert R. Ropelewski

Singapore—General upgrading of cabin services is likely to occur on scheduled commercial airline flights between the U. S. West Coast and the Orient as a result of the entry of Singapore International Airlines into this long-haul market.

This AVIATION WEEK & SPACE TECHNOLOGY editor flew a round trip with Singapore when passenger service was inaugurated between here and the U. S. West Coast in April. The airline is offering three round-trip McDonnell Douglas DC-10-30 flights a week between Singapore and San Francisco via Hong Kong and Honolulu. The airline has a well-established reputation in the Orient for outstanding cabin service, and this reputation is causing concern among the carriers with which it will be competing on transpacific routes. Pan American World Airways has added several amenities to its services to cope with the challenge.

Inauguration of passenger service between here and the West Coast marks a significant step for the rapidly growing Asian carrier, even through the aircraft used and the West Coast destination served are not optimal in the eyes of SIA executives.

SIA executives would have preferred Los Angeles rather than San Francisco as its first gateway to the U. S., with an intermediate stop at Tokyo. The airline, however, had waited eight years since its original application for a route to the U. S. When the U. S. government proposed a compromise of San Francisco and Hong Kong, SIA executives did not quibble.

The carrier is scheduled to receive this summer the first two of 12 new Boeing 747-200s it has on order, and these aircraft will allow the elimination of a Guam refueling stop presently needed for the DC-10s on the westward flight from Honolulu to Hong Kong.

While the DC-10 provides an adequate level of comfort on the route, the shorter range, compared to the 747, necessitates more stops that make a long journey even longer. Westbound passengers on the inaugural services, for example, endured a 24½-hr. flight that included refueling stops at Honolulu, Guam and Hong Kong en route to Singapore. Strong tailwinds and elimination of the Guam stop shortened the return flight by several hours, although a 3-hr. 10-min. refueling stop in Honolulu offset part of this gain.

SIA managing director Lim Chin Beng noted that the airline "very seriously considered" the smaller, longer-range 747SP, especially since Pan American operates the SP nonstop between San Francisco and Hong Kong. Pan American is the airline's prime competitor on the transpacific route.

SIA opted for the 747-200 instead, Lim said, primarily because the SP is load-limited on the Pacific runs and because seat-mile operating costs are higher than those of the standard 747. "Given the low fares now coming into the market," he said, "we need a low-operating-cost aircraft."

The Honolulu stop will allow SIA to carry a full load of 400 passengers on its 747s, as well as air freight. Its DC-10s are configured for 270 passengers.

"We realize Pan Am will carry more of the business traffic," Lim conceded. "But we will carry more of the tourist traffic. And we will also get some of the business traffic—especially those who want to stretch their legs in Hawaii" on their way to or from the U. S. mainland.

SIA executives now believe the U.S.-Singapore bilateral was signed too soon, before the U. S. airline deregulation concept was finalized. Because of deregulation, they believe the State Dept. and CAB will be more receptive to proposals for expanded SIA service to the U. S. Discussions with the Civil Aeronautics Board on this matter are expected to resume in the next few weeks.

If Los Angeles is obtained as a new gateway, SIA officials do not believe the airline would continue to serve San Francisco.

On its transpacific as well as its Far Eastern route sectors, SIA continues to stress its cabin service as its primary attraction over other air carriers. Attractive Singapore and Malaysian stewardesses, along with a small contingent of

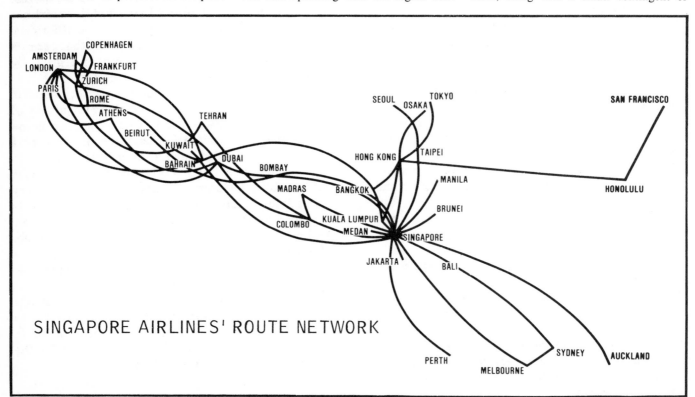

SINGAPORE AIRLINES' ROUTE NETWORK

Singapore International Airlines' route network includes Honolulu and San Francisco, to which the carrier inaugurated service last month.

U. S. Route

male stewards, provide the service. Drinks and earphones are free, and in-flight meals are a cut above standard airline fare.

To maintain a high level of service on its long and often crowded flights, Singapore uses larger than average cabin staffs. On its 747s, for example, 18 stewardesses and stewards provide cabin service. The legal FAA minimum for this size aircraft is 11, and most airlines use 14-15.

The legal minimum cabin crew on the DC-10 is also 11. Singapore uses 15. On its 707s, while the FAA minimum is four, Singapore carries a staff of seven. This allows cabin staff members to be more attentive to passenger needs and to respond more promptly to individual passenger requests. Crews are changed at each stop on the transpacific crossings, reducing fatigue among crewmembers and largely eliminating the service slump that often occurs on very long flights.

Passenger Fatigue

The duration of the transpacific flights, particularly westbound—24½ hr. from San Francisco to Singapore—is in itself physically taxing on passengers. It is difficult to overcome this factor, even with the finest service.

SIA has a partial answer for this in its 747s, which have slumberette seats in the first class section. There are only 10 of these, however, and they are reserved on a first-come, first-served basis. Seat pitch in the economy section is 32 in., which becomes confining after the first several hours on a long trip.

Except for premeal bar service, drinks on the inaugural flight consist of champagne, beer or fruit juice. On the inaugural flight from San Francisco to Singapore, and return, requests for anything else from water to liquor generally took a long time—up to an hour in some cases—to be satisfied.

Lunch and dinner menus offered two different entrees, but the cabin crew did not ask preferences beforehand. Passengers either took what came or risked the ire of the cabin staff by demanding a particular entree from the menu.

Cabin crews displayed a certain inflexibility at some points in the flight. They were impatient when meal trays were not lowered immediately into place upon announcement of meal service, and if window shades were not pulled—even at night—prior to the start of a movie.

Baggage did not appear on the carousel until 1 hr. after arrival in Singapore, and about 1½ hr. after our return to San Francisco, where Qantas is responsible for Singapore ground handling.

If such conditions exist elsewhere on the carrier's route network, they apparently

Singapore Airlines Depends on Expatriate Pilots

Singapore—Rapid expansion of Singapore Airlines' transport aircraft fleet has outpaced the carrier's ability to train flight crews, and the company remains heavily dependent on expatriate pilots as a result.

While nearly all of Singapore Airlines' first officers and flight engineers are Singapore or Malaysian nationals, more than two-thirds of the carrier's captains are expatriates—mostly British, Australian or American.

The airline has been expanding its training facilities and activities to cope with the growth, but Singapore Airlines executives do not expect to be able to phase out the expatriate pilots in the foreseeable future. Reflecting the rate in the fleet growth, 12 type conversion courses were conducted for 143 flightcrew members in the fiscal period April, 1977-April, 1978, compared with eight type conversion courses for 65 flightcrew members in the preceding year.

Singapore currently operates two six-degree-freedom-of-motion simulators with visual systems for the training of its Boeing 747 and 707 crews. Spare time on these simulators is sold to several Asian and Eastern European airlines, including Malaysian Airline System, Korean Airlines, China Airlines and the Yugoslav carrier, JAT.

Singapore Airlines has ordered a Boeing 727 simulator and McDonnell Douglas DC-10 simulator from CAE of Canada, both with computer-generated visual systems. The simulators are scheduled for delivery in August, 1980.

have not been bothersome enough to deter the strong following the airline has developed with frequent travelers. Several Asian business travelers approached by AVIATION WEEK & SPACE TECHNOLOGY all rated SIA as their first choice among Asian carriers.

Such keen passenger preference is reflected in SIA's load factors, which have been running around 75% for the company's overall route network. Oriental routes have had the highest load factors, running close to 80%. The daily SIA Boeing 747 flight from Singapore to Tokyo, for example, last year registered a year-round average passenger load-factor of 83%—up from 76% in the preceding year.

On its European and west Asian routes, SIA's thrice-weekly 747 services terminating in Amsterdam and twice-weekly 707 services to Copenhagen via Tehran registered an average passenger load factor of 74% last year. Australian and South Pacific routes using DC-10s, 707s and 747s produced passenger load factors averaging 65%.

In the first few weeks of the Singapore-San Francisco service, the carrier was averaging load factors of 75% into San Francisco and 51% out of San Francisco.

The high load factors and continuing traffic growth on regional Asian routes were the motivating factors in SIA's recent order of eight Airbus Industrie A300B4 twin-engine wide-body transports (AW&ST Apr. 16, p. 27). Those aircraft will enter service beginning in April, 1981, on routes to Bangkok, Hong Kong, Manila, Djakarta, Colombo and Madras.

The 246-seat A300s are intended to replace the Boeing 707s and 727s currently used on these routes. SIA's 10 727-200s, each with 136 seats, will be put on routes currently served by five 737-100 aircraft with 85 seats each.

Both the 707s and 737s will be phased out of the carrier's fleet between

now and 1981, along with the current fleet of 10 747s operated by the airline. This will leave the company with a relatively modern fleet of 10 747s, seven DC-10-30s, eight A300B4s, and 10 Boeing 727-200s.

SIA officials are looking for an aircraft to replace the Boeing 727s around the mid-1980s, and the leading candidates for this role are the Boeing 757 and 767 and the Airbus Industrie A310. A decision also is expected toward the end of this year on a new cargo aircraft to replace the two 707F freighters operated by SIA. Only one aircraft will be ordered initially, with the choice between the Boeing 747 and the DC-10-30 freighter.

SIA executives are anticipating capital expenditures of close to $2 billion over the next five years to cover the costs of fleet modernization and facilities expansion.

More than half of the amount will be applied to the procurement of new aircraft, including the 10 Boeing 747s, four Boeing 727s, five McDonnell Douglas DC-10-30s, and six Airbus Industrie A300s now on order. Most of the remainder will be spent on new facilities at Singapore's existing Paya Lebar Airport and the new Changi International Airport on Singapore's eastern tip.

Financing for these investments will come from several sources, including:

■ Internal funds—about one-quarter, or roughly $500 million, will come from the airline's operating revenues.

■ Sale of aircraft—Singapore is selling its seven older Boeing 747s to Tiger Air for approximately $300 million, and this income will be applied to the purchase of 10 new 747s.

■ Exim Bank—Exim Bank funding for a share of the procurement costs of the 727s and DC-10s has been arranged, and Singapore executives are now trying to convince Exim Bank officials that partial funding of the 747 purchases is justifiable as well because the 747 is a competitor to the Airbus Industrie A300 on shorter high-density routes. The existence of a competitive foreign aircraft is one of the criteria for Exim loans.

■ Private banks—About $150 million in loans from private European banks have been arranged so far, and other arrangements are still in discussion.

■ Leasing—Singapore has concluded an agreement with Japan's Orient Leasing Co. under which approximately $200 million will be made available to finance four DC-10s at 8.2% interest over 10 years. At the end of that period, a $1 payment by SIA will give it complete ownership of the aircraft. "This is different from most American-type leases," Lim noted, "where you have to pay the market price of the aircraft at the end of the lease period."

Load Factor

Airline officials generally quote 58% as the company's present break even load factor. This, however, does not include debt servicing. With debt servicing included, the break even load factor must be "well above 68%", according to Lim.

Because of the strong support the airline is getting from the traveling community, SIA officials are confident they can maintain this load factor, and they are predicting revenues will be triple those of last year by 1983.

The Singapore-San Francisco route is the latest expansion move by SIA, which has been growing rapidly and steadily since it broke away from Malaysia-Singapore Airlines (MSA) in late 1972.

The carrier's route network grew by nearly 50% between 1973 and 1978, expanding first in the Asian market, then westward to Europe, and finally eastward to the U. S. (The company began cargo flights to San Francisco in April, 1978). Available passenger capacity increased 132% during the same period, from 4.8 billion seat-kilometers in 1973 to about 11.2 billion seat-kilometers in 1978.

Aggressively promoting the quality of its in-flight services, the carrier has nearly doubled its number of passengers carried over the past five years, from 1.33 million in 1973 to around 2.57 million in 1978. Coupled with the new, longer routes, this resulted in a 230% increase in passenger-kilometers recorded, from 3.42 billion in 1973 to 8.23 billion in 1978.

New, larger aircraft added a cargo-carrying capability and cargo business logged by SIA climbed from 81.15 million metric ton-kilometers in 1973 to 275.39 million ton-kilometers in 1978—an increase of 239%.

Revenues nearly tripled during the first five years of operation, from Singapore $398.04 million in 1973-74 to Singapore $1.14 billion in 1977-78. (A Singapore dollar is worth about 48 U. S. cents.) These figures are for fiscal year extending from Apr. 1 through Mar. 31 of the following year. SIA executives anticipated

---

Higher Pacific Fares

Los Angeles—Singapore Airlines officials here are anticipating a 4-7% increase in Pacific air fares in the near future as a result of rising fuel prices.

"The recent increases in fuel prices almost wipe out any possibility of profits on these routes," a Singapore executive said here. He predicted there probably would be an increase in fares "across the board in the Pacific" in the near future to compensate for the higher fuel costs.

---

that revenues and profits for the 1978-79 fiscal year will be about 30% higher than 1977-78 once the final figures are in.

Although it is government-owned, the airline has not encountered pressures toward inflated hiring to hold down unemployment statistics. The result has been a rise of only 52% in staff during the first five years, despite the much more significant growth in capacity, traffic and revenues during that period.

SIA executives do not expect the airline's growth to continue at its previous pace, however. Lim has suggested that the growth rate in such areas as traffic, revenues and profits will probably drop to around 20% annually over the next five years. He cited several reasons for this, including cost of fleet modernization, smaller increases in productivity and a slower rate of route network expansion.

By 1983, Singapore will be operating a fleet of 40 jet transport aircraft, compared to 30 presently. Of the 40, all but a few will be less than four years old. The SIA work force of about 8,000 has little margin left for further fleet and route network expansion without building up its own employe level substantially.

With the start of passenger service to the U. S., Singapore has taken advantage of most of the existing bilateral agreements authorizing its operations to other countries. A bilateral has been signed by the governments of Singapore and New Guinea opening the way for SIA service to Port Moresby by mid-1980, and the airline would eventually like to extend its route network both southeastward into South America and southwestward to Africa. This will be a gradual process unlikely to be on a scale with the rapid route expansion of the past five years.

Given its proximity to mainland China, SIA expects to be among the new carriers that will begin operating into and out of that country in the near future. Current planning anticipates regular operations into China before the end of this year, at a starting frequency of three flights a week. Possible gateways include Canton, Shanghai and Beijing (Peking).

Singapore would begin the service using Boeing 707s, like the Chinese carrier CAAC. Eventually, Singapore executives expect to go to wide-body transports such as the DC-10 or 747 on the Chinese

---

routes. When this would occur is still unclear.

"There won't be any explosion in traffic [to China]," Lim said. "It will come slowly. There are still many problems with such things as hotels and visas. China is still limiting the number of tourists entering the country to 100,000 a year."

Other factors are also threatening to slow the growth of SIA. At the same time that the carrier was inaugurating service to San Francisco, it was feuding with the Australian government and the Australian flag carrier, Qantas, over Australia's new international civil aviation policy.

Announced in late 1978, the policy limits SIA's fifth freedom traffic rights in Australia. It also restricts the rights of other Asian carriers from the Assn. of Southeast Asian Nations (ASEAN), but Singapore would be the hardest-hit initially because of the substantial Australia-to-England traffic it carries.

Fuel Shortages

SIA's operations at the time of its Singapore-San Francisco inaugural were further complicated by fuel shortages in the United States. Because airlines operating from San Francisco were faced with fuel rationing based on their consumption a year earlier, SIA was unable to operate both its cargo and passenger services at the same time. The airline had begun twice-weekly all-cargo flights between Singapore and San Francisco in April, 1978, using a Boeing 707-320C.

The cargo flights were suspended for three weeks in late March and early April to insure the availability of fuel for the debut of passenger flights. The cargo flights resumed Apr. 16 after SIA chairman J. Y. M. Pillay received assurances that adequate fuel would be available for all of the carrier's scheduled flights.

Under the bilateral agreement concluded between Washington and Singapore in September, 1977, SIA was authorized to operate three cargo and three passenger flights a week into the U. S. Effective last month, frequencies were permitted to increase to four a week for both services, and to five a week beginning in April, 1980.

For direct services between Singapore and the U. S., which do not pass through third countries, there is no frequency restriction.

The 707 cargo flights currently are routed through Hong Kong, Guam, Honolulu and San Francisco on the outbound leg, but they bypass Hong Kong on the return trip to Singapore.

There is incentive for the cargo flights—the United States was Singapore's second largest trading partner last year, with total trade between the two countries amounting to approximately $3 billion. This was about 14% of Singapore's total world trade. Of Singapore's total air cargo last year, 6% originated from or was destined for the United States.

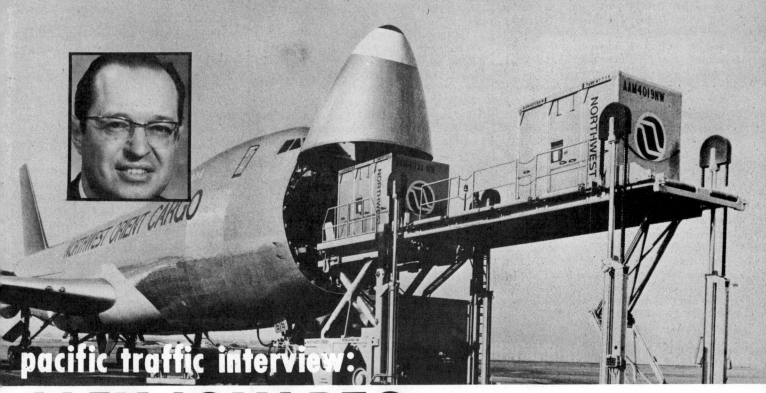

ALEX IGYARTO
Director, Cargo Sales
NORTHWEST ORIENT AIRLINES

Intermodality is not a new idea, having been practiced in the surface transportation industry for a number of years, but its application in the air freight industry is still in its infancy.

The long-range cargo objectives of Northwest Orient Airlines involve the encouragement of the intra- and intermodal use of containers. According to Northwest, the benefits to the shipper include surface flexibility blended with the speed of air; the coordination of the advantages of each mode; and an efficient pricing method that creates new markets for air freight.

Thanks to the Boeing 747 jet freighter, of course, the intermodal-type container can now move by air. With four Boeing 747 freighters on line, Northwest Orient can offer direct service from more U.S. cities to more Far East destinations than any other airline utilizing the 747F. To help fill these giant aircraft with containerized freight, Northwest has invested in its own motion picture about intermodality in action. The movie is presently available for showings to shippers in conjunction with an informative booklet, "Intermodality for Air Shippers".

In a recent interview, Alex Igyarto, Northwest's director of cargo sales, described the airline's activities in the field of intermodality and in other areas as well. His comments are, we believe, most instructive.

Eichorn: *Give our readers a little of your background in the industry.*

Igyarto: Well, I am a graduate of the University of Toledo where I majored in air transportation. I went to work for Northwest in 1950. Other than the first couple of years, I have been in air cargo sales the whole period. For the last nine years I have been the Director of Cargo Sales for Northwest Airlines' system, based in the General Office. One of my prime objectives has been to develop Northwest's air freight potential.

Basically, John, "Intermodality for Air Shippers" has been our theme for several years and to explain it, we have published a 40-page booklet which is used as a sales presentation. This booklet explains container benefits to the shipper and carrier, background and pricing concepts, present problems with governments and carriers in accepting intermodality, and its long range benefits to the industry. This booklet is used as a "desk-top" presentation to shipping executives, helping them to understand what we are trying to do to enhance their air transportation cargo services. Our local people make these presentations. A 17-minute film we recently made is used as a companion piece to the booklet. The booklet doesn't explain how containers move around in the shipper's warehouse,

but the film gives a pragmatic view of container applications on a shipper's premises.

The booklet may be used for reference purposes, but as indicated in the preface, a narrative is necessary. This booklet is the same presentation made to the members of the CAB on February 23, 1977. These presentations were made in conjunction with our Total Distribution Cost program.

Our TDC program has given us some good results. For instance, working with Circle Air Freight, Chicago, we were able to get the Upjohn Company to engage in a TDC study. The study showed Upjohn that by using air freight, money could be saved in in-transit insurance and interest costs. Consequently, we were able to acquire 300,000 pounds new westbound transpacific air freight business from this account. The TDC story is explained in the latter part of the intermodality booklet. It analyzes distribution costs and regroups them into a form where ocean and air costs are easily compared. We provide the shipper with a booklet containing the computer output, a written report explaining the analysis, and our recommendations. Of course, there are times when air is not recommended, and when this is the case, it is clearly stated. Some shippers are astounded at this, and we gain some air freight shipments as a result of the confidence our presentation generates. The TDC program was successful for Motorola. The program converted over three million pounds of cargo to air and, according to Motorola, our program helped them reduce their distribution costs.

Eichorn: *How could deregulation benefit Northwest?*

Igyarto: Northwest (and apparently most other carriers) is maintaining a wait and see attitude. We will probably stay with our already certificated points. I really think that not much real change is going to happen in 1978. We intend to continue to run our business in a way to assure a profit. Since we have four 747s, we would want to use our deregulation rights in conjunction with the transpacific flights. Our freighters are not in the California market, and almost half of all transpacific cargo business that goes by air comes and goes via California, so we may want to operate between these gateways to the Orient.

Eichorn: *Would deregulation give some leverage on the domestic leg of the flight that goes on to Tokyo?*

Igyarto: Ratewise, no. There is no point in lowering the rate and carrying twice as much for half the price. If we made a special domestic rate, it would not be exclusive for Northwest. Since any transpacific carrier can use our rate, there would be nothing to gain. There is leverage in the sense that you can make it happen, but the point is whether you are developing new traffic by doing it, or diluting existing traffic.

Eichorn: *What are your feelings on IATA? Are you going to stay out of it?*

Igyarto: We have no intention of returning to IATA. We dropped out of IATA basically because of excessive meeting and travelling expenses, with no measurable accomplishments. Somehow, some IATA members manage to retard progress for others, and it is unfortunate for the shipper and the industry.

Eichorn: *Should there be a different organization?*

Igyarto: IATA has its good points, but when it comes to ratemaking, maybe this method needs to be changed; I don't know. I understand from a recent article that the U.S. CAB is considering withdrawing anti-trust immunity for U.S. members of IATA.

Eichorn: *What's behind your emphasis on containerization?*

Igyarto: Handling volume business piece by piece is not profitable. If we doubled our pounds out of Chicago where we can't expand our freight facilities, we would be so saturated that we could not hold on to our gains because we would deteriorate our service level. Containerization helps double our business by increasing the manpower output through larger container loads. Through the stacking of 20' containers (M2s) we could use our ramp area without expansion of present real estate. Our booklet details all this information.

Eichorn: *Where does the forwarder fit in?*

Igyarto: The forwarders are basically our volume shippers—we are a volume airline, so to speak. According to ATA figures for 1976, the average domestic shipment for the industry is 303 pounds, while our average domestic shipment is 448 pounds. Containerization helps bring that about. We think the small shipper is best handled by freight forwarders. We'll stay out of that business—at least as a major effort.

Eichorn: *Do you have a small package service?*

Igyarto: Yes, we have EPS (Expedited Package Service), and we have deliberately avoided having these handled at our freight facility. Also, along that same line, we are looking into a new service called "Air Parcel Service". It is designed to compete with Federal Express. It will be handled by our ticket counter as passenger baggage.

Eichorn: *What does the economy of the Pacific Basin look like to you right now?*

Igyarto: We see steady growth, not explosive. In 1978 we want to increase 25% throughout our system. We did this in 1976. 1977 was not as strong. To achieve the 25% increase, we have to do exceptionally well during the first six months since the last quarter we expect to be saturated eastbound. Lately, our westbound increases have been good; this could help to achieve our goals if it continues.

Eichorn: *Do you think there is going to be a sizeable use for 20' containers?*

Igyarto: Economically, it is not advantageous for the shipper to use 20' containers until a new rate structure is put into effect. Of course, I am speaking of international rates.

Eichorn: *What about daylight rates?*

Igyarto: Well, daylight rates, which is shipper-loaded traffic, have been undercut by carriers who don't have adequate container capability by having a similar bulk rate for specific commodities. We just can't see why a carrier, for less money, would want to encourage shippers to give carriers their cargo as bulk. Increased costs without adequate compensation is probably a major reason why domestic cargo has not been profitable for some carriers.

Eichorn: *Which is more important, the domestic or foreign business?*

Igyarto: I suppose we could say the greatest growth could be domestic, but the big dollar is still in transpacific traffic. Not many carriers have been successful making a profit domestically. Another means of expanding this year will be our new transatlantic routes.

Eichorn: *There's more competition there than in the Pacific.*

Igyarto: I think there are 23 carriers we will have to compete with. We are going to Scandinavia, which represents about 10% of the transatlantic market.

We expect to get our share of that traffic fairly soon after entry.

Eichorn: *What do you think airlines are going to do about new aircraft? Particularly freighters?*

Igyarto: There is a lot of skepticism with regard to what deregulation can offer, and carriers are holding off on spending big amounts of money since they don't know what the future offers in terms of their investment. I think there will be some turbo prop purchases by the small carriers. Federal Express is already buying the obsolete 727QCs. I think that smaller aircraft allowed them a frequency air advantage larger carriers could not offer, and service to many cities; but with a larger aircraft, they have to give up some of these advantages.

Eichorn: *You're in the small package business, on the one hand, and you see an intermodal market for 20' containers. Where lies your largest interest?*

Igyarto: We are in the L3 and M1 container business, just like the other major truck carriers are. The 20' container has a short term rate problem. As I said earlier, we've got to get a rate first. It's a chicken and egg routine. We need some assurance that shippers will use it. Shippers are eager to use a container that resembles their truck volume, but everything depends on what the price will be to the shipper. Even if we agreed on a price, foreign governments might not agree, because the national carrier might see it differently. It costs about $180,000 for each 20' lifter, and another $8,000 for each 20' container. We are talking about millions of dollars with no assurance that rates will be approved. We would like to see an interim rate for two 10' containers (which most carriers have) equal to a 20' container. I am sure other carriers will look at their investment along the same lines. Again, I am speaking of international traffic only.

Eichorn: *What do you think it is going to take to develop air cargo? There's an awful lot of trade-offs with carriers taking cargo from each other, and nobody is developing it. What do you think the industry should be doing?*

Igyarto: Developing growth traffic through volume container rate structures; more efficient ground handling systems; and being allowed to pass on some savings, thereby lowering distribution costs. This is what the TDC program is set up to do. We know, from working with a company's surface data, what it costs them, and we know what it costs us. From this, we can determine a proper rate structure for that commodity. If all carriers were doing this, based on efficient loading system for containers, we could improve our growth substantially. Actually, our intermodality booklet explains this better than I can here in a paragraph. The booklet is 40 pages in length and offers a great number of details on the subject.

WHY THE CONFERENCE SYSTEM MUST BE CHANGED

In the December issue of DISTRIBUTION WORLDWIDE an article was published entitled "Why We Must Keep the Conference System." In rebuttal, I will attempt to differentiate between the conference *carrier* and the true *"we"* of the original article, the small shipper.

To the small shipper, the conference should be considered as two specific elements, the shipper and the carrier. Each one depends on the other in order to effectively and economically participate in the distribution system. The immediate question that arises, however, is *how* dependent is one on the other.

Granted, the shipper must utilize the carrier to transport his goods to the overseas market, and the carrier must have goods to

A small shipper explains why the conference system is not responsive to the needs of the U.S. shipper, and why it must be brought into true perspective and its obligation to the shipper restored

By ROBERT L. VIDRICK,
Manager,
International Transportation,
Robertshaw International

carry. Although this is a basic logistical concept, the difference is that when the term "conference" enters into the picture, we are not speaking of a shipper or a carrier,

but rather the titular middle-men of ocean shipping.

All transportation undergraduate students read of the rationale for the establishment of the 100-year-old conference system in their freshman transportation history course. "Monopoly," "rebate," "trade war," these are terms that always appear on semester exams as to the reason for the initiation of the conference system. Although the school solution for the establishment of the conference system never changes, even through graduate school, it must be emphasized that the modern academic and professional school solution for the purpose and need of the current system has changed.

It would be hypocritical to be-
Continued

lieve that purpose and need have not changed in 100 years, yet the professionals of the conference continually dust off their freshman exam papers when asked the reason for their existence. Today, we should be realistic and examine the conference in the era of the '70's when answering the freshman exam question.

The syndrome of "that's the way we have always done it," is as out of place in the conference system as it is in modern management theory. Modern management does something about updating; the conference, when asked to change, continually quotes history and cries "unjustified criticism."

How often the small shipper receives his periodic rate increase letter from a conference with a statement: "To preserve and to ensure the continued maintenance of the kind of service our customers desire and deserve, we must regretfully impose this charge." The shipper has yet to be asked, by a conference, as to what service is desired, let alone questioned whether he has received what he deserves.

The same letter

The conferences speak of "vital services" to the shipper. Unless we equate vital services to the academic rationale for the historical initiation of the conference, we are left with an unquantified term. The periodic conference form letters continually emanate percentages, surcharges, loss of revenue, etc. We have yet to see one that states, "A _____ percentage of your vital service, namely _____ will be reduced unless there is a rate increase."

This may sound mundane, yet if the conference continually tells us that it is providing "vital services," why can't the conference quantify these services? If a conference can proclaim a *specific* surcharge within twenty-four hours after a dock strike and further state that the revenue losses

were so serious that the *specific* surcharge must be placed in effect, we would assume that they could just as easily use the same crystal ball and tell us exactly what *specific* percentage our vital services will be impacted upon.

I must admit that I am indeed criticizing the conference. This admission now allows the carrier element of the conference to discontinue reading and revert to the "we are under attack again" philosophy. The carrier element is right, if these are their thoughts, but this attack is not from a government agency, non-U.S. country nor even from their own lines. Rather it is from the other half of the conference system—the small shipper.

Eliminate the conference system and its vital services to the shipper? Of course not! Bring the conference into its true perspective and its obligation to the shipper? The answer is yes.

The obvious solution that is oftentimes heard is to scrap the conference system. I do not agree with this channel of criticism. A system over 100 years old must have some saving graces; we contend that it does. An alternative or another approach for the current conference system, however, rests with the conference carriers.

Communication between shipper and carrier in the current system is a one-way street. The small shipper signs his contract with a conference, ships his freight according to the rules, and gets periodic increase notices. His appeals to the conference regarding increased rates and regulations fall upon the water without a ripple. When reemphasized, they become the element of criticism that the conference speaks of continuously.

Why? Because the conference carriers are more concerned with the other aspects of their operation that are up for criticism by government and outsiders. I have yet to read in any professional journal that the conference is un-

der criticism by the small shipper and is attempting to resolve difficulties.

The small shipper has only one alternative; if he doesn't like the system, he can drop out. The problem is that by doing this with some conferences, his cargo would sit at the dock or be shipped at a non-conference rate with a conference carrier. The element of monopoly fought against 100 years ago still prevails on some routes in these modern times, regardless of what the freshman textbooks argue.

The greener grass

The small shipper resents the innuendo that is oftentimes cast by the conference regarding the criticism of the conference, that the "grass is always greener on the other side, but if you got there you would find it isn't so." The small shipper is not looking to the abolishment of the conference, but rather a right to be heard.

The conference must untie its umbilical cord from the minority and stand upright with the support of the majority—the small shipper. The tip of the iceberg approach to the problem of the conferences will not sink the conference; what will sink it is the unknown criticism of the small shipper that is submerged and not listened to by the carriers.

The shipper is for a viable conference where he has a voice, not one that is based on one-way communication. The small shipper is prepared to help if asked, but only if listened to. I have taken the liberty of paraphrasing an adage to illustrate what the shipper can do for the conference if called upon. "If you treat the conference as it is, it will remain as it is—if you treat it as if it were what it could be and should be, it will become what it could, should be."

A representative of the real "we" in "we must keep a conference system" has stood up, but will his words continue to fall on deaf ears? ■

Liner cargo changing patterns

JOHN R. IMMER

John R. Immer is president of Work Saving International, management consultants of Washington, D.C. and chairman of the board of Caribe Trailer Systems, Inc. He is the author of "Container Services of the Atlantic" and other books on cargo handling and industrial management.

Fundamental changes now taking place in the distribution pattern of waterborne liner cargo will have a major effect on the future development of each United States port. Liner cargo, as opposed to tramp, irregular or tanker services, places a much greater demand upon all port services and, by the same token, contributes more to the prosperity of the port.

Liner exports consist predominantly of manufactured or processed products and materials. The largest single source for these products in the Western Hemisphere is the great "Heartland" of the North American continent — an area consisting of the North Central states of the U.S. and the province of Ontario in Canada. This is the area whose entry ports have been changing and will continue to change.

The entire trade to and from this area is subject to diversion and rapid changes of distribution pattern. The area is highly reactive to new methods, improved service, lower costs and more efficient methods of transport and distribution. Imports for processing and fabrication to be used in manufacturing will have the same distribution pattern as the exports. Imports for consumption will be distributed more on the basis of regional income levels. Imports for the Heartland will be drawn to the same services and facilities developed to attract the exports.

Summary of changes

From 1970 to 1977, the ports of the North Atlantic, Gulf and the Great Lakes lost 6.8 million long tons of liner cargo. During the same period the Pacific ports gained nearly 4 million long tons. The ports of the South Atlantic gained 623,000 long tons. Stated percentagewise, the loss of the North Atlantic, Gulf and Great Lakes ports amounted to 21.5 percent of their total 1970 liner cargo while the Pacific ports increased their liner cargo traffic by nearly 54 percent. The trade from South Atlantic ports increased nearly 16 percent. This constitutes a drastic change in the pattern of distribution for liner cargo and indicates that strong forces are at work.

There are several forces at work to cause these changes. The first of these involves basic demographic changes. A major shift in population has been taking place for some time. More factories are opening and expanding in the South Central and Pacific areas than in the Middle West and North East regions. If this were the sole determinant, however, the Gulf and South Atlantic ports should have had the greatest increase during this period. This did not happen because of another factor. The Gulf ports delayed too long in setting up the port structures required for containerization and it will take some doing to catch up.

Perhaps the most important single force in causing these changes has been the impact of the railroads. Piggyback is most efficient at greater distances, thus its growth minimizes the negative aspect of distance and makes the far-distant port more competitive with the nearer port. Shorter distances tend to be served more by truck than by rail, hence increasing labor costs causing immediate truck rate increases which favor the distant port over the nearer port in the long run. A part of this picture is the aggressiveness of the Western and Canadian railroads and the shambles of the railroads connecting the Middle West with the North Atlantic and Gulf ports. There is a correlation between the success of the Southern and Family Railways and the growth of traffic through the South Atlantic ports.

Changes in the Great Lakes traffic have been due to the fact that shipping companies have begun to realize that it takes longer to go from Montreal to Chicago than it does from Halifax to Liverpool. This reduces the round trips per year and the total tonnage a ship can transport per year. Work Saving International showed in 1962 that liner cargo could be carried more cheaply by rail from Chicago to Halifax than it could be carried by water. This study resulted in the development of Halifax as a container port and the formation of the Dart Containerline.

The character of the total services of a port has facilitated or stimulated changes in the traffic patterns. In the past, traffic patterns have tended to remain rigid. Strikes and arbitrary labor conditions encourage companies to try new routes, new ports and new shipping services. Once tried, sometimes they like the new route better and a permanent traffic change has occurred. Such conditions have hurt Boston and New York particularly and do not seem likely to change. Improvement in container handling and processing through the port is more likely to occur in Southern and Western ports which will cause the trend toward those ports to continue.

Changes in exports

The regional changes in the volume of exports of liner cargo from 1970 to 1977 are summarized in Table I. This table is based upon the specific tonnage figures for each major port as shown in Table III. Total liner exports declined for the period from 28,875,000 long tons to 25,199,000 long tons, a decrease of 3,676,000 long tons or 12.7 percent. The North Atlantic, Gulf and Great Lakes regions lost 4.8 million long tons and the Pacific ports increased their output by 2.0 million tons.

North Atlantic. Between 1970 and 1977 the North Atlantic ports lost nearly 20 percent of their total export liner cargo. This was a loss of 1.6 million long tons. The greatest loser was New York City which found its share of the total export pie reduced from 14.4 percent to 13.2 percent. With the exception of Newport News the other ports retained or slightly increased their share of the traffic. Most of New York City's loss was probably to the western or to the Canadian ports with a small amount southward.

South Atlantic. The South Atlantic ports increased their share by 22 percent. Total liner exports increased from 2,118,000 long tons to 2,586,000 long tons, an increase of 468,000 long tons. This increase could have been due almost entirely to the growth of industries in the South Central and South Atlantic states with a small amount diverted from the more northern ports.

Gulf Ports. The Gulf ports suffered the greatest loss of any region. Their liner exports in 1970 of 8,653,000 long tons dropped to 5,915,000 long tons in 1977, a loss of 2,741,000 long tons or 31.6 percent. By far the greatest part of this loss is believed to have resulted from the diversion of manufactured cargo from the Heartland to the West Coast. The loss was also caused by the failure of the Gulf ports to provide adequate cranes and equipment for the increased use of van size containers. Also, a lack of promotional effort, on the level of the West Coast and Canadian ports and railroads, contributed to the scale of the loss.

South Pacific. The South Pacific ports had the greatest increase in liner exports. Their liner exports increased from 2,844,000 long tons in 1970 to 4,282,000 long tons in 1977, an increase of 1,438,000 long tons or 50 percent. Although there was some increase in local manufactures during this period, the greatest part of the increased trade is believed to have come from the North Central states.

North Pacific. The North Pacific ports had the same percentage of increase in liner exports from 1970 to 1977 as the

TABLE I

REGIONAL CHANGES IN VOLUME OF LINER EXPORTS
1970-1977

Region	Change in 1,000 Long Tons	% Change in Volume	Change in % of Total
North Atlantic	− 1,645	− 19.3	− 2.3
South Atlantic	+ 468	+ 22.1	+ 3.0
Gulf Ports	− 2,738	− 31.6	− 6.5
South Pacific	+ 1,438	+ 50.1	+ 7.2
North Pacific	+ 492	+ 49.6	+ 2.5
Great Lakes	− 470	− 63.9	− 1.5

Source: Table III.

TABLE III

U.S. WATERBORNE EXPORTS — LINER CARGO
Bureau of the Census, SA 705
(1,000 Long Tons)

Region / Port	1970	Percent of Total	1974	Percent of Total	1977	Percent of Total
NORTH ATLANTIC						
Boston	110	.4	149	.5	118	.5
New York City	4,168	14.4	4,860	17.3	3,319	13.2
Philadelphia	670	2.3	879	3.1	539	2.1
Baltimore	1,639	5.7	1,828	6.5	1,529	6.1
Norfolk	1,278	4.4	1,249	4.4	1,060	4.2
Newport News	472	1.6	211	.8	127	.5
TOTAL	8,337	28.9%	9,176	32.6%	6,692	26.6%
SOUTH ATLANTIC						
Wilmington, N.C.	85	.3	110	.4	165	.7
Moorehead City, N.C.	167	.6	78	.3	83	.3
Charleston	402	1.4	709	2.5	807	3.2
Savannah	932	3.2	997	3.5	903	3.6
Jacksonville	238	.8	162	.6	234	.9
Miami	210	.7	338	1.2	296	1.2
San Juan	84	.3	174	.6	98	.4
TOTAL	2,118	7.3%	2,568	9.1%	2,586	10.3%
GULF PORTS						
Tampa	1,007	3.5	285	1.0	289	1.1
Mobile	654	2.3	525	1.9	313	1.2
New Orleans	3,632	12.6	3,477	12.4	2,681	10.6
Port Arthur	163	.1	182	.6	136	.5
Beaumont	380	1.3	189	.7	36	.1
Houston	2,088	7.2	1,859	6.6	1,990	7.9
Galveston	729	2.5	593	2.1	470	1.9
TOTAL	8,653	30.0%	7,110	25.3%	5,915	23.5%
SOUTH PACIFIC						
San Diego	138	.5	157	.6	10	—
Los Angeles	996	3.4	1,187	4.2	1,294	5.1
Long Beach	405	1.4	974	3.5	1,055	4.2
San Francisco	593	2.1	795	2.8	362	1.4
Oakland	621	2.2	953	3.4	1,549	6.1
Alameda	91	.3	41	.1	12	—
TOTAL	2,844	9.8%	4,107	14.6%	4,282	17.0%
NORTH PACIFIC						
Portland	556	1.9	516	1.8	526	2.1
Seattle	435	1.5	709	2.5	957	3.8
TOTAL	991	3.4%	1,225	4.3%	1,483	5.9%
GREAT LAKES						
Milwaukee	198	.7	94	.3	129	.5
Detroit	111	.4	33	.1	32	.1
Chicago	427	1.5	130	.5	105	.4
TOTAL	736	2.5%	257	.9%	266	1.0%
TOTAL ABOVE PORTS	23,679		24,443		21,224	
TOTAL U.S.A. PORTS	29,875		28,113		25,199	
Listed Ports % of U.S.	82.0%		86.5%		84.2%	

TABLE II

REGIONAL CHANGES IN VOLUME OF LINER IMPORTS
1970-1977

Region	Change in 1,000 Long Tons	% Change in Volume	Change in % of Total
North Atlantic	− 1,011	− 10.3	− 5.2
South Atlantic	+ 155	+ 8.6	+ .6
Gulf Ports	− 123	− 4.1	− .7
South Pacific	+ 1,495	+ 52.5	+ 6.9
North Pacific	+ 539	+ 79.6	+ 2.7
Great Lakes	− 732	− 70.1	− 3.5

Source: Table IV.

TABLE IV

U.S. WATERBORNE IMPORTS — LINER CARGO
Bureau of the Census, SA 305
(1,000 Long Tons)

Region / Port	1970	Percent of Total	1974	Percent of Total	1977	Percent of Total
NORTH ATLANTIC						
Boston	505	2.4	340	1.5	270	1.3
New York City	6,350	30.2	6,392	28.5	5,740	27.0
Philadelphia	1,203	5.7	932	4.2	600	2.8
Baltimore	1,180	5.6	1,786	8.0	1,253	5.9
Norfolk	536	2.5	802	3.6	892	4.2
Newport News	44	.2	44	.2	53	.2
TOTAL	9,818	46.6%	10,296	45.9%	8,808	41.4%
SOUTH ATLANTIC						
Wilmington, N.C.	236	1.1	208	.9	240	1.1
Moorehead City, N.C.	17	.1	218	1.0	2	—
Charleston	346	1.6	422	1.9	463	2.2
Savannah	370	1.8	586	2.6	564	2.6
Jacksonville	252	1.2	272	1.2	206	1.0
Miami	169	.8	280	1.2	254	1.2
San Juan	413	2.0	307	1.4	229	1.1
TOTAL	1,803	8.6%	2,293	10.2%	1,958	9.2%
GULF PORTS						
Tampa	195	.9	177	.8	62	.3
Mobile	288	1.4	453	2.0	167	.8
New Orleans	1,461	6.9	1,656	7.4	1,495	1.0
Port Arthur	5	—	1	—	19	.1
Beaumont	13	.1	1	—	16	.1
Houston	974	4.6	1,670	7.4	1,017	4.8
Galveston	101	.5	177	.8	138	.6
TOTAL	3,037	14.4%	4,135	18.4%	2,914	13.7%
SOUTH PACIFIC						
San Diego	51	.2	25	.1	6	—
Los Angeles	1,243	5.9	1,371	6.1	1,730	8.1
Long Beach	566	2.7	923	4.1	1,364	6.4
San Francisco	580	2.8	400	1.8	348	1.6
Oakland	295	1.4	555	2.5	853	4.0
Alameda	112	.5	115	.5	41	.2
TOTAL	2,847	13.5%	3,389	15.1%	4,342	20.4%
NORTH PACIFIC						
Portland	218	1.0	243	1.1	153	.7
Seattle	459	2.0	625	2.8	1,063	5.0
TOTAL	677	3.0%	868	3.9%	1,216	5.7%
GREAT LAKES						
Milwaukee	116	.6	32	.1	37	.2
Detroit	459	2.2	97	.4	102	.5
Chicago	469	2.2	131	.6	173	.8
TOTAL	1,044	5.0%	260	1.2%	312	1.5%
TOTAL ABOVE PORTS	19,226		21,241		19,550	
TOTAL U.S.A. PORTS	21,061		22,445		21,294	
Listed Ports % of U.S.	92.4%		94.6%		91.8%	

South Pacific ports. Their 1970 liner exports increased from 991,000 to 1,483,000 long tons in 1977, an increase of 492,000 long tons or 50 percent. Practically all of this increase is believed to have come from the North Central states, traffic which formerly went south or east or through Great Lakes ports.

Changes in imports

The regional changes in the volume of imports of liner cargo from 1970 to 1977 are summarized in Table II. This table is based upon the tonnage from the various major ports shown in Table IV. Total liner imports remained about the same during this period. However, there was a considerable change in the share of the various regions. This change, for the most part, followed the pattern for exports.

North Atlantic. Between 1970 and 1977 the North Atlantic ports lost 10 percent of their import liner cargo. Imports declined from 9,818,000 long tons to 8,808,000 long tons, a loss of 1,010,000 long tons. New York City declined by 10 percent but Philadelphia dropped to one half of its 1970 rate. Baltimore and Norfolk managed to increase their import liner cargo slightly.

South Atlantic. During this period, the South Atlantic ports increased their liner imports by 8.6 percent, increasing from 1,803,000 long tons in 1970 to 1,958,000 long tons in 1977. Charleston, Savannah and Miami increased their imports while Jacksonville and San Juan fell behind. This increase for the region was in line with the growth of income for the region for the period.

Gulf Ports. The Gulf ports had only a small loss in imports, about 4 percent, compared to its loss of exports for the period of 31.6 percent. Perhaps this was due to the fact that in 1970, imports were only 35 percent of the level of its exports so there was less to lose. This may also be due to the possibility that imports for the North Central area historically came through North Atlantic or Great Lakes ports. Hence the diversion of traffic would have been more to Canadian and Pacific ports.

South Pacific. Liner imports through South Pacific ports increased nearly 1.5 million long tons, from 2,847,000 long tons to 4,342,000 long tons for an increase of 52.5 percent. As total

163

imports for the country remained fairly constant during the period, it must be assumed that a substantial part of the 2 million long tons of liner imports picked up by the Pacific ports must consist of the 1.8 million long ton decrease noted by the North Atlantic, Gulf and Great Lakes ports (see Tables II & IV).

North Pacific. Line imports increased from 677,000 long tons to 1,216,000 long tons, an increase of 539,000 long tons or 79.6 percent. The greater part of this increase went east to replace the loss of the North Atlantic and Great Lakes ports.

Great Lakes. The loss of liner imports from the Great Lakes ports was even greater than its loss of exports. Its liner imports dropped from 1,044,000 long tons to 312,000 long tons, a loss of 732,000 long tons or 70.1 percent of its 1970 trade. As consumption increased in the Great Lakes during this period it is doubted that there was much of a decline of total imports brought into the trade area. The loss to its ports was made up by increased traffic from Canadian and Pacific ports. As the services upon which this traffic depends continue to

decrease there seems to be little likelihood of a reversal in this trend.

The prospects

The total U.S. traffic in liner cargo may not be much greater five years from now than it is in 1978. There will be pressure from the government to increase exports, particularly of manufactured goods. On the other hand, there will be the decreased buying power of developing countries due to higher oil prices and a saturation level of foreign debts. Worldwide competition for these markets will become intensified by both the other developed countries and by the developing countries themselves.

As trends in manufacturing change slowly, it can be assumed that most of the liner exports will come from the same regions they come from today, except that there is still a trend toward the Southern states. The South Atlantic ports are expected to have the highest rate of increase of any of the regions during the next five years. This will be due to the increase in manufacturing in the South Atlantic and South Central states and the acquisition of additional traffic from the North Central and South Central states.

It will be interesting to see how much of its own regionally manufactured exports the Gulf ports will be able to recover and how much cargo it can recapture from the North Central states. Minibridge traffic works both ways and traffic from the Pacific ports via rail may increase the total movement through the Gulf ports. This will depend, to some extent, on the increase of additional services from the Gulf ports to Europe, the Middle East, Africa and the east coast of South America.

The Pacific ports will be hard pressed to retain the additional traffic they have gained so far. The increase in their own manufacturing capability will help maintain the local traffic, but this will be a small part of the increase these ports have had in the seven years.

The Great Lakes may continue to lose its liner cargo so that it may become entirely dependent upon foreign tramp services for any waterborne movement to and from the Great Lakes ports. There will be more pressure from the Canadian ports and from traffic down the Mississippi River for whatever liner cargo is left.

OCEAN SHIPPING'S COLD WAR

OR – –

are you preparing to ship with the Russians – – (when there's nobody else left)?

Whatever you, as your company's transportation executive, might think about the Soviet Union as a world power and as an adversary of the United States of America, you must acknowledge that the past growth of its merchant fleet has been and continues to be phenomenal. Pacific Traffic believes that a comprehensive and factual examination of the motives behind this dramatic increase in Russian shipping activity would contribute to your better understanding of the potential seriousness of this controversial worldwide problem

Accordingly, Pacific Traffic will editorialize, in detail, the entire background and potential impact of the Soviet merchant marine on not only our own shipping industry but the entire free world's.

The following article is the first in a series. A great deal of research has been compiled by the editorial staff of Pacific Traffic which will allow you to better evaluate the seriousness of the situation and hopefully result in some positive approaches to solving the problem.

After all, it is the shipper and his ocean freight forwarder who are supporting the Soviet merchant marine. We believe that this is very probably a short-sighted approach. We also can demonstrate how, in the long run, it can be highly damaging to the free enterprise system under which, in spite of its faults, we all prosper today.

It's important to understand that Russia has never been very easy to get along with. Numerous invasions of the country throughout its history have made its people secretive and suspicious of foreigners. The problem was compounded by the fact that for a long period of time the country did not have convenient access to a warm water port, and until

Peter the Great 'opened a window to Europe' within comparatively recent history, the country was in effect cut off from the civilized world, especially in terms of trade. But even with access to warm open water through the Baltic Sea and the Black Sea, Russia still had to be concerned with how easily those routes could be cut off. All in all, it's not surprising that the Russian people are influenced by the traumatic and uncertain nature of their maritime history.

In the years immediately after the Second World War, the Russian merchant marine was mainly limited to domestic service, and was practically an unknown factor in world shipping. The Russian merchant fleet was a motley assortment of pre-war Russian vessels, various craft captured during the war or handed over as German reparations, and a few American Liberty ships. By comparison with the rest of the world's fleets, much of which had been rebuilt because of the war, a large percentage of the fleet was over 25 years old. The average size was smaller, and only seven percent of the ships had a speed of over 14 knots. The variations between the different types of ships made them difficult to effectively maintain, and a great deal of time, ingenuity and expense was required to keep them at sea.

Shipbuilding technology takes time to develop under the best of circumstances, and most of Russia's shipyards were destroyed during the war. Even when they were rebuilt, much of their capacity was devoted to military uses, and therefore, the rapid expansion of the Soviet commercial fleet did not gather its full momentum until the early 1960s.

THE EXPANDING OPERATIONS
of
Russia's Merchant Fleet
(Millions of Tons)

	1960	1968
Liquid cargo	32.5	70.1
Dry cargo		
Coal	7.1	9.0
Ore	7.5	11.7
Timber	3.3	9.3
Metals	2.8	5.8
Machines & equipment .	.9	2.3
Other dry cargo	20.7	38.0
Total dry cargo	42.3	76.1
Total liquid & dry cargoes	74.8	146.2
Average length of voyage (miles)	935	2161
Ton/Miles (billions)	71	317

Source: Soviet Ministry of the Merchant Marine

However, as long as Russia remained relatively isolated, nobody really cared what its merchant marine did. But after the death of Stalin in 1953, the country became more outward looking and somewhat less politically isolated. One result of a more relaxed foreign policy was an increased volume of foreign trade.

DEVELOPMENT OF RUSSIA's
FOREIGN TRADE
(Billions of Rubles)

	1947	1952	1957	1962	1967	1968
Total	1.4	4.8	7.5	12.1	16.4	18.0
w/socialist countries	0.8	3.9	5.5	8.5	11.1	12.2
w/industrially developed countries	0.5	0.7	1.3	2.2	3.4	3.9
w/developing countries	0.1	0.2	0.7	1.4	1.9	2.0

Source: Official Soviet trade statistics.

The immediate result of the demand for sea transport that developed along with the increased levels of Russia's foreign trade was a decline in the proportion of the foreign trade carried by the country's own ships.

DISTRIBUTION OF RUSSIA'S
FOREIGN TRADE CARGO

	1950	1955	1960	1967
Percentage carried by Russian ships	50	30	40	52

Source: Soviet ships on World Sea Routes

Chartering foreign tonnage produced a heavy drain on currency reserves which might otherwise have been used to finance more trade or to purchase the Western technology that Soviet industry needed so badly. It also produced a dependence on the "whims of the capitalist freight market". The concern this caused was aggravated by an American decision to embargo all shipping involved in Communist trade after unfavorable developments took place in Cuba during President Kennedy's tenure. A number of the free world's shipping lines reneged on their obligations to the Russians, who as a result resolved never to be vulnerable to outside shipping again. The Russians also found that control of their own merchant fleet was a good way to control the means by which their increasing amounts of technical, military and economic assistance was provided to the countries they hoped to influence.

Viewed in this light, and considering the importance of a strong merchant marine as a support for the country's rapidly growing navy, there is nothing surprising about Russia's decision to expand its merchant marine. What is more difficult to explain is the scale of the expansion.

A study published in 1976 by Lambert Brothers, a British ship-brokerage firm, offers a possible answer. According to the study, the Soviet merchant fleet is characterized by basic inefficiency, ignorance and bad planning, and its development was incompatible with Soviet foreign trade, world trade and world shipping trends. For example, at the time of the study the Soviet Union had only some 1.2 million tons in its bulk carrier fleet, while its bulk trades amounted to some 40-50 million tons per year. Meanwhile, the cargo liner fleet had grown in recent years by some 30 percent per year, to total 27 percent of the total Soviet fleet. But the cargo carried by that liner fleet has only increased 10 percent. In other words, "tons of cargo carried per ton of shipping space available has declined".

The Russians developed their merchant fleet not only as a means of stopping a drain of foreign currency, but as a deliberate means of earning it. As former Minister of the Merchant Marine Victor Bakayev said: "Every country connected with sea transport tries to have its own fleet, so as to secure economic and political independence for its external trade, and, in favorable circumstances, to increase the income side of its balance of payments".

That this is a right that cannot be denied to any nation is undeniable. After all, are the Russians any different from any other cross-trader? The Scandinavians, for example, have a fleet which is more than adequate to serve their own domestic shipping needs, and which is also a vital source of currency revenue.

However, the Russian sales pitch to the free world's shipper somehow manages to hide the country's undisguised hostility to the free enterprise system.

As far as we know, the Russians have never abandoned their goal of the eventual overthrow of capitalism. The nature of their system enables them to commit as much of their resources as they desire to this goal, and they have demonstrated that opportunities for internal dissent are extremely limited.

Typical of the Russian attitude is a statement by the Admiral of the Soviet Navy, Sergei Gorshov to the effect that the goal of Soviet sea power is to "effectively utilize the world ocean in the interest of building communism". Gorshov also claims that the Soviet Union

"will have superiority of position over the enemy by building up a maritime base system". That's hardly the language of which peaceful coexistence and detente are made. Who do you suppose the "enemy" is?

These statements and the actions backing them up, have not been lost on many observers. As early as 1964, a report on the Soviet merchant fleet by the Committee on Commerce of the U.S. Senate began with the assertion that "Soviet Russia rapidly is emerging as a major maritime power, dedicated to economic, political and strategic objectives, and committed to disrupting and ultimately dominating world trade". And in 1966, Edwin M. Hood, president of the Shipbuilders Council of America, was asked whether he saw anything more than commercial motives behind the buildup of Soviet shipping capacity. "Yes", he responded. "There has been no decline in the objectives of international communism. The dialect may have changed, but the goal of world domination has been reiterated with every change of command at the Kremlim. To that end, Russian shipping and shipbuilding are regarded as important instruments of national policy, and the Soviet Union is moving rapidly to control the oceans and trade routes of the world. Because of her enormous fleet expansion, she will soon be able to manipulate ocean freight rates at will, and through a superiority in terms of numbers of ships in-being and mobility, she will be on the road to economic domination of the world". The situation hasn't improved in the 12 years that have passed since that statement was made.

The most recent warning as to the sinister nature of the Soviet merchant fleet's activity came from Suzanne Oetting, a House Merchant Marine Subcommittee staff member. According to her report, despite the Kremlin's claim that the main task of their merchant marine is to serve the demands of their coastal and international trade, their commercial fleet is operated as a naval auxiliary, giving the Russian Navy a ready made intelligence capability that can operate anywhere in the world. For example, in 1961 only two Soviet ships visited Hong Kong, in 1974-75 there were 123 ship visits, which the Chinese and British interpreted as a growing involvement of Soviet merchant shipping with the actitivtes of the KGB (the Russian CIA).

In the U.S. cross-trades, the KGB employs agents in practically every port, and according to John Barron, an authority on Russian intelligence operations, there has been a 50 percent

increase in the number of Communist bloc intelligence officers operating in this country since the dawn of detente in 1972, when the ports of the United States were opened to Soviet ships. "KGB agents disguised as seamen have been able to step onto American soil almost at will", he said. "In 1972, more than 25,000 Russian crewmen came ashore. Because it is impossible to keep so many people under surveillance, U.S. security officials have no idea how many were engaged in KGB missions or how many remained here as spys". Thus, there would seem to be an obvious connection between these "seamen" and subversion which "in magnitude and intensity exceeds any that the Russians have mounted against us since World War II", according to Raymond Wannall, former FBI director of counterintelligence. Intelligence sources also report that Soviet freighters routinely smuggle arms and espionage agents into other non-Communist countries.

The close ineraction between Russia's merchant marine and Navy has also been documented.

Russia's modern fleet of several thousand ships are fully prepared to operate with the Soviet Navy in time of war because they have consistently and systemically operated with the Navy in peacetime, Ms. Oetting said. In addition to an extensive civilian maritime training program, with over 30 modern, ocean-going training vessels, cross-training between the navy and the merchant marine is a common practice. Regular naval officers serve as merchant captains, and Soviet merchant ship officers remain close to their country's military efforts by continuing their active participation as naval reserve officers. Career naval personnel are assigned to freighters as a matter of routine procedure.

Commercial ships participate directly in large-scale Russian naval exercises, in addition to providing logistic support for the Russian Navy worldwide. Three-fourths of the over 200 surface vessels involved in a recent naval exercise were non-combatants which were requisitioned for the purpose.

The military and commercial fleets have technically autonomous administrative structures, with the civilian sector's ongoing concerns focusing on the attainment of civilian tasks and the successful meeting of planned economic quotas. However, military advisers are attached to the higher planning organizations of civilian fleets. Day-to-day coordination of military and civilian tasks is conducted through special committees within the Soviet bureaucracy, with naval representatives as part of the organization. Important decisions concerning the Soviet merchant marine are ultimately made at the Ministry of Defense level.

The Soviet shipbuilding industry is characterized by thorough standardization and interchangability of the components of naval and merchant ships, which are procured through the defense industry ministries. Specifications from civilian fleet offices are channeled through the Military Industrial Commission, which is responsible for the meshing of civilian and naval requirements.

This means that most Soviet commercial vessels are particularly suitable for transporting troops and military equipment. Russia's "long hatch" cargo ships, which can accommodate heavy artillery, aircraft, tanks and nuclear-warhead missiles, were used to carry ballistic missiles to Cuba, under the cover of a "technical assistance program to augment Cuban fisheries". Fortunately, the Soviet Union was forced to carry the missiles back home at the time of the "Cuban crisis". That particular international "incident", however, was what really made the Soviet Union recognize the importance of sea power and caused them to implement the massive build-up of both their navy and merchant marine.

More recent was the role of the Soviet merchant marine in arming both North Vietnam and still more recently the Cuban forces in Angola. Many of the tanks and artillery which conquered South Vietnam were carried to Haiphong by Soviet merchant vessels. And part of the large Soviet Ro-Ro fleet was recently used to carry tanks to Angola. The U.S.S.R. also demonstrated a high degree of proficiency in its readjustment of shipping allocations from programmed commercial schedules to meet its resupply operation in the Middle East. There's no denying that Russia has developed seapower in its fullest sense, and that it has altered the balance of world power by the superior ability of its merchant marine to carry troops and military equipment overseas— complemented by a navy to protect it.

Even the Lambert Brothers, who maintained that one of the main reasons for the growth in the Soviet merchant fleet was sheer incompetence, said that no matter what the excuse, the effect on western shipping is still the same. "A sinister influence is not incompatible with inefficiency", they said. "Gross instances of inefficiency ultimately attract odium under socialism as well as capitaliism, and the one way in which the Soviets can improve the performance of their particularly under-utilized liner ships is by diverting them to cargoes secured from western shippers by rate cutting. In the broader political context, we are confronting an alien system which is pledged and on record to strive for the dissolution of our way of doing things".

In all fairness, our merchant marine also played an import part in supplying the Vietnam War, and we are not suggesting that Russia's method of operating its merchant marine should be adopted in the United States. But it is interesting to compare the two systems. There is comparatively minimal cooperation between the U.S. Navy and our merchant marine, if not outright hostility. Government agencies such as the Justice Department seem determined to break up the conference system. Our merchant marine training system has been tainted with political corruption, while our shipbuilding industry is not internationally competitive. As Congressman Paul N. McCloskey, Jr., said in these pages last month, there is an almost glaring lack of focus and coordination in our maritime policy.

That's a problem Russia does not have and the advantages that it allows the Russian fleets, both naval and merchant marine, leaves little doubt as to the end result if pursued to the end—that of a complete demise of the free world's merchant shipping fleets and economic chaos.

Shipbuilding: Study Finds Prospects Dim,

European and Asian shipbuilders will build a 'probable' total of 3,855 ships during 1977-1987, concludes a recent Frost & Sullivan survey of world shipbuilding outside the United States, entitled "Shipbuilding Markets in Europe and Japan."

On a low-probable-high projection for the period, the low estimate sees 1,410 ocean carriers being launched, and a total of 6,300 vessels for the high end.

Under the "probable" scenario for 1977-1987, 3,260 tankers, ore-and-bulk and bulk/oil ships are expected to be constructed, and 595 liquefied natural gas (LNG), liquefied petroleum gas (LPG) and container ships equipped for specialized fleet work.

The major activity will be tankers, with a predicted demand of 2,000 for oil transport, with 800 ore-and-bulk carriers and 400 bulk/oil vessels.

The greatest percentage growth will be in LNG, LPG and container ships as world demand increases for LNG and LPG and shipping trends continue use of containerization.

There are two major factors determining the shape of the shipbuilding industry in the next decade use the study finds: (1) The demand for world shipping capacity, and (2) the growing trend toward government involvement in the industry. There is a building overcapacity of nearly 50 per cent and the shipbuilding nations of the world are struggling against each other to capture their shares of a shrinking market. The battle between the traditional in-

dustrialized shipbuilding countries of Europe and their chief rival, Japan (the number one builder) tends to over-shadow the threat to both groups from the growing shipbuilding industries in both the less-developed countries and the "command" economies of the USSR and other Comecon countries.

The problem of the next 10 years is to build demand, and the prospects appear dim, according to the study's figures. Shipping demand is based upon the transportation of oil, the major product carried by ship, and of five dry bulk products—iron ore, coal, grain, phosphate rock and bauxite/alumina. Oil sets the pace for the industry; it accounts for nearly half the seaborne transportation requirements. The five major dry bulk products comprise about 90 per cent of the dry goods transported by sea.

Three factors influenced demand over the past six years, changing the shipping and shipbuilding industries dramatically. The first was the oil crisis of 1973. Oil prices tripled and even quadrupled and changed the patterns of world growth and trade. Oil suddenly transformed from an inexpensive commodity into an expensive necessity. Because the shipbuilding industry normally fluctuates on a two-year cycle, it was not until 1975 that the full effect of the crisis became obvious.

Two other factors influenced demand during the same period: The unexpected reopening of the Suez Canal and the port congestion that developed in the sud-denly rich oil-producing nations as they began importing vast amounts of goods from the rest of the world. The Suez shortened trade routes between certain parts of the world, particularly from the Middle East oil producers to Europe. This lessened the demand for ships, as voyages could be made in shorter times. During the eight years the Suez was closed, huge supertankers had been developed, because of their inherent economies of scale in carrying large amounts of oil over long distances. These supertankers were now too large to transit the Suez.

The composition of the world fleet has changed in recent years, both in ship types and the flags under which they are built and carry on trade. The changing pattern of world trade between the industrialized countries and the developing countries leads the world towards the opposite ends of the ship design spectrum. At one end are the very simple ships, the tankers and bulk dry product carriers, which essentially hold one product loaded directly into a large open hold. At the other end are the increasingly sophisticated ships, requiring either complex design of the ships themselves or complex and expensive land-based support facilities.

New Construction by Major Ship Types 1977-1987

Ship Types	World Fleet 1976 No.	'000GRT	Orderbook 30 Sept. 1976 No.	'000GRT	Case A Low 1982	1987	Case B Probable 1982	1987	Case C High 1982	1987
Bulk Fleet										
Tankers	7,020	168,161	419	25,806	50	500	60	2,000	150	1,050
Ore & Bulk	3,513	66,714	655	15,140	60	400	100	700	150	1,050
Bulk/Oil	419	25,023	46	3,000	15	100	40	360	100	600
Specialized Fleet										
LNG	33)				25	35	40	45	40	60
	)	3,377	177	5,200						
LPG	400)				60	100	100	250	300	600
Containers	433	6,685	n/a	2,500	35	35	90	70	180	120
TOTALS	19,952	269,960		51,646	240	1,170	430	3,425	870	5,430
Total, decade					1,410		3,855		6,300	

Shipbuilding Forecast by Country 1977-1987

Country*	# Ships **	(000) # GRT	Case A Low 1977-82	1983-87	Case B Probable 1977-82	1983-87	Case C High 1977-82	1983-87
1 Japan	1,087	20,344.5	96	460	170	1,370	375	2,295
2 USA	216	4,624.9	13	55	15	80	44	105
3 Sweden	88	4,618.7	4	20	10	40	18	100
4 UK	215	4,230.6	13	35	17	100	32	150
5 Spain	374	4,129.5	4	20	10	60	18	100
6 France	104	3,699.4	14	64	27	205	52	325
7 Brazil	220	3,403.6	28	130	48	450	90	620
8 W. Germany	199	2,826.2	12	55	20	130	40	220
9 Italy	109	1,831.5	4	18	9	40	16	105
10 Poland	165	1,819.6	25	152	50	460	90	680
11 S. Korea	94	1,532.6	23	141	48	450	85	630
12 Denmark	81	1,391.3	4	20	6	40	10	100
TOTALS	2,952		240	1,170	430	3,425	870	5,430

* Ranked by orderbook standing as of 30 Sept. 1976
** Existing orderbook and ships under construction 30 Sept. 1976

These ships include the liquefied gas carriers and what are termed unit load carriers. The cargo is carried in modular containers, or is rolled on and off the ship via a lowered stern or side ramp, or is loaded on barges which are floated to the ship in the harbor and then loaded onto the ship by a shipboard crane. These unit load ships are the ones that eased port congestion so dramatically.

There are three major groups of countries engaged in shipping and shipbuilding. These are the in-dustrialized countries, which are members of the Organization for Economic Cooperation and Development (OECD), the lesser developed countries (LDCs), and the state controlled countries. Most countries enter ship-building for any or all of four major reasons: First, to provide a defense force; second, to provide employment for large numbers of people; third, to control their own seaborne trade; fourth, to provide a favorable balance of payments through earning export dollars from ships. For these social, political, and economic reasons, the industrialized countries are turning more and more to protectionist measures to combat the growing competition from the LDCs and state-controlled shipbuilders, says the F & S study.

In studying the world economics into which the various nations must integrate their shipbuilding industries, the oil crisis of 1973 and the subsequent world-wide recession stand out as the primary influencing factors. With the high cost of oil, nations had little left for other goods. Thus, world trade declined and many countries, particularly the LDC,s borrowed heavily to finance their oil

Maritime Administration's 1978 Construction Summary of U.S. Ships

Total large merchant type vessels under contract in private U.S. shipyards as of July 1, 1978

NEW CONSTRUCTION

	Total	Intermodal[1]	Freighters	Tankers	LNGs	Dry Bulk[2]	Others[3]
Total	53	10	3**	14	14	9	3
Government	0	0	0	0	0	0	0
Private	53	10	3**	14	14	9	3

CONVERSIONS

	Total	Intermodal	Freighters	Tankers	LNGs	Dry Bulk	Others
Total	0	0	0	0	0	0	0
Government	0	0	0	0	0	0	0
Private	0	0	0	0	0	0	0

SHIPS COMPLETED[4]

(October 1, 1977—July 1, 1978)

Ship Name	Type	Dwt.	Cost[5]	Delivered	Owner	Shipyard	Govt. Aid
OVERSEAS OHIO	T	89,700	30.0	10/20/77	Shipmor	NASSCO	MI
AMERICAN INDEPENDENCE	CT	265,000	81.4	11/18/77	Gulf	Beth Steel-SP	CS(40.93%)
ANTIGUN PASS	T	164,000	66.7	11/22/77	Shipco 2295	Avondale	MI
LNG ARIES	LNG	63,000	89.6	12/13/77	LNG Trans.	GD-Quincy	CS(23.7%),MI,CCF
CHEVRON LOUIS	T	35,000	16.1	12/22/77	Union Bk.	FMC	None
OVERSEAS NEW YORK	T	89,700	30.0	12/08/77	Shipmor	NASSCO	None
KEYSTONE CANYON	T	164,000	66.7	2/27/78	Shipco 2296	Avondale	MI
BT ALASKA	T	188,500	67.0	3/14/78	Shell	NASSCO	None
OVERSEAS WASHINGTON	T	89,700	30.0	3/15/78	Shipmor	NASSCO	MI
EL PASO SOUTHERN	LNG	63,460	106.6	5/31/78	El Paso Southern	Newport News	CS(25.74%),MI
BROOKS RANGE	T	164,000	66.7	5/21/78	Shipco 2297	Avondale	None
MAUAI	Cn	26,600	50.7	5/25/78	Matson	Bath	None
TONSINA	T	118,300	25.0	5/11/78	Shipco 668	Sun	None
LNG CAPRICORN	LNG	63,600	89.6	6/22/78	Liquegas Trans.	Quincy	CS(23.7%),MI,CCF
LEWIS W. FOY	O	62,600	32.5	6/7/78	Beth Steel	Bay	None

15 vessels   1,647,760   848.6

CONVERSION/RECONSTRUCTION

(October 1, 1977—July 1, 1978)

Ship Name	Type	Dwt.	Cost	Delivered	Owner	Shipyard	Govt. Aid
GOLDEN BEAR	Cn-p	39,500	5.1	11/30/77	PFEL	Beth Steel-SF	CS(42.64%)
AUSTRAL ENVOY	Cn-p	27,480	20.1	12/06/77	Farrell	Avondale	CS(36.73%)
JAPAN BEAR	Cn-p	39,500	5.1	3/14/78	PFEL	Beth Steel-SF	CS(42.64%)
THOMAS C. CUFFEE	Cn-p	39,500	5.1	6/30/78	PFEL	Beth Steel-SF	CS(42.64%)

4 vessels   145,980   35.4

Key: B—Bulk; C—Cargo; c—Conversion; CCF—Capital Construction Fund; Ch—Chemical Carriers; Cn—Containership; CP—Cargo Passenger; CS—Construction Subsidy; CT-Crude Tanker; DS—Deep Sea Mining Ship; F—Freighter; L—Lighter-Aboard Ship; LNG—Liquefied Natural Gas Tanker; MI—Title XI Vessel; PT—Product Tanker; RO/RO—Roll-on/Roll-off; SB—Sea Barge; T—Tanker; TB—Tug Barge; Cn-p—Partial Containership; O—Ore Carriers; OBO—Oil-Bulk-Ore.

[1] Includes types: RO/RO, LASH, Seabee, Containership.
[2] Includes OBO and ore carriers.
[3] Includes tug barges and pipe-laying vessels.
[4] In shipyards having facilities to build vessels 475 by 68 feet.
[5] Million of dollars estimated.
** Cargo break-bulk vessels.

purchases. The recession lasted longer than expected, and little capital investment was made. Because of financial pressures, many governments have intervened in their monetary systems, resulting in a widening shift in the relative values of the world's major currencies.

Each country approaches the over-capacity situation and future building plans somewhat differently, the study points out. The one common characteristic of all shipbuilding countries is that there is increasing government involvement in the industry, ranging from financial incentives, subsidies and loans to outright nationalization.

Japan became the largest and most efficient of all the builders through strong government direction and policy setting. Today it has the capacity to fill all of the world's shipbuilding requirements through 1980, but has ordered cutbacks of 35 per cent throughout its yards. The cutbacks are being achieved through reductions in worker hours, so actual capacity is held intact. Japanese shipyards are part of vertically-integrated industrial conglomerates, giving them financial strengh and the ability to shift resources

The United Kingdom, once the world's largest shipbuilder, was brought under state control in 1976. Examples of some of the world's most efficient and some of the most inefficient shipyards can be found in the United Kingdom. There is reason to believe that nationalization will only delay the necessary elimination of those yards which were marginally productive even in better times.

In France, the government initiated a strong modernization program that might be a model for other countries. Modernization had two main criteria — to reduce the number of yards and to build more sophisticated yards. France achieved both objectives, improved its output and became the leading builder of liquefied natural gas (LNG) carriers.

The West German government has intervened strongly in the country's shipbuilding industry, forcing mergers between shipbuilding companies and with associated industries, such as steel.

In Italy, the shipbuilding industry is entirely state-controlled, and builds only for its own national needs. The government had planned an export program in large oil tankers, but the oil crisis rendered that plan unworkable.

Some of the other OECD countries are shifting their shipbuilding resources to other industries — Norway in particular, despite its long history of strength in shipbuilding.

Among the Comecon countries, the USSR is developing a large fleet of container and roll-on/roll-off ships. Its ability to cut rates below those of the free-world countries makes this large fleet a major threat on some of the established trade routes. Poland has developed a major shipbuilding industry that ranks twelfth in the world in terms of orders outstanding at the end of 1976. The developing countries, Brazil and South Korea in particular, have increased their share of new orders in recent years at the expense of the traditional shipbuilding countries of Europe.

The conclusions reached in the study are that demand for new ships will be minimal, consisting mainly of replacement vessels as the current fleet ages, and that government involvement will continue to grow. Oil prices will remain high, and though there will be a rise in other sources of energy, no substitute source will replace oil. There will be changing oil distribution patterns; the increased use of pipelines and the Suez Canal to transport oil will reduce the demand for ships, as will the shortened haulage routes of Alaskan and North Sea oil to their markets. In dry goods transportation, the trend will continue toward unit load vessels, particularly in the industrialized countries.

There will be a shift of orders for simple bulk vessels to the developing countries, where costs are low, and of the more sophisticated vessels to the traditional shipbuilding countries, which have the necessary technology and skilled labor.

The major labor problem is in productivity and practices. The Japanese became the top builders because they were more efficient than others.

There will not be any major technological advances the study predicts. Increased use of computers for both design, building, and maintenance scheduling will be seen.

Reduced to its simplest terms, the problem of the next ten years is to build demand, the F & S study concludes.

Survey: Exports, Imports and Ports

"Many times we lose a bid to our competition in Europe because the freight from the U.S. is too expensive," wrote one respondent to *Traffic World's* survey of export and import managers. "U.S. carriers have to make a profit, but they shouldn't price themselves out of the market. If we don't get the business, the carrier doesn't get the business. I think the American flag fleet situation is serious. Someone had better do something about that soon."

In an attempt to find out who was getting the business (perhaps in both senses of that phrase) and who was doing something about it, *Traffic World* recently surveyed a random selection of 350 firms with export and import departments, or "titles" in their executive ranks. Ninety-four questionnaires had been returned by cut-off date, a rate of return of 27 per cent.

The nine-question questionnaire covered a variety of topics of particular concern to importers and exporters and concluded with an invitation to comment on any of the issues touched on in the

survey. Respondents were offered annonymity for these comments if they wished—an offer which the majority of them accepted. Not surprisingly, comments from the survey group were devoted exclusively to two questions, Questions 8 and 9. Both of these questions concerned regulatory policy and the federal government's relationship to export/import shipping and usually prompted respondents to summarize their "philosophy" on these topics.

The results of the survey are tabulated on the following pages. The figures shown are actual numbers of replies rather than percentages. With a response group of 94, converting the figures to percentages would show only insignificant, decimal-point differences from the number of responses.

Comment

Question 8. Do you think the "conference" system of setting ocean freight rates benefits or penalizes your company's export/import business?

Steamship conferences are beneficial to carriers and shippers because they maintain stable rates. However, there must be sufficient non-conference service available to insure a competitive rate situation. Steamship companies must be permitted to operate at a reasonable profit and I do not believe a U.S. Shippers' Council or a Cabinet-level Department of International Trade bureaucracy would be able to determine "reasonable" rates any better than individual shippers.

* * *

Something has to be proposed to change the present "conference" system of establishing ocean freight rates behind doors closed to shippers. If industry is prohibited from "fixing prices" on manufactured goods by government regulations, why shouldn't the same rules apply to steamship conferences?

* * *

I would be in favor of setting up any type of forum whereby shippers could more effectively communicate with steamship conferences relative to rate proposals. The present system is very time-consuming, cumbersome and unrewarding.

* * *

A more competitive level, rate-wise, between conference and non-conference lines would be of benefit, as service, for the most part, is consistent regardless of rate.

* * *

The balance of payments is hurt by lower inbound rates. American producers are hurt by low inbound rates which then prejudice outbound movement where higher rates are charged (required). In practice higher outbound levels subsidize inbounds. I favor "cost" related pricing with minimum and maximum rates with FMC jurisdiction (See ICC).

* * *

When conferences monopolize a trade rate, eg. U.S.-West Africa, shippers and trade suffer.

* * *

I view the entire proposal to amend existing practices, i.e. closed conferences; expanded bilateral shipping agreements; shippers' councils and the attack on state-owned carriers as an attempt to reduce competition. I favor the conference system but believe the right of independent action is essential.

* * *

We need a firm belief in and support for the free enterprise system, with the market place controlling price levels. Equitable maritime laws to permit U.S. flag lines to be competitive, and thereby deserving of the support of the American shipping public.

* * *

The U.S. government should demand equal flag treatment on cargo for every country that requires national flag as prerequisite for reduced duties or special privileges. Also, U.S. should give throught to single carrier (air) representation rather than private U.S. firms competing with the national flag of other countries.

* * *

Currently, the conference system, and the FMC are unresponsive to shipper and day to day shipper activities.

* * *

The advantages of conference rate policies are questionable and presently subject to discussion. If "Shippers' Councils" are authorized, the conference system would be a disadvantage. At present you could consider it a necessary evil.

* * *

Major problem is imbalance of export vs. import rates (in favor of other countries). The U.S needs a specific, strong U.S. foreign policy to protect U.S. carriers and shippers. For too many years, the U.S. State Department has made sacrifices in this area to make gains in others. The position of the Justice Department in international affairs is naive and impractical.

* * *

The conference system is the best known system at the present time but there is no doubt it does have some deficiencies, however. It is like democracy, we do not know a better way of doing it right now.

* * *

Even though we normally do not pay the freight, the freight can be a determining factor as to whether or not we will obtain an order. Two years ago 28 percent of our business was export, last year it was 13 percent.

QUESTIONNAIRE

1. In 1977, approximately what was the dollar amount of your company's freight transportation bill for exports/imports?

1,000 to $100,000	$101,200 to $500,000	$550,000 to $1,000,000	$1,100,000 to $10,000,000	More Than $10,000,000	No Response
6	9	8	45	14	12

2. How did that bill break down by carriers?

	None	1-25%	26-50%	51-75%	76-100%	No Response
Rail (Canada/Mexico)	56	33	2	1	1	1
Truck (Canada/Mexico)	39	46	4	1	3	
Ship	7	13	12	16	45	
Air	20	55	9	5	5	
Forwarders/Agents	52	30	None	3	8	

* 3. How is your company's export/import shipping handled? What is the title of the person responsible?

Through International Division or Subsidiary	Through General Traffic Department	Others	No Response
39	45	12	5

4. Approximately what percentage of your waterborne export/import freight moved by foreign-flag operators. By U.S.-flag operators?

	None	1-25%	26-50%	56-75%	76-100%	No Response
Foreign-flag		11	20	29	27	7
U.S.-Flag		33	27	19	8	7

* Question #3 — Titles of individuals in charge (general traffic department):

Assistant Traffic Manager (2); Corporate Transportation Manager; Director of Overseas Traffic; Director of Transportation; Distribution Supervisor; Export Coordinator (2); Export/Import Manager; Export/Import Traffic Manager (4); Export Operations Manager; Export Traffic Manager (3); General District Manager & District Service Manager; General Traffic Manager; International Traffic Supervisor; International Transportation Manager (3); Manager (2); Manager—Corporate Transportation; Manager—International Traffic (2); Manager—Marine Systems; Manager—Marine Transportation; Manager—Overseas Transportation; Manager—Transportation (2); Physical Distribution & Transportation—International Traffic Dept.; Supervisor Expediting & Traffic; Traffic Manager—Marine; Traffic Manager (8); Traffic Supervisor.

Titles of individuals in charge (international division or subsidiary):

Administration International Dept.; Director of Export; Director International Distribution; Distribution Manager; Distribution Traffic Manager; Export Distribution Supervisor; Export Manager (7); Export Traffic Manager (4); International Traffic Coordinator; International Traffic Manager (7); International Traffic Supervisor; International Sales Coordinator (2); Manager—Export Traffic; Manager Export/Import Traffic; Manager International Customer Services; Manager International Distribution; Order Services Manager—International President—Manager Supervisor; Supervisor Export Administration; Traffic Manager (3).

Other-Titles: Separate International Divisions by Product, Manager Export/Export Traffic Corp.; Individual Divisional Export Departments; Ocean Freight Dept., Ocean Freight Manager; Imports

More Often by Supplier/Vendor; Freight Forwarder; Export Services Group Under Marketing, Regional Director; Through Traffic Department, Traffic Manager; International Transportation, Manager; Export Manager; Traffic Department Export, Export Transportation Manager; Branch Traffic Department, Traffic Manager; Engineering and Services, Purchasing Division, International Dry Cargo Transportation; Section, Supervisor-IDCT.

5. Approximately what percentage of your import/export freight is containerized?

	None	1-25%	26-50%	56-75%	76-100%	No Response
Import	22	14	7	5	35	11
Export	5	14	21	20	27	7

6. To and from what parts of the world do your air and waterborne export and import shipments move?

	Export to—by			Import from—by			No Response
	Air	Water	Rail	Air	Water	Rail	
Western Europe	61	73		43	54		5
Canada	34	11	41	20	9	22	
Central America	46	64	5	11	12	3	
South America	51	71		22	23		
Japan	53	67		24	35		
Other Asiatic Countries	34	57		11	15		
Middle East	34	59		8	7		
Australia-New Zealand	43	70		13	14		
Africa	35	57		8	8		
Soviet-Bloc Countries	8	21		2	3		

7. Which U.S. ports do you use most frequently?

Baltimore 46	Houston 36	New Orleans 40	Savannah........22
Boston 5	Long Beach 21	Norfolk 31	Seattle 10
Charleston, S.C...28	Los Angeles 29	Oakland 27	Stockton 1
Chicago 13	Miami 33	Philadelphia 19	Tampa 3
Detroit 7	Milwaukee 2	Portland, Ore.....7	Wilmington, N.C..6
Galveston........3	Mobile 10	San Francisco 26	Others...........11

Others:

Baton Rouge, LA	Coos Bay, OR	Laredo, TX	Portsmouth, NH
Beaumont, TX	Eureka, CA	Oswego, NY	Richmond, VA
Brunswick, GA	Jacksonville, FL	Panama City, FL	Searsport, ME
Buffalo, NY	Harvey, LA	Pascagoula, MS	Texas City, TX
Cleveland, OH	Lake Charles, LA	Pensacola, FL	West Palm Beach, FL

8. Do you think the "conference" system of setting ocean freight rates benefits or penalize your company's export/import business?

Benefits	Penalizes	Both	No Response
32	42	6	14

9. Are you in favor of setting up (a) A U.S. "Shippers' Council" to deal with steamship conferences on behalf of importers and exporters? (b) A Cabinet-level Department of International Trade?

	Favor		Oppose	No Response
Shippers Council	Cabinet Level	Shippers Council	Cabinet Level	
63	39	17	28	11

Question 9. Are you in favor of setting up (a) A U.S. "Shippers Council" to deal with steamship conferences on behalf of importers and exporters? (b) A Cabinet-level Department of International Trade.?

It is discouraging to our company to watch the behavior of carriers serving certain trade markets. For example, the Pacific-Australasian route. Something along the lines of Question Nine must be done. *Keith Clark, General Traffic Manager, The Toro Co., Minneapolis.*

* * *

We believe both proposals would be very beneficial to our export operation. Almost all of our exports are on a job-to-job basis. Therefore we have very little need for conference shipping. We are more concerned with expeditious shipping than with reduced rates for using same conference time and time again. *Dennis A. Velie, J. B. Webb International Co.*

* * *

While the vast majority of our international trade involves importing crude gypsum rock from Canada and Mexico, our other international markets (of finished goods for the most part) would benefit greatly from shippers' councils. We have long advocated a system where shippers have some say in rate structuring and price increases which in the recent past have masqueraded as fuel surcharges, port surcharges, strike surcharges, and currency adjustments. *Richard B. Mooshie, District Service Manager—Eastern Region, Gold Bond Building Products, Buffalo, NY*

* * *

We are favorable to a "Shippers' Council" as long as its influence is not mainly in behalf of the larger importers and exporters. As there are presently at least five federal agencies involved with international trade, we do not need another bumbling group in Washington wasting tax payers' money. A forceful attempt should be made to get the FMC functioning properly. *L. Pauksta, Traffic Manager Export/Import, Nichimen Company, Inc., Chicago, IL*

* * *

We are strongly in favor of (a) and (b) provided they are structured to be truly effective in their respective functions. We favor only "limited" Shippers' Councils. By limited, we mean rate activities limited to only general rate increases. I will negotiate my own individual commodity rates. Such Councils *must* be regional or by conference to avoid domination by the "biggies" and to assure that the council understands the unique problems of a port, region or a trade route. If not limited or regional—it's "no go."

I think industry should serve as its own organizer-administrator-spokesman in international trade. With a Cabinet-level Department exercising influence, too many policies would be based on political rather than economic or industrially-wise considerations.

* * *

The proposed Shippers' Council will not negotiate rates on specific commodities. It will discuss surcharges etc.

* * *

Instead of establishing still more organizations, we need to make the current ones work—conferences, FMC, etc. Shippers must awake to the need to demand of the FMC action when conferences decline a shippers request that is paramount to securing foreign business. Conferences, are unresponsive they must become responsive. Shippers have not used the FMC—they must.

* * *

I'm not holding my breath in anticipation of getting much help for our exports via a Shippers' Council, but *anything* that's designed to support shipper interests is welcome. We must keep alive the admittedly-feeble stirrings of competitive activity in the ocean trades (general cargo, of course). We don't need closed conferences, pools or any other devices which tend to smother competition.

* * *

We do not feel that either proposal in its present form will represent or be indicative of, benefit to American shippers' interests. What is needed is more joint jurisdictional authority areas for the ICC and FMC and for the FMC to havd definite enforcement authority so it can enforce and make decisions effective.

* * *

We favor "A Cabinet-level Department of International Trade" only if there is a mandate for department to find ways of making it more economically advantageous to export.

* * *

Would prefer to see less government regulation.

* * *

Would favor a "Cabinet-level Department of International Trade" if it did not increase the Federal bureaucratic population and in fact consolidated international trade functions now performed by others.

* * *

Neither. I believe if conferences were more responsive to shippers' needs, there would be no need for a U.S. "Shippers' Council" to deal with steamship conferences on behalf of importers and exporters or a "Cabinet-level Department of International Trade."

One Company's Views on HR 11422

We appreciate the opportunity to give our views on HR 11422, which we consider to be of the utmost significance to the promotion of American export trade.

Closed Conferences: The bill could permit carriers presently plying a particular trade route to form a closed conference, if they so desired. Once a closed conference is formed, any carrier desiring membership would have to apply, fulfill the membership requirements and be subject to vote among the member carriers on admittance. Any carrier who does not desire to join a conference would be free to ply the trade route as an independent. Any American flag carrier who desires to join a closed conference would be automatically a member of that conference, not subject to an admittance vote.

Closed conferences with strong shipper tying agreements would be a powerful force in controlling American exports. Pfizer's experience around the world with closed conferences is that we almost always sign shippers' agreements with the conferences because we find it impractical to stay out and use independents. We have also found that where there is no counterbalancing force to the conference, the carriers are not responsive to shippers' needs. We believe that if Congress authorizes the establishment of closed conferences without authorizing the establishment of a U.S. Shipper's Council, as proposed in HR 11422, our ability to export goods promptly and at reasonable cost will be frustrated because we do not have, as an individual company, sufficient tonnage to influence a strong conference.

We believe that the present conference system in the U.S. trades does not work. Too often we find that carriers, in their desire to attract cargo, waste money on duplicate services for which we as shippers must pay in the form of higher rates. We also believe that permitting anyone to dump vessels into a trade to pick up U.S. dollars by "skimming" high revenue cargoes is detrimental to the shippers' long term needs for a shipping service that will be available at reasonable rates.

Rationalization: Because of the nature of our business, we need a reliable service that has sailings at regular intervals. We find that in many trades, the lines for competitive reasons sail against each other, and cargo must be delayed until a vessel sails. If the members of the conference were allowed to rationalize their sailings without losing their individual share of the market, the shippers would get more frequent and total service. This would, of course, require a revenue pooling agreement among the member lines based either on total lift or traditional market share. The only stipulation the Federal Maritime Commission should require to allow rationalization would be that the carriers must provide enough "lift" to carry all the cargo offered plus say 15 per cent to allow for immediate expansion, and must sail as scheduled unless utilization per sailing drops below, say, 60 per cent for over a stipulated period.

Intermodalism: We believe conferences should be allowed to offer intermodal services to shippers and to set "through" rates in conjunction with overland carriers. The shipper, however, should be allowed to choose freely whether or not he wishes to use this service without losing his rebate privileges. For example, a shipper in East St. Louis, Ill. shipping to Japan would have his choice between Far East Conference port-to-port service, Far East Conference intermodal service, Pacific Westbound Conference port-to-port service or Pacific Westbound Intermodal service. He would not lose his FEC rebate just because he shipped on PWC or vice versa. Even if he only had a contract with one conference, it would still not jeopardize his position. He would, however, lose his rebate privileges if he shipped on an independent from an East Coast port or that independent's intermodal service if he had a contract with the Far East Conference.

Shippers' Council: It is imperative that the shippers have a strong voice in determining the availability of services and general level of rates to be charged by the carriers. We strongly endorse the organization of a U.S. Shippers' Council along the lines proposed by the New York Chamber of Commerce and Industry's International Traffic Committee. We request that the shippers be allowed to organize with full anti-trust immunity on an equal basis with the carriers. The proposed organization would give full protection to individual shippers without discrimination and still allow a sound council enough power to deal with conferences on an equal basis. Any disputes arising between the council and the conferences which become stalemated can be resolved by the Federal Maritime Commission.

Chapter 7
Physical Distribution and Logistics

MANAGEMENT

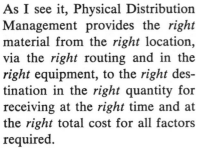

Defining distribution

By DR. E. GROSVENOR PLOWMAN

As I see it, Physical Distribution Management provides the *right* material from the *right* location, via the *right* routing and in the *right* equipment, to the *right* destination in the *right* quantity for receiving at the *right* time and at the *right* total cost for all factors required.

In effect, Physical Distribution Management manages the logistical activities within a gap area between the production and the consumption or end use of a company's products. The gap area may be large or small in geographic extent. It could range, geographically, from an intercontinental to an intracity gap area depending upon a company's bid to do business. The gap area may have few or many decision/action management variables. The tasks of managing in a gap area involve three elements:

● Receiving, recording, and storing. Included in this element are management functions that involve inbound transportation from outside sources (vendors/ suppliers) as well as from intracompany production locations; inventory paperwork which now is being performed, increasingly, by computer; maintaining raw material quality during storage for production; internal movement and placement of material at proper locations to assemble or create the products; successfully handling hazardous ma-

terial where applicable; adequate security measures for material and proper safety measures for personnel; and, risk management paperwork.

● Customerization. This element begins at a convenient location where company products (finished goods) or goods-in-process are assembled for outer protective packaging in order to move as a shipment within the gap area. For example, shipping to a private or a public warehouse or distribution center. It ends with an accurate and efficient meeting of customer needs as stated in specifications that are written, oral, or otherwise decided by policy.

● Customer service. This element is primarily one involving time and place factors management. The final functions within this element include transporting company product and material from the initial gap area locations; re-assembly in the field— at a warehouse or distribution center—to meet customer specifications; transit routing and costing; quality control measures to avoid or minimize obvious and concealed damage to the product; order acceptance and assembly governed by a company's inventory policies; and, customer delivery paperwork.

(Next month, the segment concept of Physical Distribution Management inter-relationships.)

We're pleased to announce that Dr. E. Grosvenor Plowman will preside over this new monthly column. In his first of the series, he suggests a right definition, and a meaningful purpose and place, for Physical Distribution Management. Welcome, please, Dr. Plowman.

FEBRUARY 1978

DISTRIBUTION WORLDWIDE
FOR TRAFFIC AND PHYSICAL DISTRIBUTION MANAGEMENT

INBOUND MATERIALS MANAGEMENT

A recent seminar of experienced distribution managers clearly
indicates that the function of moving raw materials and components into
the plant must be more closely aligned with the logistics umbrella

By JIM DIXON, Managing Editor

"Too many traffic managers," said A. H. Odeven, Western Electric manager, transportation east & administration, "fail to understand that purchasing people can't enlist the help of knowledgeable transportation people if they don't understand the transportation function itself.

"The lack of understanding of each other's functions in some companies is absolutely appalling," continued Odeven, speaking at a recent seminar of the New York Chamber of Commerce and Industry. "This is especially so if you consider that the long-range goal of both traffic and purchasing is to obtain material when required, and deliver it at the point needed at a particular time in good condition at the lowest cost."

The seminar was staged at an appropriate time, as physical distribution managers throughout industry are becoming more and more convinced that the management of inbound materials—the area of materials management—must be more closely allied with, if not actually placed under, the logistics umbrella.

Over a year ago, Don Bowersox, professor of marketing and transportation at Michigan State University, delivered a keynote speech *(see "The Need for Innovative Distribution Management," DW, December 1977)* before the National Council of Physical Distribution Management, calling for the Council to be a leader in placing greater emphasis on inbound materials management as part of the functional responsibility of forward-looking distribution management.

The Commerce & Industry seminar brought some 65 of these "forward-looking" distribution managers together to provide some strong support for this view along with examples of just how the functions can work together.

"To paraphrase Peter Drucker," said PPG' Industries' Leonard C. Heisey, manager, distribution-development supply, "controlling the inbound materials flow is really the 'last frontier.' There are great opportunities for saving money. But few of us know enough about it."

Western Electric's Odeven went on to say that some sort of transportation education program for purchasing people is absolutely essential, if optimum results are to be obtained. Such a program should teach the gamut of transportation services. There has to be a new understanding of such essentials as expediting, tracing, routing, claims, rate adjustments, and the like.

Ed McGrath, of Johnson & Johnson, told the group that his company, long one of the leaders in forward-looking distribution management, has gone a step further. Johnson & Johnson has established a formal Purchasing Traffic Department, which he heads up.

McGrath's department selects and controls carriers moving raw material to his three manufacturing sites (New Jersey, Illinois, Texas) and various subcontractors in the U.S., Canada, Mexico and Puerto Rico. Purchasing Traffic also moves finished-goods' production from subcontractors back to distribution centers. Thus, McGrath budgets freight expense for all inbound raw material *plus* the aforementioned finished-product shipments.

His department reports to General Traffic, which is a function of Johnson & Johnson's Sales & Distribution Services organization. (There is no *corporate* traffic or purchasing department, *per se.*) But Purchasing Traffic is physically located in the Purchasing Division; it functions as an oper-

Continued

INBOUND CONTINUED

ating department guiding the outlays of Purchasing freight dollars. (All carrier tariff work and freight payments are located elsewhere.) McGrath outlined the advantages of being located with Purchasing as:

"1. We have direct access to Purchasing buyer's planners and accountants, and they to us—the lines of communication are very open.

"2. Our carrier-routing selections follows those being used in our branch and customer-shipping operations. Benefits accrue to our carriers and all of our own operating departments.

"3 . . . As our Vice President of Purchasing reminds us, we are with the Purchasing Division to challenge their transportation decisions by furnishing carrier costs and service information on a timely basis."

John Barry, manager, Physical Distribution Coordination, GTE Products Company put it this way: "We are becoming increasingly materials' sensitive. Material—the purchasing, transportation, inventory control and the like at this time takes in excess of 50% of the sales' dollar. We've seen our costs in the last couple of years constantly multiply; a 121% increase in class rates (rail) between 1966 and 1976, for one example." He noted that rate increases do not guarantee higher service levels.

Barry went on to say that, as a result of several GTE studies, he feels "private carriage has to be the best friend purchasing ever had. It provides an unusual opportunity—not only to reduce costs, but to increase your service levels to the point that you become very dependent on it.

"The way you coordinate purchasing and physical distribution is to look at the total cost; its coordination. How do we impact on that total cost? It's pretty darn ridiculous to go to a new vendor and get a reduction in price, then end up paying more for the product because of transportation," Barry continued.

"All too frequently in the past, we at GTE have looked at the functions of purchasing, physical distribution—transportation and inventory control as three separate and distinct functions. And they are *not*. They are part of the total flow of material—from the time a decision is made to purchase material to the time that material is delivered to the ultimate customer.

"We've got to control the whole ball of wax.

"Reporting to our materials manager is the manager of purchasing, the manager of production—inventory control and the manager of physical distribution. He has the responsibility of making those hard economic decisions concerning the *total flow* of materials; what's the best thing to do," Barry added.

A lot of sites

This management arrangement applies to all GTE divisions—from a $25 million unit to a $250-million-a-year unit, a total of 138 manufacturing sites.

What is the basic role played by this person in charge of inbound materials management? Ed McGrath's description of "functional responsibilities" in Purchasing Traffic at Johnson & Johnson is an excellent guide:

"We have given emphasis to two considerations, carrier cost and carrier service. The Purchasing Traffic Expeditor handles the bulk of service activities. His duties include the handling of all tracing-expediting, coordinating the movement of leased hopper cars, investigating and handling carrier claims and coordinating sales-promotion shipments.

"The tracing-expediting requests," McGrath continued, "represent an excellent opportunity to challenge the intended use of excess-cost routings. Oftentimes, we can produce desired service results at regular freight expense; at other times, excess cost routings are used but we can question who should absorb the added charges—ourselves or the supplier?

"All inbound freight budgets, cost studies and cost-improvement projects are performed by the manager," McGrath added.

An ideal purchasing-traffic liaison for inbound materials management would produce forecasts for all future freight charges—both for raw materials and subcontractors' finished goods' movements. Such budgeting is the linchpin for practical future-cost improvement and freight cost-control efforts.

That's the Johnson & Johnson method. Each raw material is coded with a budgeted freight rate. But a computerized worksheet first goes to each buyer, so

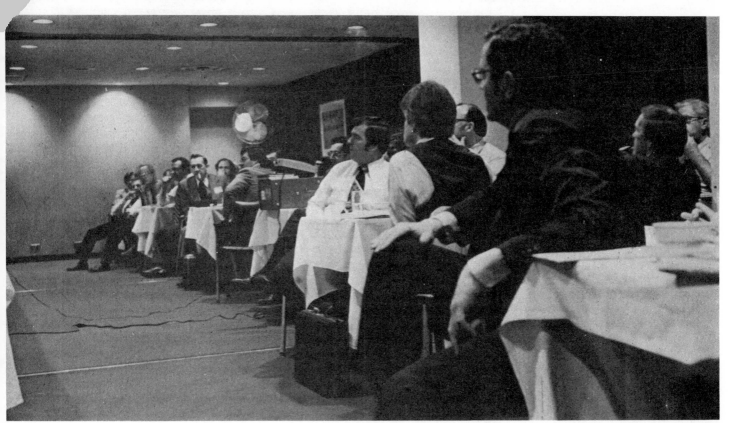

Western Electric's A. H. Odeven probed the problems and opportunities of inbound-materials' management before more than 60 "Fortune 200" distribution executives at New York Commerce & Industry Association seminar recently.

that he may verify the following data on a code-by-code basis:
—Vendor shipping point.
—Freight terms.
—Pounds/M purchase units.
—Estimated shipping weights.
—Estimated shipping frequencies.

Each finished goods' buyer reviews future-year shipping expectations on a subcontractor-by-subcontractor basis. Then data furnished by purchasing is compared against year-to-date freight payment records on a supplier-by-supplier basis. From this review, a base rate for each supplier—which is then increased by anticipated freight rate changes—is budgeted as the next year's figure.

This budgeted data—shipping point, freight terms and the like—is used to challenge the authenticity of future freight payments.

Another key factor in inbound management is the freight payment control system. And an important consideration here is the liability control report. At Johnson & Johnson, this report is used to identify what inbound freight bills are Purchasing Traffic's responsibility. Each shipment at the company's own or subcontractors' docks has its own receiving information recorded on the "receipt" side of the computer report.

Then, on receipt of a carrier freight bill, this report is used to verify payment responsibility, and freight bills are paid or returned.

Monthly summary reports allow accounting to (1) allocate freight expense by raw material or finished-goods' codes, (2) accrue freight expense against "receivals" still not paid, (3) explain freight variance reports with the help of the next report and (4) question non-receipt of carrier billings.

A lot of goals

Ed McGrath's system also generates reports covering: Inbound purchased finished-goods shipments, non-standard raw materials' shipments, high-volume material codes' expenses and carrier revenue.

In sum, such an inbound reporting system has four goals: Furnish historical data for future budgets, identify causes of freight variances, highlight freight cost-improvement opportunities and furnish a data base for all transportation development studies.

Western Electric's Odeven and GTE's Barry spiced their conversation on inbound with practical examples based on their own recent experience. "The significant factor," said Barry, "is the increased cost of transportation; our costs are over double what they were four or five years ago."

He's found the biggest impact for GTE's Sylvania Division "is the common-carrier truck. In establishing our own private carriage operation, we'll trim millions of dollars in costs. Also we're coming up with a method to use the advantages of our collective size to impact on the vendor community and the transportation community to get a reduction in costs."

Odeven observed: "The purchasing organization should adopt a policy of purchasing FOB origin, unless it's more advantageous to do otherwise. At the least, this policy will separate the cost of the product and the cost of transportation. It is surprising how many
Continued

181

RIGHT: Flowchart shows manufacturing-inbound interface.

FAR RIGHT: Example of inbound cost study at Western Electric.

INBOUND
CONTINUED

people think that material purchased FOB 'destination' is delivered free. They should know that there is no such thing as a free lunch.

"For example, we have a supplier in Albany, N.Y. who must ship to our locations in New York City, Indianapolis, Chicago, Denver and San Francisco. If we want to purchase FOB destination, the supplier must build in a factor to recover his transportation costs. In real life, he certainly isn't going to build in the cost to New York City. More likely, he will build in the cost to Denver, to play it safe.

A lot of waste

"An analysis of this problem," Odeven continued, "shows that 50% of the shipments will be for New York, 20% for Indianapolis and 15% for Chicago. Therefore, on 85% of the shipments, too much transportation cost is built into the selling price." *(See Chart.)*

What about the interface with buyers (purchasing)?

"In order to evaluate laid-down costs when considering quotes of several suppliers," Odeven said, "the buyer will have to come to transportation for rate quotations. But, your people should not merely quote the freight rates requested. They should discuss the problem the buyers are working on with him and request their input.

"Obviously, they will want to know the weight and frequency of the shipments. However, they may be able to ship from a particular supplier via an established consolidation, which would drastically reduce the cost, making that supplier more competitive, even though he is farthest from the destination. Another valuable input could be the present freight rates, plus an estimate of the lev-

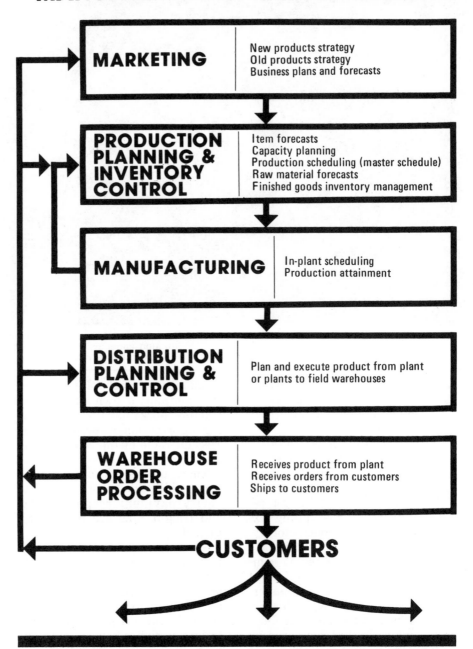

FLOW OF EVENTS
MANUFACTURING ORGANIZATION

MARKETING
- New products strategy
- Old products strategy
- Business plans and forecasts

PRODUCTION PLANNING & INVENTORY CONTROL
- Item forecasts
- Capacity planning
- Production scheduling (master schedule)
- Raw material forecasts
- Finished goods inventory management

MANUFACTURING
- In-plant scheduling
- Production attainment

DISTRIBUTION PLANNING & CONTROL
- Plan and execute product from plant or plants to field warehouses

WAREHOUSE ORDER PROCESSING
- Receives product from plant
- Receives orders from customers
- Ships to customers

CUSTOMERS

el of rates that might be negotiated with a carrier."

Odeven continued: "At this stage of negotiations, the transportation man should discuss not only the freight rate, but various routing options, service requirements and packing, if appropriate. He should also furnish a firm bill-of lading description, which should be included in the contract for use by the vendor to insure proper transportation costs.

"If hazardous materials (as de-

fined in Title 49) are involved, a great deal more education is required for the buyer, as well as instructions to the supplier. Other items that should be discussed pertain to the classification of certain chemicals—such as carbon tetrachloride, which is rated class 100 in carboys, as opposed to class 55 in steel drums.

"Once the quotations have been analyzed on a laid-down basis, the approval of the award should be thoroughly documented," Odeven said. He adds that once a contract

RESULTS OF DENVER TRANSPORTATION FACTOR BURIED IN PRICE

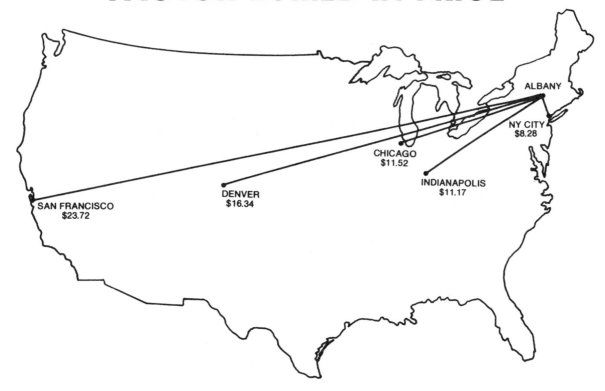

DENVER FACTOR—F.O.B. DELIVERED

Total of 100 shipments @ $16.34 each $1,634.00

F.O.B. ORIGIN

City	No. of Shipments	Chg. per Shipment	Total Charges
NEW YORK CITY	50	$ 8.28	$ 414.00
INDIANAPOLIS	20	11.17	223.40
CHICAGO	15	11.52	172.80
DENVER	10	16.34	163.40
SAN FRANCISCO	5	23.72	118.60
TOTAL	100		$1,092.20
		LOSS	$ 541.80

has been decided, all individuals and departments involved should sign the award.

"The transportation organization should become deeply involved in fitting the purchased goods into the transportation pipeline. This means that specific routing should be applied to the purchase order, either manually or on a computerized basis. The following should also be considered:

—"Where an item is dual-sourced, transportation should be consulted to determine which source will produce the lowest laid-down cost before the purchase order is placed.

—"In routing the purchase order, full advantage should be taken of any established consolidation and distribution programs, as well as any private carriage operations.

—"The expediting function should be coordinated."

Odeven's conclusion: "The transportation department and the purchasing department *can* work together to accomplish your company's goals."

PPG's Len Heisey had his own conclusion: "I think that distribution personnel that have outbound responsibilities have, to some extent, overlooked the opportunities of inbound. These opportunities include both improved costs and service. In sum, it's all really a matter of dollars *or* cents."

The 'last frontier'? It is, as Heisey says, "a matter of dollars or cents." ∎

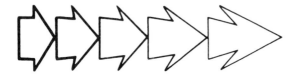

A way to move
physical distribution
ahead faster

By JOHN F. SPENCER, *editor emeritus*

A little analysis of influences which account for present success suggests ways to speed up progress

When P.T. Barnum retired, at the age of 44, he was famous, wealthy, and dwelt in the house of his dreams. He had built the house as an almost exact copy of George IV's famous Pavilion at Brighton, which still wows the tourists. Barnum had not only become famous as a showman and impressario, but had headed banks, manufacturing companies, civic organizations, and he was known as a patron of the arts.

Barnum summed up the talents which won this success in a few simple words. He wrote,". . . I have *managed,* while my vocation has been that of *manager."*

If we accept Barnum's assessment, it was his ability to manage that made his varied, sometimes bizarre, enterprises profitable. We do accept that, and also a corollary—that *good management is the most valuable asset that any business organization can have.* Think of that the next time you hear petulant carping at the "enormous" salaries paid to some managers.

Barnum was not, however, in any way a modern manager. The last of his ten rules for success was "Do not depend on others." He could believe this rule because his era ended just at the beginning of the upsurge of the modern business corporation.

The corporation, one of the most important economic developments of all time, soon produced business organizations of a size rarely seen in the proprietorships, partnerships, and stock companies of earlier days.

As the information in the box on page 56 suggests, the upsurge came because the corporate form could attract capital in quantities previously unavailable. With increased size came new demands upon management, and one of these was certainly the need of all managers, from top to bottom, to depend heavily on both their subordinates and their superiors. It is possible to look at the history of management, over the last century, as a record of progress along a road toward greater economic efficiency. The milestones on this road are the successive improvements which allowed managers to look upon this dependence with greater confidence.

The first answers to size were answers to the raw problems of control. To assure control, corporations borrowed from another ancient institution, the military. Two devices were copied. One was the idea of dividing the organization into "staff" and "line" activities. The staff was an extension of the chief officer's planning, memory, and supervisory abilities; the line carried out operations. Another borrowing was the differentiation and departmentalization of line activities—in the military the separation

About business corporations . . .

The concept of the corporation is neither new nor complex. It was a device which the ancient Romans used, and the legal foundation of modern corporations comes from Roman law. The corporation is an association of natural persons, and most of the legal rights, and restrictions, of a person; it can continue to exist, however, as long as it has any person as a member. This deathlessness is one important attribute. Another is the business corporation's ability to possess property, incur debts, and conduct business like a person. Equally important is the fact that while the corporation may owe debts, liability for such debts does not extend to the members. For many hundreds of years most corporations were guilds, municipalities, and associations of religious persons, whose members had no direct claim to the property owned by the corporations. From the time of the renaissance to the end of the eighteenth century, commercial ventures were mostly proprietorships or "stock companies." The stock companies were, legally, partnerships, and each stock owner was liable for the debts to the extent of his entire fortune, just as sole proprietors and partners are liable. Moreover, withdrawal or death of a stock holder could terminate a stock company legally, just as it does any other partnership. These disadvantages—limited life of the organization and unlimited liabilty—hampered the development of companies until the stock company form of ownership was combined with the principles of the corporation—continuing existence, and no extension of liability to stock owners. Because the stockholder in a commercial corporation has at risk only the amount of money he paid for his shares, and since the incorporated business offers superior stability in time, this economic invention proved highly popular. It attracted the capital which made industry on a modern scale possible. Legally the limited liability was at first regarded as a great hazard to the creditors and customers of a business corporation, and it is for that reason that English law required the word "limited" or "ltd." to appear on all legal documents and invoices, bill heads, letterheads, and other communications, after the name of the corporation.

not only of combat units from supply and service, but separation of combat types—infantry, artillery, cavalry, and so on. In business organization this functional departmentalization went even farther, so we have finance, accounting, procurement, sales, production etc., and then in production the foundry, the machine shop, the assembly line, packaging, etc. In a large corporation the departments could number in hundreds.

This pigeonholing helped top managers discern what they had to control, and how the parts could fit together. It worked, and with the advent of "scientific management" at the turn of the century, worked pretty well. But—

There were weaknesses. Those familiar with the physical distribution management concept are well aware of the shortcomings of the traditional organization pattern for business. In part these are the result of faulty communication. More serious, however, is the risk that under traditional methods the interests of subordinate managers can become contrary to the interests of the organization as a whole, and that the manager can further his own interest at the expense of the whole organization without being detected—sometimes even the offender himself is not fully aware of the undesirable nature of his activities.

The usual pattern is activity by the subordinate manager which decreases unit costs in his operations, but increases unit costs disporportionately in areas beyond his jurisdiction. That is, on the surface we have Mr. Doe who is seen to be a "good manager" because he cut costs, and came up with a splendid record for his "profit center." Never mind that Doe caused poor performance in other profit centers, and ultimately cost the company more than he saved it.

Sometimes there is no "Doe" at all, but simply a company practice which seems to minimize a cost, when actually hiding that cost. You still hear people from smaller companies say "We have no transportation costs; we buy everything on a delivered basis, so our suppliers pay the freight, and we sell everything F.O.B. our dock, and let our customers pay their freight."

Physical distribution management arose when some thinking managers perceived and began trying to find ways of overcoming these problems. They arrived at a concept of total physical distribution management. It sought to find and understand such conflicts of interest, and to produce balanced solutions to them, so that the whole system would always gain, never lose, from resolution of the conflicts; in physical distribution terms, this is the process of making acceptable trade-offs.

Sometimes this aim is expressed incorrectly, as in the statement, "we try to maximize customer service and minimize inventory costs." Mathematically it is not possible (except by accident) to maximize or minimize two related variable elements of an equation simultaneously. Therefore the statement should emphasize *system* and should run something like this: "the purpose is to maximize a desired product of the system, through proper balance of elements and functions in the system." Usually the end product which managers desire to maximize is profit, but even in this there is a pitfall; profit has to be defined with reference to a duration of time, else an unscrupulous manager may show high profits for a limited period, by neglecting maintenance and replacement.

These considerations were clear to those who

which would benefit demonstrably from the change. The success of the first change could then be a springboard for launching into the next improvement, and by a succession of such advances the gradual spread of the principle would ultimately produce the full benefits desired.

A new aspect. All this is history, widely known and not news. There are aspects of it, however, which have never been sufficiently emphasized. The ideas which Fredericks advocated did not come from any classroom, or laboratory, or scholar's study. They came from the field. Indeed, going back to the origins of the physical distribution concept, the discipline seems to have grown from practical experiences rather than from the pale cast of thought. The doctrines of the business schools were antici-

---

Physical distribution management arose in the corporation when some thinking managers . . . sought ways to find and develop acceptable trade-offs in customer service and inventory costs.

---

first began to apply the ideas of physical distribution management, almost forty years ago. The concept really took hold in the late 1950s, and in the 1960s an increasing number of companies began to apply the concept to their management methods. By this time the theory was spelled out plainly, there being textbooks like that of Smykay and Bowersox. Enthusiasts sought to apply the theory as a whole, and to whole company managements. On paper this looked fine. In practice it failed more often than it succeeded. The physical distribution management concept was essentially a reform, and as a reform it implied a management revolution. The reformers were few, and those to be reformed were many. In consequence the world did not turn topsy turvy at once, but great confusion arose. Some of the theorists were even ready to abandon the whole concept, as impossible to apply.

The correct answer did come, however, from some managers who remained convinced of the soundness of the concept in spite of great difficulty in putting the ideas into practice. Critiquing their own experiences, they came to a conclusion which really saved the day. The best analysis of this new thinking was offered in an article by Ward Fredericks, who advocated gradualism in application of the ideas.

In essence Fredericks said that the reform had to start with one small part of the company's activities, a part in which the need was fairly obvious, and

pated in the field, in the minds of managers actually working to control inventory, to reduce storage costs, to improve the financial performance of distribution activities. It was in a food company that the computer was first devoted, on a large scale, to physical distribution activities.

This orientation of the conceptual development to actual practice can be observed also in the organization of the physical distribution people. When it was founded, the National Council of Physical Distribution Management was heavily influenced by the fine leadership of several scholars in the field. This scholarly influence is still undoubtedly of importance, but in proportionate numbers, and in leadership, the academic side has never kept pace with the participation of those active in the field. At the most recent annual meeting of the NCPDM, more than 80 percent of those who were speakers or discussion leaders were individuals employed in the field, in profit-making companies, in physical distribution functions. Only about ten percent of the speakers and discussion leaders came from college or business school faculties.

From these observations a number of truths seem to emerge. One is that actual experience—success or failure of projects in progress—produced the physical distribution concept and contributed to many of its steps of development. This process of learning from experience, and developing precepts and principles on the basis of what is learned in practice, continues to be vitally important in physical distribution. It appears that the practitioners are fitted, by their experience and education and by facilities at their command, to do adequately for themselves what might in another discipline be left largely to research specialists and theorists.

If these observations are true, then it seems desirable to add to the extent of the process which takes place. The national NCPDM meeting takes place only once a year, and the local or regional NCPDM Roundtables give limited exposure to ideas and information. Up to this date the publications devoted to physical distribution have offered some supplement, but one which must be difficult for the manager who seeks an audience. Not many could describe, for example, the process by which Ward Fredericks found a place to publish his important article. Any examination of the contents pages of

A number of problems cry for discussion through physical distribution management dialog.

the appropriate periodicals reveals that such articles have not hitherto been sought and published on a planned, scheduled, regular basis. The record shows that, as a forum for the exchange of physical distribution management ideas, the publications might be very effective in one issue, and a blank tablet in the next.

Is there really a need? A question might be raised as to whether there is really a need for a year round, national platform continuity for discussion of the management of physical distribution. Perhaps it is better to allow discussion to peak once a year, at the annual NCPDM meeting, and then supplement only sporadically in print.

When we look at the number of problems which cry for discussion, and measure their importance, it seems better to improve the in-print dialog, in order to focus the issues for face-to-face discussion at the national NCPDM meeting and elsewhere. To cite a few of the topics—

The problem of accounting practice. Accounting continues to be dollar-oriented, to be historical, and to be a record of assets, liabilities, expenditures and receipts, which have very limited utility for many management needs. A simple example is the matter of inventory reporting. Reports in dollar figures can conceal significant facts. In one industry it was discovered that though both inventories and sales rose in terms of dollar amounts,

in the same period the quantities in terms of number of cases of the product on hand and sold was dropping sharply. At one time it was probably too much of a burden on accounting people to ask for more than dollar figure reports.

In our day, with the computer, it should be possible to obtain, at little increase in cost, many additional statistics, in greater detail, than ever before. Such an advance could advance by a quantum leap those data underlying decisions relating the balancing, or "trade-offs," which make the total system approach so useful.

The problem of antitrust restrictions. Our antitrust laws are an impediment to the best application of the physical distribution concept. Many savings, especially in transportation costs, could be achieved if it were possible for companies, including competitors, to work together, on a day-to-day basis, to make better use of facilities which can be shared. No compromise of true competitiveness is needed. A simple example might be the unit train. Suppose we have two coal users in the same area who are competitors, and who obtain coal from another general area. Neither alone has a volume which justifies the most efficient use of a unit train, but together they could make excellent use of such a facility. Antitrust restrictions make it difficult to get the benefit from such an arrangement at present. Now, with the computer, it is possible to raise efficiencies not only in situations like that of the unit train, but in the movement of all kinds of cargo. Waste of transportation capacity in backhaul movements can be reduced, and costs thereby reduced for both shippers and carriers.

The problem of personnel development. Application of the physical distribution concept has been slowed by shortages of trained and competent personnel; this shortage has existed not only at the graduate degree level, but in many subordinate specialties; there appears to have been a decline in the availability of courses in traffic and transportation subjects. It is also apparent that an insufficient number of women, and of individuals representing minorities, is being trained for physical distribution functions. At the core of the problem is the need to motivate young people, in high schools and colleges, to choose to prepare themselves for careers in transportation and distribution.

Did you guess the happy ending? Finding effective means of attack on such problems would accelerate progress toward maximum gains from good physical distribution management. Many problems exist, and are recognized by those who are active as physical distribution managers. A continuing discussion in print can serve to bring such problems to light, and often can uncover solutions. ∎

An effective marketing and distribution relationship

By DANIEL F. McNAMARA, *manager, distribution planning, Chrysler Corporation*

**2nd Prize
$250**

When your division's primary responsibility is to market and supply parts and accessories to an automotive aftermarket of nearly 4,800 dealer/distributors, you've got to constantly search for ways to improve operations.

Our Service and Parts Division, of which I am the distribution planning manager, believes that a prerequisite to successful marketing and distribution operations is "control"—particularly as it applies to providing consistent, high-quality service for our dealers. This, we believe, results in improved dealer and customer loyalty and increased sales for our division.

Recently, however, our division encountered difficulties in maintaining control over the transportation aspects of our distribution operations as common carrier service inconsistencies began surfacing at an increasing rate.

What our division did to counter this problem, reassert control over distribution operations, and relieve our frustrated dealers and irate customers is the subject of this paper. But first, to set the stage, here is some critical background.

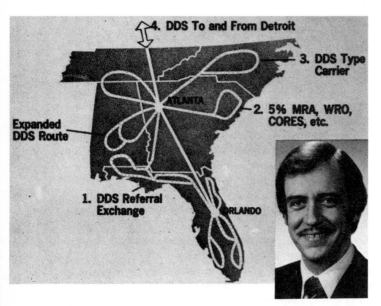

This Dedicated Delivery System features cloverleaf routing, unattended delivery, and reusable containers, says author Daniel McNamara, pictured above.

Distribution system background. Our distribution system is multi-echelon. It is geared to move parts from our plants and suppliers through a central packaging and warehousing complex in Detroit.

Nineteen field warehouses or "depots" receive replenishment inventory of nearly 30,000 parts and accessories from this central facility which carries a line totalling 170,000. (See distribution chart.)

Our service policies call for same, next, or second day shipment of parts, depending on the order type designated. The depot closest to a customer can, on an average, accomplish over 85 percent fill. An extensive referral network of alternate depots results in a 97 percent total system fill on all orders.

Shipments from our depots to dealers average 47 pounds. A typical shipment mix goes out 70 percent UPS, 25 percent LTL, and five percent TL. Our dealers are located in over 3,000 cities throughout the 50 states.

Our computer system has provided us with considerable control over our distribution operations through forecasting, procurement, material tracking, stockkeeping, order processing, and accounting. And, standards on order fill, inventory levels, and replenishment through-put have provided even further thrust to our efforts to provide consistent service for our dealers and customers.

Defining the problem. Getting back to the thrust of this paper, however, common carrier service inconsistencies were throwing a damper over our otherwise relatively controlled, consistent distribution operations. While many carriers, for example, performed up to par, others did not. And, even the best of carriers fluctuated service levels to some degree; i.e. delivery at 10 a.m. today but 2 p.m. tomorrow.

With our division's emphasis on "control" and our belief in its relationship to dealer and customer loyalty and improved divisional sales, one can readily see why this set of circumstances provided substantial frustration not only for our dealers and customers, but in turn for our division.

To solve this problem, we implemented a concept designed to provide our dealers with parts delivery on an unattended basis—preferably in the evening. This, we believed, would not only provide our dealers with more consistent delivery service,

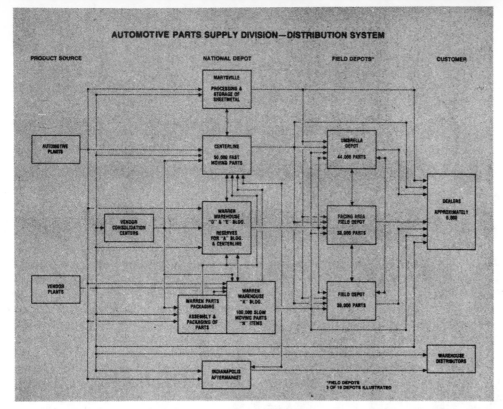

AUTOMOTIVE PARTS SUPPLY DIVISION—DISTRIBUTION SYSTEM

This multi-echelon distribution system is designed to move parts and accessories from manufacturing plants and suppliers through a central warehousing, packaging, and distribution facility in Detroit. This facility feeds a replenishment inventory of approximately 30,000 parts to 19 field warehouses or "depots". The total number of parts housed in the central facility, however, exceeds 170,000.

but also permit their service managers to schedule repair work more accurately on the basis of needed part availability first thing each morning.

Solution specifications. The concept was first tested in Florida out of our Orlando Parts Depot. We utilized private carriage with leased drivers to run five cloverleaf routes three and five days per week.

Reuseable tote bins, steel cages, lift gates, and dealer security areas made the unattended, nighttime delivery feasible. The system was subsequently converted to contract carriage.

Our dealers reacted very favorably to this system (which we've subsequently labeled DDS—Dedicated Delivery System). In fact, as word of the system's success spread, more and more of our dealers began pressing for nationwide implementation.

The costs of expanding this DDS service at first seemed prohibitive, however. But again we managed to overcome these obstacles by approaching them from two directions; marketing, and operations.

Marketing considerations. Much to our chagrin, our initial analysis of the dealers involved in DDS service failed to reflect any significant improvement in either dealer loyalty or sales.

A second analysis and survey, however, did, in fact, reflect considerable increases in both regards. The difference between the two studies, we discovered, was timing.

The first analysis was conducted for the 90 days immediately following the system's inception. The results of this study, we determined, were distorted because the dealers were actually depleting their own inventories, based on the improved reliability of the DDS distribution system.

Real sales growth was, in fact, occurring, we concluded. And, the resulting incremental profits were indeed helping to offset the costs of DDS.

Operations considerations. With parts depots able to provide for particular dealers/customers only 85 percent order fill, we recognized the need to further exploit the system's fixed costs.

Our traffic department juggled schedules to include the transport of dealer returns (due to obsolescence, etc.) into the system. Later, warranty items and certain core items (transmission cores, etc.) were also being transported back from dealers to depots via this system.

Once several systems were operating out of the various depots, routes were rescheduled around common meeting places where a driver out of one depot could exchange referral shipments with a driver from a neighboring one. Each driver then would return the referral shipments to his home for reshipment via the next day's routes.

To round out this system, several common and contract carriers were added to our system because they offered customized operations into areas too low in volume to justify private carriage or consistent common carriage transportation service. These carriers permitted us to provide most of the advantages of DDS to dealers located in these otherwise unreachable areas.

Summarization of benefits. Because of DDS and our distribution system improvements, we've regained control over the factors influencing consistent dealer/customer service.

Our overall warehousing strategy—warehouses constructed to supplement inferior quality common carriage service between key markets—has subsequently come under detailed review.

And, to make the most of the expanded capabilities of our distribution network, we are also conducting an optimization study using Geoffrion's MILP model and an in-house model to determine the optimal depot configuration. ■

189

SO YOU'RE THE NEW DISTRIBUTION MANAGER!

You've got the job. It's a nice promotion. It's more money. It's a new company, and it's a real challenge. So how do you make sure you start off on the right foot?

By MICHAEL PREGMON, JR., Director of Distribution, Citrus Central, Inc.

How does an experienced Distribution Manager approach the task of taking on a new responsibility? That this happens frequently in our industry is borne out by the 1977 LaLonde-Levy survey *("Distribution Career Patterns," DW, December 1977)* which indicated that 64% of the executives reported from one to four or more moves during the past ten years.

When the situation arises, it can be a particularly unsettled time for the first-time mover. He is, of course, elated by the selection and the accompanying higher compensation. But he is perhaps somewhat uncomfortable with his new environment and particularly the challenge to prove himself. For the old-timer or the individual who has moved before, these same feelings are not uncommon. Each new job change brings new challenges. So, likewise, this unsettled feeling reoccurs. The mere environment of a different organization—or particularly unfamiliar people—tremendously enhances this feeling.

There have been many volumes and articles written to help the Distribution Manager overcome some of the technical problems. But relatively little information has been printed to help bridge the gap in job change situations. If you find yourself facing the problem, here's an approach you might take to make a smooth and effective transition.

Obviously, the key is to move along the learning curve as quickly as possible in order to enhance department improvement and productivity. However, much of what is suggested depends upon you as an individual, your familiarity with the people you will be associating with, as well as the new company and its business philosophy.

It is implicit that you will first want to meet personally the

190

Phase I—Where are we?
- Meet key personnel throughout the company or division, etc.
- Get to know subordinates and department personnel
- Schedule orientation program with other company managers
- Study company policies & procedures
- Establish a personal reading file
- Initiate weekly staff meeting
- Schedule monthly department meeting
- Hold bi-weekly or monthly Distribution/Marketing Department coordination meetings
- Undertake the customer service surveys

Phase II—Where do we want to go?
- Analyze the customer service items such as order handling system, inventory turnover, loss and damage, etc.
- Detail study of departmental personnel and staffing needs

Phase III—How are we going to get there?
- Devise the distribution strategy to overcome system weaknesses and capitalize on the strengths
- Institute required organization and structure changes

Phase IV—When will it be done?
- Establish specific objectives with deadlines which will satisfy the agreed stragegy. Insure these objectives are controllable by the Distribution Department and are reasonable and attainable.

people with whom you will be dealing. Secondly, you will need to learn as much about your department and the company as quickly as possible. How can you best expedite this process? To answer this you must first answer four basic planning questions.

Where are we?
Where do we want to go?
How are we going to get there?
When will it be done?

Initially, as the new Distribution Manager, you should impose upon your immediate supervisor to provide you with personal introductions throughout the company. If the company is significantly large, obviously this initial introduction will be restricted to those with whom you will have a working interchange.

The initial introduction quite often becomes the responsibility of the Personnel Manager. But it certainly is more effective if it is performed by the immediate supervisor.

Your next objective must be to spend some time with your subordinates. During these initial periods, you should be more concerned with getting a feel for the personalities and how they fit into the structure. In so doing, you will also get some exposure to the operational involvements. However, a more detailed and in-depth analysis of this area logically follows at a later time.

Why the concern about the people and how they fit into the organization? Studies have shown that a vast majority of personnel terminations have resulted, not from the individual's quality of work, but from the inability of an individual to relate with others in the organization. This aspect is ever so important because the success of any manager or supervisor is determined by his ability to get things done through others. A new Distribution Manager will almost certainly bring new ideas and his own management style into the structure. Certainly, not all work will be completely delegated. But a large majority must be carried out by others through his guidance.

After you are fairly familiar, personally, with those in your immediate department, you're ready to study the organization and other inter-departmental relationships. This can most effectively be done by what may be referred to as an "orientation program."

Simply, as the new Distribution Manager, you set up a series of personal visits with other department heads and executives throughout the company. This may be established by letter or memo to each person you are to visit. For example, you would certainly want to spend some time learning about the specific involvements of the Sales or Marketing Manager.

You may want to spend time with specific regional or product sales managers. Individuals such as the Controller, Internal Auditor, Budget, Data Processing Manager, and the like would also be included, along with such key people as the Personnel, Training, and Planning Managers.

It must be emphasized that these visits need not necessarily be scheduled all consecutively, although they may be. Usually, the Manager benefits most by scheduling these visits over a brief period of time—say two or three weeks. In fact, it probably would be rare to find each of these individuals available in a single week
Continued

NEW DM
CONTINUED

or so due to travel schedules and commitments.

What benefits accrue from this program? First, in addition to learning more about the individual personalities, you will also quickly learn of areas for Distribution Department improvement. This results naturally from the dynamics of human behavior.

Since you are new to the company, you are not personally responsible for any of the prior programs or problems. Individuals who interact with the distribution functions usually will become more open to discuss problems and challenges requiring corrective action with someone who has not been involved previously.

Here's a specific example: A Distribution Manager, during one of his inter-departmental discussions, learned of a significant "buck-passing" attitude which had developed among Distribution personnel. This was specifically prevalent in the Customer Service section of the department. When salesmen or customers confronted department individuals with problems or even questions, these questions were invariably passed on to others for handling.

Identifying problem areas

This was first learned by the Manager during his orientation sessions when many regional sales managers complained of getting a "runaround." It's easy to envision the impact upon customer service when a customer calls for information and his phone call is transferred among four, five or six different people.

Secondly, as the new Distribution Manager you will certainly have been provided with an excellent opportunity to learn more about the individuals and their specific responsibilities. Further, your exposure to and understanding of the organization, its structure, policies, proce-

WHERE ARE WE, AND WHERE DO WE WANT TO GO?

dures and philosophies will certainly be accelerated.

Next, you must make a point of specifically studying and becoming familiar with operating policies and procedures. If a company has a formal policy or procedures program, your reveiw of these guidelines will be invaluable. Additionally, an excellent method for familiarization becomes available through the use of a reading file. Your secretary merely needs to keep a file handy of all correspondence she prepares. After some specified period—perhaps initially daily or weekly—she can pass this file on to you for review as time permits. A simple review of these memos, letters and other correspondence will certainly enhance your understanding of the departmental involvements.

Depending on the size of the department, it is generally most helpful for the Distribution Manager to establish a weekly staff meeting and a monthly department meeting. The staff meeting

will further help to speed organizational understanding. The department meeting can be used simply as a vehicle to keep personnel updated and abreast of what's happening in the department and company. It will help subordinates to get to know their boss more quickly. Further, this single meeting often does much to enhance morale and improve communication throughout the department.

In suggesting such meetings, I surely do not want to give the impression of scheduling meetings for meetings' sake. However, a periodic meeting of distribution personnel and key marketing and sales personnel will certainly serve its purpose well. In actual fact, such meetings do more to avoid the so-called "fire-fighting" exercises so often evident in distribution departments. Such benefits as information dissemination, market strategy, planned promotions, price changes, etc. are very often learned during such meetings.

ANALYZE COMPANY POLICIES & PROCEDURES

Without this opportunity, these programs often become surprises to distribution managers and their staff.

Learning from other managers

Another advantage of such meetings offer is in gaining insight in the company's competitive environment. The sales people who will attend these meetings will provide an excellent resource for distribution personnel regarding its company's competition. This information is vital for the Distribution Manager when it becomes necessary to devise the distribution system strategy you will employ for your new company.

The next major involvement by the Distribution Manager will entail a customer service survey. This may be one of the most detailed and time-consuming undertakings during the early period referred to as "Where Are We?". The survey results should provide you with the feedback needed to get on with the job. It will also provide very powerful testimony to support improvement programs.

Certainly, as you become more familiar with your company; many other improvement areas will surface. Many of these will be internal, too. However, none will be as significant as those improvement areas or problems identified by the company's customers. After all, one of the Distribution Manager's major responsibilities is that of "keeping customers."

Experience has dictated that this survey needs to encompass a bilateral dimension. A detailed survey should be directed to the buyers or purchasing agents of the firm's customers. A much shorter survey depicting general order handling, carrier service and packaging adequacy should be directed to the customers' receiving warehouse personnel. The former, a more detailed survey, can be simply mailed to those individuals; whereas, the latter may be a brief return-addressed post-card conspicuously attached to a package in the shipment.

It is not uncommon to find a high survey response from those directed to buyer and purchasing agents. This may be in the area of 45% response or greater. A relatively low response (approximately 10% to 15%) can be expected for surveys directed to warehouse personnel when the postcards are attached to invoices. A better response (approximately 35%) from warehouse personnel will be obtained when attaching short post-card survey questionnaires to a package in the shipment. But, the postcard survey must be conspicuously placed on a pallet or case in the shipment. If this goes unnoticed at the time of receiving, the chances for getting a response are slim.

Obviously, both surveys need to be correlated to authenticate the data responses. Above all, a Distribution Manager must be well versed in survey techniques before a survey is undertaken. Certainly, an ill-conceived or poorly devised survey can do more harm than good. It could be both expensive and ineffective. A word of caution beforehand: Survey questions should and must be pre-tested before customer mailing. And, most important, survey randomness must be insured.

With the above information in hand, you are now ready to move into the second phase.

Deciding where you want to go

At this stage, it will be necessary to determine what customer service level the firm desired to satisfy. It is best if this decision emanates from top management. And the service level should be in concert with the philosophies of the marketing, production, materials and distribution areas. It may also be necessary to obtain specific information regarding shipments, loss and damage in-
Continued

193

cidences, order handling time, track record of stock-outs and inventory turnover, etc. Further, the Distribution Manager may find it necessary to delve specifically into the area of order handling control. This latter area is vital in most industries such as the highly inventory-sensitive grocery products industry.

Generally, grocery industry wholesalers and chains have the most intricate inventory control systems. As a result, missed deliveries quite often result in store level stock-outs—a very disconcerting phenomena for the store manager. Similarly, these customers demand accurate and timely order handling information. So, the effective distribution function must be aware of the order status of all orders at all times. Should a channel miscue result, customer service will be improved by notifying the customer before he becomes surprised by the missed delivery.

Essentially, the information received from customers, marketing and sales representatives, order handling, research, loss and damage, etc. will clearly define "Where We Must Go" to improve the company's market share.

Getting where you want to go

This is truly the enjoyment part of a Distribution Manager's responsibility. This is when the strategy is both devised and deployed. But, before you will reap the full enjoyment of any system improvements, you must insure that you have adequately assessed your internal distribution department structure and organization. Most important, you need the right people in the right jobs. Sometimes this stage usually requires the longest period of time for completion.

A typical distribution system example of this is the requirement to effectively consolidate warehouse operations into major

MAKE YOUR IDEAS KNOWN AT MEETINGS

geographic distribution centers. Experience dictates that it is best to undertake these changes on a step-by-step basis to avoid irrepairable customer disservice. As an example, one manufacturer programmed this strategy over a period of five years. In this fashion, each distribution center service area was changed, consolidated and placed on-stream before the next was undertaken. Certainly, this is not necessary in all cases, but such changes must be cautiously undertaken.

At this point, the many volumes of technical information available may be utilized by the Distribution Manager. He must analyze his particular situation and devise the strategy best suited for his firm. It is not unusual for these improvements to span a time frame of three to five years. When will it be done?

Perhaps the most important of all, however, is the scheduling phase. This is when specific milestones or objectives are devised. It is imperative these be specifically written and documented. Further, a completion date or month should be identified for each objective.

You must insure that each objective is reasonable and attainable. It is ironic that many managers have devised outstanding improvement plans but the plans seemingly never get completed. Simply, these fail because a deadline or completion time frame was not established.

Many managers have integrated the "Management by Objectives" (MBO) program into this phase. It can be done. But a results-oriented manager can successfully devise a plan and see it through completion. It is not necessary that the devised plan be ironclad and unalterable for successful completion. Obviously, business decisions and policy-making must be flexible. But parameters must be established for a frame of reference. Only through such regimentation does a realistic plan and program become reality. ∎

Chapter 8
Traffic Management

How Traffic Managers Select Carriers

By **ROGER E. JERMAN,** Associate Professor of Transportation,
Graduate School of Business, Indiana University
RONALD D. ANDERSON, Associate Professor of Marketing,
Graduate School of Business, Indiana University
JAMES A. CONSTANTIN, David Ross Boyd Professor of Marketing and Transportation,
Distribution Research Program, University of Oklahoma

An in-depth survey of traffic managers reveals that shippers consider a
wide variety of "selection variables" when they choose a carrier, from
how courteous the driver is to past experience with freight damage and loss

The traffic manager has many duties in his job design, but perhaps the most important is that of purchasing reliable transportation.

The product the traffic manager purchases is really a service, and a rather subjective one that is very difficult to evaluate.

So, how does the traffic manager select the carriers he uses? Which service variables making up the carrier's product offering are important to the traffic manager when he makes his carrier selection?

To find out how traffic managers actually perform the complex function of choosing carriers, the authors conducted an in-depth survey of shippers all over the country.*

Six underlying carrier selection areas were studied:

1. Carrier charges and privileges
2. Carrier past performance
3. Carrier image
4. Carrier cooperation in rate adjustment
5. Carrier routing capability
6. Carrier knowledge

There were 26 specific questions covering these six areas. Responses to the questions were rated on a scale of one to five expressing the perceived importance of the specified carrier selection variable. A value of five was considered extremely important, a value of one was not important and the numbers in between expressed degree of differences.

Charges and privileges

As part of their product offering, common carriers can offer a group of services which are accessoried to the line-haul. Fig. 1 shows the importance evaluations of selected supplemental services.

The traffic managers thought that diversion and reconsignment privileges were important in their choice of carrier. A shipment using reconsignment and diversion moves at the regular published rate from origin to final destination, plus, in some cases, a reconsignment charge. This is what makes the privilege valuable, for the through rate is ordinarily less than the rate to diversion or reconsignment point plus the rate from there to final destination.

The remaining three questions in Fig. 1 involve transit privileges. The establishment of transit privileges permits the movement of many different commodities from origin to destination, with a stop at an intermediate point, where the commodities are unloaded, stored, processed, reloaded and reforwarded. Two separate transportation movements are involved, but the transportation
Continued

The data are based upon responses from surveys of two professional transportation and traffic organizations. Questionnaires were sent to the entire membership of the American Society of Traffic and Transportation, excluding those with academic affiliation. Nine hundred seventy-six usable questionnaires were returned for a response rate of 48 percent. Questionnaires were also sent to a random sample, excluding educators, of 2,000 members of the Delta Nu Alpha Transportation Fraternity. Six hundred sixty-four questionnaires were returned from Delta Nu Alpha members for a response rate of 33.2 percent. From the two groups 270 respondents indicated they were traffic managers. These 270 responses were used to summarize how traffic managers evaluate certain carrier selection variables.

Carriers CONTINUED

from origin to final destination is considered to be an interrupted through movement.

Historically, one of the most popular in-transit arrangements has been fabrication or milling in-transit privileges. This allows the traffic manager to stop a shipment enroute to enable some process or operation to be performed on the article, and of re-shipping to final destination at the through rate applicable from the original shipping point to destination. The traffic managers viewed fabrication in-transit privileges as minor in importance in their choice of common carriage.

Storage-in-transit privileges have taken on new relevance because of the tremendous growth in distribution centers, and the increasing emphasis on inventory control and locational analysis. Again, the traffic managers did not place much emphasis on storage-in-transit privileges in their carrier selection process. The traffic managers also indicated that the amount charged for storage privileges was of minor importance. This implies that while the traffic managers viewed storage-in-transit as minor in importance, if they needed to use this service, they would be relatively insensitive to price.

Past performance

A carrier's product is a service which can best be evaluated by the traffic manager after the service has been tried. Fig. 2 shows traffic managers' evaluations of specific past performance questions.

The perceived importance of past performance of a carrier in the carrier selection process was viewed as very important by traffic managers. One of the key variables in the carrier selection process is the incidence of loss and damage. Again, the traffic man-

agers considered past experience with the amount of freight loss very important in their continued patronage of a common carrier. The traffic managers gave even a higher importance rating to past experience concerning freight

damage with a carrier in their choice of carriers. In addition, traffic managers ranked frequency of service to key points in a shipper's market as the most important selection variable of the ones classified under the cate-

Fig. 1 **CARRIER PRIVILEGES AND CHARGES**						
Selection Variable	5	4	3	2	1	Mean
Diversion and reconsignment privileges	12.5%	25.1%	33.9%	20.7%	7.7%	**3.14**
The amount of storage charges	9.0%	12.7%	26.1%	32.1%	20.1%	**2.58**
Storage in-transit privileges	9.3%	13.7%	24.4%	21.5%	31.1%	**2.49**
Fabrication in-transit privileges	7.1%	11.6%	18.4%	21.7%	41.2%	**2.22**

Fig. 2 **CARRIER PAST PERFORMANCE**						
Selection Variable	5	4	3	2	1	Mean
Frequency of service to key points in a shipper's market area	30.7%	50.4%	17.0%	1.5%	.4%	**4.10**
Past performance of a carrier	28.9%	50.7%	17.4%	2.6%	.4%	**4.05**
Freight damage experience with a carrier	29.6%	48.9%	17.4%	3.7%	.4%	**4.04**
Freight loss experience with a carrier	29.9%	46.5%	19.9%	3.0%	.7%	**4.02**

Fig. 3 **CARRIER IMAGE**						
Selection Variable	5	4	3	2	1	Mean
Carrier reputation for dependability	32.8%	50.6%	12.5%	3.3%	.7%	**4.11**
Carrier reputation for quality service	22.6%	53.7%	17.0%	5.6%	1.1%	**3.91**
Scheduling flexibility of a carrier	22.3%	42.8%	29.0%	5.6%	.4%	**3.81**
Carrier-shipper discussions at professional meetings	20.7%	39.3%	26.3%	10.4%	3.3%	**3.64**
Courtesy of vehicle operators	16.6%	34.3%	36.5%	11.1%	1.5%	**3.54**
Neatness of vehicle operators	5.5%	16.2%	45.0%	24.7%	8.5%	**2.86**

5 = Extremely Important   4 = Very Important   3 = Moderately Important   2 = Slightly Important   1 = Not Important

197

gory of past performance in Fig. 2.

Carrier image

The importance profiles for the traffic managers' responses to six carrier selection variables that were grouped under the topical area of carrier image are displayed in Fig. 3.

The traffic managers placed strong emphasis on the selection variable of the reputation of a carrier for dependability. The

Fig. 4 **COOPERATION IN RATE ADJUSTMENT**						
Selection Variable	5	4	3	2	1	Mean
Carrier assistance in obtaining rate or classification changes	32.5%	52.4%	12.5%	1.5%	1.1%	**4.14**
Carrier's leadership in general rate adjustment proceedings	22.6%	51.5%	19.6%	5.2%	1.1%	**3.89**
Carrier's participation in general rate adjustment proceedings	19.6%	47.8%	26.7%	4.8%	1.1%	**3.80**

Fig. 5 **CARRIER ROUTING CAPABILITIES**						
Selection Variable	5	4	3	2	1	Mean
Carrier ability to quickly trace shipments	43.2%	41.3%	13.3%	1.8%	.4%	**4.25**
Total transit time for the shipment	43.2%	36.9%	18.1%	1.8%	0	**4.21**
Carrier honoring a shipper's routing request	36.3%	44.8%	14.4%	3.3%	1.1%	**4.12**
Feedback from the consignee to the shipper about the quality of service given by specific carriers	22.5%	41.0%	26.6%	9.2%	.7%	**3.75**
Nearness of carrier offices to the shipper	4.8%	13.7%	34.8%	28.1%	18.5%	**2.58**

Fig. 6 **CARRIER KNOWLEDGE**						
Selection Variable	5	4	3	2	1	Mean
Cooperation between carrier and shipper personnel	50.2%	44.7%	3.7%	.4%	0	**4.46**
Knowledge of a shipper's needs on the part of a carrier representative	29.9%	49.4%	17.0%	3.0%	.7%	**4.05**
Carrier attitude toward accepting small shipments	23.0%	38.9%	22.6%	9.6%	5.9%	**3.63**
Regular calls by a carrier salesman	4.1%	18.8%	9.5%	25.8%	11.8%	**2.77**

5 = Extremely Important   4 = Very Important   3 = Moderately Important   2 = Slightly Important   1 = Not Important

traffic manager purchasing transportation is interested not only in the extent of the services offered by a carrier but also the consistency of the service because consistency is akin to uniformity in a non-service oriented product. This uniformity permits more orderly planning with other functional areas with which the traffic managers must coordinate.

As an extension of the dependability variable, traffic managers were asked to evaluate the importance of the scheduling flexibility of the carrier. The majority of the traffic managers rated carrier scheduling flexibility as very important.

One of the common methods used to locate shipping prospects is for the transportation salesman to become a member of, and attend the meetings of, numerous business groups, luncheon clubs, and other professional organizations where the opportunity to meet traffic men exists. When asked their attitudes on the importance of carrier-shipper discussions at professional meetings, the traffic managers thought that this informal relationship with common carrier representatives was important.

The courtesy and neatness of vehicle operators can represent a real problem area for the marketing portion of common carrier management. These two variables fall under the jurisdiction of the operations function of common carrier management. Union relationships also influence these two variables. When asked about the importance of the courtesy and neatness of the vehicle operators, traffic managers thought that courtesy was somewhat influential in their choice of a common carrier but that neatness was not all that important in their carrier selection process.

A common carrier produces an
Continued

Carriers CONTINUED

intangible service rather than a physical product. This means that customer confidence in the ability of the common carrier to provide quality of service in large part is really the traffic manager's perception of the general competence of the management of the common carrier. As one might anticipate, the responding traffic managers thought that the reputation of the carrier for quality of service strongly influenced their choice of carrier.

Cooperation in rate adjustment

In general, common carriers do not use pricing as a direct strategy element to bring about favorable market reaction. Therefore, instead of asking directly the importance of pricing or rates in the traffic manager-carrier interface, three questions grouped under the importance of carrier cooperation in rate adjustments were asked. These three variables stress the service aspects connected with regulated common carrier pricing, and the findings are illustrated in Fig. 4.

Traffic managers thought that carrier assistance in obtaining rate or classification changes was very important and the most important of the three variables. Next in importance was the carrier's leadership in general rate adjustment proceedings. The traffic managers also acknowledged the importance of a carrier's actual participation in general rate adjustment proceedings.

Routing capabilities

One of the early specialties of the traffic manager was both a skill and expertise concerning rates and routes. Fig. 5 presents the results of traffic managers' evaluations of five variables grouped under the topical area of routing capabilities.

Tracing means keeping track of the location of a shipment on the part of the carrier. The ability of the carrier to quickly trace shipments was ranked the most important of the routing capability variables. This is consistent with the high ranking given carrier dependability in an earlier section. Carrier ability to quickly trace shipments is a major vehicle the traffic manager can use in accomplishing reliability for his procurement—distribution system.

The honoring of a route request and the total transit time for the shipment were both considered important by traffic managers. Feedback from the consignee to the shipper about the quality of service given by specific carriers was evaluated by traffic managers as only moderately important. In addition, the importance of having carrier offices close to the shipper was considered of minor importance by responding traffic managers.

Knowledge of carrier

Fig. 6 presents the results of four carrier selection variables grouped under the topical area of carrier knowledge.

The traffic managers ranked cooperation between carrier and shipper personnel the most important of these variables. One of the problems which constantly plagues shippers is the problem of sending and receiving small shipments. Traffic managers thought that small shipment service was important in their shipper-carrier interface.

The remaining two questions asked traffic managers to evaluate common carrier salesmen. Knowledge of a shipper's needs on the part of a carrier representative was ranked very important by traffic managers in their continued use of a specific common carrier. Traffic managers were also asked whether they thought regular calls by a carrier salesman were important. The responding traffic managers thought that these regular calls by carrier salesmen were of minor importance. Evidently the traffic manager is deluged with calls and visits from the various carriers. Apparently the traffic managers would prefer fewer calls and when that call is made prefers that the carrier salesman be better informed about the service his own line holds out to the public and how this service can fit into the traffic manager's procurement—distribution system.

Conclusions

The results of this survey will most certainly be of interest to carriers interested in improving their marketing efforts, but the traffic manager should also be able to use the results to improve his ability to select reliable carriers. There are undoubtedly selection variables included in this survey that many traffic managers have overlooked or have not fully considered.

Understandably, past performance, to include freight loss and damage experience and frequency of service to key points, ranked very high.

There were also a number of less obvious, and perhaps surprising, selection variables that the respondents considered important. The traffic managers polled thought carrier-shipper discussions at professional meetings, courtesy of drivers, carrier cooperation in rate adjustments and carrier willingness to accept small shipments were all very important.

The reader can reach his own conclusions, but the overall message of the survey seems to be that shippers want more than transportation from the carrier. Traffic managers expect a high degree of cooperation from carriers in all matters. ■

Consolidated Freightways

LOSS AND DAMAGE

What to do when

When it comes to freight damage claims, the carrier may have your money but you probably have the law on your side. If you know the law.

William J. Augello, executive director and general counsel of the Shippers National Freight Claim Council, Inc. (SNFCC), was a little abrupt with the questioner. The setting was a warm, well-packed meeting room in a large motel near Cincinnati. The group of about 60 traffic managers from six states was assembled for one of a series of SNFCC seminars.

One attendee, giving the background to his question about a claim he had filed, explained that he had declined a complete shipment when he observed that the first few pieces off-loaded were seriously damaged. Said Mr. Augello:

"I can't stress enough the importance of accepting a shipment that's damaged unless it's practically worthless. Yes, this places a heavy burden on the consignee to determine the extent of the damage, the remaining value, etc. But that's the law. And that's your job. You have to make serious decisions in this business."

Freight claims represent one of the biggest and most mishandled problems in distribution. Traffic people deal with large and small claims every day, but many of them are working in the dark when it comes to knowing where they stand under the law. As Mr. Augello says, "Once you start thinking like a lawyer instead of a layman, you'll be better off."

Now neither you nor we sport law degrees on our walls. So don't start preparing a court brief to file suit against that carrier and don't take these guidelines for any more than that—guidelines. But shippers and receivers still need to know where their own responsibilities begin and where the carriers' end. Being aware of the basic precepts of freight claim law can help you avoid some thorny complications. Shippers shouldn't be intimidated by carriers, but neither should they get in trouble out of ignorance.

Prevention first. Freight claim headaches can be minimized by taking a few logical precautionary measures. Instruct your receiving department to **go**

the carrier says NO

By PATRICK GALLAGHER, *associate editor*

through a simple, rigorous inspection of every shipment. They needn't open every carton, but they should be on the lookout for dents, bulges, punctures, flattened corners, and short counts.

They should note any and all discrepancies on the carrier freight bill before signing it and turning it over to the driver. If they can get the driver to initial each discrepancy, so much the better. A camera might not be a bad thing to have around either.

Caution your receiving department to sign only for the number of cartons it actually receives or for the number in good condition. A shipment might be signed for as "10 cartons missing," or "10 cartons crushed," or "10 cartons on bottom layer damp."

Make clear your standard procedures for receiving freight. Especially when dealing with concealed damage, you may be called on to prove that the damage did not take place while the goods were in your hands. The greater the value of the shipment, the more careful your receiving department should be.

If you notice that a shipment is short or is damaged, call the carrier immediately. Request an inspection of the goods. Do not throw away the shipping container or inner packing until the carrier has inspected them or waived his right of inspection. He has 5 days to act. After that time, prepare your own inspection report. You can get blank inspection forms from any carrier.

No single established form exists for filing a claim. It simply must be in writing and it has to specify an exact (or determinable) amount of loss or damage. If you can't determine the exact value of the damage, estimate liberally and file for that amount. The carrier can modify the amount after he inspects.

Send a carrier a letter saying "We intend to file claim for X shipment for loss of $100 more or less," and you'll probably get your letter back labeled "incomplete claim." The carrier is right, your claim is incomplete. But he's wrong if he thinks you haven't filed a valid claim with him.

The American Trucking Associations' National Freight Claim Council and the Association of American Railroads have issued procedures for filing freight claims. You may want to get copies. But use common sense. State your claim clearly and completely. Include all pertinent information: certified copies of original shipping documents, a copy of your inspection report, a copy of the invoice to establish value, a statement of nondelivery, etc.

His move. When you discover loss or damage some time after accepting the goods, notify the carrier immediately. For all land surface carriers, you have 15 days from delivery to file notice before the burden of proving the damage falls to you, the claimant. Until then, the law assumes that the damage occurred while the goods were in the carrier's possession.

The final limit for filing a loss, damage, or delay claim on any shipment moving by land is 9 months from delivery. For nondelivery, the limit is 9 months plus a reasonable time for delivery. Claim filing rules for air and steamship carriers vary.

If you are in danger of missing a claim deadline, hand-deliver your claim or send it express mail. But get it delivered in writing within the 9 months, and the sooner the better.

Once the carrier receives your claim, he has 30 days to acknowledge it. Don't hesitate to send him a claim tracer including all pertinent information if he doesn't respond. If your original claim lacks some necessary supporting documents, the carrier must inform you that your claim is incomplete. He can't pay the claim until he has all the information—but neither can he properly deny it solely on those grounds. The statute still starts running, though.

The law requires a carrier to investigate every claim. And he must make periodic reports on the progress of settling each claim and the reason for any delay. He has 120 days to dispose of a claim—to either reject it, modify it, or pay it. If he fails to act, complain to the ICC.

Rejected. Filing was easy—but suppose the carrier says, no? He rejects your claim outright. You now have two years plus one day to file suit in a court of law for loss, damage, or delay. Keep close track of your claims, because nothing will stop the running of the statute.

Well, almost nothing. A recent court case allowed

201

a suit to be filed after two years had passed because the carrier had inadvertently misled the claimant. *(Cordingly v. Allied Van Lines.)* But don't count on being so lucky.

The laws regulating common carriage strongly favor the shipper. Carrier liability is stringent. The contract terms of the motor carrier uniform bill of lading clearly state that the carrier is liable for any loss or damage except as specifically provided in the contract. Some tariffs include language which attempts to limit a carrier's liability. Ignore it. The Supreme Court has ruled that nothing can be added or subtracted from the law by limitations or definitions stated in tariffs. The carrier is the ultimate insurer.

God and other exceptions. Because they have more at stake, carriers are generally more knowledgeable about the law than shippers, especially smaller shippers. Don't be bullied. It is not a proper claim disallowance for the carrier simply to state that "there is no carrier liability because damage was not 'caused by it' as provided in Section 20(11) of the Interstate Commerce Act." Even if it proves that one of the five allowable exceptions was the cause of the damage, the carrier still must prove that it was not negligent. These are the five exceptions:

Act of God. Says Mr. Augello: You'll never know the answers to some of these act-of-God questions until one of the cases goes to court. But you should ask yourself: Could the event have been anticipated? Was it normal? Was there advance warning? Was negligence involved? Perhaps the key question is: What was the sole and proximate cause of the damage—the act of God or the carrier's negligence?

The weather the past two winters may provide a bumper crop of act-of-God cases. Mr. Augello cites one: A railcar is delayed and gets caught in a flood as a result. The contents are destroyed. In one such case, the court ruled that the flood, not the delay, was the proximate cause of the damage. *Intervention of a public enemy.* The carrier reports his trailer was hijacked by an organized crime ring—they are public enemies, right? Therefore, he is not liable. . . . Wrong. By U.S. law, only a nation at war is a public enemy.

Intervention of law. Same situation as before, but the FBI catches the thieves and recovers the trailer intact. Except the court holds the trailer and its contents as evidence for two years. Is the carrier liable? Yes, because he is still liable for failure to protect the load in transit. The intervention of the authorities was not the proximate cause of the delay.

Inherent vice. This exception means that a product is of its nature subject to damage under certain normal conditions beyond the control of the carrier. Sample situations: product delivered frozen; product damaged by heat or condensation; product rusted.

If a carrier denies your claim because of an

Where to Find

Interstate Commerce Commission
If you have a problem involving motor carriers, freight forwarders, railroads, or small shipment carriers, contact your local Interstate Commerce Commission office. There are 78 around the country. You may also want to direct a letter to the ICC, Section of Insurance, Washington DC 20043. This office will attempt to help the parties straighten out misunderstandings of ICC law. They will also furnish you with name and address of the insurance company covering the carrier or freight forwarder (railroads do not carry insurance). However, remember: the ICC is a regulatory body. They will not adjucate your claim for you.

Civil Aeronautics Board
The CAB regulates domestic and international air transportation. Several individuals there may be able to help you. The CAB is in Washington DC 20428.
- Brad Smith, director of special projects
- Chris Browne, chief legal division, Bureau of Enforcement
- Jack Yohe, consumer division-cargo (202) 673-5526
- Ezekial Limmer, consumer division-domestic cargo
- Herb Aswall, consumer division-international tariffs.

Associations
For assistance with claim problems of a general nature involving the respective modes, contact the following people. However, don't expect them to help you with a specific complaint against a carrier. Their concern is improving shipper/carrier relations in the area of claims for their particular association. They may be able to offer you some legal explanations, and they will almost certainly provide you with information to help your company ship with a minimum of damage or loss—and fewer claims.

inherent vice of your product, check your bill of lading. Does it carry clear instructions about proper handling? A phrase like "protect from freezing" is probably adequate. But what does "protect from excessive heat" mean?

Also go back to your bill-of-lading contract. Did the carrier have any protective service provisions

Aid and Advice

Association of American Railroads
J. C. Hindman
Freight Claims Division
59 East Van Buren St.
Chicago, Illinois 60605
(312) 939-0770

Air Transport Association of America
Glenn E. Stephan
Manager-Packaging & Claims Prevention
1709 New York Ave. N.W.
Washington, DC 20006
(202) 872-4235

National Freight Claim Council
of the American Trucking Associations
John V. Lund
Executive Director
1616 P Street N.W.
Washington, DC 20036
(202) 797-5302

Other possible sources of relief are state public utility commissions and state offices of consumer affairs. Finally, the shipper's newest ally is the independent Shippers National Freight Claim Council. Even if you're not a member, they'll probably try and help you.

Shippers National Freight Claim Council
William J. Augello
Executive Director/General Counsel
120 Main St. (Box Z)
Huntington, NY 11743
(516) 549-8984

The secretaryship of the Transportation Arbitration Board (TAB) alternates between NFCC and SNFCC. Until August 1978, contact Mr. Augello at SNFCC. TAB assesses each party a $25 fee for its services. ■

in his tariffs? If the carrier is soliciting goods even with no tariff provision, he is still liable if he picked up the freight.

Is past experience valid evidence against a carrier's denial based on inherent vice? If you've been shipping your product the same way for years, and suddenly the railroad denies a damage claim saying your product is inherently susceptible to normal shock and vibration, you've got a pretty strong case. *Act or omission by the shipper.* These disallowances are usually cases of inadequate packing or packaging or improper loading. The shipper is responsible by law to protect freight over and above minimum packaging requirements. Doing this can lead to expensive overpackaging if you're not careful. You may be able to establish performance-related packaging requirements based on drop tests, vibration tests, etc. Most carriers won't waive the rules, but should the situation arise, you will have strong evidence to support your position.

So who files? The party who holds title to the goods at the time of loss or damage is the one authorized to file a claim. If you suffered the loss, you file the claim.* Don't spend money on claims covering goods purchased FOB your plant. Simply pass along any necessary papers to the consignee or supplier. After all, that's one of the advantages of buying FOB destination and shipping FOB origin.

You file the claim with the carrier who made the delivery right? Yes, if he is solvent. If not, the law permits you to hold the origin carrier liable.

This issue grows sticky when merchandise moves on two bills of lading with a distributor as intermediary. You have no basis for presuming that the damage was caused by the delivering carrier and not a previous carrier. The package has probably not been opened and examined since it left the manufacturer's dock and that may have been several months earlier.

The American Trucking Association suggests that claimants hold the distributor responsible for sorting out the claim. If the prior carrier or the distributor refuses to cooperate, don't expect the delivering carrier to pay more than a sum representing his portion of the entire move, says the ATA. Their legal ground is shaky, according to the ICC's ruling in Ex Parte 263.

Getting your due. Generally, the carrier must return the claimant to the position he would have been in had the shipment been delivered as promised.

An exception to this—by its own request—is United Parcel Service. UPS prefers that the shipper always file the claim with them.

If the carrier lost an entire shipment, the claimant should file for the invoice price of the goods, for any freight charges paid, and for any duties paid and unreturnable.

If the carrier damaged part of a shipment, the claimant should file for the invoice price of the goods less any salvage value, the freight charges on the damaged portion, any duties paid and unreturnable, and the cost of repairing or repackaging the damaged portion of the shipment.

To repeat what Mr. Augello said earlier, a consignee cannot and should not refuse to accept a shipment unless it is practically worthless. One of the responsibilities of the owner of the goods is to minimize the carrier's loss by salvaging whatever he can. Consider your own interest as well. Refuse

The SNFCC Roadshow

"This has been the most articulate claims seminar I've ever attended."
"Fantastic. Still making me think more."
"This was head and shoulders above any previously attended."

So say attendees of the claims seminars sponsored at sites around the country by the Shippers National Freight Claim Council. The seminars are hard-hitting affairs with SNFCC Executive Director William J. Augello presiding. He prefers the "case method" and the long day—from 8 to 5 for two days and no cocktails for lunch either.

Some of those in attendance are SNFCC members; others quickly become new ones. In four short years, 700 shippers and carriers have joined the organization. For their investment they receive—

● a unique encyclopedia of freight claim information

● monthly freight claim news bulletins

● copies of important court decisions and legislative and regulatory actions

● comprehensive index to claims subjects.

The 1978 seminar roadshow gets underway next month in the following cities. Call or write SNFCC for more information.

Minneapolis—Sheraton Airport Inn (Bloomington). May 1-3.
San Jose—Holiday Inn-Park Center Plaza. May 3-5.
Dallas—Sheraton Dallas. May 8-10.
Detroit—Sheraton-Southfield. May 10-12.
Pittsburgh—Ramada Inn. May 22-24.
Boston—Holiday Inn (Peabody). June 12-14.

delivery and you surrender control over the fate of those goods. You may also subject your company to product liability suits for sale of defective goods.

Once a carrier has attempted delivery, his liability is reduced to that of a warehouseman. "Warehouseman's liability" is less stringent than that of a carrier. A carrier is the ultimate insurer; a warehouseman need only protect goods as a prudent man would protect his own property under similar circumstances.

Conversely, a carrier cannot take possession without your consent of goods that are damaged, dispose of them, then offer you the salvage proceeds. That is an improper practice and a potentially dangerous one.

If inflation or something else increases the expense of replacing the lost or damaged goods, by law you are entitled to the higher amount. However, a carrier cannot be held responsible for what are called "special damages" unless written notice is given on the bill of lading specifying the amount of potential damage and the conditions of the demands. As a rule of thumb, special damages are those incurred by the owner (loss of profit, for example) over and above any damage to the freight itself. The carrier is not responsible for your problems. He is charged with delivering your goods with "reasonable dispatch."

Thus, a carrier could probably not be held liable for a civil fine or other penalty suffered by the owner of the goods because of delay or non-delivery. Recently, however, we heard that a Canadian court awarded $50,000 in damages when an air courier was three hours late delivering a bid for a project. The bidder lost out on the project and successfully sued the courier.

Not too late to arbitrate. Faced with a completely recalcitrant carrier, bringing suit may be your only recourse. However, if you and the carrier are agreeable, consider arbitration. It is faster, cheaper, and less trying than going to court. Make your own arrangements with the carrier or use one of several services available. Just be careful the two-year statute doesn't run out while you're discussing arbitration.

The Transportation Arbitration Board (TAB) arbitrates claim disputes between shippers and motor carriers. The two parties execute an agreement and submit the claimant's brief and exhibits, the carrier's response, and the shipper's rebuttal to the TAB. Two arbitrators are selected from lists supplied by SNFCC and NFCC. They have 30 days to come to a unanimous decision. TAB has accepted 40 cases so far and settled them all. ■

Private fleet a good fit at Levi Strauss & Co.

A lesson in how the strategic use of private trucks can enhance service and cut expenses

By PATRICK GALLAGHER, senior editor

Truck arrives at Levi's* Panatela Sportswear Div., Little Rock, Ark.

*Levi's is the registered trademark of Levi Strauss & Co.

What's the secret to the success of Levi Strauss & Co., the jeans maker that became the largest apparel company in the world? The short answer is, basic quality products backed by a trademark known in Rio as well as in Racine.

A longer answer, though, would have to include mention of a tightly run distribution system that has kept pace with the company's incredible growth and expansion in recent years.

Transportation and distribution personnel have had to keep up with net sales that jumped 7.3 times in ten years—from just $213 million in 1968 to $1,559.3 million in 1977.

The map on page 33 illustrates what this growth has meant in terms of the company's facilities: five large distribution centers and better than 50 sewing plants arrayed across the southern tier of the country. The Sportswear Division's Little Rock distribution center just opened in 1974. And the Henderson, Nevada center is even newer—it opened only last year.

The thread that holds this extended distribution network together is a hard-working proprietary fleet of 30 tractors and 180 trailers. Hauling in conjunction with dozens of common carriers, this private fleet provides Levi's distribution operations with the flexibility it needs.

Corporate Traffic & Transportation Director Joseph Gray and his staff of 11 at Levi's plush San Francisco headquarters have devised a closed-circuit system that supplies the sewing plants with material, the distribution centers with inventory, and thousands of retailers with jeans, shirts, and other apparel articles, and does it with a minimum of delay.

So service is the motto of the private fleet, although not at the expense of efficiency. Levi's trucks run loaded 85 percent of the time,

Experience has taught us that we can operate much cheaper than a common carrier in many cases.

---

states Mr. Gray. That figure compares favorably with most common carriers and tops the average private fleet by a good margin.

Keep it lean

A private fleet is virtually a necessity when a company's facilities are located in a lot of out-of-the-way places like Brownsville, Texas, and Clovis, New Mexico. However, necessity is no guarantee of effectiveness.

A three-pronged strategy to achieve the most effective use of the fleet might be described, cansisting of:
- inbound consolidation
- pool distribution
- tight cost control.

Mr. Gray and Corporate Transportation Manager Robert M. Amos keep the fleet lean by constant comparison with what the common car-

rier "competition" is offering.

"We know that we can operate much cheaper than a common carrier in many cases," says Mr. Amos. "Experience has taught us that." Levi's private trucks can get in and out on schedule or at odd hours, and the company can boost driver efficiency with incentives.

"Yet a carrier may come in with a good rate," notes Mr. Gray, "and if we can't compete with it, we don't bother. We'll give them the business. Our savings have to be some percentage less that it would cost to move it by common carrier.

"Sometimes, I'll be meeting with our drivers," says Mr. Gray, "and I'll get out the blackboard. We're moving it from here to here, I'll say. So is the common carrier. Here's our cost; here's his cost. See that spread? That's what it was a year ago—want to see it today? You're competing with the common carrier. In two more months, that won't be our traffic; it'll go back to him."

Mr. Gray is now experimenting with a new method of allocating the expenses of the private fleet that has one of the company's divisions paying a fixed rate: 85 percent of the common carrier rates and charges. The policy reiterates the idea that the fleet must operate efficiently, while also making life easier for the divisional traffic managers.

Until last year, expenses were allocated back to the division at cost. But the traffic managers find themselves unable to calculate their freight expenses in advance. A truck might make a run from one of the Womenswear sewing plants down in the tip of Texas to the Amarillo distribution center and then deadhead to El Paso to pick up a shipment for the Jeanswear distribution center in Henderson.

The cost for the empty miles between Amarillo and El Paso is split between the two divisions. It

happens constantly and it adds up. Now the transportation department charges its 85-percent rate and may wash back any surplus "profit" to the divisions semi-annually, or annually.

Levi's gets a lot of work out of its fleet (7.3 million miles run in 1978, with less than 15 percent empty miles), but the fleet still accounts for less than 25 percent of the company's total domestic transportation bill. The balance is divided among motor common carriers, United Parcel Service, and Parcel Post.

Rail is a minor factor at Levi's, as is air. Only occasional samples sent to the San Francisco headquarters or rush orders for the sewing facilities move by air; they add up to less than one percent.

A strict division between Levi's U.S. Group and International Group keeps imports and exports to a minimum. Almost everything sold here is made here, and everything sold abroad is manufactured abroad.

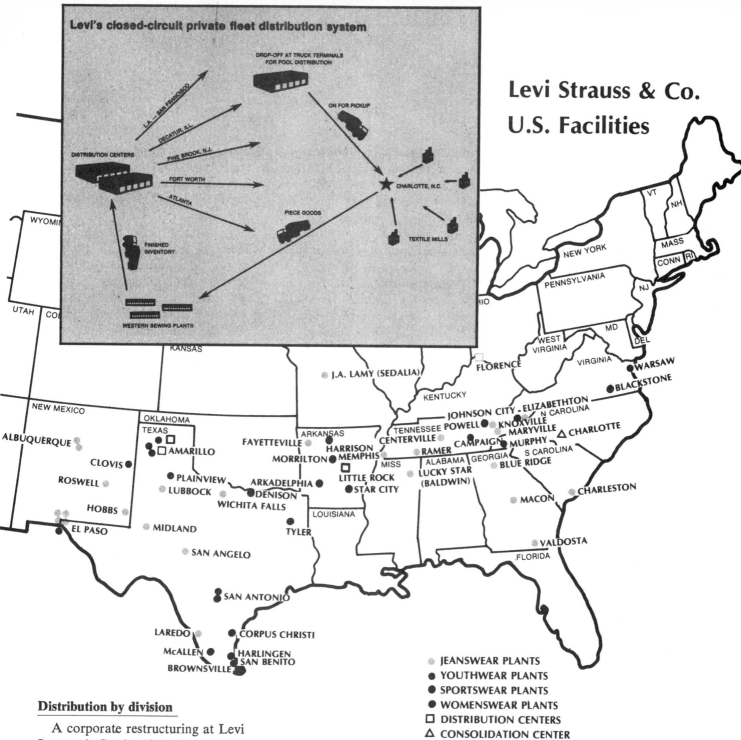

Levi Strauss & Co. U.S. Facilities

Levi's closed-circuit private fleet distribution system

DROP-OFF AT TRUCK TERMINALS FOR POOL DISTRIBUTION

ON FOR PICKUP

DISTRIBUTION CENTERS

L.A. — SAN FRANCISCO
DECATUR, ILL.
PINE BROOK, N.J.
FORT WORTH
ATLANTA

CHARLOTTE, N.C.

PIECE GOODS

TEXTILE MILLS

FINISHED INVENTORY

WESTERN SEWING PLANTS

Map labels:

WYOMING · UTAH · COLORADO · KANSAS · NEW MEXICO · OKLAHOMA · TEXAS · ARKANSAS · LOUISIANA · MISS · ALABAMA · GEORGIA · FLORIDA · TENNESSEE · KENTUCKY · OHIO · WEST VIRGINIA · VIRGINIA · N CAROLINA · S CAROLINA · MD · DEL · NJ · PENNSYLVANIA · NEW YORK · CONN · RI · MASS · NH · VT

J.A. LAMY (SEDALIA) · FLORENCE · WARSAW · BLACKSTONE · JOHNSON CITY - ELIZABETHTON · POWELL · KNOXVILLE · MARYVILLE · CHARLOTTE · MURPHY · CAMPAIGN · RAMER · CENTERVILLE · FAYETTEVILLE · HARRISON · MEMPHIS · MORRILTON · LITTLE ROCK · STAR CITY · LUCKY STAR (BALDWIN) · BLUE RIDGE · MACON · CHARLESTON · ALBUQUERQUE · CLOVIS · ROSWELL · HOBBS · EL PASO · AMARILLO · PLAINVIEW · LUBBOCK · DENISON · WICHITA FALLS · ARKADELPHIA · MIDLAND · TYLER · SAN ANGELO · VALDOSTA · SAN ANTONIO · LAREDO · McALLEN · BROWNSVILLE · CORPUS CHRISTI · HARLINGEN · SAN BENITO

○ JEANSWEAR PLANTS
● YOUTHWEAR PLANTS
● SPORTSWEAR PLANTS
● WOMENSWEAR PLANTS
□ DISTRIBUTION CENTERS
△ CONSOLIDATION CENTER

Distribution by division

A corporate restructuring at Levi Strauss & Co. in 1972 that created the U.S. and international groups also realigned domestic operations into four marketing divisions: Jeanswear, Youthwear, Sportswear, and Womenswear.

Distribution activities proceed autonomously along these divisional lines. Traffic managers in each of the five distribution centers (the Jeanswear division has two) control the flow of products from Levi's sewing facilities into their distribution centers as inventory and then out again for retail distribution.

They report to the distribution center managers who in turn report to divisional presidents or vice presidents.

In this setup, the corporate traffic and transportation department acts as a service function, operating the proprietary fleet and providing a corporate overview on traffic and rate matters.

Perhaps from a pure physical distribution point of view, this is not the best possible world. But for a marketing-oriented company like

Levi Strauss, it works very well. There are the usual communications problems between the main office and the divisions, says Mr. Gray, but nothing significant.

"We are in a good position here to see the total picture. First, all the operating division staffs are right in the building—their national production people, their inventory people, all the raw materials schedulers. We have contact with them on a constant day-to-day basis. Then our people at each one of the

207

Here, unit loads are staged for shipment to major market areas for breakout to retailers.

Each distribution center may move more than 3,000 shipments on an average day, including many small orders like these.

three fleet bases have contact with each of the plant and D.C. managers and with the major mills.

"So we see the overall picture," says Mr. Gray, "whereas the people in the field at the distribution centers are probably aware of it, but not as aware as we are."

From this vantage, Mr. Gray has been able to institute several innovations in the use of the private fleet since he came aboard five years ago.

Levi Strauss had been operating its own trucks since 1961, but responsibility for the fleet was scattered. The distribution center manager in Amarillo controlled trucks based there, the Knoxville production manager had his trucks, and the Memphis manager had his. The trucks were used simply to supplement the common carriers, with little thought given to overall cost.

"While we had the responsibility for running it," says Mr. Amos, "we still didn't have real control. The drivers still reported locally to the respective production or D.C. manager. We decided to bring it all in under central management and take complete control."

Inbound consolidation

More recently, the traffic department undertook a study of the volume and movement of the piece goods Levi's buys from various suppliers like Burlington Industries and Cone Mills, located primarily in the Carolinas.

Levi's controls the transportation of the material through piece-goods schedulers in each division who report their purchasing and scheduling activities. Mr. Gray's traffic department then routes the shipments by the Levi's fleet or by common carrier and notifies the sewing plants as to the routings.

The study of these inbound ship-

ments showed that Levi's was moving about 30 million pounds of LTL piece goods each year out of the Carolinas area to points west of the Mississippi.

Pointing to the map, Mr. Gray indicates some of Levi's far-flung plants. "If you can see where some of these are located, say, down in that southern tip of Texas around Brownsville and Corpus Christi, you can understand why we were having problems.

"It was taking anywhere from 15 to 20 days to get something there on an LTL basis," he says. "The shipments were going through two or three carriers on an interline, and by the time the goods got there at all, they were in no shape to be used."

Here's what Levi's did: First, they searched around for a carrier who could provide the broadest coverage of the major mill locations in the Southeast at a good rate. They found it in Standard Trucking, of Charlotte, N.C.

Standard now handles most of this traffic, supplemented by various other carriers for those movements outside of its tariffs.

Levi's set up shop with a supervisor at their leased facility in Charlotte. The piece goods are delivered there from the mills, consolidated, and reloaded onto Levi's private trucks or common carrier for straight runs to the distant sewing plants. Those particular trucks in this service had been domiciled in Knoxville before, but were scheduled to be relocated to the new Charlotte base. That has now been done.

"We sometimes have to hold the goods two or three days to get a full truckload," says Mr. Gray, "but even so, we get it down to Texas and that area much quicker and much more cheaply.

"The studies told us we could probably handle 50 percent of these movements on our own equipment. In fact, we are moving 80 percent of it on our trucks."

A failure of common carrier service? No, just that Levi's has been extremely successful in using these movements to balance out their east-bound movements of finished goods. Putting the purchased piece goods onto the private trucks completes the circuit and offers better service at the same time.

So far, the transportation department has concentrated on consolidating those piece-goods shipments less than 20,000 yards (about 20,000 pounds), and even that has been almost too much to handle. But Mr. Gray affirms that he hopes "to tighten things up a little bit and control those movements ranging between 20,000 and 30,000 pounds as well."

Eastern drops

As for the other half of the private fleet circuit, it's working pretty well too. Levi's runs major pool distribution drops from four of the five distribution centers to several strategic points around the U.S. where local motor carriers provide the delivery service to retailers in these big marketing centers.

The delivering carriers are selected on the basis of the breadth of their coverage in the particular area and on their willingness to put in distribution rates, says Mr. Gray.

In the Southwest, Levi's is using Merchants Fast Motor Express. California Motor Express handles the pool distribution in California while AAA Trucking serves the big Mid-Atlantic region and up into New England. Another pool drop is made to Spector Freight in Decatur, Ill., and Suburban in Indianapolis, for breakout in the Midwest and East.

A profile

Only in recent years has private carriage been given due credit for the key role it plays in corporate distribution strategy and in the overall transportation system. This isn't news to Joe Gray, however.

Levi Strauss & Co.'s director of traffic & transportation has managed more than a few private company fleets during the 30 years he's been in the transportation business.

"I've always handled my job more or less as a consultant," he says. "I was in consulting years ago in Philadelphia, and I've been with a number of major companies across the country handling private fleets. I like the overview a consultant has."

A big straightforward man, he makes his points carefully, leaning back in his chair. The expanse of the San Francisco waterfront gleams through his office window.

It can be a touchy business, he explains, since in theory a private fleet manager's primary task is trying to negotiate rates and contracts with various carriers to lessen the company's dependence on the private fleet.

Of course in the real world today, matters almost never get to that point because the good manager is simultaneously trying to make his fleet as strong as possible.

But, Mr. Gray emphasizes, this paradox demands that the private fleet manager be something of a diplomat in his dealings with his employees, the ones who make it all work.

"My basic philosophy is to show them the economics of what they're doing. We say, help us run this fleet as efficiently as we can. It's your security."

Unlike many private fleet managers, Joe Gray's background isn't the trucking business. He is a graduate of the Wharton School at the University of Pennsylvania, majoring in transportation and ocean shipping. He is also an ICC practitioner.

Prior to joining Levi Strauss & Co. in 1974, Mr. Gray worked for such companies as American

Joe Gray

Metal Climax, Phillip Morris, Container Corporation of America, and Pennwalt. He worked for the government for a time, too. His well-traveled career has brought him into contact with many local traffic associations. Before moving on from Phillip Morris, he served as president of the Piedmont Traffic Club of Virginia.

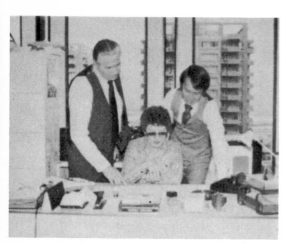

Joe Gray checks over a report with Corporate Transportation Manager Bob Amos and Administrative Assistant Rebecca Chrisman.

Right now, Mr. Gray is working with Traffic Services Manager Don Miller on a plan to bring United Parcel Service into the pool drop. Skids to be slugged to UPS terminals in the various regions could be added to Levi's trucks when they are loading for their regular pool drop runs. The truck bound for AAA in Pine Brook, N.J., could make that drop and shoot over to the UPS terminal in Carlstadt, N.J.

So far, there have been some difficulties in getting our distribution center personnel acclimated to the new UPS arrangement, admits Mr. Gray, but it's done elsewhere and the benefits would be great.

"It's a question of service, making these pool drop runs," he says. "In some cases, it would be cheaper to give it to the common carrier, but it might be switched or transloaded through several breakbulk points across the country to New York. If it's LTL, you know damn well it's going to Oklahoma City or Dallas from Amarillo and from there—where? Who knows, it depends on the carrier. It may then be broken out in Cleveland or Columbus and then again in New Jersey somewhere.

"Whereas, if our truck leaves Amarillo at midnight, 36 to 40 hours later it's going to be in Pine Brook (N.J.)," says Mr. Gray. "If it's going to New England, it will be broken out across the dock and on its way to Boston for delivery that evening."

When UPS shipments are integrated into the plan, Levi's expects to be able to move on a daily scheduled basis.

"Our salesmen love these pools," says Mr. Gray. "They can now go to the carrier and say, I know when this was shipped from, say, Amarillo. It was on Trailer No. K-19,

Pool Run No. 16, due to arrive such and such a day and hour. Can you give me disposition of the movement?

"And the carrier can supply the information. Before, we could give it to a common carrier on a direct LTL basis and tracing the shipment was a real problem."

The fleet

When we talked with Levi's, they were in the process of ordering 28 pieces of highway power equipment for expansion and replacement. The fleet's power units are all Kenworths—some owned, some finance-leased. Ryder provides the maintenance for the whole fleet on contract at each of the bases.

The trailer fleet includes both 40- and 42-footers, but the shorter ones are being phased out and replaced with 45-footers to gain the extra cube and to better match the "competing" common carriers' 45-foot capability.

As Levi's has gotten more into fashion goods, it has retrofitted some trailers with racks to take hanging garments. Carpeted floors in all the hanging garment trailers is another extra that makes sense for Levi's.

After all, this is an expensive commodity and easily damaged. In fact, the high value thieves put on Levi's jeans may be one of the less-often mentioned incentives for utilizing private trucks.

Therefore, the company has taken such precautions as eliminating all markings from the outside containers and keeping the packing slip inside the box.

These and other administrative changes have been successful in keeping Levi Strauss' distribution operations in fit form in recent years when explosive growth threatened to burst some seams. ■

Editorial

Freight Loss and Damage and Carrier Profits

When he made a speech at the fifteenth regular meeting of the Mountain-Plains Shippers Board last February 15, in Denver, H. D. Knudson, assistant manager of freight claim prevention for the Burlington Northern, gave the members of his audience a well-prepared assortment of information and advice about prevention of freight loss and damage as a means of preserving profits — for shippers as well as for carriers. He probably gave no thought to the possibility that his speech, as reproduced in the board's "Proceedings," published several weeks after the February meeting, would provide material desired by this writer for use on this page. In any event we are thankful for the help he has given us.

Several of the points made by Mr. Knudson on the subject of profit-conservation through careful handling of freight shipments have been made on many other occasions by many other speakers over a period of many years. Nevertheless, those points need to be restated often and forcefully. We think Mr. Knudson did an excellent job, at the shipper board meeting in Denver, of giving fresh and vigorous impetus to what should be a spirited and unceasing campaign, conducted cooperatively by carriers and shippers to reduce sharply the "FL & D" losses that can be attributed to inadequate loss-or-damage-prevention efforts. Who would contradict Mr. Knudson's assertion that rail losses in the form of freight claim payments constitute massive, unadulterated economic waste?

"The survival of our transportation industry or any other business," Mr. Knudson said, "is based on economics. It is the profit dollar that keeps us alive and active, and this is exactly why loss and damage prevention is of primary importance, not only to Burlington Northern, but to all carriers. It should be equally important to the manufacturers and shippers and, finally, to the consumer.

"Every dollar that carriers pay out in loss and damage claims is a profit dollar. In other words, figuring at a 6-per-cent profit, for every $100 paid out in claims the marketing department has to generate approximately $1,700 of new business, whereas with a good damage-prevention program the same $100 profit can be returned by a reduction in claims of $125."

What does good claim-prevention mean for shippers (who in some instances have only themselves to blame for delivery of their goods in damaged condition to the consignees, or for non-delivery of the goods)? Mr. Knudson pointed out that the shipper is in business to make a profit, that his profit depends on getting the product to the right place at the right time and in the proper condition, and that arrival of the product in unsatisfactory condition makes it for all practical purposes the wrong product, so that the seller has a dissatisfied customer who rarely has to look far to find other sellers who may serve him better. And, Mr. Knudson added, although claims for loss or damage may be paid in full, the shipper is not compensated for lost production or for the cost of filing the claims; manufacturing schedules are delayed; employes of the shipper may be laid off because of a temporary shortage of materials caused by the in-transit damage or loss of in-

bound freight; the profit from a sale is lost, and seasonal markets may be lost completely.

As noted by Mr. Knudson, there are cases of "blundering incompetence" among shippers as well as among the railroads. There are companies that don't package their products adequately, companies that don't load or unload their goods properly, companies that load a damaged product (apparently expecting the carriers to perform a miracle and deliver the product in undamaged condition), and "companies that just don't give a damn."

Another aspect of the "FL & D" problem that's a cause of growing concern, said Mr. Knudson, is the fact that since 1969 the losses from theft, pilferage and vandalism that the nation's carriers have experienced have increased by 480 per cent. The outlook for any substantial decline in this loss category, he said, is not good, overall crime having increased seven times faster than the U.S. population. Trailer hijackings and the disappearance of entire carloads of cargo account for less than 10 per cent of the national dollar value of freight cargo losses, while pilferage (committed in some instances by employes who regard pilgerage as a vested interest of their employment) accounts for about 80 per cent of the shipping industry's cargo losses, the Mountain-Plains board was told.

Forming especially noteworthy parts of Mr. Knudson's speech were his delineations of actions taken by the BN to halt pilferage and in oher ways to cut down its payouts for freight loss and damage.

The railroads' total freight claim bill for 1977, according to the Association of American Railroads, was $277,793,469, with a ratio of $1.29 spent on claim payments out of each $100 of revenue.

"Burlington Northern's share of this claim bill totaled $14.5 million, and we had a ratio of 88 cents per $100 of revenue," said Mr. Knudson. "Compared to the year 1976, we had a reduction in claims of $3.5 million and a ratio-to-revenue decrease of 32 cents. . . . Claims are not always paid in the year damage occurred; therefore, the results of any prevention effort must be viewed as a long-term effort. In this light, had the Burlington Northern paid claims in 1977 at the same ratio as were the claims paid at the time of merger, 1970, our claim bill would have amounted to $25 million."

Loss and damage prevention on the BN, it was stated, is "a staff function reporting directly to senior management," and in each of the five BN regions there is a trained damage-prevention staff. The training is built on "a foundation of skills and attitudes," and an important part of it is in the area of customer contact, "where the necessary cooperative effort starts and is maintained."

The record of accomplishment by the BN in making an impressive reduction of the ratio of the claim payment total to the revenue total, as reported by Mr. Knudson, proves that the "FL & D" situation is far from being hopeless and that it's possible for carriers, no matter how large or small they may be, to increase their profit-dollar totals by making forceful and tenacious claim-prevention efforts that are well managed. Such efforts should also be well rewarded.

In the Wake of 'Toto'

by Colin Barrett
Transportation Consultant

". . . The rule that motor carrier operating authority is not to be granted to an applicant who intends to use it primarily as an incident to carriage of its own goods and its own business is rejected. . . ."

With these words the Interstate Commerce Commission in the spring of 1978 opened up a new option for private motor carriers—an option which had previously been denied them for more than 40 years. Henceforth, the ICC ruled, private carriers will have the same opportunity as anyone else to haul federally regulated traffic on a for-hire basis.

The case in which the Commission issued its precedent-shattering decision is docket MC-141414 (Sub-No. 1), entitled Toto Purchasing & Supply, Inc., Common Carrier Application, embracing MC-142108 (Sub-No. 1), Avon Corrugated Corp. Contract Carrier Application (report published at 128 MCC 873)—known for short as the Toto case. Subsequently the ruling was affirmed in a proceeding docketed as Ex Parte MC-118 with the formidable title of "Grant of Motor Carrier Operating Authority to an Applicant Who Intends to Use It Primarily as an Incident to the Carriage of Its Own Goods and Its Own Non-Transportation Business'—The Grant of Authority case.

The Toto and Grant of Authority decisions give the private carrier a new potential way of balancing its operations—hauling ICC-regulated traffic. As a result, many private carriers are faced with a difficult decision to make: Should they, or should they not, seek to fill out their empty backhauls by providing transportation service for others? It is a decision that has not for the most part heretofore confronted the private carrier.

Pre-Regulation Era

In the early days of motor carriage few, if any, restrictions were imposed on what a truck operator might haul. Advertisements in many business publications read, in effect, "Have truck, will travel"—and that was about the way the business worked in those days. A truck oeprator would get a load going from here to there, and he was on his way.

There are those who believe this is the way things should still be today. But unfortunately this way of operating led, as the trucking industry grew, to some chaotic conditions. Large shippers whipsawed one truck operator against another, forcing rates far below realistic levels as related to costs; small shippers had to take what was left over, sometimes at rates the truckers pegged defensively high. Neither shippers nor carriers prospered, especially after the Great Depression of the 1930's struck, and both began clamoring for controls to stabilize the industry.

Motor Carrier Act

In 1935 Congress passed, and President Roosevelt signed, the so-called Motor Carrier Act, now Part II of the Interstate Commerce Act. It gave the ICC authority to control interstate transportation of freight by motor vehicle; from then on no trucker might haul goods which crossed state lines unless authorized to do so by the Commission.

There were exceptions to this law. For example, agricultural commodities—raw farm produce—could still be transported

Basic Issues in Hot Debate

The Interstate Commerce Commission's recent decision in the so-called "Toto case"—reaffirmed in a rule-making proceeding late last year—makes a major change in the basic fabric of motor carrier regulation. For the first time, it allows private motor carriers to apply for operating rights to provide regulated for-hire service as common and contract carriers.

To private carriers, the ruling opens up new ways of filling out empty backhaul movements and otherwise improving the economics of their motor transport operations. To existing common and contract carriers, it creates a new body of potential competitors for their business, as well as encouraging more companies to shift their own traffic to private carriage.

The ruling goes into effect on January 19. Meanwhile, the American Trucking Associations has asked a federal court to overturn the Commission's ruling.

This article outlines the basic issues that are involved in this debate. It is extracted from a new book entitled "The For-Hire Option for Private Carriers." The book is available from the author, a transportation consultant, 11764 Indian Ridge Road, Reston, Va. 22091, at $29.50 postpaid.

without regulatory authority.[1] And businesses which used their own trucks to haul their own goods were also exempted from the ICC's jurisdiction.[2] But by and large the bulk of all interstate highway transportation had been placed under the Commission's control. When the various states, one by one, followed suit with respect to traffic moving within their own boundaries (indeed, some state laws even pre-dated the Federal statute), the pioneering era in motor transportation, with its associated freedoms, was at an end.

A relatively small number of companies had, even then, already started their own trucking operations, hauling their own goods to their customers or from their suppliers. Because this type of service was often a one-way operation—with the company having a substantial volume of traffic headed from point A to point B, but nothing, or next to it, coming back from B to A—some of these private truckers had also started handling a little backhaul traffic for others. Under so-called "grandfather" provisions of the law, this handful of private truckers was eligible for operating authority to continue providing the same service that they had previously provided.[3]

For-Hire Ban on Private Carriers

But then the ICC slammed the door. In the future, it said, no company that was primarily in a non-transportation business and used trucks principally to haul its own goods would be permitted to transport traffic for anyone else.[4] Once again, the states largely followed suit, and the "great divide" between private and for-hire motor transportation was established.

[1] 49 U.S.C. 10526(a)(6) (Section 203(b)(6) of the IC Act).

[2] 49 U.S.C. 10102(13) (section 203(a)(17) of the IC Act).

[3] See, for example, Bowar Bros., Inc., Contract Carrier Application, 11 MCC 123 (1939); H. V. Grantham & Sons Extension of Operations, 20 MCC 457 (1939); Chas. Maronna & Co., Inc., Common Carrier Application, 26 MCC 281 (1940); Edgar A. Gill Extensionof Operations, 26 MCC 593 (1940); Southern Utah Produce Co. Common Carrier Application, 29 MCC 767 (1941); Irving A. Villaume Contract Carrier Application, 30 MCC 92 (1941); Thomas F. Buzby Contract Carrier Application, 33 MCC 226 (1942), and Thomas W. Watkins & Son, Inc., Common Carrier Application, 41 MCC 564 (1942).

The rule wasn't quite absolute; every once in a while the ICC opened the door a crack to let a private carrier into the for-hire business under what it referred to as "special circumstances." For example, in several cases it found that private carriers could transport for-hire traffic so long as the private and for-hire operations were not "complementary"— that is, the private operations weren't predominantly in one direction, with the for-hire service filling out what would otherwise be an empty backhaul.[5] A private carrier that operated on a strictly seasonal basis was allowed to offer for-hire service during the balance of the year.[6] Where the for-hire operations were the carrier's primary business, with private carriage constituting only a relatively small part of the traffic, operating authority was granted in several cases.[7] The same was done where there was no existing common- or contract-carrier service to compete with the private carrier's for-hire operations.[8]

But, although (as the ICC phrased it in the Toto decision) "riddled with exceptions," the basic rule that private carriers may not haul goods for others on a for-hire basis remained paramount for

[4] See James C. Duros Contract Carrier Application, 2 MCC 406 (1937); Charles F. Geraci Contract Carrier Application, 7 MCC 369 (1938), and Lorene C. Bales Common Carrier Application, 9 MCC 709 (1938). Geraci is usually considered the "lead case" in this regard.

[5] See, for example, Brooks-Gillespie Motors, Inc., Common Carrier Application, 14 MCC 631 (1939); George E. Biddison Contract Carrier Application, 28 MCC 205 (1941); W. P. Ross & Sons Contract Carrier Application, 31 MCC 473 (1941); The James Gibbons Co. Contract Carrier Application, 31 MCC 635 (1942), and Garrison Elevator Co., Inc., Extension, 69 MCC 99 (1956). There were also several other cases where the Commission found in other respects that the private and for-hire carrier operations would be essentially unrelated, and hence not debarred by the Geraci doctrine: See R. B. Zimmerman Contract Carrier Application, 27 MCC 650 (1941); Harry A. Thrun Extension of Operations, 46 MCC 484 (1946); Fuller Contract Carrier Application, 73 MCC 716 (1957); Preston K. Moyer Common Carrier Application, 83 MCC 83 (1960), and North-eastern-Malden Barrel Co., Inc., Contract Carrier Application, 83 MCC 705 (1960). Such grants of operating rights have ben upheld by the courts; see Beard-Laney v. U.S., 338 U.S. 803, affirming 83 F.Supp. 271.

[6] See Good Roads Co., Inc., Contract Carrier Application, 10 MCC 183 (1938).

[7] See, for example, Carl Dohrman and Bernard L. Dohrman Common Carrier Application, 31 MCC 680 (1941); Redland Oil Co., Inc., Contract Carrier Application, 91 MCC 771 (1963), and Wycoff Co., Inc., Extension, 92 MCC 549 (1963).

[8] See, for example, Charles C. Wood Common Carrier Application, 10 MCC 389 (1938), and L. Zeisloft Common Carrier Application, 12 MCC 13 (1938).

40 years. The average private carrier that sought authority from the ICC to handle traffic as a for-hire common or contract carrier faced the prospect of having its application denied almost automatically.[9]

Since state regulatory agencies largely followed the ICC's lead, the private carrier's options were severely restricted. It could try to balance its operations with its own traffic—such as by hauling finished products from its plant or warehouse at point A to its customer at point B, and then hauling supplies back from B (or somewhere near there) to its plant at A. Or it could seek to pick up unregulated loads of agricultural products, which were exempt from ICC control, for the backhaul movement. Or it could simply accept the prospect that its trucks would move loaded only half the time.

But not every private trucker was fortunate enough to have its customers located within reasonable proximity of its suppliers, so many could not combine trips that way. Agricultural products move largely on a seasonal basis, and in many cases agricultural markets didn't jibe with the private carriers' backhaul routes. And moving private-carrier equipment empty on most or all backhauls does a good deal of violence to the economics of private trucking.

This is what the Toto and Grant of Authority decisions have changed. They have afforded private carriers, at last, a fourth option—the option of handling regulated traffic for others on their backhaul movements.

Reasons for the Ban

At the time it made its original rule that private carriers should be barred from transporting traffic for-hire for others, the ICC gave three reasons:
"(1) It would be an anomalous situation under which a single operator of motor vehicles would at one and the same time, as to different parts of its operations, be a private carrier not subject to regulation and a (for-hire) carrier subject to regulation. The difficulties which such a status would present with reference to accounting, statistics, issue of securities, unifications and the like are obvious.
"(2) Apart from this objection to such a combination of functions, it is clear that the public interest, as declared in the policy of Congress, requires motor carriers able to supply 'adequate, economical and efficient service' to the public 'without unjust discriminations, undue preferences or advantages, and unfair or destructive competitive practices.' A private carrier has the advantages of an assured traffic ob-

[9] In recent years the Geraci doctrine was re-examined twice by the Commission, in Ralph A. Veon, Inc., Contract Carrier Application, 92 MCC 248 (1963), and Stilwell Canning Co., Inc., Common Carrier Application, 123 MCC 614 (1975). Both times it was reaffirmed.

tained without solicitation expense, freedom from the expenses which public regulation necessarily entails, and often an overhead or management expense shared with the commercial enterprise for which the hauling is being done. A disadvantage which it often suffers is lack of a well-balanced traffic in both directions. If the private carrier be able to overcome this disadvantage by operating as a (for-hire) carrier in one direction, it is evident that advantages which it enjoys in its private carriage will enable it to compete on better than even terms with most contract carriers (and) common carriers.
"(3) . . . Many private carriers are associated with large industries. If private carriers generally were permitted to engage in (for-hire) operations, . . . it is clear that the results might seriously affect the maintenance of adequate and efficient service by the motor common carriers upon whom the general public must depend, and by the contract carriers who do not also engage in private carriage. We are of the opinion that such a mixture of private-carrier and (for-hire) operations is definitely inconsistent with the public interest. . . ."[10]

Fallacies of the Ban

Not until 1978, in its Toto and Grant of Authority decisions, did the Commission publicly acknowledge what many had long believed—that these arguments were full of holes through which (quite literally) a truck might be, or at least should be, driven.

For example, the Commission admitted that point No. 1—the difficulty of separating a company's private and for-hire transport activities—could be overcome quite simply. All that is necessary, it concluded, is to require that each private carrier "conduct its for-hire motor carrier activities and its other activities independently, and . . . maintain separate records of each."[11]

The remaining points posed some tougher issues, forcing the ICC to make some extraordinary adjustments in its regulatory posture. The first of these is, basically, just what duty the Commission owes to the common and contract carriers subject to its control. In other words, to what extent should the Commission protect them from competition?

This question lies at the heart of the regulatory debate that is currently raging in the Congress as well as numerous public and industry forums. For decades the ICC's view has been that, basically, it must defend the regulated for-hire carrier industry against competitive incursions in order to protect its economic stability—even at the cost of higher rates and poorer service to shippers than more open

[10] Geraci, 7 MCC 369 at 372.

[11] Toto, 128 MCC 873 at 881.

competition might allow. With this commitment toward the carriers under its aegis, the Commission understandably looked askance at the prospect of non-transportation firms entering the for-hire trucking business as something of a "sideline," taking business away from the full-time carriers.

Add to this the ICC's traditional antipathy for private carriage, which it has appeared to feel contributes next to nothing to the overall U.S. transportation system. For decades private carriers learned to expect that, in any close decision involving private carriage, the ICC was sure to come down against them. The Commission seemed to take its statutory mission to protect the public interest in a curiously literal-minded sense: the broader a section of the public a carrier served, the more the ICC was wont to favor that carrier. And private carriers, being the most restrictive of all in their range of service, wound up at the bottom of the totem pole.

Why the ICC Changed Its View

Two major factors caused the ICC to re-examine its stance in these areas. First there is the growing disfavor into which regulation has fallen philosophically. The once-prevalent belief that a controlled oligopoly is needed for transportation stability is giving way to a view that freer competition will not lead to serious instability and may result in better service and lower rates for the public. The current climate of economic inflation has given this thesis a considerable boost, especially with opponents of regulation asserting vigorously that too-strict controls push rates excessively high.

Of more immediate concern is the heavy focus on U.S. energy problems that has featured the post-1973 era. Our last three Presidents have strongly emphasized the national need to conserve energy, and particularly petroleum-generated energy – a point on which they have garnered considerable support from both Congress and the public at large. In the face of this broad-based drive for energy conservation, ICC policies that force oil-burning trucks

to run empty for long distances, no matter what the reason, are highly unpopular.[12]

Confronted with these pressures, the Commission took another look at its competitive concerns. On second thought, it said, the private carrier probably won't have any insuperable competitive advantage over its for-hire brethren; after all, it must assume the same problems and costs as anyone else in the handling of regulated traffic. And it found that private carriers aren't likely to use "low-ball" pricing techniques simply to fill up their empty backhauls, for this would come into conflict with the modern "profit center" concept of management – the view that every aspect of the business must seek to maximize its contribution to overall corporate profits. Finally, it noted, "the Commission can police any threatened abuses in this area through its ratemaking functions."[13]

Relying on the Shipper's Judgment

But that still left one issue to be considered – the possibility that private carriers entering the for-hire market might operate in a discriminatory fashion, favoring their own traffic over that of others. It was here that the Commission made perhaps its most extraordinary concession.

Going back to beginnings, the Interstate Commerce Act was written, and the ICC was created, primarily for the purpose of preventing unjust discrimination in the transportation industry. The possibility that a carrier might give preference to one shipper over another is anathema to this concept, and the Commission has long taken the view that even the threat of such discrimination (or, as it's sometimes phrased, "undue preference and prejudice") was enough to disqualify a proposed operation. The public, it has long held, must be protected at all costs from the possibility of such discrimination.

With this long history, it is almost shocking to hear the Commission saying that perhaps the public is smart enough to protect itself in some cases. But here are its own words:

"We can find little to be realistically concerned about when the shippers intending to use the (carrier's) services are aware that the carrier is controlled by another shipper. The shipper presumably knows the theoretical risks involving in using a carrier which also hauls its own goods. Some deference must be accorded to the business judgment of the shipper in deciding to

use the service. *Indeed, we believe it entirely possible that the shipper's judgment in such matters may be better than ours.*"[14]

Thus, with some important changes in its attitude in several respects, the ICC opened a new era for private carriers.

The decision is not quite a *carte blanche* for private carriers to get into the for-hire transportation business. Under the Toto decision, private carriers seeking to haul traffic for others will have to meet the same standards as any other applicant for motor carrier authority – and those that fail to meet these standards must expect their applications to be denied. Furthermore, the private carrier must keep its private and for-hire operations strictly separate, and must maintain "separate records for each."[15]

But these are relatively minor drawbacks when compared with the disqualifying rule that was invoked against private carriers for so long – in essence, little more than the normal problems any other applicant for common or contract operating rights must face. No private carrier who genuinely wants to enter the for-hire trucking business should find them impossible obstacles to surmount.

So the decision is now a managerial one, which must be made by the management of each private carrier: Should it, or should it not, transport traffic for others as well as for itself? There are many factors which must be taken into account in the course of making that decision, and – especially for managers who have never before had this option to consider – it will often be a very difficult one.

---

[12]The Commission made a special point of discussing the energy question in its Grant of Authority decision: "We are convinced that the high cost of energy, now and into the foreseeable future, requires us to pay close attention to the need for greater operating efficiency, not only in the for-hire sector, but in all interstate surface transportation. Energy efficiency . . . is best achieved by integration of all the existing systems of surface transportation, not by continued segregation of the private trucking sector." Grant of Authority, p. 11 (43 F.R. 55051 at 55053).

1/8 3/8 Toto, 128 MCC 873 and 883.

[14] Toto, 128 MCC 873 at 882; emphasis added. This language was reiterated verbatim in Grant of Authority, p. 8 (43 F.R. 55051 at 55052).

1/8 5/x Toto, 128 MCC 873 at 883-4; these requirements were reiterated in Grant of Authority, p. 1 (43 F.R. 55051).

Chapter 9
Mass Transit

FREE FARES
WILL
IT WORK?

by Thomas Crosby

From John D. Simpson's utilitarian fifth floor office, he can spot all the clues that make Denver's single-minded reliance on automobiles a frustrating reality.

Simpson's building on six-lane-wide Colorado Avenue is within a bus token's throw of four fast food restaurants, a three-story block-long parking lot stuffed with cars, two car dealerships, two car washes and a service station.

As general manager of Denver's Regional Transportation District (RTD) for the past five years, Simpson, like other transit executives nationwide, has been seeking the formula that will alter his city's automobile dependent habits. And, although all the evidence is not yet in, Simpson may have found the answer—free fares.

From Feb. 1, 1978, through Jan. 31, 1979, every person riding an RTD bus rode free, except during rush hours. It was the first year-long, system-wide, free-fare transit experiment in a major American city and it boosted RTD's daily ridership from 101,800 to 146,500—the area's highest public transit ridership total in 20 years.

"We won't know whether our experiment was a success or not for several months, after all the data has been analyzed," said Simpson. "The real question is how many people who were induced to travel in the off-peak hours when it was free, will stick with us now that it costs money."

So far, the outlook is promising. In the first week after the 25 cent off-peak fare was re-instated, ridership averaged 133,400 a day—down only 13,100. If ridership remains steady, it will mean approximately $1 million a year more in RTD farebox revenues.

According to surveys, another benefit was a shift of 24,000 people during the free fares from their automobiles onto the bus.

In the RTD area, which covers portions of six counties and the city-county of Denver, decreased automobile driving is significant because of the "brown cloud," an infamous mass of pollution 90 per cent created by automobile exhaust fumes that periodically hover over the city for days when the wind isn't blowing in the proper direction, causing some of the worst air pollution in the United States. When the "brown cloud" appears, public officials plead with commuters to ride RTD but rarely is there any reduction in the 291,000 cars that enter Denver's one-square-mile downtown area daily.

An unexpected benefit from the free fares was a boost in sales at several downtown stores, apparently because people found free transit superior to driving downtown and facing the hassle of traffic and finding a parking space.

In evaluating Denver's free fare, extra RTD ridership and future revenue from converted transit users, reduced automobile driving and increased downtown sales are definite long-range pluses but there were also some minuses.

The experiment cost $5 million, mostly in lost revenue; bus vandalism caused by school children increased; bus drivers objected to driving overcrowded buses; bus scheduling problems surfaced; and regular paying riders complained bitterly about no longer being able to find a seat.

These drawbacks, many of which were resolved during the course of the experiment, will be carefully studied by the Urban Mass Transportation Administration (UMTA), which for years has been intrigued with free fares, pumping millions into fare-free transit projects on a smaller scale and shorter time frame than Denver, which will cost UMTA $3.4 million.

Free fare can be a powerful promotional gimmick, luring people out of cars and onto public transportation, according to James I. Scheiner of Simpson and Curtin, the transportation consulting division of Booz Allen and Hamilton, Inc., which has a $200,000 contract with RTD to gather data on the free-fare program.

"I don't see free fare as a give-away," said Scheiner. "I see it as a habit breaker so that over the long run you actually increase revenue."

Scheiner feels transit systems should have a five-year plan to increase revenue and he believes that six months of free fares is long enough to break old transportation habits, with enough riders converted by then to easily cover the cost of free fares over the

next five years. Simpson agrees, noting that whatever riders free fares are going to attact "happens very quickly. We were up to 145,000 riders in less than two months."

Once the dynamics are understood, free fares may become a superior marketing technique for transit systems. Deleuw, Cather, & Co., under contract with UMTA's Transportation Systems Center, is doing the evaluation and analysis on the Denver project.

"We're looking for insight into ways of providing periodic off-peak free service, if we can understand what makes them stay with us (after free fares end)," said Simpson. "I doubt that we would ever go to sustained off-peak free service. There are too many problems."

One surprise problem was bus scheduling. While ridership totals stabilized quickly, ridership patterns never settled down. Passengers reacted to day-to-day events—shopping promotions, sports events, cultural activities or the weather—causing major ridership jams on specific bus routes and forcing drivers to fall behind schedule.

While all of Denver's 622 buses are radio equipped, at first drivers were reluctant to call in and say they were running late because they feared they might be disciplined, but eventually they learned there wasn't going to be any management backlash.

In order to bolster service on these ever-changing routes, RTD kept a mobile fleet reserve of 20 buses that could be dispatched to augment service on an overcrowded route or replace a broken bus.

However, six months after the program started, about one-third of RTD's 900 bus drivers signed a petition calling for an end to the experiment because of vagrants, vandalism and crowds. And at least one RTD board member also called for an end to the experiment, but it continued.

In most cases, drivers just gritted their teeth when a problem arose, like at 3 p.m. when a high school ended its day and all the students, who normally would walk several blocks home, decided to play the modern version of how many bodies can be crammed into a phone booth, Volkswagen or . . . RTD bus.

In at least one incident, Simpson said regular adult riders all abandoned the bus when they saw several hundred students waiting at a bus stop.

"We got letters from regular riders objecting to the free fares," Simpson said. "They were able to get a seat before and then they couldn't even get on a bus."

And the students brought vandalism.

"In April and May vandalism shot up 75 per cent, even though ridership had gone up only 50 per cent," Simpson said. Before free fare, vandalism costs for RTD averaged $100,000 a year and RTD officials conservatively estimate free fares will add $15,000.

At one junior high school, the bus was a shambles for five days in a row after picking up students who boarded with sharp objects and attacked the bus, even bringing tools and one day removing two bus seats that had been bolted to the floor.

A plainsclothes policeman was assigned to the bus the next week and by pre-arranged secret signal, the bus driver was to head for the nearest police precinct once the policeman was able to identify the people doing the damage.

However, when the students—some of whom were not participating in the vandalism—saw the bus wasn't taking the regular route, they panicked and started pummeling the bus driver, who hunched himself over and drove on.

At the police station Simpson said students kicked out the bus windows and started jumping to the ground as policemen poured out of the precinct to chase them.

"It was a Keystone Kops comedy," said Simpson. "It sounds funny now but at the time it wasn't."

As a result of that incident and others, RTD officials instituted an anti-vandalism campaign in the schools using speeches by Denver Bronco football players. In addition, teen-age "courtesy aides" were hired with federal Comprehensive Education Training Act (CETA) funds to ride buses on troubled routes during the summer. This two-pronged approach worked and the number of vandalism incidents dropped dramatically.

A winter problem was vagrants, who boarded the warm buses to sleep instead of curling up in a chilly doorway. Usually, drivers summoned police on the bus radio and the vagrants, often drunk, smelly and obnoxious, were removed.

217

fares

Aside from the vagrants, others who fell in love with free fares were the young, the low income and the senior citizens. Middle income riders generally opposed it, according to on-bus surveys.

Half of the riders were less than 24 years old, with a yearly income of $10,000 or less, taking the bus to or from work and with limited access to a car. More than a third were regular transit riders who shifted their travel times from the 50-cent-a-ride peak hours (6 a.m. to 8 a.m. and 4 p.m. to 6 p.m.).

Strangely, the peak hour ridership of roughly 60,000 a day never diminished, Simpson said. One theory is shoppers would ride downtown for free, then pay to ride home during the evening rush hours. Another theory is that as more seats became available during rush hour travel, infrequent transit commuters became regular riders.

During the free rides, ridership boomed between noon and 2 p.m. on Colfax Avenue, Denver's major east-west downtown feeder, apparently with shoppers and "lunch bunch" executives going to the better downtown area restaurants.

One major downtown Denver store experienced a 15 per cent increase in gross retail sales and an eight per cent increase among its half-dozen suburban stores.

"They could find no explanation for the increase in sales except free bus service," said Simpson, who is considering in the future having department stores fund free rides for shoppers during major sales.

Denver's RTD already has a good working relationship with the area's businessmen. Between mid-1975 and mid-1976, free fares were offered in downtown Denver and Boulder, just northwest of Denver, in exchange for the businessmen plugging RTD in their advertisements. It cost RTD $50,000 for the free rides but they estimate they received $300,000 worth of advertising from the businessmen.

The RTD undertook the free-fare year after they discovered a $200,000 windfall in their 1978 budget when they had to pay lower than expected interest rates on the sale of $45 million in bonds in 1977.

"The board of directors had been toying with special marketing incentives in the past but had never found a means to do it," said Simpson.

The timing was also right because in later 1977 pollution in Denver reached alarming levels and the state legislature considered ordering free transit during air pollution alerts but no one offered extra funding to support it.

"That was troubling to us," said Simpson. "They were reacting to the problem as a gut issue and no one was dealing with it in an economic way. We wanted a marketing venture approached in a sensible way."

After offering one month of free transit in Denver, UMTA decided to help fund a year's experiment, putting up $3.4 million to pay half the expected cost. The final price tag, however, was only $5 million.

Denver's RTD was able to support the program because it receives its deficit financing from a one-half of one per cent sales tax and has authority to levy a property tax to make up deficits, if necessary.☐

Thomas Crosby covers transportation, among other subjects, for the Washington Star, *and is the author of a new book on the* National Zoo.

Newest Santa Clara County Transit District buses are GM RTS IIs.

Santa Clara County Transit District — A rapidly expanding bus system

Santa Clara County (California) Transit District (SCCTD) will host the 1979 Annual Western Bus Maintenance and Purchasing Forum February 27—28 at the San Jose Park Center Plaza Holiday Inn. Chairman and Transit Moderator of the Forum will be Peter Shambora, SCCTD's director of fleet operations.

SCCTD has a rapidly expanding system providing service to a county of 1,300 square miles and 1.2 million people, one of the nation's fastest growing population centers. The county's "Silicon Valley" is home to a majority of the nation's micro-miniature electronic companies.

January, 1973 was the date SCCTD began operations, after buying out San Jose City Lines, Peninsula Transit Lines (Palo Alto) and Peerless Stage Lines' intracounty service. The District is governed by the Santa Clara County Board of Supervisors and is part of the County Transportation Agency which has responsibility also for general aviation airports, county roads and expressways, bikeways, carpooling and transportation planning.

Operating approximately 900 miles on 44 routes connecting the county's 15 cities, SCCTD in 1978 carried in excess of 13.4 million passengers — a 17 percent increase over the previous year. During fiscal

Passenger shelters in the Santa Clara system will number 45 when the current contract is complete, and 30 more will be installed by the end of this year.

year 1977-78 the transit system operated some 9.9 million miles on the 44 routes. Service included 18 major arterials, 7 local routes, 2 intercounty routes (to Menlo Park and Fremont), 1 regional arterial (to Gilroy), 10 midday routes, 1 express route, 1 route with special service for the handicapped and, in the rural South County area, 3 mini-arterials and Dial-A-Ride service. The arterials provide service at 15 and 30 minute intervals on weekdays and less frequently on evenings and weekends.

October and November 1978 brought several service improvements signalling the start of the "516 — Bus Plan" implementation. Then December saw the inauguration of a brand-new arterial and January brought the District's second and third express routes as well as other improvements.

Over the next two years, additions and extensions will be made monthly until the level of service has more than doubled and over 77 percent of the County's population will live within 1/4 mile of the bus line.

During 1978 the County introduced operational improvements as it installed an "Opticom" signal pre-emption system along portions of one bus line. Twelve intersections were equipped with optical detectors which turn traffic signals green when activated by a device on the coaches. Still in the process of being refined, "Opticom" will be carefully evaluated and may serve as a model for other major transit corridors.

In the interest of increasing passenger comfort, safety and operational efficiency, SCCTD continues to upgrade its 4300 bus stops and to plan for an additional 1700 stops in its expanded system.

Improvements to date include signs at all stops, 200 benches, 430 concrete pads, 180 trash con-tainers, 45 shelters and 82 "duck-outs" (pavement widenings). Pole-mounted signs bearing detailed schedule information have been installed at 90 stops and 17 large information displays have been mounted in passenger shelters.

During the past year, the District constructed its first Park and Ride facility and plans during the current year to build three more. Among other major improvements scheduled for 1978 are three bus transfer centers, two of which will be located adjacent to Southern Pacific commuter rail depots.

The District's current bus fleet numbers 250 and is scheduled to expand to 520 by 1981. Recently released transit studies indicate the need for at least 750 buses and a light rail starter line by 1990.

To bring the fleet up to 520, SCCTD is currently awaiting bid results on an award for 50 ADBs (Advance Design Buses) and will soon invite bids for additional ADBs and 30-foot coaches. Concurrently, the District is transitioning from primarily propane to primarily diesel.

Vehicles in service at this time include the GMC RTS II, Gillig Neoplan, GMC "New Look," Twin Coach and FMC. Some of the District's coaches have the "kneeling" feature and passenger lifts.

Expansion of the bus fleet is being accompanied by expansion of support facilities. Under construction is a major overhaul and repair shop scheduled for completion in February 1979. This 65,000 square foot facility will include a 10-bay body repair area, a 14-bay major overhaul area, a unit repair shop and the District's main parts warehouse. The facility is built on the central core concept for maximum efficiency. Under design is a new 250-bus garage and minor maintenance facility which will replace the original, now functionally

Between 1974 and 1978 the backbone of Santa Clara's transit system was the medium-weight Twin Coach, which is now being phased out in favor of larger, heavier vehicles. Pictured here are Twin Coaches in downtown San Jose.

Santa Clara's fleet will soon include 131 Gillig-Neoplan buses, all with the kneeling feature and 50 with passenger elevators folding out from the front steps.

obsolete, Central division inherited from the former private operator. A third garage will be built in 1979 to serve the small fleet serving the south part of the county.

Upon completion of the current construction program, SCCTD will have four minor maintenance facilities and one major overhaul and repair shop. Any increase in fleet size beyond the planned 520 will require additional minor facilities or expansion of an existing one. Only servicing, inspections and unit changeouts will be performed at the minor maintenance facilities while major or heavy maintenance work will be centralized. SCCTD chose this maintenance scheme after researching "deadhead" costs and fixed asset requirements.

The District's scheduling of bus maintenance is accomplished at the various facilities by use of computer and visual display systems. SCCTD will incorporate CRT monitors into each maintenance control center, allowing the schedulers access to "real time" information on every vehicle. This maintenance system will also interface with the computerized parts system, constantly updating inventory.

Soon to be implemented by the District is a component repair program which will compile data on selected components in order to identify bit and piece items which cause failure, establish "mean time between failures" and provide precise warranty management.

SCCTD, like most transit operators, finds that hiring experienced bus mechanics is next to impossible and that training personnel is a major endeavor. The District is working closely with local union officials in an attempt to design a comprehensive training program to include (1) familiarization training related to new equipment and basic coach knowledge, (2) promotional training to allow employees with incentive to advance at a faster rate and (3) on-the-job training with follow-up instruction and training unique to the shop floor. The new overhaul facility will house a maintenance training center where the resources of vendors, instructors and employees will be used to accomplish the training goals.

The District's maintenance supervisors recently participated in a joint training program conducted by the Regional Transit Association of the Bay Area (RTA). It included supervisors from San Francisco Muni, Golden Gate Transit, San Mateo Transit, AC Transit and BART. SCCTD found this joint supervisory training and the accompanying interchange of ideas very valuable.

Realizing that many of the problems and circumstances associated with growth are not unique to the District, Santa Clara County looks forward to increasing its knowledge and sharing its experience with others in the upcoming maintenance forum. ∎

The new Santa Clara County Transit District (SCCTD) Agnews Terminal begins to take shape in the foreground. Beyond is the new 65,000 square feet major repair and overhaul facility. Harvis Construction Company of South San Francisco is the construction contractor.

The new SCCTD Terminal building, left foreground, and new fueling facility, extreme right, frame the new facility in the background. It will also house the District's main parts warehouse.

The SCCTD North Division maintenance facility features seven bays. When operational, the new facility will relieve major repair pressures from this North Division and the aged Central Division. In addition a 250 coach yard is being designed for the rapidly expanding transit system.

The Bus That Bends

By Deborah H. Noxon

It's front end looks like a regular bus—a new, shiny one with big windows.

The surprise comes toward the back. Just where you would expect a normal-sized bus to end, there's a flexible connector, and hooked on the rear is another half a bus.

This "bus that bends in the middle"—known more officially as an articulated high-capacity transit bus—is the Department of Transportation's newest addition to its arsenal of programs to ease the problems of congested urban streets and rising operating costs.

The rear-end extension makes the articulated buses quite a lot longer than standard U.S. buses—55 to 60 feet long instead of the conventional 40 feet—but the hinge allows for easy maneuvering on crowded downtown streets.

A big plus is the fact that one driver can handle 50 percent more passengers in these buses.

Popular for a long time in Europe, articulated buses are used extensively in such cities as Stockholm, Barcelona, and Munich, but they are just now beginning to appear on American streets.

Back in the old days, when fuel was plentiful and labor costs were low, there wasn't much interest in the United States in these newfangled buses.

Seattle Metro

Above, the first of Seattle Metro's articulated buses went into service in July 1978.

Left, German buses were shipped to this plant in Texas, where the interiors were outfitted and the exteriors were painted.

In the Middle

Before World War II, Twin Coach produced experimental articulated buses, but few were ever sold. In the early 1950s, Continental Trailways also put some articulated buses on its intercity routes, but all of them were retired from service around 1960.

One successful use has been in Washington, D.C., where a small fleet of articulated tourist buses has been taking sightseers around the city since 1967.

The breakthrough into serious mass transit use came in 1965, when AC Transit of Oakland, California, bought one of the Trailways articulated buses, made some extensive modifications to meet its needs and federal safety regulations, and started it running across the bay into San Francisco. After 500,000 miles of service, the bus is still rolling, to a chorus of cheers from riders and operators alike.

AC Transit's success prompted other U. S. transit operators to take another look, and the result is that articulated buses are now on the streets of Seattle and Los Angeles.

Getting them there wasn't easy.

The effort started back in 1972, when a group of transit operators joined in a consortium with the Department of Transportation's Urban Mass Transporta-

tion Administration to develop specifications for "high-capacity" buses for the U. S. market.

The original members of the consortium were AC Transit, Chicago Transit Authority, Dallas Transit System, New York City Transit Authority, Port Authority of Allegheny County (Pittsburgh), Southeastern Michigan Transportation Authority (Detroit), and Southern California Rapid Transit District (Los Angeles). Seattle Metro Transit joined the consortium in 1973. These eight organizations operate 25 percent of the nation's buses and move nearly half the transit riders in the country.

The consortium members had three primary objectives in mind when they started looking into the use of high-capacity buses: to increase the productivity of their work forces, to shorten total trip times, and to give riders more places to sit (a move that some transit operators think would be the most dramatic improvement in buses since the introduction of air conditioning).

The initial budget for the project—including study and design development—was $330,000. The Urban Mass Transportation Administration paid for two-thirds of this, and the members of the consortium put up the rest.

223

Articulated buses have been used successfully for years to take tourists around Washington, D.C.

Uniphoto

The first order of business was debating the merits of the two kinds of high-capacity buses under consideration—articulated buses and double-deckers. Since there wasn't enough time or money to experiment with both kinds, the consortium had to make a choice. Studies showed that articulated buses could serve 90 percent of the U.S. market, whereas double-deckers, because of height limitations in many cities, could serve only 30 percent.

Having settled on the articulated bus, the consortium began deciding on specifications. American operators insisted that the major components be American-made to simplify maintenance work and parts inventories. And the location of the engine was a crucial factor that had to be worked out satisfactorily for the American market.

European articulated buses use a "pancake" engine mounted under the floor of the front section. However, this location makes the floor too high to meet U.S. standards. The floor in the Daimler-Benz coach is 35.4 inches from the ground, and the floor in the German M.A.N. (Maschinenfabriken Augsburg-Nurnburg) is 37 inches high. No pancake-type engines are produced in the U.S., and the flattest available American engine would raise the bus floor to about 40 inches, a height clearly unacceptable in view of the Department's efforts to promote low-floor vehicles that are easily accessible to elderly and handicapped persons. Therefore, the consortium's consulting engineers examined a number of other possibilities, including the typical U.S. rear-mounted engine.

The final specifications for a U.S.-made articulated bus were published in October 1974—just at the time the Urban Mass Transportation Administration was developing specifications for a low-floor Transbus. In order to make the two projects complement each other, the specifications for the articulated bus were revised to include the low floor and other special features of the Transbus. These revised specifications for an "Articulated Transbus" were issued in September 1977. They call for a seating capacity of 74; operation by one person; a length of 60 feet (with an optional 55-foot model); a maximum floor height at the front door of 22 inches, with a kneeling feature that can take it down to 18 inches; a front door width of at least 44 inches; and an area where wheelchairs can be tied

down. The hinge mechanism has to be able to bend 80 degrees horizontally and 20 degrees vertically. And the bus has to meet all applicable federal, state, and local emission and safety standards.

The location of the engine was left to the discretion of the manufacturers and operators.

The next step now is to ask U.S. bus manufacturers to submit proposals for the development of preliminary designs. Officials at the Urban Mass Transportation Administration hope that one or two of these design proposals can be produced as models so that they can be tested and costs can be estimated.

Some conditions will be attached to these requests for proposals, however. "We don't want any manufacturer to proceed with a design project unless it is willing to build and market an articulated vehicle," says Charles Daniels, Chief of UMTA's Bus Technology Development Program. "UMTA will provide most of the funding through the completion of the design phase, but after that, it will be up to the free enterprise system to actually put these buses on the road."

It will be a while before U.S.-made articulated buses are in service, but some European models are already at work here. When it became evident that the U.S. version was years away, the consortium started looking overseas for articulated buses they could begin using right away. During the summer of 1974, the consortium borrowed a European articulated bus made by M.A.N. so they could test the reactions of U.S. bus riders. Tests were run by seven of the eight members of the consortium, and the results were favorable.

Ninety-one percent of the riders surveyed preferred the articulated coach over standard 40-foot buses. Ninety percent preferred the hinged bus's larger windows and wider doors, and 81 per-

cent thought the bus was easier to board, even though this version had floors that were more than three inches higher than those on conventional U.S. buses.

Riders liked the ease with which they could move around inside the bus, the smooth ride, the low level of noise inside, the comfort of the seats, and the spaciousness of the interior. Drivers liked the way the bus handled, the ease of steering, the good acceleration, and a turning response they found superior to that of conventional buses.

The consortium was ready to go. Funded by capital grants from UMTA, the group contracted for 248 German-made articulated buses. By this time, the membership of the consortium had changed. It now included the Golden Gate Bridge, Highway, and Transportation Authority of San Francisco; San Diego; Atlanta; Minneapolis; Washington, D.C.; Phoenix; Oakland; Los Angeles; Pittsburgh; and Chicago. Seattle Metro contracted separately for an additional 150 buses. The contracts went to a joint venture by AM General, a U.S. company, and M.A.N. of West Germany—M.A.N. would provide the vehicle shells, complete with hinge mechanism and pancake engine (all of which would account for about 60 percent of the cost) and AM General would outfit the interiors and make other modifications.

The vehicles were put on ships in Bremerhaven, West Germany, bound for AM General's plant in Marshall, Texas. They arrived in Texas, were outfitted, and were sent on to the Southern California Rapid Transit District in Los Angeles and Seattle Metro. The first of Seattle's articulated buses began service on July 28, 1978, and in Los Angeles, the first day of service was October 29.

Articulated buses are now being delivered to AC Transit in Oakland, San Diego, San Francisco, and Minneapolis.

So the Department of Transportation's dream of increasing the efficiency of bus transportation through the use of articulated buses is off to a successful start.

And this season, the latest European fashion on the streets of Los Angeles and Seattle is a long bus that bends in the middle.

Deborah Noxon was formerly on the staff of the Urban Mass Transportation Administration's Office of Public Affairs.

Moving People

An expanding market—but for whom?

The business of moving people by rail in the U.S. and Canada continues to be good business for railcar manufacturers. In 1978, the authorities that operate rail passenger service in these countries took delivery of 623 cars; another 1,512 cars are on order; more than 800 additional cars are scheduled to be ordered in 1979; and a *Railway Age* survey indicates a market for 4,000 cars during the next 5 to 10 years.

All of that is, of course, good news for the carbuilders—though not necessarily for U.S. carbuilders. They have seen a good share of their market go to foreign builders in recent years, and it remains to be seen whether a "Buy America" provision written into the Surface Transporta-tion Act of 1978 will be used by the Secretary of Transportation in a suffi-ciently tough way to reverse the trend.

● **Japan next?** Of the 328 cars delivered to U.S. operators in 1978, only 10 were produced outside of the U.S. But the 1,229-car backlog of U.S. orders in-cludes 382 cars that will be produced in Canada, Italy, and France. And there is a

Bill Stokes: "A banner year for mass transit"

By B. R. STOKES
Executive Vice President
American Public Transit Association

A year ago, it was plain that 1978 could be a watershed year for the transit com-munity, but we also knew that we would have to work diligently to achieve our goals. The fact is that the transit com-munity did work hard, spearheaded by APTA's efforts, and we can write 1978 down as a banner year for mass transit.

It was a tumultuous, busy, and occa-sionally confusing year. We spent a lot of time carrying the ball on transit legisla-tion, and with the help of men like Con-gressman Jim Howard of New Jersey and Senator Pete Williams, another New Jersey Democrat, we scored a touch-down. Congress enacted the Surface Transportation Assistance Act—a joint highway-transit funding law that pro-vides $15.16 billion through 1983. The act is significant not just because of its in-crease in money, but for key features that reshape the federal transit program. The new law authorizes operating and capital assistance directly tied to the amount of rail service a city operates, and it provides for a second tier of aid for the nation's largest cities, a number of which have important rail transit or commuter rail systems that serve millions of passengers.

Even as we were persuading Congress that transit deserved greater support because of its increasingly important role in matters of energy, environment, and urban conservation, people across the country were proving our point in the simplest way—they rode transit more often in greater numbers. Paced by in-creases on the nation's rail transit systems, transit ridership has increased every month so far in 1978, with the likely result that all 12 months will show healthy increases. The passenger hikes for 1978 continue a trend from the end of

B.R. Stokes

1977, and the string now stands at 15 straight months of increases, the longest since the Arab oil embargo of 1973 and the second longest since the end of the Second World War.

Perhaps the most controversial—and still not resolved—issue that took up the attention of transit officials everywhere was the multibillion-dollar time bomb of Section 504 regulations on accessibility to transit systems for the handicapped, par-ticularly the wheelchair bound. The length and breadth of the transit com-munity dissented loudly, with the nation's rail systems perhaps the lustiest protesters of all. About 90% of the cost for meeting the rules would have been directed to rail cities, and estimated costs for major cities such as New York and Chicago were stag-gering. In Chicago, Section 504 capital costs would exceed the total amount spent

on building the system since the 1890s. In responding to this issue, transit operators amassed convincing evidence that univer-sal accessibility was not effective, effi-cient, or economical. Around the coun-try, transit officials testified that far more valuable special services could better meet the needs of the handicapped at a drastically lower price. Transit made its point eloquently, and we hope tellingly. Right now the ball is in the federal court, as they ponder the extensive material sub-mitted to them.

For the coming year, there will be no dearth of tough questions that will face transit. Already, we have begun work on the issue of the Surface Transportation Administration—the child of a marriage between the Federal Highway Adminis-tration and the Urban Mass Transporta-tion Administration. Transit operators are concerned that the transit program might get overwhelmed or just quietly lost in the proposed merger. We need to know whether STA will be a healthy heir or an illegitimate stepchild.

APTA also will be pushing hard for a supplemental appropriations act in 1979 to fill some of the gaps between the amounts authorized in the Surface Trans-portation Assistance Act and that appro-priated in Fiscal Year 1979. This is par-ticularly crucial for rail cities since one of the biggest gaps is in the rail funds appor-tioned under Section 5.

Transit officials will undoubtedly be under great demand to serve more riders, particularly in the wake of announced plans to ration some gasoline by several oil companies and the substantial OPEC price hike decided upon last month.

The list could go on. But just this list alone should make it clear that 1979, like 1978, will pose new challenges to transit. I trust that we will meet them with the same determination and spirit that made 1978 a year of success for transit.

Passenger car market at a glance

Deliveries

480 (1971)
716 (1972)
433 (1973)
294 (1974)
464 (1975)
1,131 (1976)
1,064 (1977)
623 (1978)

Backlog
(as of Jan. 1)

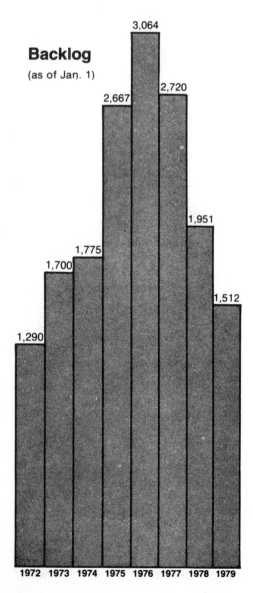

1,290 (1972)
1,700 (1973)
1,775 (1974)
2,667 (1975)
3,064 (1976)
2,720 (1977)
1,951 (1978)
1,512 (1979)

These cars were delivered in 1978:

Purchaser	No. of cars	Type	Builder
Amtrak	1	Intercity	Pullman Standard
Atlanta (MARTA)	6	Rapid transit	Franco-Belge
Chicago RTA	71	Commuter	Budd
Chicago Transit Authority	96	Rapid transit	Boeing Vertol
Mass. Bay Transportation Authority	5	Light rail	Boeing Vertol
	4	Rapid transit	Hawker Siddeley
	1	Commuter	Pullman Standard
Montreal (MUCTC)	231	Rapid transit	Bombardier-MLW
New Jersey DOT	51	Commuter	General Electric
New York City Transit Authority	74	Rapid transit	Pullman Standard
New York MTA	8	Commuter	General Electric
San Francisco Muni	11	Light rail	Boeing Vertol
Toronto Transit Commission	58	Rapid transit	Hawker Siddeley
	6	Light rail	SIG
Total	**623**		

Work goes forward on this undelivered backlog:

Purchaser	No. of cars	Type	Builder
Amtrak	283	Intercity	Pullman Standard
	10	Intercity	Bombardier-MLW
Atlanta (MARTA)	90	Rapid transit	Franco-Belge
Calgary transit	27	Light rail	Siemens-Duwag
Chicago RTA	9	Commuter	Budd
Chicago Transit Authority	8	Rapid transit	Boeing Vertol
	300	Rapid transit	Budd
Cleveland (GCRTA)	48	Light rail	Breda
Mass. Bay Transportation Authority	40	Light rail	Boeing Vertol
	186	Rapid transit	Hawker Siddeley
	59	Commuter	Pullman Standard
Montreal (MUCTC)	12	Rapid transit	Bombardier-MLW
New Jersey DOT	59	Commuter	General Electric
PATCO (Lindenwold)	48	Rapid transit	Canadian Vickers
San Francisco Muni	89	Light rail	Boeing Vertol
Toronto Transit Commission	4	Rapid transit	Hawker Siddeley
	190	Light rail	Hawker Siddeley
VIA Rail Canada	50	Intercity	Bombardier-MLW
Total	**1,512**		

These orders are likely to develop in 1979:

Purchaser	No. of cars	Type
Atlanta (MARTA)	20	Rapid transit
Baltimore Metro	72	Rapid transit
Chicago RTA	34	Commuter
Cleveland (GCRTA)	70	Rapid transit
Connecticut DOT	12	RDC
Dade County (Miami)	136	Rapid transit
Edmonton Transit	3	Light rail
New Jersey DOT	66	Commuter
SEMTA (Detroit)	3-5	Commuter
SEPTA (Philadelphia)	50	Commuter
	141	Light rail
	110	Rapid transit
Washington Metro	94	Rapid transit
Total	**811-813**	

The 5-10 year outlook:

Purchaser	No. of cars	Type
Amtrak	800	Intercity
Atlanta (MARTA)	100	Rapid transit
Baltimore Metro	20-30	Rapid transit
Calgary Transit	16-20	Light rail
Chicago RTA	88	Commuter
Chicago Transit Authority	300	Rapid transit
Cleveland (GCRTA)	10-15	Light rail
Edmonton Transit	35	Light rail
Honolulu Transit	200	Rapid transit
New Jersey DOT	20	Rapid transit
New York City Transit Authority	1,200	Rapid transit
N.Y. MTA lines (Conrail, LIRR)*	440	Commuter
NFTA (Buffalo)	30	Light rail
PAT (Pittsburgh)	89	Light rail
San Diego Transit	14	Light rail
San Juan Transit	100	Rapid transit
SCRTD (Los Angeles)	120	Rapid transit
Washington Metro	340	Rapid transit
Total	**3,922-3,941**	

*Conn. DOT shares in cost of cars used on Conrail's New Haven division

Kawasaki hopes to build 141 light rail cars like this one for Philadelphia. Nissho Iwai American Corp., representing the Japanese firm, is the apparent low bidder for the order. Its quoted price, $57,739,150 for 141 nonarticulated units, compares with a price of $84,048,000 for 103 articulated cars submitted by Budd, the only U.S. bidder.

strong probability that Japan, very early in 1979, will break into the U.S. market.

In December, the Southeastern Pennsylvania Transportation Authority (SEPTA) opened bids for the supply of light rail cars for Philadelphia. There were six bidders, only one of which, Budd, is a U.S. company. The apparent low bidder was Nissho Iwai American Corp. (whose principal subcontractor is Kawasaki of Japan), quoting a price of $57,739,150 for 141 nonarticulated cars. The high bidder was Budd, with a price of $84,048,000 for 103 articulated cars. The 30 companies from whom bids were originally solicited were asked to quote either on nonarticulated or articulated units. The other bids came from the Urban Transit Development Corp. of Toronto ($61,499,136, nonarticulated); Breda of Italy ($68,461,100, nonarticulated; $64,781,200, articulated); Hawker Siddeley Canada ($77,369,048, nonarticulated); and BN of Belgium ($81,261,323, nonarticulated; $77,947,271, articulated).

SEPTA will take 60 days from Dec. 21, 1978, to evaluate the bids. "We do not believe the Buy America Act will be operative in this case," said a SEPTA spokesman, referring to the $26-million spread between the only U.S. bid and the apparent low bid.

(The Buy America provision has been interpreted by DOT's Urban Mass Transportation Administration to authorize a 10% cost differential in favor of domestic bidders; that differential does not include import duties.)

The next major price test will come Jan. 18, when Baltimore and Dade County-(Miami) open bids for a total of 208 rapid transit cars. Both Budd and Pullman Standard are expected to go after that business; early in January, Bombardier-MLW of Canada, Franco-Belge of France, and Breda of Italy were considered to be possible contenders. U.S. transit observers hope that bid opening may provide a more clear-cut test of the Buy America provision than did the SEPTA surprise.

● **Will DOT get tough?** One transit supplier believes that the real effectiveness of the provision may not be known for some time to come. "There's a lot of discretion left to the Secretary of Transportation," he points out. "In time I believe the secretary will use that discretion to favor our own industry. But I am not certain that Secretary [Brock] Adams is yet fully aware of the problems that could be caused by the disappearance of carbuilding capability in this country. Over the long pull, I am hopeful, but over the short pull I'm afraid that more orders will be lost overseas."

This supplier, incidentally, makes a point that has been made by many others with respect to Canada: "It's a shame," he says, "that our Canadian friends are necessarily affected by the Buy America legislation. They have done business with us for a long time, and fairly."

● **The low-bid problem.** The foreign invasion is not, of course, the only reason that U.S. builders are in trouble. This was demonstrated in Chicago a few weeks ago when the Chicago Transit Authority opened bids for 300 new transit cars that are to be very similar to 300 cars CTA previously ordered from Boeing Vertol. There were no foreign bids at that opening. Budd won the contract with a low bid of $133.3 million. Boeing Vertol lost out with a next-low bid of $174.9 million. The high bidder was Pullman Standard, with a price of $248 million.

That was the last straw for Boeing Vertol, whose director of surface transportation, Arthur Hitsman, told *Railway Age* a few weeks later that the company would no longer submit bids as a prime contractor for railcars (RA, Dec. 11, p. 11). "There's something about this market that we don't understand," said Hitsman. Boeing Vertol's main complaint, he indicated, was the low-bid policy generally.

Whatever the reason, there are only two U.S. carbuilders still actively soliciting business—Pullman Standard (which has long talked about withdrawing from the field if it cannot start to show a profit) and Budd. General Electric has staged a quiet retreat. GE's big disappointment came with loss of the Atlanta order, for 100 cars, to Franco Belge. After that GE continued to turn out commuter cars but has now converted its carbuilding plant at Erie, Pa., into an off-highway vehicle facility. Before that, the Rohr Corp. quit the business, after taking losses on orders for the Bay Area Rapid Transit District and the Washington Metro. Earlier casualties were GSI's St. Louis Car Division and, many years ago, ACF.

So it may be said, at the beginning of the new year, that the predictions of past years are coming true: The U.S. passenger-railcar market is enjoying a renaissance. As much cannot, however, be said for the U.S. passenger-railcar industry. ■

Railview

"This Administration *is* committed t

(There is a strong feeling within the transit industry that while President Carter's Urban Mass Transportation Administration may not be anti-rail, it has not proved to be demonstrably pro-rail. In an address prepared for the annual Rapid Transit Conference of the American Public Transit Association in Chicago June 6, UMTA Administrator Richard S. Page attempted to put these fears to rest. Excerpts from his address follow.)

It is especially fitting that you meet in Chicago—a leader in all forms of public transportation, especially rapid rail. I was impressed as I read Railway Age's special feature, "Chicago: Rail renaissance in the making." The commitment of state, city, and regional officials to modernizing and expanding mass transit, especially rail service, should inspire all of us.

I am pleased to report that we are doing our part: Last week we cleared three engineering contracts for work on the Franklin Street subway, and we stand ready to move quickly and vigorously just as soon as Chicago completes the final Environmental Impact Statement. Yesterday I signed the long-awaited Transportation Improvement Program for this fiscal year—at $122 million of federal funds—including $32 million for the O'Hare extension, exactly what Chicago requested.

In addition to Chicago, we have rail construction projects under way in 11 other cities. Seven more are nearing the end of alternatives analysis, which may justify a new rail line or a rail extension. Add to that 11 cities in the Downtown People Mover program and 15 cities now beginning to study alternatives, and you can see that we have a big and promising agenda.

You can also see that this Administration is—how can I say it more clearly—*is* committed to rail transit. We prepared and published a special rail policy statement which the White House cleared and Secretary Adams and I signed to emphasize our support and to clarify our procedures.

I intend to discuss our rail policy more fully in a moment. First, I ask you to turn the clock back and think again of your impressions in early 1977. Compare those impressions with what I suggest are the realities of today. Early in 1977, we in the transit business were worried. I remember because I shared most of those concerns and at that point I had no idea that I would become the UMTA administrator. We were concerned by at least three things: the Administration's refusal in

February to endorse S. 208; the President's March handwritten memo to the secretary; and, in April, the failure of the energy policy message to deal with urban mass transit. In May the secretary mandated Transbus, which I am sure bothered some in this industry. These were unsettling events. But I want to suggest to you today that all of us who care deeply about public transportation should be as encouraged now as we might have been discouraged then. I especially invite you to listen to a few things that make up a solid picture today.

The Administration is committed to

"All of us want rail projects to be economical in design, reasonable in construction costs, and reliable in performance."

---

adequate long-term funding of public transit. The President endorsed last August increases in the gas tax and the idea of a trust fund for transit. The President in January submitted his own special message on legislation, calling for a five-year, $15-billion program. In March, the President made urban mass transit an integral part of his urban policy message. And last month, the President's wife rode on Metrorail in Washington, escorted by Secretary Adams. Our recommended budget for FY '79, while it may have been disappointing to some, represented $1 billion more than the UMTA budget of FY '77, and that budget President Carter had increased over the Ford budget.

The Congress acted in mid-1977 and the Administration agreed to expand the DPM program. The Congress authorized and the President signed a law extending commuter rail subsidies. Secretary Adams, in fact, had reaffirmed this Administration's commitment to the new starts launched by the previous Administration, and those new starts are funded in our budgets and our bill.

Although it is difficult to make new commitments without new legislation, I have made two in recent months. First, to expand the Miami-Dade County rapid transit system from 16 to 20 miles; it survived a second referendum, and they are

ready to build. The second commitment was to endorse the Port Authority-New Jersey package concept of transit improvements. Both of these have been submitted in writing to us, and we have responded in writing, the main condition being passage of adequate legislation this year. Big rail grants have been made in Boston, New York, Philadelphia, and Washington, D.C. The $800-million Atlanta commitment has been paid in full. Engineering funds have been committed to Honolulu and to two projects in Chicago. We are talking with Atlanta and Baltimore and PATCO about extensions....

In addition, we have done some administrative things. We have initiated a program management concept with Atlanta and offered it to Miami, Baltimore, and Washington, D.C. We have instituted a letter of credit procedure; simplified the Section 5 application requirements; published minority business, Title VI, and EEO circulars; and moved staff and authority to the regional offices. Six regional offices now have project decision and management authority. We have filled available positions to correct some of UMTA's chronic understaffing. We have a FY '78 OMB ceiling of 542 positions, and, as of today, we have 539 people onboard and over 40 pending personnel actions. We have asked for 50 additional positions for Fiscal Year 1979....

There's been some talk of our finding an ombudsman to figure out a way to move money faster within the agency. I'm interested in new ideas and hope that you will tell me when we are not doing the right job, and I have heard from many of you recently on this. But my intention through the decentralization effort is that our regional directors be the first and last UMTA word for each of you. Instead of creating an UMTA ombudsman, I like to think that we are creating 10 of them so that they can help work your problems through our procedures.

Finally, we have spent a great deal of time in recent months drafting proposed regulations pursuant to the HEW guidelines on Section 504 for accessibility of all persons to existing and new transit facilities. These were signed by Deputy Secretary Butchman yesterday and sent to the *Federal Register* for publication. They are *draft* regulations published for comment. I urge everyone to read our draft carefully and don't rely on second-hand reports....

All of us know that these regulations are first required by federal law and secondly

228

il transit"

By RICHARD S. PAGE
Administrator, Urban Mass
Transportation Administration

will have a greater impact on our capital and operating costs than almost anything we do. Please read them and give us your best advice. We plan at least a 90-day period for review and comment. We are planning hearings by the department. I am sure we would welcome proposals from APTA or anybody in this room for additional ways that we can hear your views on these regulations.

This little recital is not intended to blow our own trumpet, but simply to show that it has been a busy time. I believe much has been accomplished and much more is on the way. I think today's facts demonstrate the Administration's solid support for transit and stand in sharp contrast to those impressions of early 1977.

On the subject of rail specifically, my impression is that some of you still detect skepticism or a lukewarm attitude. If so, I think it can be traced to three obvious problems: lack of financial and political commitments, overdesign and excessive capital cost, and problems of reliability and equipment performance. All of us in this room have been shaken, and disappointed, in problems at BART, problems at Metro, problems at Boston with new cars. We know rail has advantages in certain cases—and we know those problems are being solved. Metro is on its way to being a success story—but the public, and the professionals' confidence has been shaken, and new, hard looks are being taken at rail.

That, in a nutshell, is the purpose of our rail policy: to urge that each city take a good hard look, develop a solid case, and forge the local financial and political commitments to build and pay for a rail transit system. I don't want—and cities shouldn't want—decisions for rail to be induced by 80% federal money, or by slippery optimistic data, or by political promises. And all of us want rail projects to be economical in design, reasonable in construction cost, and reliable in performance. With the talent and dedication in this industry, they can be.

We have in recent months acted on several pending rail issues. These accomplishments in the past year give promise of other successful actions in coming years:

—In March we issued guidelines for terms and conditions for rail car procurements—putting in place a project which arose in late 1975.

—We are progressing on rail car standardization, to reduce "customizing," and expect the spec to be ready next spring.

—We have directed joint car buys between Miami and Baltimore and Cleveland and Philadelphia, with WMATA going alone.

—The secretary approved in March a nationally derived reliability data bank—thanks to APTA and many in this room.

—We now require all new rapid rail and light rail cars to be tested at Pueblo.

—We have instituted a new program to adapt existing technology to provide near-term solutions: STARS (Subsystem Technology Applications to Rail Systems).

—A cost reduction program with

"Rail transit can help...to revitalize distressed cities and prepare the way for...an energy-constrained future."

WMATA has identified several millions of dollars of savings. Other technology projects in Baltimore, Dade County, Boston, Atlanta, and Pittsburgh are also paying dividends.

The purpose of these projects is to find cheaper solutions. The purpose of our rail policy is to emphasize local responsibility—for financing, for management, for related transit, highway, and land-use policies....The overriding goal is the development of rail transit projects which are justified and useful—in terms of mobility, to serve the transportation needs of a corridor and an urban area, but especially to contribute to air-pollution control, petroleum-energy savings, and urban revitalization.

Rail transit is a powerful investment tool. If used wisely and supported by policies on parking, land use, development, traffic, and bus transit, it can revitalize older, depressed parts of our cities and open up new opportunities for joint urban development, employment, and public convenience.

Our rail policy statement declares, and I quote: "To the extent that it can foster higher density, clustered development, rail transit can be a means to more efficient forms of urban settlement and an instrument of long-range energy conservation efforts.

"In short, rail transit is and will continue to be a valuable form of urban transportation in selected circumstances, provided that local public and private leaders and interests recognize and learn to exploit its unique contributions. In particular, rail transit should be viewed as part of a strategy to promote broader national purposes. Its effectiveness should be measured not just in terms of its ability to move people, but in terms of its positive influence on the urban economy and on the long-term patterns of urban growth. Specifically, rail transit can help in our nation's efforts to revitalize distressed cities and prepare the way for a gradual transition to an energy-constrained future."

Rail transit is also by far the safest form of transportation. And the *New York Times* on June 1 reported from California that "trains are luring commuters" because they save time, money, and peace of mind. A recent public opinion poll found that auto safety was the number one transportation issue in the nation—so saving "peace of mind" is an important benefit of rail transit.

The first order of business we all have this year is passage of new long-term legislation. It now appears that the appropriations committees, not the authorizing committees, will call the tune for 1979—but we must continue our mutual effort to pass a reasonable and flexible bill this year, and make sure that it doesn't get stuck somewhere in the legislative process. With the President's clear and unmistakable concern about inflation, it must be a prudent bill to get this signature.

We have a big agenda and an exciting program. I hope that you have followed the public opinion surveys. I know you follow the promising developments in your own cities, but I have been impressed by the solid steady annual increases in ridership. I have seen three public opinion surveys in the last 60 days—all of which show that there is a great deal of public support for transit. I have been impressed by the cities and the taxpayers who have voted tax increases to support public transportation.

Given the national problems of urban revitalization, of traffic safety, of air pollution, and of energy—and given the public opinion favoring public transit—I believe we stand on the threshold of a new era in public transportation. Our task is to deliver to the consumer products that work, services that are reliable, and performance that is cost effective. ■

For new and expanding systems — th

By TOM ICHNIOWSKI
Associate Editor

Across the sprawling expanse of Canada, there are only a few pockets of population dense enough to support mass transit systems. As Canada's cities have studied urban transportation alternatives and weighed their merits, what is significant is that, in many cases, the choice has been fixed guideway.

The pioneer was Toronto, which in 1954 opened the first 4.6 miles of the Yonge Street subway. In 1966, Montreal inaugurated service on 13.7 miles of subway, but where Toronto had picked steel-wheeled vehicles, Montreal decided to run rubber-tired cars. Both systems are still growing.

Now two cities in western Canada, Calgary and Edmonton, Alta., have gone the fixed-guideway route, and Vancouver, on the West Coast, is giving it consideration. Compared with the 2.8–million populations of both the metropolitan Toronto and Montreal areas, metro Calgary has only 470,000 and metro Edmonton 550,000, but both are large enough to present people-moving problems. Feeling they needed more capacity than buses would provide but believing heavy rail provided too much capacity, Calgary and Edmonton both opted for light rail lines.

Canada is definitely "into" rail transit, and here's what is happening:

●Montreal. Gerard Gascon, director of the Metropolitan Transit Bureau, the agency in charge of system construction, reports that in September the Montreal Metro will open a five-mile extension on the western end of Line 1 (RA, Dec. 13, 1976, p. 22). In addition, Gascon says, a two-mile extension to Line 2 will open in June 1979, and more is under construction.

In the summer of 1976, the Quebec provincial government had placed a moratorium on much of Metro's construction plans, evidently growing worried at escalating construction cost estimates. But this year the province partially lifted the moratorium, and Gascon expects capital projects to proceed to the tune of about $100 million per year for the next three years. That total would include subway construction and purchase of cars. Metro is currently receiving an order of 423 subway cars from Bombardier/MLW.

●Edmonton. On April 23, the city opened a new 4½-mile light rail line (RA, Dec. 13, 1976, p. 24). The price tag of the project

was $65 million, with the province of Alberta putting up $45 million and the city providing the rest. In the months since service began, how has the new line been doing? "Great," says Bob Clark, Edmonton Transit's supervisor of rail operation. "By and large it went in very smoothly." In May, the line was carrying 15,000 riders each workday. In June, the figure had risen to 16,000, and in the first part of July it was up to 17,000. Clark expects ridership to grow steadily to about 22,000-23,000 per workday this fall and winter.

The light rail line had its genesis in 1970, when a plan was advanced to build a network of freeways around Edmonton. But citizens and the downtown business community rose up in opposition to the highway proposal, saying it would kill the downtown area. Says Clark: "The alternative was to upgrade the transit system." How do officials at Edmonton Transit feel now about their choice and how it's working so far? "We're delighted with it," says Clark.

●Calgary. In May, this city started building a 4.8-mile light rail line that will have 12 stations, be about 95% on the surface, and cost about $144 million. The city

is providing $95 million of the total and the province the remainder. Rev service is scheduled to start in 1981, Jim Hemstock, planning coordinator, LRT (Light Rail Transit) division, for the city's transportation department, projects that the line will be carrying between 40,000-45,000 riders a day. One reason for building the light rail line is that Calgary is growing rapidly. "Because of the extreme growth," Hemstock says, "we're short of transportation capacity."

In considering a number of transportation possibilities, Calgary saw that light rail, though more expensive than buses, provided far superior service as well as having land-use and environmental benefits. "Calgary's sprawling," Hemstock says. "It has developed at quite a low density." Officials hope the line will direct future development, especially in the southern section of the city. Says Hemstock: "The light rail line will be basically the focus for the growth in the south part of town."

●Vancouver. Over the past 10 years, there have been various sorts of proposals for light rail in this metropolitan area of over 1.1 million. The present situation is about the same: Officials are studying the feasibility of high-capacity transit in some

oice is fixed guideway

Toronto (far left) and Montreal (left) came in first and second with heavy rail. Edmonton's light rail system (below) opened in April; Calgary's is building; and one has been proposed for Vancouver.

corridors in the region, but there are no firm plans as yet.

●Toronto—still a leader. Of all the transit cities in Canada, Toronto was the first to lay track and run trains. In many ways, it is still a transit leader. For years, it has been the North American city that observers and officials cite to demonstrate the positive impact rail transit can have on an urban area. Toronto's aerial photographs showing how high-rise development has clustered around stations on the Yonge Street line are by now legendary in transit circles. Officials at the Toronto Transit Commission, the agency responsible for building and operating the system, will tell you about the increased real estate values around those stations. Toronto is also known for a well-run operation, with the accent on full integration of bus, trolley, subway, and commuter rail.

Riding on the Toronto subway is a pleasant experience. Clean, if somewhat utilitarian, trains roll through clean, if somewhat plain, stations. To be fair, though, the most recently built stations have some pretty jazzy artwork—funded by the province of Ontario and private donors. One worth mentioning is the Yorkdale station's "Arc en Ciel"

(rainbow)—a 570-foot-long series of neon tubes that runs the length of the station's glass ceiling. As a train enters the station, the neon lights go off and on in colorful patterns. The TTC calls it "the ultimate environment."

Visitors from transit systems all over the world come to Toronto to study the system, see how it works, and learn how Toronto does it. All in all, their perception of the city's transit system is that it works spectacularly well.

The Toronto success story is an often-told tale—in Railway Age (May 9, 1977, p. 24) and elsewhere. Delegates who come to the city for the American Public Transit Association's annual meeting late in September might expect that TTC would be pretty satisfied with what they have, content just to keep a good thing going. But Metropolitan Toronto is changing, and so is its transit system.

●"A transit-oriented city." Jack T. Harvey, TTC's general manager-operations, supplies some background: "Toronto has always been a transit-oriented city. Where some of the American cities lost that transit orientation, Toronto has maintained it." As evidence, he points out that Toronto has about 166 rides per

capita per year—the highest figure among North America" transit systems.

"The first line in Toronto, the north-south Yonge line—4½ miles—certainly concentrated development in that corridor. You may say that the development would have taken place anyway throughout the city. That can be debated," says Harvey, "but one thing it did do was to control the location of the development and to maintain the viability of a tight, concentrated, downtown core."

On the Yonge Street line, development didn't begin to sprout around stations until some time after the line was in place. When the first part of the east-west line was built in 1966, development there took place along with or shortly after construction. By 1968, when the east-west line was extended, especially on the west end, Harvey remembers that "I could follow where the right of way was by watching the development—ahead of the construction."

Of course, new high-density residential and commercial structures spurred by transit benefit the city with tax dollars. And just as transit helps development, development helps transit. "The rapid transit line by its very nature needs development to support it," Harvey says.

231

In 1980, Toronto will start work on a $100-million light rail

To justify itself, a heavy rail line needs the large numbers of riders that densely populated, developed areas contain.

• **"Incremental growth."** Toronto's rail network contines to expand, but only a little at a time. It is the paradigm of the philosophy of "incremental growth" that the U.S. Urban Mass Transportation Administration has been preaching about to U.S. cities for the last several years.

On January 28, service started on a new, 6.17-mile, $220-million, heavy rail extension, called the Spadina subway. The new spur starts at the east-west subway line, heads north for a short distance, then runs in a meandering diagonal for a short stretch, and finally shoots straight north to end at Wilson Avenue.

How has the Spadina line been doing? Not as well as TTC expected. One big reason for its construction was to relieve some of the congestion on the Yonge Street trunk, and there is evidence that Spadina is succeeding at that. But TTC had expected Spadina would be carrying about 12,000 additional riders in the peak hours by next January; so far, it's only carrying 8,000 new riders in peak hours. "It's a little bit slower than we anticipated," Harvey concedes.

The opening of Spadina was slowed by an electricians' strike and affected by the harsh weather last winter. "With new equipment, and the weather conditions, the reliability of service on Spadina was lousy," Harvey says bluntly, "with the result that we turned off a lot of people. Once you turn them off, it takes you a while to get them back again."

Compounding those headaches was another problem. Spadina was the first TTC rail route that was not built along a corridor of established transportation demand. To attract riders, Harvey says, "you have to educate people and advertise a little more than you would normally do if you had had a corridor." The obvious question: Why was Spadina built where it was? Harvey's short answer: "Political."

TTC had been planning another north-south line to complement the Yonge line for some time. The commission came up with some 22 different alignments, which were subsequently narrowed down to five. What complicated matters was a freeway planned to run down from the Wilson Avenue area to downtown, and by the early 1970s part of it was even completed. Then, in 1971, the province of Ontario shifted policy and killed the Spadina expressway along with several others that were planned. The upshot was that the route finally selected for the Spadina subway generally follows the route of the aborted Spadina expressway. The final alignment was favored by the Metro Toronto government and the province but not by the TTC.

How much development has taken place so far along the Spadina line? "Very little. Very little," says Harvey, though he adds that there is room for future growth.

Meanwhile, one-station extensions are being constructed on each end of the east-west line. The eastern extension, just under 1½ miles long, is slated to be finished in June 1980; the western spur, just under a mile, in October 1980. The two short extensions will cost about $143 million. With their completion, Harvey says, "I think we've seen the end of the subway construction per se."

• **Enter "Metroplan."** From that point on, Toronto and the TTC shift gears. In 1976, the regional government produced "Metroplan," a set of guidelines for the area's future development. Explains Harvey: "The philosophy behind Metroplan is to slow down the growth of the downtown area, and in its place, put in sub-centers." These sub-centers would be concentrations of jobs and activities in sections within the boundaries of the metropolitan area, but some distance away from the downtown.

"Once you embark upon a decentralization," Harvey says, "then your method of transportation changes. You can no longer require a heavy transit line." The new choice for Toronto is light rail.

The first step towards decentralization will be the construction of a new light rail line from the western end of the east-west subway line, looping north and then west to the Scarborough Town Center, one of the target sub-centers mentioned in the Metroplan. Construction on the 4½-mile, $100-million line is to begin in 1980, with opening slated for 1982. Beyond the Scarborough route, Metroplan contains proposals for other light rail lines in the metro region, but no firm decisions have been made on them. Officials are waiting to see what happens with the Scarborough line. Asked about the likelihood of further light rail construction, Harvey replies, "I think a great deal will depend upon whether or not the concept of decentralization can actually become effective."

• **New cars.** TTC is acquiring new equipment, partly to serve the new routes, partly to replace some of its older cars. From Hawker Siddeley, TTC will be getting 190 new light rail vehicles. Of these, 20 will go into service on the new Scarborough line; the rest will replace some of TTC's streetcars.

In addition, Hawker Siddeley has almost completed delivery of 138 new subway cars for TTC. They will be used on the new Spadina line and to provide additional service on the east-west line. The new H-5 subway cars are the first TTC vehicles to have air conditioning. Harvey feels that, except for brief stretches in the summer, Toronto's climate doesn't really warrant air-conditioned cars, but he says of the H-5s, "I must admit they're rather pleasant." The cars also have chopper controls, which TTC says should provide energy savings, and solid state equipment that should reduce maintenance costs.

• **Changing times.** But Toronto is not simply adding more routes and buying more cars. Metropolitan Toronto has changed since the first segment of the Yonge Street line went into service in 1954. And TTC believes it must change, too.

In the 1950s and 1960s, the region experienced a steady growth of population—and TTC experienced a steady growth in ridership. That population growth has levelled off in the last several years, and TTC's ridership (subway, streetcar, trolley bus, and bus) has dipped slightly: Last year's total system ridership of 348.7 million was down 1.9 million, or about .5%, from 1976 totals of 350.6 million.

Harvey feels that some private companies have experienced the same trend. "They have been living in the land of growing expectations," he says. "Now they're in a no-growth area." What does no-growth mean for the TTC? Harvey answers, "You've got to start re-thinking!"

In 1977, TTC underwent what it calls an

For commuters

One hallmark of the transit system Toronto is that it is well integrated. Subways, commuter trains, buses, and street cars are all interlinked to form an efficient urban transportation network. Most of those modes fall under the operating umbrella of Toronto Transit Commission. The one that doesn't is commuter service. The Toronto Area Transit Operating Authority (TATOA) runs the commuter bus and rail service, and calls it GO (Government of Ontario) Transit. Where does GO Transit fit into the Toronto urban transportation picture? "We're the interregional guys," explains James A. Brown, TATOA's manager, rail division.

GO Transit has four main rail lines, with Toronto's Union Terminal as the endpoint. Two run along the shore of Lake Ontario: one from Hamilton in the west, the other from Pickering in the east. The third begins at Georgetown in the northwest, and the fourth (opened May 1) starts at Richmond Hill in the north.

Brown says the rail lines now carry about 37,000 fares a day, and he adds, "We've shown increases every year we've been in operation [since 1967]."

What has GO Transit's commuters buzzing is new equipment. In March, GO

encourage decentralization

organizational "renewal." One result was Harvey's promotion from general manager-engineering and subway construction to general manager-operations. Another was the creation of a new position: manager of corporate planning. The new position is held by Dr. Juri Pill, and his job is to keep an eye on TTC's long-range needs, with special emphasis on financing. He is also to analyze the pros and cons of any contemplated changes in TTC's service or organization. As an example, TTC is currently evaluating the benefits and drawbacks of a pass system.

There have been other changes thrust upon TTC by the period of slow growth. Says Harvey: "Marketing and community relations are very important. You no longer have a complaint department; you have a marketing department." With fewer potential new transit riders moving into Metro Toronto, TTC has to sell its system more aggressively than before.

● **The cost-revenue question.** The biggest problem transit operators in all parts of the world are grappling with is what to do about the spreading gap between costs and revenues. Toronto is no exception, but TTC, in cooperation with the metropolitan and provincial governments, is taking steps to tackle the cost-revenue question.

Last year, a financial plan was developed for the next five years that sets up the guidelines: 70% of the costs of running the TTC system are to come from the farebox, 15% from the government of Metro Toronto, and 15% from the province of Ontario. TTC was given the authority to raise fares to maintain the 70% cost-recovery level. In January, it instituted a fare hike of about 7%. Harvey says TTC will try to keep future hikes in line with the rate of inflation. But TTC also knows it must watch its costs tightly, because it does not want to price its service out of the reach of its riders. It feels that continuing and frequent double-digit fare increases would probably lead to a rapid spiral of declining ridership and revenues.

● **Government support.** But as it confronts the financial question and the others it faces, TTC has the benefit of dealing with a metropolitan form of government. "In order to get a successful transportation system, you need a successful government organization," says Harvey. The metro government in Toronto is responsible for providing those services, such as transportation, that are area-wide in nature. As a result, Toronto doesn't have the problem many U.S. transit agencies face of having to meld the conflicting interests of suburbs and cities into a coherent whole. "This is a problem I see with a lot of the larger American cities," Harvey says, "They just don't have that integration of government.

In Canada, the federal government provides next to nothing in the way of urban transit assistance. Instead, Canadian transit agencies look for their financial aid to the cities and the provinces. Here, TTC is blessed with an Ontario government that has taken a strong pro-transit line, as evidenced by its 1971 decision to stop construction of a number of expressways, including Spadina.

Last year, the province of Ontario took another innovative step. Realizing that it takes time to build up patronage on a new transit line, the province instituted a special start-up operating subsidy for new transit lines. For the first three years a line is in operation, the province will pick up about 50% of its operating costs. Spadina is the first TTC line to benefit under this plan. "That is a big thing," Harvey says of the new subsidy. "We're not looking over our shoulder wondering where the next buck's coming from." TTC knows it has a little cushion for three years and can direct its efforts to intensive marketing of the new route. But TTC also knows the subsidy will not be permanent, so its marketing efforts had better show some results.

● **Transit "service," not "business."** This new subsidy is another example of the re-thinking about transit that is taking place in Toronto. "When we were covering costs entirely out of the farebox," says Harvey, "we were running more like a business. If a run wasn't going to make money, it didn't go in." Now, transit in Toronto is seen differently: "You're influencing land use. You're looked upon in the conservation of energy, environmental protection." In the past, if a system ran a deficit, it was "looked upon as a sign of inefficiency," says Harvey. But since transit is also providing Toronto with environmental, energy-saving, and land-use benefits, Harvey believes that the start-up and regular operating "subsidies" are "actually a payment by the community for services the transit system renders to the community at large." Speaking about this move toward thinking of transit as service instead of as business, Harvey notes, "This is new. This is not the old railroad thinking."

Faced with a changing city and a shrinking ridership market, TTC is adapting, moving in new directions. At first, it may seem a little surprising to hear Jack Harvey, a 30-year TTC veteran, say, "We're still struggling with what are the roles and objectives of a transit system." But in another sense, the new directions are not so surprising. Toronto has always been the pioneer. ■

e Toronto area, it's GO Transit

"Extremely sexy," the new green-and-white, tapered-ended, bi-level cars Hawker Siddeley is delivering to GO Transit are luring many commuters from more conventional trains.

ransit began putting in service the first of n order of 80 new bi-level commuter cars, uilt by Hawker Siddeley. The green-and-hite cars have a striking design—though ney are double-deck cars, they taper down the ends to a single level. The tapering is ot smooth, but angular. Carl Mawby, hief of the urban transportation division f Canada's Ministry of Industry, Trade, nd Commerce, finds the new cars' design extremely sexy."

TATOA's Jim Brown says, "We have noticed a shift to trains with bi-level equipment" on the part of riders.

GO Transit has also recently received six new locomotives from the Diesel Division of General Motors of Canada, bringing its total locomotive fleet to 25. In addition, GO Transit plans a new $17-million maintenance facility at the site of its present Willowbrook shop, to be fully in operation by August 1980.

Chapter 10
Transportation Deregulation

On the road to deregulation

Is it the road to ruin or to riches? Probably neither, but getting there could be painful

By PATRICK GALLAGHER, senior editor

American industry has an enormous investment in regulated transportation. A multi-billion dollar system of physical distribution has been built over the years on the solid structure of regulation. So it's no wonder why most shippers and carriers are upset—no, furious—when a band of government reformers pushes for deregulation.

Would deregulation be a grave mistake? The question has been beaten senseless. The answer is, simply, no one really knows. It's pure speculation. The guess here is that deregulation will ultimately be neither the American Trucking Associations' disaster nor President Carter's miracle. Too many forces are at play in modern distribution for a miracle, while both shippers and truckers underestimate their own ability to adapt and respond positively to new freedoms. Many of the shipping public's greatest fears—that all but 20 or so huge carriers will be put out of business, for example—are groundless.

However, the road to deregulation could be a treacherous one, not to be embarked upon hastily. The nation's entire product distribution network cannot be transformed at the flick of a legislative switch,

no matter what air deregulation architect Alfred Kahn thinks.

Congress must carefully weigh the impact of its actions. One matter it should especially consider is the timing of reform. "If deregulation comes," says Kenneth E. Mayhew, Jr., executive vice president of $190-million Carolina Freight Carriers Corp., "it's effect will depend greatly on the economic conditions. If it comes during a recession, the impact in the short term will be severe. But if the economy is strong I don't think there would be a problem."

Unlike the railroads, which have improved their overall service only slightly in recent decades, the truck transportation business bears only a superficial resemblance to its fledgling self of 50 years ago. Service is fast and its timely availability crucial. Giant transcontinental carriers dominate. The industry has flourished. And yet in doing so, trucking has long since outgrown the morass of special privileges and restrictions that early on fostered that growth.

Once justifiable limits and duties patterned on the rail industry have become a tangle of contradictions, circuities, and hindrances. Today,

a truckline's success is often related to its ability to circumvent restrictions or use the rules to stymie competition. The Interstate Commerce Act has made the trucking industry an anachronism in the American economy—a throwback to the era of the mom and pop corner grocery store and the small local brewery. Viewed in this light, deregulation becomes convincing.

Of course when the rules are changed, economic dislocation is inevitable. "I'm of the opinion that if you deregulate, there will be one bloody rate war," says Dennis Enright, senior transportation analyst for Bache Halsey Stuart Shields Inc., in New York. "That will almost have to come to pass. It would hold true in almost any industry. At the other end of that war would be a shaking out, and the guys without the capital will be the ones who get shook out."

The casualties of transition make up the strongest argument against total deregulation. Proponents like Alfred Kahn and Senator Edward Kennedy sound very callous in their talk of inefficiency when one realizes that they are toying with people's jobs, their investments, their livelihoods.

Richard E. Edwards, president, Hemingway Transport: "A change of this magnitude should occur over a long period of time—maybe 20 years."

Contrary to what the deregulationists seem to expect, the brunt of reform will not be borne by the chiefs of the big carriers. The impact will be on their drivers and other employees put out of work or required to relocate; on the employees of their customer shippers; and on the owners of the thousands of small, undercapitalized trucking companies whose prime assets are their ICC operating certificates. There is an unusual anti-populist tinge to the whole deregulation argument that hasn't yet been fully appreciated by either side.

Is deregulation unfair? Yes it is, but as President Carter has astutely observed, "Life is unfair." Our system should not be expected to guard against the winds of change. We take our chances, some of us more than others. No one can say that truck deregulation hasn't been in the cards for some time now.

Doubtless, total motor carrier deregulation carried out in one swoop would be a major jolt to many companies and carriers. The effect would be relatively short-lived, as any economy has a natural tendency toward stability over chaos, and probably the fittest and most efficient would survive and prosper. But poorly implemented, the social price would be high.

"You've got a big system here," Richard E. Edwards, president and chief executive officer of Hemingway Transport, a New England-based, $51-million carrier. "The location of the country's manufacturing plants, warehouses, and distribution centers, the flow of products, and the development of certain markets are all related to the existence of specific transportation costs. Total deregulation would change these costs and suddenly the location of specific warehouses or plants may not make sense anymore.

"A change of this magnitude should occur over a long period of time—maybe 20 years—to allow for a major restructuring of distribution patterns. Otherwise, American industry could be completely disrupted."

Another point that has been misconstrued by many of trucking's denigrators is that, despite its imperfections, the trucking industry is hardly a bastion of rigid non-competition. In actuality, competition on many routes is intense, with at least 10 or 20 regular common carriers serving most decent-sized city pairs. Traffic managers often have to suffer the sales pitches of dozens of carrier representatives every month.

And not all of them are offering the same service. Shippers may benefit from a variety of special or volume discounts, including distribution rates, assembly rates, commodity rates, aggregate tender rates, or multiple shipment rates. A carrier may be persuaded to "flag out" and not go along with a selective bureau-wide rate increase. Such flag outs are common; about half of the 18,000 rate bureau actions last year were reductions.

Beat the system

Carriers competing for a shipper's traffic will usually match another carrier's flag out or independently filed volume discount—but not always. Joseph Gray, corporate traffic and transportation director for Levi Strauss & Co., San Francisco, notes that it is sometimes difficult to find a carrier who will put in the special distribution and assembly rates he requires.

Volume discounts are a perfectly acceptable way of doing business: the seller passes his savings along to the customer. Except that is not how non-discriminatory regulated transportation is supposed to work!

Contrary to the principles of the Interstate Commerce Act, large volume shippers do win favored treatment while carriers use the closed doors of the rate bureaus and the IC Act to deny other special services to smaller companies and smalls shippers.

Ironically, deregulation would not put a halt to the favored treatment—it would probably enhance it. ICC Chairman Daniel O'Neal told a congressional subcommittee that LTL (less truck load) rates would almost certainly rise under price decontrol. But deregulation would acknowledge the existence of natural economic tendencies, permit new solutions to old problems, and count on competition to keep rates reasonable.

If the working system is subtly tilted in favor of the big shipper, the tilt is even more pronounced in favor of the shrewd carrier with enough computerized cost-accounting horsepower to beat the convoluted industry cost structures. Today's profitable trucklines have the technical sophistication to accurately determine the unit cost of handling specific shipments between specific points. They compare the cost to the revenue allowed in the tariff and decide whether or not to pursue that business. The ICC is supposed to enforce the "duty to serve" principle and sometimes does catch carriers *in flagrante delicto,* but most easily evade the duty to serve when it suits them.

From the carrier's point of view, the object is a money-making payload every time. "You have to have all kinds of freight," says Hemingway's Mr. Edwards. "Our salesmen are encouraged to seek out a mixture so that heavy base freight can be topped off with light freight, making an economically efficient payload. But of course the more Class 125 freight you haul versus Class 100, the more money you're going to make."

The technological capability to pinpoint unit costs has only come in the last 10 years and is still not widespread. Yet as more and more carriers inevitably achieve accurate cost-accounting capability, shippers of certain undesirable commodities begin to find that their choice of carriers is limited, or alternatively, that the rates to move their goods are prohibitively high.

Organizations like the National Small Shipments Traffic Conference have been fighting cost-based rate hikes for small shipments, but it is a losing battle. In truth, carrier revenue from shipments under 500 pounds does not cover costs. And yet the regulatory system effectively prevents innovative companies from developing profitable new specialty services. Applications from United Parcel Service or Trailways buslines for broader authority are consistently protested.

Even insignificant innovations are endlessly scrutinized. Two years ago, Herman Bros., a contract carrier, asked the Interstate Commerce Commission to allow it to offer reduced rates to consignees who would accept delivery any time during a 24-hour period. In November 1977, the commission found the plan unlawful based on the opportunity for discrimination. Herman Bros. filed the plan again last spring. In December, the commission reversed itself and voted to permit the service.

Such restrictions and red tape have distorted the true picture of distribution economics, says Stan Sender, transportation counsel for Sears, Roebuck in Washington. As Mr. Sender and his assistant Ted Erfer explain, broad corporate distribution decisions include transportation as just one factor. A company operating on a low-cost trans-

Senator Howard W. Cannon, (D-Nev.), chairman of the Senate Commerce, Science, and Transportation Committee: "The agony of uncertainty is not too high a price to pay for a well-considered resolution of the issue."

Senator Edward M. Kennedy (D-Mass.), chairman of the Senate Judiciary Committee: "The timetable for deregulation is less important than moving in an irreversible direction."

portation/high-cost inventory basis might choose to allocate a greater share of its expenditures to transportation—if express LTL service were available. Regional warehouses could be eliminated in favor of relying on the distribution pipeline.

So it's not true that shipping is price inelastic, Mr. Sender concludes. There are products being made today that cannot be profitably sold through a catalog in some markets because the minimum freight charges are too high.

Prospectus for change

Three months ago, legislation calling for motor carrier deregulation looked like a sure bet for 1979. Now it appears that internal congressional squabbles and the pressure of other business may prevent a truck deregulation bill from ever coming to a vote in this session.

The urgency of truck reform is more related to politics than to economics. An objective look argues for a slow, careful approach. But for its public relations benefits, the White House and certain others would like to see transportation deregulation well underway by the end of 1980. In recent weeks, however, key members of Congress have urged caution.

"This process takes time," Senator Howard W. Cannon (D-Nev.) told the board of governors of the Regular Common Carrier Conference, ATA in February. "And it should take time. . . The agony of uncertainty about the future is not too high a price to pay for a well-considered resolution of the issue." Sen. Cannon chairs the key Senate Commerce, Science, and Transportation Committee. His claim to jurisdiction over transportation reform has bottled up—perhaps permanently—Senator Edward Kennedy's (D-Mass.) controversial bill to end motor carrier ratemaking

antitrust immunity.

Senator Cannon has stated that he would ideally like to consider transportation reform as a single omnibus legislative package. The White House is preparing such legislation through an inter-agency task force spearheaded by the Department of Transportation; the group has a mid-May target date. The more politically attuned members of the task force have let it be known that the White House will not propose radical legislation if it has no chance of passing.

Truck reform is also being nudged aside by Conrail's problems. There is a growing consensus in Washington that the railroads—specifically, Conrail—must be dealt with first. Immediate action is vital, says U.S. Railway Association President Donald C. Cole, and his concern has been echoed by Chairman O'Neal and DOT Secretary Brock Adams.

Railroad deregulation has the support of the industry itself and would prove a much easier nut to crack politically, although in actuality the railroads present a much greater challenge. The potential for disaster is much higher.

Some suspect there is a method to this political madness. Fred G. Favor, executive director of the ad hoc group against truck reform, Assure Competitive Transportation (ACT), offers a conspiracy theory.

"They're actually hoping to keep Congress away from the issues and move ahead with deregulation through O'Neal at the agency," he says. "That was their strategy all along. I don't think they ever thought they could get a bill through Congress. We're hearing that they may not send up any bills this year."

According to ACT, the advocates of deregulation would like to present Congress with a *fait accompli.*

And there is evidence to support that idea. The ICC under Chairman O'Neal has pushed through significant reforms. Route entry has been liberalized, while cancellation of joint-line agreements has been made easier. The commission has restricted competing carriers' rights of protest and will now consider rates as a factor in operating rights procedures. Contract carriers can expand, private truckers can engage in for-hire operations, and now the ICC has voted to curb collective rate-setting powers on all but across-the-board actions.

O'Neal's Box

The upshot is that the trucking industry is being significantly altered under the direction of Mr. O'Neal while the broader policy matters await formal consideration in Congress. The chairman has certainly opened a Pandora's Box with his "experiments," but it is most interesting to observe that he seems to have the full backing of not only the White House, but also Secretary Adams and the important committee chairmen in Congress.

Several recent statements make this apparent. Sen. Kennedy, for example: "It is to early to tell how our bill (to eliminate the collective ratemaking exemption) will dovetail with the administration. The timetable for deregulation is less important than moving in an irreversible direction toward more competition and less regulation."

The decision of both the American Trucking Associations and the ad hoc group ACT to take the ICC to court over its authority to reform is justified and appropriate. The ICC as a laboratory for regulatory experiments has profound implications for the trucking industry.

For one thing, trucking companies will be very reluctant to get involved in mergers with other companies or to purchase operating rights when the value of those assets is so uncertain. Also, small carriers relying on their certificates for capital will be considered poor risks by most banks. And looming ahead are higher fuel prices and even a recession.

Says Bache Halsey analyst Dennis Enright, "Until the issue is resolved, trucking earnings are going to go to hell in a handbasket. . . . I would be fearful of touching the stock right now, not knowing what's going to be coming. We're just waiting for the next shoe to drop. You don't need a trucking stock selling at seven or eight times earnings when so many other stocks offer much greater yields. Why gamble?"

But if one believes that at least partial decontrol is a certainty (as Mr. Enright does), there is this consolation: when the chips have been down, Daniel O'Neal has shown himself to be a reformer but never a deregulator. In testimony before various committees and in his strong stance on the necessity of a rail market dominance test, the chairman has emerged as the most knowledgeable and most prudent of the reformers, with the clearest understanding of the users' needs.

Many shippers and carriers might wish that the proverbial truck of state (to coin a phrase) be put back on automatic the way it was for years. That is probably impossible now. It gives some relief to know that a competent driver is behind the wheel at this crucial stage. Mr. O'Neal is a strong believer in the preservation of the ICC as the instrument of reform and regulation now and in the future. The continued existence of an authoritative and flexible commission should be the bottom line in the debate over deregulation. ∎

Daniel O'Neal, chairman, Interstate Commerce Commission: He admits that LTL rates would rise under price decontrol.

SHIPPERS VOTE DOWN DEREGULATION

In a straw vote, shippers polled for DW give a landslide victory
to continued regulation of motor carrier entry. Deregulation,
they fear, will lead to worse service and higher prices.

By WILLIAM B. WAGNER, Associate Professor of Marketing, University of Missouri-Columbia

In theory, deregulated entry into the competition among motor common carriers should increase competition. In theory, more competition should make carriers vying for business more efficient. In theory, service to shippers should increase and costs should be trimmed to the optimum for all concerned. Putting all of this theory into practice should lead to the "free marketplace."

But shippers are afraid that such a free marketplace would, in reality, be a competitive jungle in which not even the fittest may survive.

It's no secret that the shipping community is openly worried about the current rush to deregulation. A recent survey of shippers indicates that if the choice to de-regulate were put to a vote of shippers, regulation, in line with our present system, would win the ballot by a landslide.

Entry deregulation for motor carriers is one area where shippers must be heard. It is, of course, impossible to know what will happen to carrier rates and service levels. However, as such levels will be influenced by shipper demand it is imperative to know their attitudes on this issue.

Their decisions with respect to such things as modal selection and allocation, the private carriage alternative, as well as types of commodities shipped will all

"Relaxation of entry would not be a major problem if it boiled down to each point being served by a reasonable number of truck lines. Shippers need competition. But too many carriers serving at a given point may mean too little revenue to permit viable operations. Deregulation could result in too many carriers for the amount of available tonnage."

Mel McKinney,
Manager of Traffic
and Transportation
McDonnell Douglas Corp.

play a part in the success or failure of regulatory changes affecting the carriers.

Specifically, do shippers favor deregulating the motor carrier industry? Does the shipping public feel deregulation would improve or worsen service? Help or hurt carriers? Increase or decrease carrier competition? Be favorable or undesirable to their own interests?

Answers to such questions are necessary if sound public policy decisions are to be forthcoming and, as a result, public interest best served.

A study designed to provide insight into such questions has been concluded and focused on determination of shipper attitudes toward deregulation.

Of the 1200 sampled, 322 responded. When these respondent shippers were asked whether they favored regulated or deregulated entry of motor common carriers, the majority favored the former. Over three-fifths of those traffic managers taking a position (responded other than "4") favored a regulated industry. The percentage was higher among those personally interviewed.

Rationale for favoring regulation of motor common carrier entry can, in large part, be explained by responses to questions in which shippers were asked to indicate the impact entry deregulation in the long run would have.

For example, about two-thirds of those sampled felt deregulation of entry would more likely worsen service provided to the shipping public. Also, about three of five indicated they would expect entry deregulation to hurt the shipper.

Continued

The sample size for the final study was 1200 shippers with a pretest mailing to 250. There were approximately 300 useable returns for the final study. Nearly half the shippers polled had annual sales in excess of $100 million. All were heavy users of motor carriage, with 23% having annual freight bills of at least $10 million and 88% having annual freight bills in excess of $100,000.

241

DEREGULATION

CONTINUED

Nearly 80 percent of all respondents taking a position thought deregulation of entry would be harmful to carriers. Although this general finding might be expected, the degree to which shippers agreed on this issue is significant.

There is a fairly mixed reaction among shippers as to whether deregulation of entry would have a positive or negative effect on competition, with slightly more thinking it would help.

Shippers appear to be generally against entry deregulation for the motor carrier industry. Although they feel it would assist in bringing about a more competitive cli-

---

"The shipper pays the freight bill, and therefore bears the burden or reaps the benefits of whatever takes place in the regulatory environment. The shipper better pay close attention to what's happening."

A. Gail Cobb,
Director of Traffic
Chemtech Industries

---

mate for the carriers, they feel it would have a definite negative influence on the carriers themselves.

Furthermore, shippers generally feel deregulation would hurt service. And they think the shipping public would suffer if entry controls were relaxed.

If shippers think both the carriers and themselves would suffer as a result of deregulation, their modal decisions would be influenced. And if they shifted their traffic away from motor carriers as a result, the overall impact of the decision to deregulate might be much different than that which many proponents have speculated. The need for additional empirical research in the area is, as a result, becoming increasingly apparent. ■

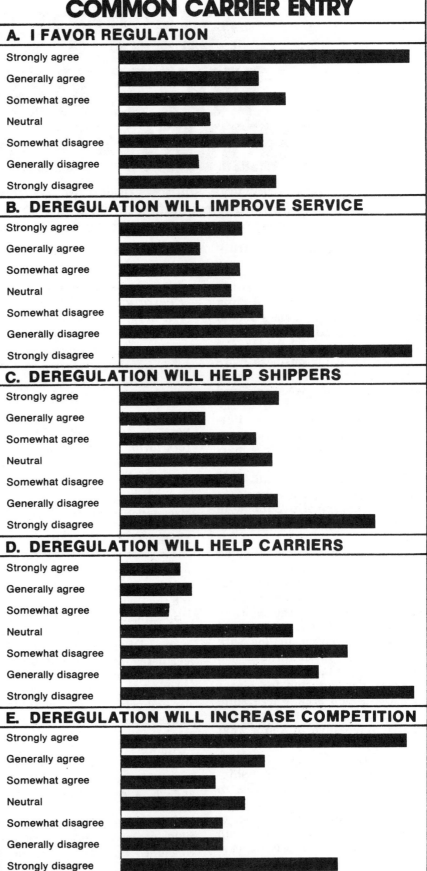

SHIPPER ATTITUDES ON DEREGULATION OF MOTOR COMMON CARRIER ENTRY

A. I FAVOR REGULATION
Strongly agree / Generally agree / Somewhat agree / Neutral / Somewhat disagree / Generally disagree / Strongly disagree

B. DEREGULATION WILL IMPROVE SERVICE
Strongly agree / Generally agree / Somewhat agree / Neutral / Somewhat disagree / Generally disagree / Strongly disagree

C. DEREGULATION WILL HELP SHIPPERS
Strongly agree / Generally agree / Somewhat agree / Neutral / Somewhat disagree / Generally disagree / Strongly disagree

D. DEREGULATION WILL HELP CARRIERS
Strongly agree / Generally agree / Somewhat agree / Neutral / Somewhat disagree / Generally disagree / Strongly disagree

E. DEREGULATION WILL INCREASE COMPETITION
Strongly agree / Generally agree / Somewhat agree / Neutral / Somewhat disagree / Generally disagree / Strongly disagree

A leading industry spokesman explains—
and defends—the stand railroads have
taken on economic deregulation.

By BENJAMIN F. BIAGGINI
Chairman and Chief Executive Officer
Southern Pacific Co.

Deregulation: Analysis and critique

The railroad regulatory apparatus—both the statutory framework and the system of implementation which for years have disfavored railroads while favoring their competitors—*must be changed and changed quickly.*

Congress has already received the message that the transportation industry should be deregulated. It has already applied the concept to the airlines, and the horror stories advanced by opponents of airline deregulation have not come true. The Interstate Commerce Commission also has taken note of the strong movement toward deregulation, and it has adopted some specific changes in that direction with respect to the trucking industry.

Here I must insert a note of caution, that if the commission's full deregulation program for truckers is adopted and no comparable move is made for the railroads, the plight of the railroads will be even worse than it is today while the truckers gain even more advantages than they now have. Moreover, we must have in mind that the majority of truck traffic already is largely exempt from economic regulation.

President Carter and other leaders of his Administration have stated that a railroad deregulation program should be adopted by Congress in the interest of a proper national transportation policy. Yet, until the last few days, spokesmen for the commission have been making public statements that were in my view having a decidedly "chilling" impact on the future of railroad deregulation. The commission spokesmen placed emphasis on the potential use of the provisions of the 4R Act that were adopted in 1976.

Then on Feb. 27 the commission, as you know, reviewed rail regulatory issues and options. While I welcome this critical review of the present railroad regulatory structure, I truly believe that the required changes are so fundamental that they should be adopted by Congress, rather than through placing excessive reliance on commission policy which may be both uncertain and unpredictably changeable.

Adapted from an address at the Transportation Law Seminar of the Bureau of Investigations and Enforcement of the Interstate Commerce Commission in Bethesda, Md., March 7, 1979.

It is absolutely essential that the railroad industry be returned to economic viability. By that I mean that it must be allowed to earn a rate of return comparable to the rate earned in other industries, instead of the dangerously low one-half of one percent on investment earned last year by the nation's railroads, excluding Conrail and the bankrupts.

I am happy to report that—after months of intensive study of the economic and legal framework in which the industry operates, and all its problems including the huge capital shortfall which were so well pointed out by the Depart-

> **"Railroads should have substantially complete rate freedom, on both the 'down' and the 'up' side."**

ment of Transportation in its "Prospectus for Change in the Railroad Industry" last year—the Association of American Railroads has adopted a deregulation program which should be enacted by Congress this year.

The first point of this program calls for greater freedom in ratemaking.

The system of rate regulation which we have today proceeds from a railroad monopoly premise which, although perhaps valid a hundred years ago, is certainly not valid today. Almost all serious and analytical observers agree that competition in the transportation industry today is strong and pervasive in most markets and with respect to most commodities and shippers.

Market forces dictate price levels in other industries, and there is no reason why this same force of the free market cannot be relied upon to control pricing decisions in the railroad business. Therefore, the railroads should have substantially complete rate freedom, on both the "down" side and the "up" side.

In those rare instances where competition does not exist, the railroads should have the right to increase rates annually within a 20% zone—that is, we should have a 20% "yo-yo" provision, instead of the present 7%. Thus, where effective competition exists, or even where it does

not exist but the carriers remain within the 20% zone, the commission would not have any right of suspension or unilateral investigative power. Moreover, the railroads should be able to change prices on very short notice.

I use the term "effective competition" in the practical sense. The commission has been slow in recognizing that all kinds of competition must be considered, but I am much encouraged to note that in Ex Parte 320, decided Feb. 5, 1979, it finally agreed with the rail industry that present railroad and intermodal competition, potential competition and private carrier competition are *all* competitive factors.

You may ask: What's wrong with the 7% yo-yo of the 4R Act? Apart from the fact that the 7% zone of reasonableness is too narrow, the problem with the present provision is that it can only be used—as you know—if the railroad lacks "market dominance." The definition of this term, which I believe the commission has made far more restrictive than ever intended by Congress when it passed the 4R Act, has prevented not only use of the yo-yo but also the general use of greater rate discretion by carrier managements. Although the commission's right to define the term "market dominance" was upheld in court review of Ex Parte 320, that does not mean that its regulations carried out the intent of Congress.

The effect of the commission's presumptions has been to create a very unreal world in which the railroads, by definition but not in fact, are deemed to have market dominance on the great bulk of railroad traffic, and have had the burden thrust on them to disprove market dominance.

Market dominance simply is not widely prevalent. If it were, railroads would not be losing business to the other for-hire modes or to private carriage; their financial results would be better; and we probably would not be here discussing the need for new legislation to avoid very serious industry problems.

One more comment about rates and market dominance is called for. In no event should individual rate adjustments be considered a substitute for general rate increases, which are the only way the rail industry can recover, on a timely basis, increases in labor, material, and fuel costs which affect all carriers alike.

While the 4R Act did introduce a number of new concepts of rate regulation for the purpose of permitting more flexibility in pricing of railroad services, I question whether we can really find many significant advances in this area. The Act left the ICC with broad discretion in implementing ratemaking reform, and in my view the commission has used that discretion to interpret the provision restrictively and narrowly, and even to impose more onerous requirements for more detailed evidentiary presentation than ever before.

No single carrier, alone, can afford to bear the brunt of a major shipper's actual or threatened traffic diversion while that carrier tests the murky water of the long, tedious, and very uncertain ICC procedure on a rate adjustment. Under present rate regulatory practice, a major shipper has a decided advantage, because the delays inherent in making rate changes keep the railroad pricing officer from handling matters in an expeditious and orderly manner. Contrast this, if you will, with the normal process in general industry where one company tests the market with a price change, with no advance notice, and in a day or a week either goes ahead or retreats, depending upon the actions of the competition and the customers.

Some have suggested that the railroads have not tried to use the 4R Act. In response I would observe that we tried and were frustrated by the commission's delay (ever since our filing on March 9, 1978) in acting on our request for an exemption under Section 207 of the 4R Act, for movements of agricultural commodities co-extensive with the agricultural exemption which the law grants to the truckers. Further, we were disappointed that the commission did not see fit to grant the full exemption which was requested. To be sure, we do favor the limited exemption of perishables from railroad regulation which the commission has proposed in its recent decision in Ex Parte 346.

I hope the commission's proposal concerning perishables does go into effect—and the sooner the better. We are looking forward to using the freedom the commission has proposed in an innovative way. We are going to do the best we can to offer better service to shippers and to bring back to the railroad the perishables we once moved in volume, but which we lost to the unregulated truckers. Optimistically, we may have a chance to compete, and we plan to compete.

I was pleased to see in the commission's review of policy options on Feb. 27 that it is considering other exemptions, such as TOFC, COFC, and manufactured commodities such as automobiles and auto parts. Careful consideration of this sub-

ject, I am sure, will lead to the conclusion that all commodities should be deregulated.

Although the industry is not entirely agreed on the point, I believe that another important ingredient of ratemaking freedom should be to allow a railroad which wishes to cancel or change its portion of a joint rate to do so, provided certain conditions are met. Various proposals have been made which would continue the present right and duty for the railroads to arrange joint rates and routes.

DOT's plan, which some railroads like, is simply to scrap the whole joint rate setup and allow a railroad unilaterally to cancel in order that it may escape a situation where it is locked into providing service at a loss. Several plans have been suggested, ranging from abolishing joint

---

The ICC's case-by-case proposal on contract rates "does not go far enough to do any real good."

---

rates altogether to allowing a dissatisfied railroad to impose a unilateral tariff change or surcharge without the consent of the other joint rate partners. The importance of through route and joint rates being available to the shipping community cannot be overlooked. We see some hope and a preferred approach in an industry system adjusting such rates by surcharges, either arrived at jointly or unilaterally, and operating within a predetermined zone.

Another aspect of the AAR's program would allow railroads to make contract rates, without commission approval. The commission's new proposal on Nov. 9, 1978, in Ex Parte 358-F, which would permit contract rates on a case-by-case basis with commission approval, in my judgment does not go far enough to do any real good. There is no good reason why shippers and railroads should not be allowed to contract among themselves completely free of regulatory review.

The chairman has expressed disappointment over the railroads' use of the "Special Rate" provisions. The reason they have not been used is that the commission's restrictions place railroads at a competitive disadvantage. An example is the commission's requirement that peak demand rates be published upon 30 days notice. Although the commission approved a 20% peak-period grain rate increase, which now is being appealed to the courts by the shippers, it was subject to a 30-day notice. This simply continues the advantage of the truckers of grain, since they can change their rates at will without any notice.

To be practical in the rate field, we must retain the rate bureaus, or some other mechanism or forum with antitrust immunity providing proper legal procedures are followed. This is necessary because joint-rate partners must be allowed to talk to one another and come to agreement without being made subject to the technicalities of the antitrust laws. In this regard, Congress and the public should appreciate that railroads are truly unique in that they have a statutory duty to interconnect and exchange traffic. This duty is important to the maintenance of a national transportation system, and to the public interest, especially when we still lack any transcontinental single-line railroads.

Some say that the price of deregulation should be a loss of antitrust immunity, but those proposing this do not recognize the truly unique interdependence of the railroad industry. Actually, the immunity should be extended to include *intra*state ratemaking to the extent that *intra*state rates affect *inter*state commerce.

Another change that should be made is elimination of the long- and short-haul clause of the Interstate Commerce Act. The railroads are often criticized for the excessive empty back-haul of their equipment, but the long- and short-haul clause deprives them of a powerful and effective tool to meet this problem. Thus, this provision inhibits innovative ratemaking, and it is unnecessary in a competitive transportation environment. Motor carriers have never been subject to any such provision, and I see no reason why railroads should not be allowed to compete on the same basis.

Another major topic of discussion and a part of the AAR legislative program calls for easier market exit, through deregulation of abandonments.

Although abandonment procedures have been simplified under the 4R Act, there should be an absolute right to abandon if a specific line does not achieve a sufficient rate of return to justify its existence. There is pervasive competition by other modes, which service practically every hamlet across this country, so there is no longer a reason to require continuance of unprofitable railroad branch lines. Even the present simplified procedure, in its totality, is far too expensive and time-consuming, although it is a welcome improvement.

Another point of the AAR program calls for elimination of ICC jurisdiction over car service and compensation matters.

Recently, the commission more and more has been dictating the conduct of day-to-day railroad operations—ranging from how quickly cars must be moved to how to repair them, and from orders to acquire railroad equipment to how to conduct yard operations. These matters are interrelated with the economics of railroading and, of course, good service and adequate equipment supply can only be provided if the carriers earn an adequate rate of return. Per diem, car service matters, and compensation for shipper-owned cars can be handled efficiently and expeditiously by the industry under contracts with provisions for binding arbitration.

My next point is that Congress should liberalize the merger and unification procedures.

Mergers are one of the useful tools to restructure and revitalize the railroad industry. But if the tool is to work, the present time limits for decisions must be shortened. The criteria for judging mergers and consolidations should be

---

"All barriers to intermodal ownership should be removed. They serve no purpose in today's environment."

---

changed to encourage mergers rather than delay or discourage them.

Mergers are needed to shape the future of the railroad system. End-to-end mergers make carriers stronger and promote both intramodal and intermodal competition. Transcontinental mergers will eliminate much of the argument about divisions and through joint rates. With a new statute properly written and defining a pro-merger national policy, and less time-consuming administrative procedures, I believe mergers could be consummated in months rather than years.

A further point—and I think a non-controversial one in this forum—is that the law should eliminate ICC jurisdiction of the issuance of securities.

No useful purpose is served by continuing the dual jurisdiction over railroad securities which are generally subject to SEC jurisdiction. Major companies in all other fields are subject to SEC jurisdiction, and there is no separate and distinct interest in railroad securities which justifies a separate statutory framework.

Another type of financial constraint which should be eliminated is the commission's assertion of authority over railroad holding companies. While there has been criticism of the holding company type of organization, true abuses of railroads at the hands of their parents have been hard to find. As a matter of fact, the commission has been most liberal in permitting at least two holding companies to shed their railroad operations. Holding company regulation is an unnecessary expansion of regulatory

authority and it should be stopped by statute.

Next, the AAR's program of immediately needed legislation calls for eliminating the restrictions on ownership by railroads of other forms of transportation.

All barriers to intermodal ownership should be removed. Whether they originate in the Panama Canal Act, the Civil Aeronautics Act, or the extant body of administrative law, they serve no purpose in today's transportation environment and should be eliminated.

As a final point I shall mention, the rail industry firmly believes that state law should be preempted in railroad regulatory matters.

Incident to enactment of the package of reform legislation I have already discussed, all state power to regulate rates, service, abandonments, and securities should be removed. This will make certain that the flexibility which is being sought at the federal level is not restricted or eroded by state actions with respect to interstate carriers.

In the changes I have suggested above, it is contemplated that the ICC should retain control for some finite period of time until, say, 1985, when both the country and the railroads will have learned how to operate under this vastly reduced system.

After that, railroads generally would be treated no differently than other business-for-profit corporations. In the interim, during the period while the new legislation is in effect, there will be full opportunity to appraise the effectiveness of the new program and to determine what, if any, part of the limited regulatory scheme should be retained permanently.

Plainly, the system of regulation for the railroads that was begun in 1887 and extended by such landmark legislation as the Transportation Acts of 1920 and 1940, as well as the Motor Carrier Act of 1935 along with other legislation, simply has not worked. At least it has not worked from the standpoint of providing an efficient, dynamic, and healthy railroad system. Instead, it has produced a system on the verge of financial crisis and one which, in the very near future, may need massive federal funds for the continuance of essential rail service. And instead, it has compelled the expenditure since 1921 of well over 475 billions of dollars on the never-to-be completed highway system of the nation and over 21 billions on the domestic waterways.

I am not naive enough to think that the railroad system could take care of all the country's transportation needs. But I sincerely feel that a railroad system responding to the forces of free markets would have been able to hold onto its traffic, and some of the billions of dollars spent on facilities for the other modes of transportation could have been saved. ■

'Deregulators,' ICC Criticized Sharply In Speech by Head of Teamsters' Union

Frank E. Fitzsimmons, Addressing New York Audience, Offers Own Proposals for Meeting Transport Needs, Voices Firm Opposition to 'Inane Tampering' With 'World's Most Efficient Transport System.'

An 11-point legislative program for transport service betterment that the Teamsters' Union advocates was outlined by Frank E. Fitzsimmons, general president of the International Brotherhood of Teamsters and militant opponent of transport deregulation actions taken or proposed by the Carter Administration and the Interstate Commerce Commission, in a speech made in New York City on May 18.

Mr. Fitzsimmons took part in the Syracuse University Salzberg Conference, in the Plaza hotel. His legislative proposals included provisions that would prohibit shippers, as private carriers, from operating as ICC-certificated common carriers and would also prohibit deregulation of truckload traffic and the use of lower rates as the sole or principal basis for granting of motor carrier operating rights.

Sharp criticism was directed by Mr. Fitzsimmons against "deregulators" and against Chairman A. Daniel O'Neal, of the ICC. His union, he said, opposes vigorously "foolish and inane tampering with the most efficient transportation industry in the world, because it would destroy the financial integrity of the companies from which our members and their families derive their livelihoods, and because experience, both in this country and in other nations, proves that while a regulated industry well serves our transportation needs, a deregulated industry is a foolish experiment we cannot afford."

Mr. Fitzsimmons noted, early in his talk, that he had asked President Carter to ask Chairman O'Neal, of the ICC, to resign. Further assailing the ICC chairman's performances, the Teamsters Union chief said:

"Encouragement of fair wages and equitable working conditions is required by the National Transportation Policy established by Congress. Over many years the Commission's decisions reflected this policy. However, under the chairmanship of Dan O'Neal, the ability of the industry to pay fair wages and benefits has been seriously threatened. . . . Mr. O'Neal has also obtained Commission approval for drastic changes in long existing Commission policies which can only adversely affect wage earners and sound economic conditions in the industry. Among such changes is the granting of authority on a promise by an applicant to publish lower rates."

Mr. Fitzsimmons said that there is a vast difference in safety attitudes between professional truck drivers and bureaucrats who propose deregulation. Continuing, he said:

"I have yet to hear or read a statement by a professional deregulator which seriously addresses the effect of deregulation on the lives and safety of those who make a living driving intercity trucks or the motoring public which shares the highways with them.

"Deregulators are almost cavalier in their attitude about the effect of flooding highways with tens of thousands of independent truckers, responsible to no one, and under extreme economic pressures to avoid the expense of keeping equipment in safe condition.

"Because it is committed to highway safety, my union joined others and encourage Professor Daryl Wyckoff of Harvard University to do a study of 10,000 truck drivers. His survey demonstrated that drivers for regulated carriers have the best safety record on every score. . . . During 43 years of regulation, no one has devised a means of bringing exempt carriers into compliance with federal and state regulations.

"The Department of Transportation spends far more money on safety than did the ICC, but DOT has achieved no appreciable improvement in the safety of the trucking industry. . . .

Enforcement Problem

"Teamsters favor increasing the number of safety inspectors on the highways, but we do not believe that anything short of an army of such inspectors would be able to enforce highway safety.

"Union drivers for regulated companies have the best safety records, primarily because the regulated carrier must maintain high safety standards if it is to obtain additional operating authority from the Commission."

After observing that an ICC policy change, designed to save motor fuel by eliminating an empty backhaul, involves granting to shippers engaged in private carriage authority to transport regulated commodities on the return movement, Mr. Fitzsimmons said:

"Granting a backhaul authority to a private carrier only results in the loss of a fronthaul by a regulated carrier. The empty movement remains. It is shifted to the regulated carrier. The common carrier with an obligation to serve the general public . . . is forced to assume

the burden and the cost of empty movements. The private carrier with no obligation to serve the public is presented with a windfall.

"And in an energy starved nation, deregulation would put thousands more trucks, all burning fuel, out on the road chasing the same amount of freight. The logic of that escapes me.

Correction of 'Abuses' by ICC

"The Teamsters Union intends to recommend legislation designed to correct the administrative abuses of the Interstate Commerce Commission during the last 18 months. Some of our proposals we regard as constructive reform; others we regard as correcting changes in long established policies of the Commission which seriously threaten the efficiency, the service, the economic stability and the safety of motor carrier transportation. . . .

"We recommend that the activities of the motor carrier rate bureaus be open to the public and that the restrictions placed upon the activities of the rate bureaus by the Commission to date be enacted into law so that the right to independent action by individual carriers is not restricted and those carriers not participating in a rate would be precluded from voting.

"In addition, we will recommend that Congress enact legislation providing that:

"1. All workers in surface transportation be given equal treatment under the nation's labor laws, and also that lower rates may not be used as the sole or principal basis for a grant of authority.

"2. Shippers engaged in private carriage may not obtain a certificate from the Commission.

"3. The right of employes and the carriers by whom they are employed to protest and participate fully in proceedings involving applications for authority to duplicate service offered by an existing carrier may not be restricted.

"4. Applicants for authority to serve agencies of the United States shall be subject to the same standards of public convenience and necessity as all other applicants.

"5. Efficiency of operation, fuel consumption, adequacy of existing service and highway safety shall be considered by the Commission in every application proceeding.

"6. The Commission's present limitation of intercorporate hauling may not be enlarged; otherwise large corporate conglomerates would be granted a preferential competitive position at the expense of smaller competitors and at the expense of motor, rail and water carriers.

"7. Every common carrier shall be required to live up to its common carrier responsibilities or to surrender the common carrier authority granted to it by the Commission.

"8. The Commission may not deregulate truckload traffic. This area of traffic probably has the greatest amount of competition and, therefore, least justifies deregulation. The rates charged by truckload carriers have increased far less than the cost of living in recent years and the services offered by such carriers have been satisfactory to shippers. Truckload traffic has not been marked by concentration, and finally, it is truckload traffic which competes most directly with railroad traffic.

"As everyone knows, rail rates already are depressed and many railroads are either in bankruptcy or subsidized by the federal government. If there were deregulation of truckload traffic, cutthroat competition would take further traffic from the railroads.

"9. Owner-operators under lease to certificated carriers should be granted more, not less, protection. We will ask Congress to enact our recommendations that the Commission has heretofore rejected.

"10. Finally, we will ask Congress to direct the Commission or some outside agency to determine the nature and level of costs encountered by owner-operators. We believe drivers in this segment of the nation's transportation, particularly those that do not have the protection of our union, are ignoring many of the costs that they encounter and this is a major reason for the high rate of bankruptcies among them. . . ."

Is it true that experience is the best teacher?

If so, Garrett Freightlines has as much or more knowledge and know-how when it comes to motor freight transportation than any other common carrier. After 66 years experience, Garrett has earned the respect from both carriers and shippers alike for our leadership in the industry. But one of the important things that experience teaches is that a successful business cannot continue to operate this year with the same equipment, methods and ideas as it did last year. Our fast changing world dictates a continuing drive for utilization of these changes to provide progressively better motor freight service.

Also in our 66 years experience, we have become convinced that total deregulation in our industry is not in the best interests of the people. There is no magic in the word "deregulation." The small isolated communities and shippers will not suddenly be transformed into profitable operations. If the freight volume and/or back-haul doesn't exist, deregulation won't magically provide it. These people will suffer while the big shippers and cities will be in a more advantageous position.

Another fact of transportation is that there is only a certain volume of freight at a given period. Deregulation will not appreciably increase that volume in the similar way that lower rates in the airline industry increases the number of people who fly. The political emphasis today is to aid the unfortunate, the disadvantaged, the handicapped and the minorities . . . but who is speaking for the exact same categories in the transportation field: the small shipper, the isolated or small community and small freight companies?

We have built the American Motor Freight Transportation System into the best and most efficient in the world. We can now destroy it with one word . . . "DEREGULATION!"

Since 1913

GARRETT *FREIGHTLINES, Inc.*

EXECUTIVE OFFICES - 2055 GARRETT WAY ● POCATELLO, IDAHO 83201

Editorial

Questions Our Lawmakers Must Not Ignore

The kind of activity by transportation professionals that's needed to prevent the serious mistake Congress would make if it were to adopt a total or almost-total transportation deregulation program is being demonstrated by Frank N. Wilner, director of traffic of the Public Service Commission of North Dakota (Capitol Building, Bismarck, N.D. 58505). He is a former transportation consultant who is as familar as anyone we know with the operations, problems and requirements of transport service suppliers and with those of shippers and receivers of freight.

We have at hand the text of a letter written by Mr. Wilner on February 28 to each member of the transportation subcommittee of the Senate Committee on Appropriations and to each member of the surface transportation subcommittee of the Senate Committee on Commerce, Science and Transportation. In this letter Mr. Wilner makes forceful arguments against repeal of the Reed-Bulwinkle Act. We believe that holders of responsible positions in transportation companies and in industrial or commercial traffic or physical distribution departments can help the cause of preservation of sensible regulatory laws for transportation by bringing to the attention of the federal legislators serving their respective states or districts the points made and the questions asked by Mr. Wilner in his letter.

After stating that Senator Edward M. Kennedy (D-Mass.) is sponsoring a bill that would end the antitrust immunity now afforded domestic common carriers in the area of collective ratemaking, Mr. Wilner noted in his letter that the Reed-Bulwinke Act (49 U.S.C. 10701) allows railroads, motor carriers, domestic water carriers and freight forwarders to confer and discuss among themselves rate levels that are further subject to federal and state regulatory approval. The mechanics of such collective ratemaking are closely regulated by the Interstate Commerce Commission and by various state public service commissions and are the result of written agreements pre-filed with and approved by the ICC or state commissions, he said.

Though assailed by supporters of the "unwise" Kennedy bill as anti-competitive and by the Justice Department as a price-fixing medium, said Mr. Wilner, the Reed-Bulwinkle Act is in fact "one of the most misunderstood and unfairly maligned pieces of legislation we have." He described collective ratemaking under the Reed-Bulwinkle Act as a direct result of the pressures of the market place, because, he said, "individual shippers play a key role in carrier collective ratemaking."

"Individual carriers," he continued, "are free to join or not to join in such activities and, even after joining, individual carriers are guaranteed in writing the right of independent action—the ability to set a level of rates differing from those agreed to by other parties to the ratemaking agreement. You would be amazed at how often this occurs, and I urge you develop data on independent filings."

While the ICC and the state commissions have the right to suspend or cancel any unreasonable rates, Mr. Wilner wrote, "the ultimate check lies with the shipper, who can provide his own private carriage, enter into contract carriage, offer his freight to another common carrier . . . or even switch modes."

"As a state regulator," he continued, "I am neutral in my outlook, as my responsibility is to both the carriers and shippers. I bring to my job many years of managerial experience with rail and motor carriers, and as a consultant to shipper groups I have been intimately involved with common carrier rates and collective rate-making since 1964, and have also taught the subject at a state college in Virginia."

Mr. Wilner said in a footnote in his letter that the views he was expressing did not necessarily reflect the views of the North Dakota PSC or its individual elected commissioners.

Not only carrier officials, but also large and small shippers embrace the collective ratemaking concept and support its continuation, he said.

"Does it not seem curious to you," he asked the senators, "that an activity alleged to be anti-competitive by a few politicians and bureaucrats with obvious vested interests and ambitions is supported by the very shippers the activity is alleged to injure? These shippers support collective ratemaking under Reed-Bulwinkle because it is essential to the smooth flow of commerce in our nation."

Carrier collective ratemaking begins with publication of proposals and notification to all interested shippers, who are encouraged to take part and state their views, and the shippers have access to carrier cost data and are among the nation's most knowledgeable groups of shippers, Mr. Wilner wrote. Then he addressed to the senators these questions: "Are you aware that there are upwards of 16,000 regulated motor carriers in our nation? Could you imagine a traffic manager having to consult thousands of price charts each time he had a shipment to move?"

"Without collective ratemaking," he counseled, "traffic managers would choose carriers much as consumers would buy merchandise without the benefit of advertising. . . . Collective ratemaking allows through rates to be published, which are one-factor rates from origin to destination, regardless of the number of carriers or modes that handle the shipment."

Mr. Wilner advised the senators to ask the professional traffic managers in their own states, whose names and addresses they could obtain from Carter M. Harrison, executive director of the American Society of Traffic and Transportation at (312) 939-2491, how collective ratemaking affects their responsibility for finding dependable and predictable transportation at reasonable rates for their firms.

"These," he wrote, "are the folks who represent industry and, ultimately, the consumer. These are the folks who supposedly suffer from the alleged evils of Reed-Bulwinkle. So why aren't they supporting repeal of Reed-Bulwinkle? Doesn't this concern you? Shouldn't you investigate thoroughly before committing your vote? Make sure, Senator, that *everyone* is playing with a full deck."

Better advice will never be received by any member of the Senate or House in the U.S. Congress.

Acknowledgments

Brock Adams, "Modal Excellence: Key To Transport Policy." Reprinted by permission from **Handling and Shipping Management** (April, 1978).

William T. Coleman, Jr., "Meeting The Needs of Commerce." Reprinted by permission from **Handling and Shipping Management** (April, 1978).

John H. Jenrich, "Passenger Transportation: People In Perpetual Motion." Reprinted by permission from **Nation's Business** (May, 1979). Copyright 1979 by **Nation's Business**, Chamber of Commerce of the United States.

Bernard J. LaLonde and Jerome J. Cronin, "Distribution Career Patterns." Reprinted by permission from **Distribution Worldwide** (March, 1979).

"A Transportation Career — An Honorable Calling." Reprinted by permission from **Traffic World** (February 12, 1979).

Thomas A. Foster, "On-Line, Over The Road." Reprinted by permission from **Distribution Worldwide** (September, 1978).

"Highway Transportation: Technology Fuels Conservation." Reprinted by permission from **Handling and Shipping Management** (February, 1978).

"Harvester's Patrick Kaine Looks at Truck Design of the Future." Reprinted by permission from **Transport Topics** (March 19, 1979).

Robert J. Franco, "Truck Lease-Rental Business Expected To Grow In Next Decade." Reprinted by permission from **Transport Topics** (January 29, 1979).

Richard D. Eads, "Managing Specialized Carriers." Reprinted by permission from **Motor Freight Controller**, (February, 1978).

Paul Ross, "Improving Urban Traffic Through Truck-Oriented Measures." Reprinted by permission from **Public Roads** (December, 1978).

Chalres F. Scheffey, "New Directions for the Federally Coordinated Program of Highway Research and Development." Reprinted by permission from **Public Roads** (September, 1978).

Gus Welty, "The Great Railroads: The Rio Grande." Reprinted by permission from **Railway Age** (September 11, 1978).

Benjamin F. Biaggini, "13 Steps Toward a Sane Transportation Policy." Reprinted by permission from **Railway Age** (January 16, 1978).

Gus Welty, "Mass Transport For Bulk Commodities: Doing What Rails Do Best." Reprinted by permission from **Railway Age** (July 31, 1978).

Gus Welty, "Coal: Questions Begging For Answers." Reprinted by permission from **Railway Age** (April 30, 1978).

Frank Malone, "New Peaks For Piggyback." Reprinted by permission from **Railway Age** (October 30, 1978).

"How Shippers View Rail Mergers." Reprinted by permission from **Railway Age** (October 30, 1978).

"How Shippers View Contract Rates." Reprinted by permission from **Railway Age** (February 26, 1979).

A. Daniel O'Neal, "A Short Step Down A Long Trail." Reprinted by permission from **Railway Age** (April 30, 1979).

Isabel H. Benham, "A New Way To Measure Performance — And What It Shows." Reprinted by permission from **Railway Age** (November 27, 1978).

"Amtrak's Boyd: Congress Must Make Up Its Mind." Reprinted by permission from **Railway Age** (January 8, 1979).

Fred H. McCusker, "New Dimensions In Air Cargo Traffic." Reprinted by permission from **Transport 2000** (September/October, 1978).

"Federal Express Parts Bank." Reprinted by permission from **Pacific Traffic** (March, 1978).

"Will Airfreighters Hit The Road?" Reprinted by permission from **Go West** (April, 1979).

James J. Haggerty, "Air Transports: The New Generation." Reprinted by permission from **Aerospace** (Fall, 1978).

Frank Kortum, "365 Days After Deregulation." Reprinted by permission from **Pacific Traffic** (November, 1978).

Michael Feazel, "Deregulation Sparks Criticism." Reprinted by permission from **Aviation Week and Space Technology** (April 2, 1979).

Marsha D. Banovetz, "How To Schedule An Airline." Reprinted by permission from **Pacific Traffic** (April, 1979).

Joan M. Feldman, "Access Looms As Critical Problem For U.S. Airports." Reprinted by permission from **Air Transport World** (April, 1979).

"Pipelines Energize America." Reprinted by permission from **Handling and Shipping Management** (February, 1978).

Donald B. Bright, "West Coast Crude Oil Pipeline Systems: Projects and Problems." Reprinted by permission by **Traffic World** (November 27, 1978).

"Bid Competition on Barge Delivery." Reprinted by permission from **American Shipper** (September, 1978).

"Comparison Chart of Cargo Capacity of Barges, Railroads, and Trucks." Reprinted by permission from Iowa Department of Transportation.

"The Fitzgerald Sinking: Two Views." Reprinted by permission from **The Seaway Review** (Vol. 7, No. 1, 1977).

"The All-Season Seaway Draws Closer." Reprinted by permission from **Traffic World** (September 18, 1978).

"A Freight Forwarder Offensive." Reprinted by permission from **Distribution Worldwide** (October, 1978).

"Expert Middleman." Reprinted by permission from **Via Port of New York — New Jersey Magazine** (March, 1979).

"The Essentials of Export Documentation." Reprinted by permission from **Distribution Worldwide** (October, 1978).

Patrick Gallagher, "Middle East Distribution — No Arabian Nightmare." Reprinted by permission from **Handling and Shipping Management** (July, 1978).

Brock Adams, "International Air Policy — Between The Lines." Reprinted by permission from **International Business** (March-April, 1979). Published at 14842 First Ave. S., Seattle, Washington 98168.

Robert R. Ropelewski, "Singapore Emphasizing Cabin Service on U.S. Route." Reprinted by permission from **Aviation Week and Space Technology** (May 7, 1979).

"Air Cargo At Northwest Orient Airlines." Reprinted by permission from **Pacific Traffic** (April, 1978).

Robert L. Vidrick, "Why The Conference System Must Be Changed." Reprinted by permission from **Distribution Worldwide** (March, 1978).

John R. Immer, "Liner Cargo Changing Patterns." Reprinted by permission from **American Seaport** (December, 1978).

"Survey: Exports, Imports and Ports." Reprinted by permission from **Traffic World** (September 18, 1978).

"Shipbuilding: Study Finds Prospects Dim." Reprinted by permission from **Traffic World** (September 18, 1978).

"Ocean Shipping's Cold War." Reprinted by permission from **Pacific Traffic** (Feburary, 1978).

E. Grosvenor Plowman, "Defining Distribution." Reprinted by permission from **Handling and Shipping Management** (October, 1978).

Jim Dixon, "Inbound Materials Management." Reprinted by permission from **Distribution Worldwide**, (February, 1978).

John F. Spencer, "A Way To Move Physical Distribution Ahead Faster." Reprinted by permission from **Handling and Shipping Management** (May, 1978).

Daniel F. McNamara, "An Effective Marketing and Distribution Relationship." Reprinted by permission from **Handling and Shipping Management** (March, 1978).

Michael Pregman, Jr., "So You're The New Distribution Manager!" Reprinted by permission from **Distribution Worldwide** (August, 1978).

Roger E. Jerman, Ronald D. Anderson, and James A. Constantin, "How Traffic Managers Select Carriers." Reprinted by permission from **Distribution Worldwide** (September, 1978).

"Freight Loss and Damage and Carriers Profits." Reprinted by permission from **Traffic World** (August 7, 1978).

Patrick Gallagher, "What To Do When The Carrier Says No." Reprinted by permission from **Handling and Shipping Management** (April, 1978).

Patrick Gallagher, "Private Fleet A Good Fit At Levi Strauss & Co." Reprinted by permission from **Handling and Shipping Management** (February, 1979).

Colin Barrett, "In The Wake of 'Toto'." Reprinted by permission from **Traffic World** (January 15, 1979).

Thomas Crosby, "Free Fares, Will It Work?" Reprinted by permission from **Mass Transit** (May, 1979).

"Santa Clara County Transit District — A Rapidly Expanding Bus System." Reprinted by permission from **Bus Ride** (February/March, 1979).

Deborah H. Noxon, "The Bus That Bends." Reprinted by permission from **Transportation USA** (Winter, 1979).

Richard S. Page, "This Administration Is Committed to Rail Transit." Reprinted by permission from **Railway Age** (July 10, 1978).

"An Expanding Market — But For Whom?" Reprinted by permission from **Railway Age** (January 8, 1979).

Tom Ichniowski, "For New and Expanding Systems — The Choice Is Fixed Guide Way." Reprinted by permission from **Railway Age** (August 14, 1978).

Patrick Gallagher, "On The Road To Deregulation." Reprinted by permission from **Handling and Shipping Management** (April, 1979).

William B. Wagner, "Shippers Vote Down Deregulation." Reprinted by permission from **Distribution Worldwide** (January, 1979).

Benjamin F. Biaggini, "Deregulation: Analysis and Critique." Reprinted by permission from **Railway Age** (March 26, 1979).

"Deregulators, ICC Criticized Sharply In Speech By Head of Teamster's Union." Reprinted by permission from **Traffic World** (May 28, 1979).

"Is It True That Experience Is The Best Teacher?" Reprinted by permission from Garrett Freightlines, Inc.

"Questions Our Lawmakers Must Not Ignore." Reprinted by permission from **Traffic World** (March 19, 1979).

Index